# Science and Pseudoscience in Social Work Practice

**Bruce A. Thyer, PhD, LCSW, BCBA-D,** is a professor and former dean, College of Social Work, Florida State University. He is a licensed clinical social worker and a board-certified behavior analyst. He has served in elected national leadership roles with the Society for Social Work and Research (SSWR), the Group for the Advancement of Doctoral Education in Social Work, the Council on Social Work Education, and the Association for Professional Behavior Analysts. He is a fellow of the American Psychological Association, the Association for Psychological Science, the Social Work Academy of the National Academies of Practice, and the SSWR. Dr. Thyer founded and continues to edit one of social work's premier journals, *Research on Social Work Practice.* He has written more than 250 articles in professional journals and more than 100 book chapters, and has produced more than 35 books. His research interests involve the promotion of evidence-based practice, evaluation research, applied behavior analysis, and clinical social work theory and practice.

**Monica G. Pignotti, PhD, LMSW,** is a licensed master social worker in the state of New York. She has taught social work practice, social work research, and diversity in social work courses. She has authored numerous book chapters and articles in professional journals, and keeps a blog on potentially harmful and other questionable therapies. She is a member of the Association for Psychological Science and the Society for a Science of Clinical Psychology.

# Science and Pseudoscience in Social Work Practice

Bruce A. Thyer, PhD, LCSW, BCBA-D
Monica G. Pignotti, PhD, LMSW

SPRINGER PUBLISHING COMPANY
NEW YORK

Springer Publishing Company, LLC
11 West 42nd Street
New York, NY 10036
www.springerpub.com

*Acquisitions Editor:* Stephanie Drew
*Composition*: Newgen KnowledgeWorks

*ISBN:* 978-0-8261-7768-1
*e-book ISBN:* 978-0-8261-7769-8

15 16 17 18 19 / 5 4 3 2 1

**Library of Congress Cataloging-in-Publication Data**
Thyer, Bruce A.
  Science and pseudoscience in social work practice / Bruce A. Thyer and Monica G. Pignotti.
     pages cm
  Includes index.
  ISBN 978-0-8261-7768-1
1. Social service—Practice. 2. Pseudoscience. 3. Social case work. 4. Social work educa-tion. I. Pignotti, Monica. II. Title.
  HV10.5.T49 2015
  361.3′2—dc23                                                                       2015003622

Printed in the United States of America by Gasch Printing.

# Contents

# Foreword

This book is long overdue. In *Science and Pseudoscience in Social Work Practice*, the authors suggest that "clinical social work has matured to the point of being able to take a blunt look at some of the more disreputable elements to be found within the profession" (Preface, p. xxiii). They describe an alarming variety of questionable practices used by social workers and argue for a housecleaning—decreasing use of ineffective and/or harmful practices and increasing use of effective interventions. Harming in the name of helping by professionals is by no means limited to social work, as the history of other professions readily shows (e.g., Jacobson, Foxx, & Mulick, 2005; Lilienfeld, Lynn, & Lohr, 2014; Scull, 2015). More often than not, such harm is not intended. This book is informed by surveys that the authors as well as others conducted regarding interventions social workers report using, for example, for posttraumatic stress disorder. They examined the evidentiary status of such interventions. The authors also discuss the underlying theory related to interventions used. Is this well argued and well tested? Is it compatible with empirical data? Their illustrations indicate that the life-affecting decisions made regarding interventions are often neither theoretically nor empirically well grounded. Some interventions reported as being used have been critically tested and shown to be harmful. Use of such practices does not seem to be a result of errors and mistakes that are inevitable both in science and in the helping professions

(Skrabanek & McCormick, 1992). Most seem to be related to negligence—not taking due diligence to become informed about crucial assessment and intervention concerns such as evidentiary status. The authors identify theories and interventions that have been critically appraised and found to help clients, which are available as alternatives to use of harmful or ineffective methods. But are these available to social workers? And if not, why not? This call for and modeling of transparency is a welcome one—one that is matched by trends in other helping professions and, indeed, concerning research itself, as illustrated by the creation of METRICS (Meta-Research Innovation Center at Stanford), designed to combat the enormous waste of money and effort conducting research that cannot answer questions raised (see Ioannidis, 2005, 2008, 2014).

Those in the helping professions claim to help people who seek or are forced to use their services. Social workers offer most of the mental health services in the United States today. They work with vulnerable clients in many different contexts. Claims of special expertise are integral to the helping professions. Do social workers have such expertise? Claims about what is true and what is not are integral to all helping professions. Claims are made about the accuracy of assessment methods, probability of risk, and effectiveness of intervention programs. The accuracy of these claims has life-affecting consequences for clients. Are they true? Are they false? And on what criteria are decisions based? Should professionals rely on intuition and, if so, what type, informed or uninformed (Hogarth, 2001)? Should they rely on what they learned during their professional education and in continuing education programs? Should they be "evidence informed" and, if so, what does this mean? Who is to say what "evidence" is? In psychiatry and social work, unlike most other helping professions, professionals are often double agents—agents of the state as well as agents of clients, as in child welfare and enforced psychiatric commitment. What boundaries are set on services offered and who reviews their quality and based on what criteria? This book *Science and Pseudoscience in Social Work Practice* deals with such questions. It highlights the importance of setting boundaries on what individual practitioners offer to their clients and the harms that result when these are absent, including deaths of clients.

The authors argue that a focus on identifying interventions that are effective is not enough—that there is also a need to identify interventions that harm and/or are ineffective and so hinder the initiation of effective methods. Their many examples clearly show that using ineffective or harmful methods is not benign in consequences for clients. This book highlights the vital role of assessment in understanding concerns and the harm that can result from drawing on bogus assessment theories and related methods that are dismissive of available knowledge, for example about behavior and how it is influenced and can be altered (e.g., Madden, 2013; Thyer, 2005). Social workers interact with some of the most impoverished individuals and families, those who struggle daily to make ends meet in our vastly unequal society. What percentage of those who seek help receive help? What percentage of those who graduate from accredited schools of social work are competent to offer such help and what percentage advocate for more resources when help is not available? What percentage of decisions made are well reasoned? Too often, an uninformed client (regarding questions to ask about services) meets an uninformed social worker who works in an agency that lacks transparency about what services are sought and what are offered to what effect (e.g., by posting such information on their websites).

As the authors note, books drawing attention to use of questionable and bogus methods in the helping professions have appeared over the centuries (e.g., Porter, 2000). These, as well as the current book, make for engrossing and alarming reading. *Pseudoscience* (use of the trappings of science without the substance) is closely related to *quackery*—the promotion and marketing, for a profit, of untested, often worthless, and sometimes dangerous health products and procedures, by either professionals or others (Jarvis, 1990; Young, 1992). Both are related to beliefs in the paranormal (events considered to be beyond scientific explanation) and the occult (the supernatural, mythical). Pseudoscience shares many similarities with these other areas, including lack of connectivity with critically tested theory, use of ad hoc hypotheses, and a focus on confirmation rather than on falsification. Quacks, as well as those who promote pseudoscience, are master salespersons using social influence methods such as a confident, empathic manner, vivid testimonials, and striking case examples. Quacks take advantage of factors that give an illusion that an intervention is responsible for a positive outcome, such as the self-limiting course of most complaints (e.g., many get better over time). Contributing biases include sunk cost bias and over simplifications (Gambrill, 2012a). The misuse of appeals to science to sell products or encourage certain beliefs (pseudoscience) is a form of propaganda (Gambrill, 2012b). Fraud takes advantage of pseudoscience and quackery. Fraud is so extensive in some areas that special organizations have been formed, newsletters written, and websites created to help consumers evaluate claims (e.g., National Council Against Health Fraud, Transparency International).

I do not think we can understand why professionals use harmful and/or ineffective methods nor develop effective strategies to decrease such use unless we understand related functions. Why do practitioners who are bound by codes of ethics to help clients and avoid harm use questionable methods, and how can we use this information to decrease reliance on such methods? Reasons suggested by Jarvis (1990) in his discussion of quackery in dentistry include:

- *Boredom.* Daily work can become humdrum. Pseudoscientific ideas can be exciting.
- *Reality shock.* Social workers regularly see very troubling situations. This requires psychological adjustments. Some helpers are simply not up to it.
- *The profit motive.* Quackery can be lucrative.
- *The prophet motive.* Viewing oneself as a specially gifted guide to difficult life situations.

Singer and Benassi (1981) suggest four influences that encourage a reliance on the occult: (a) media promotion of the occult; (b) cognitive biases and heuristics such as availability, jumping to conclusions, confirmatory biases, and the illusion of control; (c) environment and motivation influences, such as allaying anxiety and permitting predictability and control; and (d) deficiencies in science education (see also Irwin, 1993). All these influences also contribute to belief in pseudoscience and quackery. Consider, for example, talk shows and product advertising (e.g., Korownyk et al., 2014; Offit, 2013).

The commodification of pain and suffering (e.g., Timimi, 2012), encouraged by promotion of fear and anxiety about health, together with the promise of products, such as therapy, to allay discomfort and increase well-being, fosters consumption of related products. Most related pitches emphasize internal (psychological) causes, ignoring or minimizing the influence of environmental variables, such as poor educational opportunities, limited health and recreational services, and low wages. Indeed, Hansen, Bourgois, and Drucker (2014) argue that poverty has been pathologized by requiring a mental illness diagnosis to attain welfare. Contextual analyses emphasize the role of culture and other environmental reasons for beliefs and related actions that may harm rather than help clients. Social work practitioners and educators as well as clients are influenced by related pitches and framings of life problems rendered ever more pervasive by novel communication technologies, including the Internet with its plethora of advertisements. The extent of this influence is illustrated by the minimal attention in social work to the science of behavior, in which the role of environmental variables is illustrated and emphasized (e.g., Madden, 2013; Staats, 2012).

We must keep in mind the gravity of problems that confront many social work clients, often directly related to environmental circumstances such as lack of basic resources, including housing and health care, as well as the uncertainty that may surround decisions about what is effective. Helping takes place within an interpersonal encounter with all the complexities of such an encounter. Most social work interventions have not been critically tested; common factors such as warmth, the alliance, and empathy account for many of the positive effects of therapy (Duncan, Miller, Wampold, & Hubble, 2010). Without the values, knowledge, and skills needed to constructively handle the inequities and uncertainties involved in helping people, professionals are likely to fall for pseudoscience and quackery. There is pressure to offer something. In the absence of needed material resources and knowledge regarding a well-tested theory and related empirical data, for example, concerning human behavior, as well as related intervention skills, social workers are in a difficult position. To reduce uncertainty and helplessness, they may seize on the latest pseudoscientific or quack theory or intervention. This, combined with telling students that they are "experts" when they are not (which I have witnessed in my school of social work), encourages a dangerous (because unwarranted) confidence in their ability to identify and offer what is helpful and avoid what is harmful, especially in view of common self-inflated assessments (Dunning, Heath, & Suls, 2004).

Thus, the very reasons that encourage people to become social workers, a desire to help and to decrease inequities, may encourage use of dubious methods. This is especially true in the context of an education that fails to help students to become critical thinkers who can recognize flaws and biases in their own thinking or in the inflated claims in the professional literature or to understand what science is, how it differs from pseudoscience, and why people accept paranormal beliefs and fall for magical displays. Propaganda is not confined to fringe healers. Indicators such as inflated claims of knowledge and censorship of competing views are in ample display in the professional literature. Ioannidis (2005, 2008) argues that most claims in the peer-reviewed literature are false. Bias and selective reporting are rife. Most research in psychology either has not or cannot be replicated. Retractions of material in peer-reviewed journals are common (e.g., see Ferguson, Marcus, & Oransky, 2014). Retraction Watch (retractionwatch.com, 2014) just received $400,000 from the MacArthur Foundation to catalog the thousands of retractions in articles published in peer-reviewed journals. Social and economic pressures on researchers encourage claim inflation, data fudging, and other practices that misinform. Science is not necessarily self-correcting (Ioannidis, 2012). The term "evidence based" has become a slogan used to sell products—articles and books with hyped claims about "what works." Promotion of evidence-informed practice and policy will do more harm than good if the promoters are not well informed about political, social, and economic influences that shape the pool of literature available, including peer-reviewed publications, and so are not appropriately skeptical about what they read. Otherwise, they themselves become advertisers for inflated, misleading claims of knowledge, including those about problem framing.

The most important lapse in social work education highlighted by harmful and ineffective methods described in *Science and Pseudoscience in Social Work Practice* is the lack of a sound education in science and related critical thinking, values, skills, and knowledge. Without such an education, social workers are readily lured into quackery and pseudoscience, including bogus claims of knowledge in the professional literature (and perhaps even fraud), therefore violating ethical obligations described in the National Association of Social Workers (2008) *Code of Ethics.* This is especially concerning given that social workers are often double agents in whom poor and disadvantaged clients are coerced into contact. Many students, including doctoral students, do not know what science is and what it is not and are often misinformed by instructors and by what they read in the professional literature written by authors who also do not understand what science is and what it is not. Giveaway words include "prove," which implies that we know something for sure. Surveys show that many people do not understand the basic characteristics of science (National Science Foundation, 2006). Even some academics confuse logical positivism (abandoned decades ago) and science as we know it today (e.g., Phillips, 1992).

Not understanding science, we are open to influence by "scientism," for example, "slavish adherence to the methods of science even in a context where they are inappropriate" and a "false or mistaken claim to be scientific" (Phillips, 1987, p. 206). Not understanding science, social workers do not know that the essence of scientific objectivity is criticism. Not understanding science, they fall for claims that "x is well established," based on two well-designed clinical trials, when indeed the next trials may reveal different results; they do not have a robust recognition of uncertainty and are uncomfortable with it rather than recognizing it and acquiring constructive ways to handle it. Science is often misrepresented as a group of facts or a specific methodology. It is often hyped, as in "scientism." These misrepresentations obscure the value and humility of science as an imperfect but valuable problem-solving method. Popper (1994) suggests that "we are all equal in our vast ignorance." Environmental contingencies such as negative reactions from others in response to probing questions often work against this type of humility. Nor are social work students informed about the role of propaganda in our technological society and how it chips away at critical thinking skills (Gambrill, 2012b). We live in a society in which advertising and public relations are huge industries, the products of which are ever more present in the many gadgets we use every day. Stivers (2001) argues that in a technological society, technology itself assumes magical functions (e.g., just changing a management style is viewed as a success whether or not outcomes change).

Providing a sound education in science and related critical thinking skills would require social work educators to become informed, for example, about the many biases that may cloud our thinking. Not understanding science, social workers do not understand the role of anomalous findings in science (Bauer, 2001). They do not realize that controversy is integral to science and that social and political factors intrude, encouraging inflated claims of knowledge within science itself. Not understanding science, social workers confuse this with authority, when science is antithetical to reliance on authority. Science rejects a reliance on authority (e.g., pronouncements by officials or professors) as a route to knowledge. "Science is the belief in the ignorance of experts" (Feynman, 1969, p. 16). Authority and science are clashing views of how knowledge can be gained. Mistakes are inevitable both in science and in the helping professions. However, if a profession is authoritarian, "truth is vested in an authority. An authority is not expected to err" (so errors tend to be hidden; Skrabanek & McCormick, 1992). Not understanding science, social workers do not know what questions to ask about different types of claims (e.g., about risk, problem framing, effectiveness of intervention methods, validity of assessment measures); they do not know what claims can be tested and how and what cannot (e.g., Is there a God?). Ignorance about what science is and what it is not combines with an anti-intellectualism to hinder thinking critically about claims. The portrait of the latter in the United States by Richard Hofstadter (1963) continues to be relevant today. Both contribute to misunderstandings that foster pseudoscience and quackery in the helping professions, including social work. Intellect itself is often suspected in social work, just as it is in the arena of everyday politics in the United States.

Science is a way of thinking about and investigating the accuracy of assumptions about the world. It is a process for solving problems in which we learn from our mistakes. The essence of science is creative, bold guessing followed by rigorous testing in a way that offers accurate information about whether a guess (conjecture or theory) is accurate. Scientific statements are refutable or testable. Theories can be falsified only if specific predictions are made about what can happen and also about what cannot. The scientific tradition is the tradition of criticism (Popper, 1994, p. 42). Criticism (self-correction) is the essence of science. Popper (1994) argues that "What we call *scientific objectivity* is nothing else than the fact that no scientific theory is accepted as dogma, and that all theories are tentative and are open all the time to severe criticism—to a rational, critical discussion aiming at the elimination of errors" (p. 160). Uncertainty is assumed. Because further tests of a hypothesis may show that it is wrong, knowledge is always tentative. Indeed, the history of science and medicine shows that what we often accept as the truth has been wrong and what has been rejected as "bunk" has been correct. Consider, for example, reactions to Semmelweis's discovery that failing to wash one's hands between examinations of patients was the direct cause of death of many women (Loudon, 2013). Although we can justify the selection of a theory by its having survived more risky tests concerning a wider variety of hypotheses (without being falsified), compared with other theories that have not been tested or that have been falsified, we can never accurately claim that this theory is "the truth." Some tests are more rigorous than others in controlling sources or bias and so offer more information about what may be true or false. Theories differ in the extent to which they have been tested and in the rigor of the tests used.

The view of science presented here, critical rationalism, is one in which the theory-laden nature of observation is assumed (i.e., our assumptions influence what we observe—observation is always selective) and rational criticism is viewed as the essence of science (Miller, 1994; Popper, 1972). Concepts are assumed to have meaning and value even though they are unobservable. A critical attitude, which Karl Popper (1972, 1994) defines as a willingness and commitment to open up favored views to severe scrutiny, is basic to science, distinguishing it from pseudoscience. If an agency for the homeless claims that it succeeds in finding homes for applicants within 10 days, you could accept this claim at face value or systematically gather data to see whether it is true. It is assumed that the soundness of an assertion is related to the uniqueness and rigor of related critical tests.

The history of science and medicine shows that the results of experimental research involving systematic investigation often free us from false beliefs that harm. Scientists are skeptics. They question what others view as fact or common sense. They ask for arguments and evidence. They do not have sacred cows.

> Science … is a way of thinking. … [It] invites us to let the facts in, even when they don't conform to our preconceptions. It counsels us to consider hypotheses in our heads and see which ones best match the facts. It urges on us a fine balance between no-holds-barred openness to new ideas, however heretical, and the most rigorous skeptical scrutiny of everything—new ideas and established wisdom. (Sagan, 1990, p. 265)

Scientists and skeptics seek criticism of their views and change their beliefs when they have good reason to do so. The history of science highlights that which was thought to be true, such as the cause of ulcers, was often found to be false. It also shows that new ideas are censored and that those proposing them have great difficulty getting a hearing for their views in scientific journals and in the media. Thus, there is science as open criticism, and science as propaganda—for example, censorship of competing well-argued views. Confusing these may have harmful results for clients. Indeed, history shows that prestigious journals often rejected the work of scientists who overturned prevailing beliefs. Bauer (2004, 2012) suggests that entrenched research cartels may guard turf, hampering exploration of new (and more accurate) ideas.

Critical thinking and science go hand in hand. In both there is an openness—even eagerness—to learn by discovering that one has been wrong, a desire to accurately understand, present, and learn from other viewpoints, a deep curiosity about the world, and a willingness to say "I was wrong." In both, there is recognition that claims should be critically appraised in terms of their accuracy, especially when, if acted on, they affect clients' lives. These characteristics are at odds with authority-based decision making in which bogus claims are uncritically promoted and those who raise questions are attacked, ignored, or ridiculed. This in part explains why critical thinking attitudes, skills, and knowledge are not taught in most (any?) schools of social work or many other schools. There may be the labels, but not the substance.

Historians of science differ regarding how to demark the difference between pseudoscience and science. Some such as Bauer (2001) argue that the demarcation is fuzzy, as revealed by what scientists actually do, for example, fail to reject a favored theory in the face of negative results (e.g., perhaps a test was flawed) and the prevalence of pseudoscience within science (e.g., belief in N-rays). He contrasts natural science, social science, and anomalistics. He suggests that anomalistics shares some of the characteristics that all interdisciplinary searches for knowledge possess. Popper uses the criterion of falsifiability to demark what is or could be scientific knowledge from what is not or could not be. For example, there is no way to refute the claim that "there is a God," but there is a way to refute a claim that assertive community services for the severely and chronically mentally ill reduce substance abuse. (For further discussion of this issue, see, for example, the entry on science and pseudoscience in the *Stanford Encyclopedia of Philosophy* [2014].) Teaching students about the paranormal as well as about science may decrease beliefs in the former (Lilienfeld, 2005; Morier & Keeports, 1994). However, Impey, Buxner, Antonellis, Johnson, and King (2011) found that the level of scientific knowledge did not correlate with pseudoscientific beliefs. Many people accept a justification approach to knowledge development, focusing on gathering support for (justifying, confirming) claims and theories. Popper (1972) argues that falsification (attempts to falsify, to discover the errors in our beliefs) by means of critical discussion and testing is the only sound way to develop knowledge. Confirmations of a theory can readily be found if one looks for them.

We need more books that take a critical look at social work practice guided by empirical data regarding what social workers do. We have far too many of the other kind—books that exaggerate the evidentiary status of services and so misinform readers. Critics of social work are often ignored; the more penetrating the critique, the more likely it is to be ignored and/or distorted, as illustrated by reactions to *A Dream Deferred: How Social Work Education Lost Its Way and What Can Be Done* by Stoesz, Karger, and Carrillo (2010). *Science and Pseudoscience in Social Work Practice* highlights the importance of increased transparency regarding exactly what social workers do and to what effect. What types of parent training programs are offered to parents forced to be involved in the child welfare system? Are parents informed that the programs to which they are referred are not likely to improve their skills but will give them false assurances that their skills have improved? Evaluations of students by their supervisors in the agencies in which they work, which I have seen, are typically vague. For example, they do not describe how many clients each student saw, what problems these clients desired help with, what specific outcomes were pursued, and how many were attained based on ongoing monitoring. Avoiding calls for accountability is routine in the social service sector, even though there is a great deal of rhetoric about being accountable. And too seldom do social workers and their educators ask the question: Would they refer their loved one to a social worker who uses methods such as those described in this book?

*Science and Pseudoscience in Social Work Practice* has a clear and vital message: The vulnerable are often made more vulnerable because of social workers' avoidable ignorance and/or lack of caring. Throughout, the authors document avoidable harming in the name of helping, in direct violation of professional code of ethics, often involving clients already disadvantaged. It is not an easy book to read. The reader wants to draw back and deny that the harms described, typically unintentional, were carried out by those who have degrees from accredited schools of social work. We must care enough to move beyond good intentions. As Feynman (1974) suggests: "The first principle is that you must not fool yourself and you are the easiest person to fool" (p. 4). The authors' descriptions of the use of dubious and harmful practices and neglect of effective methods on the part of social workers have profound implications for related venues. Some, such as professional education, are discussed in Chapter 7. Egregious correctable lapses in social work education have been noted in earlier publications (e.g., Stoesz et al., 2010). Recognition of social, political, and economic influences (e.g., to make money and gain status) on "claim making" about what helps and what harms and in affecting what is published and what services are offered to clients is vital to avoid naive uncritical acceptance of claims that, if acted on, may harm clients.

Thinking critically about claims, no matter who makes them, is vital. It roots out vagueness that may hide harmful and ineffective practices imposed on vulnerable clients. Avoiding confirmation biases (the tendency to search only for data that confirm our views and to ignore data that do not) requires seeking evidence against favored views and considering well-argued alternative views. If criticism is the route to knowledge, we must value getting closer to the truth more than winning arguments, making money, and maintaining status. Only through criticism can we discover our errors and perhaps learn how to do better in the future. Collecting systematic data concerning service outcomes provides a guide for decisions and allows social workers to discover whether they are helping, harming, or having no effect. Such outcome monitoring has been shown to enhance positive outcomes (Lambert, 2010). But criticism is often feared and resented by those who prefer winning an argument or protecting turf more than discovering what helps and what harms clients. Critical thinking is dangerous. Critical thinkers raise questions such as "Where's the evidence that this method helps clients?" and "Could this practice harm clients?"

In social work, those who raise questions are often criticized as "confrontational"—too academic. A wedge is drawn between caring and questioning when indeed one cannot care if one does not question. All these dysfunctional reactions maintain a lack of transparency as to what social workers do and to what effect. Thus, we have no idea what percentage of services offered represent pseudoscience and quackery. Questions such as "What percentage of problems brought by clients to our agencies is resolved and how do we know?" and "What do you mean by_____?" may reveal that an agency is offering ineffective services to clients. It may reveal that interventions described as "evidence based" are authority based. That is why critical thinking is typically not encouraged in schools of social work; we have the name but not the essence, just as we have the trappings of science but not the essence in pseudoscience.

Social workers should graduate with well-honed critical appraisal skills, allowing them to be expert detectors of bogus claims of knowledge in addition to acquiring assertive skills needed to raise important questions, even in environments in which those who raise questions are viewed as troublemakers, even turncoats. Demonstration of minimal related competencies in these areas, such as recognizing flaws in their own thinking, should be required. Without such knowledge, skills, and the motivation to use them, social workers are patsies for bogus claims and, as suggested in the study of quackery, become advertisers for dubious products and practices (Barrett & Jarvis, 1993). We cannot assume that claims made in published literature—even peer-reviewed journals—are accurate. We must think for ourselves. This requires both the motivation and related critical appraisal and assertive skills to do so. Keeping our eye on helping clients enhance the quality of their lives will contribute to the courage to raise vital questions, as will working with others who value this aim in coordinated efforts.

Even with much-needed improvements in social work education, history shows that other paths must also be taken to improve services for clients, including continued exposure of harmful methods and failure to provide effective methods. The need for whistle-blowing and involvement of clients in pressing for effective services is described by the authors in their concluding chapter. Let us hope, as the authors note in the Preface, that shedding light on dubious practices in social work will decrease them and increase the use of effective methods. Social work has a long history of social reform and helping efforts. Let us continue this by paying attention to the important message of this book.

*The truth does not change according to our ability to stomach it.*—FLANNERY O'CONNOR (1955)

*Eileen Gambrill, PhD*
School of Social Welfare
University of California at Berkeley

## REFERENCES

Barrett, S., & Jarvis, W. J. (Eds.). (1993). *The health robbers: A close look at quackery in America.* Amherst, NY: Prometheus.

Bauer, H. H. (2001). *Science or pseudoscience: Magnetic healing, psychic phenomena and other heterodoxies.* Urbana, IL: University of Illinois Press.

Bauer, H. H. (2004). Science in the 21st century: Knowledge monopolies and research cartels. *Journal of Scientific Exploration, 18,* 643–660.

Bauer, H. H. (2012). *Dogmatism in science and medicine: How dominant theories monopolize research and stifle the search for truth.* Jefferson, NC: McFarland.

Duncan, B. L., Miller, S. D., Wampold, B. E., & Hubble, M. A. (Eds.). (2010). *The heart & soul of change: Delivering what works in therapy* (2nd ed.). Washington, DC: American Psychological Association.

Dunning, D., Heath, C., & Suls, J. M. (2004). Flawed self-assessment: Implications for health, education, and the workplace. *Psychological Science in the Public Interest, 5*, 69–106.

Ferguson, C., Marcus, A., & Oransky, I. (2014). Publishing: The peer-review scam. *Nature, 515*(7528), 480–482.

Feynman, R. P. (1969). What is science? *The Physics Teacher, 7*, 313–320. Retrieved April 2, 2015, from www.fotuva.org/feynman/what_is_science.html

Feynman, R. P. (1974). *Cargo cult science* [Caltech commencement address]. Retrieved from http://neurotheory.columbia.edu/~ken/cargo_cult.html

Gambrill, E. (2012a). *Critical thinking in clinical practice: Improving the quality of judgment and decisions* (3rd ed.). Hoboken, NJ: John Wiley & Sons.

Gambrill, E. (2012b). *Propaganda in the helping professions.* New York, NY: Oxford University Press.

Hansen, H., Bourgois, P., & Drucker, E. (2014). Pathologizing poverty: New forms of diagnosis, disability, and structural stigma under welfare reform. *Social Science & Medicine, 103*, 76–83.

Hofstadter, R. (1963). *Anti-intellectualism in American life.* New York, NY: Vintage.

Hogarth, R. M. (2001). *Educating intuition.* Chicago, IL: University of Chicago Press.

Impey, C., Buxner, S., Antonellis, J., Johnson, E., & King, C. (2011). A twenty-year survey of science literacy among college undergraduates. *Journal of College Science Teaching, 40*, 70–76.

Ioannidis, J. P. A. (2005). Why most published research findings are false. *PLoS Medicine, 2*(8), e124.

Ioannidis, J. P. A. (2008). Why most discovered true associations are inflated. *Epidemiology, 19*, 640–648.

Ioannidis, J. P. A. (2012). Why science is not necessarily self-correcting. *Perspectives on Psychological Science, 7*, 645–654.

Ioannidis, J. P. A. (2014). How to make more published research true. *PLoS Medicine, 11*(10), e100174.

Irwin, H. J. (1993). Belief in the paranormal: A review of the empirical literature. *The Journal of the American Society for Psychical Research, 87*, 1–39.

Jacobson, J. W., Foxx, R. M., & Mulick, J. A. (Eds.). (2005). *Controversial therapies for developmental disabilities: Fad, fashion, and science in professional practice.* Mahwah, NJ: Lawrence Erlbaum.

Jarvis, W. T. (1990). *Dubious dentistry: A dental continuing education course.* Loma Linda, CA: Loma Linda University of Dentistry.

Korownyk, C., Kolber, M. R., McCormack, J., Lam, V., Overbo, K., Cotton, C., … Allan, G. M. (2014). Televised medical talk shows—what they recommend and the evidence to support their recommendations: A prospective observational study. *British Medical Journal, 349,* g7346. doi:10.1136/bmj.g7346.

Lambert, M. J. (2010). Yes, it is time for clinicians to routinely monitor treatment outcome. In B. L. Duncan, S. D. Miller, B. E. Wampold, & M. A. Hubble (Eds.), *The heart & soul of change: Delivering what works in therapy* (2nd ed., pp. 239–266). Washington, DC: American Psychological Association.

Lilienfeld, S. O. (2005). *The 10 commandments of helping students distinguish science from pseudoscience in psychology.* Retrieved from www.psychological-science.org/observer

Lilienfeld, S. O., Lynn, S. J., & Lohr, J. M. (Eds.). (2014). *Science and pseudoscience in clinical psychology* (2nd ed.). New York, NY: Guilford Press.

Loudon, I. (2013). Ignaz Phillip Semmelweis' studies of death in childbirth. *JLL Bulletin: Commentaries on the history of treatment evaluation.* Retrieved April 2, 2015, from http://evaluation.www.jameslindlibrary.org/articles/ignaz-phillip-semmelweis-studies-of-death-in-childbirth

Madden, G. J. (Ed.). (2013). *APA handbook of behavior analysis.* Washington, DC: American Psychological Association.

Miller, D. (1994). *Critical rationalism: A restatement and defense.* Chicago, IL: Open Court.

Morier, D., & Keeports, D. (1994). Normal science and the paranormal: The effect of a scientific method course on students' beliefs. *Research in Higher Education, 35,* 443–453.

National Association of Social Workers. (2008). *Code of ethics.* Silver Spring, MD: Author.

National Science Foundation. (2006). *Surveys of public understanding of science and technology: 1979–2006.* Retrieved August 22, 2011, from http://www.ropercenter.uconn.edu

O'Connor, F. (1955). Letter to Betty Hester, September 6, 1955. *This Day in Lettres.* Retrieved from http://theamericanreader.com/6-september-1955-flannery-oconnor/

Offit, P. (2013). *Do you believe in magic? Vitamins, supplements, and all things natural: A look behind the curtain.* New York, NY: Harper.

Phillips, D. C. (1987). *Philosophy, science and social inquiry: Contemporary methodological controversies in social science and related applied fields of research.* New York, NY: Pergamon.

Phillips, D. C. (1992). *The social scientist's bestiary: A guide to fabled threats to, and defenses of, naturalistic social studies.* New York, NY: Pergamon.

Popper, K. R. (1972). *Conjectures and refutations: The growth of scientific knowledge* (4th ed.). London, UK: Routledge & Kegan Paul.

Popper, K. R. (1994). *The myth of the framework: In defence of science and rationality* (M. A. Notturno, Ed.). New York, NY: Routledge.

Porter, R. (2000). *Quacks: Fakers & charlatans in English medicine.* Charleston, SC: Tempus.

retractionwatch.com. (2014). Retrieved from http://retractionwatch.com/ 2014/12/15/retraction-watch-growing-thanks-400000-grant-macarthur-foundation/

Sagan, C. (1990). Does truth matter? Science, pseudoscience, and civilization. *Skeptical Inquirer, 20*, 1–10.

Scull, A. (2015). *Madness in civilization.* Princeton, NJ: Princeton University Press.

Singer, B., & Benassi, V. A. (1981). Occult beliefs: Media distortions, social uncertainty, and deficiencies of human reasoning seem to be at the basis of occult beliefs. *American Scientist, 69*(1), 49–55.

Skrabanek, P., & McCormick, J. (1992). *Follies and fallacies in medicine* (2nd ed.). Chippenham, UK: Anthony Rowe.

Staats, A. (2012). *The marvelous learning animal: What makes human nature unique.* Amherst, NY: Prometheus Books.

*Stanford Encyclopedia of Philosophy.* (2014). Science and pseudo-science. Retrieved February 2015 from http://plato.stanford.edu/entries/pseudo-science/

Stivers, R. (2001). *Technology as magic: The triumph of the irrational.* New York, NY: Continuum.

Stoesz, D., Karger, H. J., & Carrillo, T. (2010). *A dream deferred: How social work education lost its way and what can be done.* New Brunswick, NJ: Transaction.

Thyer, B. (2005). The misfortunes of behavioral social work: Misprized, misread, and misconstrued. In S. A. Kirk (Ed.), *Mental health in the social environment: Critical perspectives* (pp. 330–343). New York, NY: Columbia University Press.

Timimi, S. (2012). Children's mental health in the era of globalization: Neoliberalism, commodification, McDonaldisation, and the new challenges they pose. In V. Olisah (Ed.), *Essential notes in psychiatry* (pp. 1–27). Rijeka, Croatia: InTech. Retrieved January 2, 2015, from http://www.intechopen .com/books/essential-notes-in-psychiatry

Young, J. H. (1992). *American health quackery.* Princeton, NJ: Princeton University Press.

# Preface

We offer this book, *Science and Pseudoscience in Social Work Practice*, to multiple communities—practicing social workers, members of the social work professoriate, undergraduate and graduate students, the members of other health care professions, and the general public. Our hope is to illustrate the extent to which the practice of clinical social work has matured to the point of being able to take a blunt look at some of the more disreputable elements to be found within the profession, with the idea that shedding light on these practices will serve as a form of disinfection and perhaps of inoculation: *disinfection* in that the more science-oriented members of the field will be stimulated to actively work toward uncovering and eliminating harmful theories and therapies currently being offered to the public by members of our profession; *inoculation* in that, by reading this book, students and practitioners will be less prone to adopt pseudoscientific methods of intervention and treatment. Through recognizing the hallmarks of incredible therapies, readers will be less prone to uncritically accept highly unusual claims, and more prone to require suitable evidence before adopting novel practices or following the more conventionally accepted practices that lack empirical support.

We view this book as the latest in a series of similarly themed books that have appeared for several hundred years, volumes that have dealt with charlatans, fake cures, snake oil salesmen, faith healers, and bogus psychotherapies. Some are quite antiquated, such as Menken (1715/1937), others simply older classics, as in Barnum (1865) and Randi (1982). Some books of this genre address a single profession, such as medicine (e.g., Bausell, 2007; Brock, 2008) or chiropractic (Smith, 1969). Other critical books focus on subdisciplines within a broader field, such as the practice of psychiatry, a subfield of medicine (Fisher & Greenberg, 1989; Johnstone, 1989; Ross & Pam, 1995; Valenstein, 1986). Lilienfeld, Lynn, and Lohr (2015) address the practice of pseudoscience within clinical psychology, and the broader interprofessional field of psychotherapy has been skeptically examined by Dawes (1994) and Mercer (2014). Some authors have addressed specific instances of pseudoscientific treatments being provided to individual clients, as in Mercer, Sarner, and Rosa's (2003) accounting of the smothering death of Candace Newmaker at the hands of her social worker psychotherapist applying so-called rebirthing therapy as part of a brutally intensive "attachment therapy" culminating in her death, or of Nathan's (2011) exposé of how Shirley Mason's psychiatrist, Cornelia Wilber, fabricated the notorious story known as *Sybil*, the famous multiple personality disorder case. Another variation is where authors provide an overview of pseudoscientific treatments used to treat particular disorders, such as autism (Offit, 2008). And yet another approach is to focus on the careers of individual purveyors of bogus treatments, as in Brock's (2008) review of the profitable career of Dr. John Brinkley, who became wealthy transplanting goat testicles into men seeking to revive their virility, or of Dr. Robert Battey's introduction in the late 1800s of the eventually widespread practice of removing the healthy ovaries of women with psychological disorders (Thierry, 1998).

There has been limited attention to pseudoscientific practices within the profession of social work. *Where Do People Take Their Troubles?* (Steiner, 1940, 1945) surveyed the sorry state of psychological and psychotherapeutic practice in general toward the end of World War II. Anyone could set up a practice as a psychologist or psychotherapist, and bogus training institutions and degrees abounded. Steiner describes how the worried well were preyed upon by unscrupulous "therapists," claiming expertise in solving problems related to relationships, unemployment, romance, and improving one's personality. "Treatment" was provided via one-to-one therapy, in groups, via postal mail correspondence, handwriting analysis, palm reading, astrology, and numerology, through the use of trances and via communicating with spirits, and through radio programs. Another work was titled *Trick or Treatment: How and When Psychotherapy Fails* (Stuart, 1970) and is in some way a precursor to Dawes (1994). Social worker Richard B. Stuart discussed the very limited evidence then available demonstrating the effectiveness of conventional, insight-oriented verbal psychotherapy, and how many of the claims made by the psychotherapy industry were grossly exaggerated. The brilliant work of social work professor Eileen Gambrill stands out as an exemplar within the field dealing with the topic of teaching skills in critical thinking. The ability to think critically is of course a prerequisite to recognizing pseudoscientific theories and practices, and Dr. Gambrill's numerous contributions in this oeuvre are without parallel and most highly recommended (e.g., Gambrill, 2010, 2012a, 2012b, 2012c).

A number of social workers have coauthored original research studies evaluating complementary or alternative therapies. For example, Margolin et al. (2002) conducted a randomized controlled trial of acupuncture for cocaine addiction, concluding that "acupuncture was not more effective than a needle insertion or relaxation control in reducing cocaine use. Our study does not support the use of acupuncture as a stand-alone treatment for cocaine addiction or in contexts in which patients receive only minimal concurrent psychosocial treatment. Research will be needed to examine acupuncture's contribution to addiction treatment when provided in an ancillary role" (p. 55). Another research group including a social worker coauthor, Taylor et al. (2003), evaluated the herbal remedy Echinacea as a treatment for upper respiratory tract infections in children, using a randomized controlled trial. Their conclusion? "*Echinacea purpurea,* as dosed in this study, was not effective in treating URI symptoms in patients 2 to 11 years old" (p. 2834). We laud such studies as the kind of strong evidence needed to sort out the useless pseudoscientific chaff from genuinely effective interventions and encourage other social workers to engage in this kind of difficult, rigorous, and highly important research. It may well be that some of the psychosocial treatments described in this book as currently lacking strong evidence of their helpfulness will, in time, through being subjected to controlled investigation, be shown (provisionally) to be effective. We will be among those applauding such developments. The attitude of scientific skepticism is that of doubt, not denial—of demanding credible evidence before accepting an unusual claim, but not asserting prior to such research that the claim is, by default of its apparently pseudoscientific features, false.

The survival of pseudoscientific and occult beliefs is widespread among the general public (see Doering-Mateuffel, 2011; Schein, Li, & Huang, 2014), and it is unrealistic to expect that social workers should somehow be exempt from such influences, any more than physicians, nurses, or psychologists would be. However, the essence of a true profession is the possession of knowledge and skills not usually available to the lay public, skills acquired through an arduous process of academic and clinical training, resulting in someone with an ability to deliver genuinely helpful care that is more effective than simply having access to a sympathetic ear or exposure to placebo treatments. We wrote this book in the hope of contributing to the advance of social work practice as an effective human services profession. It has two functions—to deter the uptake of pseudoscientific techniques and to promote the uptake of legitimately effective methods of care. If you have any further suggestions to help us in this process, feel free to contact either author. We hope you enjoy your reading, and pass the book along to colleagues. You may find parts of it provocative, but we had no intention of promoting needless angst or intradisciplinary criticism. However, some things *are* worth being distressed over, and then taking action. The promotion of science within social work and discouraging pseudoscience are two such issues.

# REFERENCES

Barnum, P. T. (1865). *Humbugs of the world: An account of humbugs, delusions, impositions, quackeries, deceits and deceivers generally, in all ages.* Landisville, PA: Coachwhip Publications. (Facsimile published in 2008)

Bausell, R. B. (2007). *Snake oil science: The truth about complementary and alternative medicine.* New York, NY: Oxford University Press.

Brock, P. (2008). *Charlatan: America's most dangerous huckster, the man who pursued him, and the age of flimflam.* New York, NY: Crown.

Dawes, R. M. (1994). *House of cards: Psychology and psychotherapy built on myth.* New York, NY: Free Press.

Doering-Mateuffel, S. (2011). Survival of occult practices and ideas in modern common sense. *Public Understanding of Science, 20,* 292–302.

Fisher, S., & Greenberg, R. P. (1989). *The limits of biological treatments for psychological distress: Comparisons with psychotherapy and placebo.* Hillsdale, NJ: Lawrence Erlbaum.

Gambrill, E. (2010). Evidence-informed practice: Antidote to propaganda in the helping professions. *Research on Social Work Practice, 20*, 302–320.

Gambrill, E. (2012a). *Critical thinking in clinical practice: Improving the quality of judgments and decisions* (3rd ed.). New York, NY: John Wiley.

Gambrill, E. (2012b). *Social work practice: A critical thinker's guide* (3rd ed.). New York, NY: Oxford University Press.

Gambrill, E. (2012c). *Propaganda in the helping professions.* New York, NY: Oxford University Press.

Johnstone, L. (1989). *Users and abusers of psychiatry: A critical look at traditional psychiatric practice.* New York, NY: Routledge.

Lilienfeld, S. O., Lynn, S. J., & Lohr, J. M. (2015). *Science and pseudoscience in clinical psychology.* New York, NY: Guilford Press.

Margolin, A., Kelber, H. D., Avants, S. K., Konefal, J., Gawin, F., Stark, E.,...Vaughan, R. (2002). Acupuncture for the treatment of cocaine addiction: A randomized controlled trial. *JAMA, 287*, 55–63.

Menken, J. B. (1937). *De Charlataneria Eruditorum* [The charlatanry of the learned]. Translated from the German by Francis E. Litz, with notes and an introduction by H. L. Mencken. New York, NY: Knopf. (Original work published 1715)

Mercer, J. (2014). *Alternative psychotherapies: Evaluating unconventional mental health treatments.* New York, NY: Rowman and Littlefield.

Mercer, J., Sarner, L., & Rosa, L. (2003). *Attachment therapy on trial: The torture and death of Candace Newmaker.* Westport, CT: Praeger.

Nathan, D. (2011). *Sybil exposed: The extraordinary story behind the famous multiple personality case.* New York, NY: Free Press.

Offit, P. A. (2008). *Autism's false prophets: Bad science, risky medicine, and the search for a cure.* New York, NY: Columbia University Press.

Randi, J. (1982). *Flim-flam: Psychics, ESP, unicorns and other delusions.* Amherst, NY: Prometheus Books.

Ross, C. A., & Pam, A. (1995). *Pseudoscience in biological psychiatry.* New York, NY: John Wiley.

Schein, P. P., Li, Y.-Y., & Huang, T.-C. (2014). Relationship between scientific knowledge and fortune-telling. *Public Understanding of Science, 23*, 780–796.

Smith, R. L. (1969). *At your own risk: The case against chiropractic.* New York, NY: Pocket Books.

Steiner, L. R. (1940). Where do people take their troubles? *American Journal of Orthopsychiatry, 10*, 805–809.

Steiner, L. R. (1945). *Where do people take their troubles?* New York, NY: Houghton Mifflin.

Stuart, R. B. (1970). *Trick or treatment: How and when psychotherapy fails.* Champaign, IL: Research Press.

Taylor, J. A., Weber, W., Standish, L., Quinn, H., Goesling, J., McGann, M., & Calebrese, C. (2003). Efficacy and safety of Echinacea in treating upper respiratory tract infections in children: A randomized controlled trial. *JAMA, 290*, 2824–2830.

Thierry, M. (1998). Battey's operation: An exercise in surgical frustration. *European Journal of Obstetrics and Gynecology, 81*, 243–246.

Valenstein, E. S. (1986). *Great and desperate cures: The rise and decline of psychosurgery and other radical treatments for mental illness.* New York, NY: Basic Books.

# Acknowledgments

The authors gratefully acknowledge the professionalism and expertise of the editorial staff at Springer Publishing Company in bringing about this book. We have been positively influenced by many individuals over our own respective careers.

For Bruce, the life and work of Eileen Gambrill make her stand out as one role model, impossible to emulate but still profoundly inspirational. Scott Lilienfeld, James Randi, Michael Shermer, and Penn and Teller also loom large as crusaders against pseudoscience, and their unknowing role modeling has been most appreciated. Bruce also recognizes and admires the life and work of Monica G. Pignotti, his former PhD student and now valued colleague and coauthor (and the admiration is mutual). To all of the aforementioned individuals, he owes a profound intellectual debt.

Monica would like to acknowledge the many helpful and inspiring people in the scientific mental health community, including Bruce A. Thyer, Scott Lilienfeld, Steven Jay Lynn, Eileen Gambrill, James Herbert, Brandon Gaudiano, Jeffrey M. Lohr, Cathleen Mann, Jerry Rosen, Richard Gist, R. Christopher Barden, Carol Tavris, Richard J. McNally, Jean Mercer, Elizabeth Loftus, and others who have had the courage to take a stand on this very important issue, even when it has not been easy to do so.

# CHAPTER 1

# Characteristics of Science and Pseudoscience in Social Work Practice

*At the heart of science is an essential tension between two seemingly contradictory attitudes—an openness to new ideas, no matter how bizarre or counterintuitive they may be, and the most ruthless skeptical scrutiny of all ideas, old and new. This is how deep truths are winnowed from deep nonsense. The collective enterprise of creative thinking and skeptical thinking together keeps the field on track.*— CARL SAGAN (1996, p. 304)

## WHY SHOULD SOCIAL WORKERS CARE ABOUT PSEUDOSCIENCE?

When we disclose to our colleagues our concerns regarding pseudoscience and the practice of questionable interventions in social work, sometimes there is encouragement, curiosity, and support; other times we meet with indifference or, in some cases, even hostility. Questions we are frequently asked and comments often include:

- Why should we, as social workers and people who consult social workers, care about this topic?
- This is a dead issue. Evidence-based practice is already being used in most agencies that cannot get funding without empirical evidence (this question comes mostly from academics).

**1**

- Why are you being so negative?
- Social work is a profession that does not need to utilize research.
- Isn't it enough to accentuate the positive and focus on treatments that work?
- It is the therapeutic relationship that really determines efficacy, not the particular form of intervention.

In response to why we feel it is valuable to press on with this issue, one proponent of science and critical thinking stated:

> If people believe something that's clearly wrong about the world, it's worth trying some civil persuasion to convince them otherwise (and more impassioned persuasion in the case of more dangerous beliefs). (Quantheory, 2011, p. B18)

The feedback we have received from colleagues in our profession clearly indicates that there are great differences as to how the need for evidence-based social work practice is perceived. On the extreme sides of this issue, although some view evidence-based practice as a done deal, others still completely disregard the need for it, do not view social work as a profession that needs to utilize research, and feel that sharing of clinical experiences is sufficient and, of course, there are those who fall somewhere between these two extremes. This is indicative of what has been referred to as the gap between research (science) and practice (Lilienfeld, Lynn, & Lohr, 2014). However, from both sides of this gap, we often hear a lack of understanding as to why it is important to pay attention to pseudoscientific interventions. Among some advocates of a research-based approach, the implication seems to be that if we just focus on empirically supported treatments, it will be sufficient, and the more questionable practices will fall away on their own without further efforts to educate people on pseudoscience. Some feel that raising the topic of questionable interventions will just hurt people's feelings, something most of us in the helping professions are very reluctant to do. Others believe that all interventions are equally helpful, and it is the therapeutic relationship that makes most of the difference; hence, it makes no difference which intervention we choose. The belief seems to be that if we form a strong therapeutic alliance with our clients, all will be well.

In the spirit of Carl Sagan, we wish to encourage scientifically based innovation and openness to new ideas, yet subject all such claims to rigorous scientific scrutiny before putting them on the market and making claims. Often, social workers believe that their own clinical experience is enough to decide which interventions to use (Pignotti & Thyer, 2012) and are not aware of the many factors that can make an intervention seem effective when actually it does not help or even may be harmful (Lilienfeld, Ritsche, Lynn, Cautin, & Latzman, 2014). Our purpose in drawing attention to these issues is not to exude negativity, create conflict, or hurt our largely well-intentioned colleagues' feelings. Rather, our intentions are to remain loyal to our social work values and obligation to our clients, which require us to deliver the interventions that are most likely to help them and least likely to harm and/or mislead them. We cannot fulfill this obligation unless we are able to recognize interventions that may make claims to be scientific and help, but in fact, lack evidence of being able to do so. The National Association of Social Workers (NASW) *Code of Ethics* requires us to utilize research findings in our practice and put our clients' interests first, above our own feelings and interests if there is a conflict, although we believe that our approach ultimately is in the best interest of any honest practitioner as well as his or her clients. In order to best serve our clients, we should not only identify treatments that have support, but also treatments usually delivered by well-intentioned practitioners, which nevertheless lack support and may even harm clients.

A recent survey of 367 licensed clinical social workers (LCSWs) throughout the United States revealed both good and bad news (Pignotti & Thyer, 2012). The good news is that 97% of respondents surveyed reported having used, within the past year, at least one intervention that had some basis in credible research evidence. Although the survey was based on self-reported practices and we obviously do not know what these LCSWs were actually doing in their sessions with clients and whether they were using actual empirically based treatments, it is encouraging that they were at least naming interventions that do have empirical support. However, 75% of the LCSWs surveyed also reported having used at least one novel unsupported therapy within the past year—that is, therapies that lacked evidence to support their efficacy and yet made unsupported claims that went beyond the evidence.

Moreover, when our participants were asked to rate their reasons for selecting interventions, they rated clinical experience of success overwhelmingly higher than the results of research published in peer-reviewed journals. Although this is just one survey and it might not be representative of the practices of all social workers, other studies performed on mental health professionals from a variety of different disciplines that have included social workers and studies that surveyed licensed psychologists have produced similar results. The fact is that firsthand experience is very compelling to us as human beings. We discuss the reasons for this and how such experience can be deceiving later in this chapter.

At this point, readers might wonder why the existence and proliferation of pseudoscientific practices should matter, because many LCSWs appear to be combining questionable practices with ones that have more research support. Isn't it enough that effective treatments are being delivered? We do not believe so. There are compelling reasons why the flip side to evidence-based practice should be examined and is important in its own right. The most obvious reason is that some of these interventions have been shown to do more harm than good. For example, coercive restraint therapies were employed by two master's-level social workers, Connell Watkins and Julie Ponder, which resulted in the death of Candace Newmaker, a 10-year-old girl who was undergoing a 2-week intensive "attachment therapy" in Colorado (Mercer, Sarner, & Rosa, 2003). This is commonly described as a "rebirthing" session death, because the child was smothered to death during a so-called rebirthing session, while being wrapped in blankets and sat upon by four adults who ignored her protests that she could not breathe. In actuality, what many people are not aware of is that rebirthing was just one technique used in a highly brutal 2-week therapy intensive, much of which was videotaped and brought out as evidence at the trial. The renowned skeptic Michael Shermer (2004) referred to Candace's death, we believe correctly and fundamentally, as "Death by Theory," also the title of his article, which had to do with much more than just the one technique that killed her. As Shermer put it, she was "killed by pseudoscience" (p. 48).

The road to Candace's death began with a bad decision made by a child welfare worker to permanently separate her from her mother for neglect, rather than attempting to work with the mother, despite the fact that there was no evidence of abuse. When the child was adopted and began to have serious emotional and behavioral problems after being separated from her birth mother, her adoptive mother sought help from mental health professionals. A bogus assessment procedure consisting of a symptom checklist that had no empirical support was administered to the adoptive mother over the telephone, leading to a supposed diagnosis of "attachment disorder." This diagnosis was given without ever having communicated with the child, and it went far beyond the *Diagnostic and Statistical Manual of Mental Disorders,* Fifth Edition (*DSM-5;* the fourth edition, text revision [*DSM-IV-TR*] in print at the time this incident occurred) definition of reactive attachment disorder (American Psychiatric Association [APA], 2000, 2013). The intensive "treatment" was equally unsupported and never properly tested for safety and efficacy. The "rebirthing" session, although ultimately fatal, was only a minor part of the many highly problematic and abusive treatments employed in the days leading up to her death. More details are provided in Chapter 3, but suffice it to say for now that the reason Candace's therapists gave for not releasing her from the pillows and blankets was that they believed she was just being manipulative, an alleged symptom of their bogus diagnosis that had virtually no empirical basis. They did not believe her, due to their pseudoscientific theories on "attachment," and thus, she died. The two therapists, who each held master's in social work degrees, were ultimately sentenced to 17 years in prison and barred from ever practicing again. Although it was ultimately the rebirthing session that killed Candace, that session was made possible through a series of poor decisions that included the questionable removal of the child from her birth parent, the use of pseudoscientific assessment procedures, and the use of an "intensive" therapy based on pseudoscientific theories in which the therapists strongly believed, which ultimately led them to not believe their frightened and tightly bound child-client when she told them she could not breathe.

There are many more instances of children and adults dying or being seriously harmed by similar pseudoscientific practices. Nevertheless, people might still wonder about practices that do not appear to be directly harmful and yet make unsupported claims. Although seemingly positive effects may be due to positive suggestion and other factors having nothing to do with the treatment itself, people may ask: So what? Isn't the bottom line that the person has gotten better or at least has not been harmed? We point out that what people need to consider are indirect ways in which such treatments can be harmful, which the psychologist Scott Lilienfeld has called opportunity costs. For one thing, such treatments may be contended to be proprietary trade secrets and very expensive, wasting a client's money, draining an agency of financial resources, and also wasting time. Although such treatments might bring about a temporary placebo effect, they may deprive the client of treatments that have been demonstrated to work, through well-designed, controlled, and independently conducted research published in reputable peer-reviewed journals. Some pseudoscientific practices may seem quick and easy compared to some of the empirically supported approaches, such as exposure therapy. Furthermore, some conditions, if left untreated, may result in deterioration. Thus, such deterioration may occur during a treatment that is, in and of itself, harmless, but does not help. Such quick, seemingly painless fixes can be very seductive to the client, although not ultimately helpful. Recently, Scott Lilienfeld et al. cataloged a host of reasons why an intervention may appear to work when in fact it does not, which they call "Causes of Spurious Therapeutic Effectiveness" (Lilienfeld, Ritsche, et al., 2014, p. 355) or CSTEs. We will be providing examples throughout this book of such treatments and how they have indirectly harmed clients.

## WHAT IS PSEUDOSCIENCE?

Richard J. McNally (McNally, 2003a) has noted that pseudoscience, like pornography, may be difficult to define, but we know it when we see it. That being said, in the interest of greater precision, we would nevertheless like to begin by offering our readers some definitions and indicators of pseudoscientific practices as guidelines for determining whether a practice ought to be of concern.

Essentially, pseudoscientific practices are practices that give the superficial appearance of being derived from science and yet lack an actual scientific basis. The philosopher of science, Mario Bunge, defines pseudoscience as, "a body of beliefs and practices whose practitioners wish, naively or maliciously, pass for science although it is alien to the approach, the techniques, and the fund of knowledge of science" (Bunge, 1998, p. 41). As we can see from Bunge's definition, the practitioner's intention is not necessarily malicious. Well-meaning people might engage in the practice of pseudoscience simply because they do not recognize it as pseudoscience and believe that their own personal and clinical experience of success is enough to validate what they are doing. We operate on the premise that this is the case with most social workers who have taken up the profession with the sincere intention of helping others and who are engaging in practices that they truly believe are helping their clients.

Unfortunately, however, sincerity on the part of a practitioner does not necessarily mean that the client is truly being helped.

Gibbes (1925) addressed the topic of quacks and quackery in medicine, and his observations from almost 90 years ago are relevant to social work today. For example:

> There seem to be two main avenues through which quackery finds access to human credulity. It is either through the claim of a divinely inspired personality or the development of doctrine concerning the cause and cure of disease which differs radically from the commonly accepted ideas, the doctrine being surrounded with words and phrases which have a euphonious sound and little meaning.... The claims are not always the product of cupidity; in fact the success which attends them often depends on the fanatical sincerity of the testifier. (p. 535)

and

> Germs of psychological truths have been magnified into distorted doctrines of cause and cure of disease, electrical phenomena have stimulated the imagination to weird ideas in connection with its application to the seeking after health...sincerity seems to be the rule rather than the exception in the founders of these cults. In most instances, brooding or hysterical individuals, acting against the deficiencies of regular medicine, or having *experiences* which appeal to them as revelations, enthusiastically launch their ideas, and they find a sympathetic reception in the minds of other brooding or hysterical people who have suffered from the failures of doctors or medicine. On the other hand, we shall find instances of undoubted malicious exploitation. (p. 536)

How do we recognize whether a practice is pseudoscientific as opposed to scientific? Lilienfeld, Lynn, et al. (2014) have provided us with a list of indicators, based on the work of Mario Bunge and others, and adapted to the mental health field. Note that none of these indicators, in and of itself, means that a practice is necessarily scientific, because legitimate practices may also contain some of these indicators.

As a rule of thumb, however, the more indicators a practice contains, the more likely it is that you are looking at a pseudoscientific practice, especially if the practice also lacks independently conducted, well-designed randomized controlled clinical trials. These indicators are:

1. *"An overuse of ad hoc hypotheses designed to immunize claims from falsification"* (p. 7). This means that when evidence is produced that disconfirms a particular practice and runs contrary to its claims, ardent believers in it come up with what are essentially excuses to explain the negative or null results away. A less formal popular term for this is *mental gymnastics*. These excuses take the form of after-the-fact explanations rather than the predetermined hypotheses on which a scientific study is normally conducted. Doing so, at least in the eyes of the believers, protects the claims from falsification.

   When new information comes in that contradicts cherished beliefs, cognitive dissonance occurs, and adding new cognitions to explain them away is one way we, as human beings, have of minimizing cognitive dissonance (Festinger, 1985). One common way this may be done is by adding new rules to the procedure that are often unwarranted generalizations from personal experience or anecdotes rather than scientific evidence. For example, one therapy that involves finger tapping on acupressure points on the body, which is described in more detail later in the book, claims to cure a variety of different conditions within minutes. However, when such a cure does not occur or the results do not hold up over time, this is explained away by the notion that the person has come in contact with a "toxin" (something such as a common food the person is eating, drinking, or inhaling). Additional levels of training and procedures were developed to test for these alleged "toxins," which leads the person into more expensive, time-consuming treatments, which also remain untested and, thus, have no scientific evidence to support their effectiveness. Suddenly, a therapy advertised as taking at most, only a few sessions, ends up going on for several months or even years for some individuals on a quest for finding the right "toxin" and that staying away from that "toxin" will produce the hoped-for cure.

   Something similar may occur in legitimate science. However, the key difference is that in science the new hypotheses are systematically tested, rather than just assumed to be true based on experience. For example, blood type theory holds that type O is the universal donor. That is, people with type O blood may donate to people of any other blood type. This theory, however, appeared to have been falsified when it was found that sometimes the blood of people with type O actually ended up killing people of other blood types. This led to the discovery of the Rh factor that explained these deaths. That is, a type O Rh-positive donor to someone of another blood type with a negative Rh factor was not compatible, due to the Rh factor. Hence, the claim that all people with type O blood are universal donors was falsified. As a result, the theory had to be modified to incorporate this new discovery of Rh factor and now we commonly know that a person with type O Rh-negative blood is the universal donor. Were these scientists engaging in pseudoscience by coming up with this after-the-fact hypothesis? Of course not; there is a major difference. Unlike pseudoscience, such discoveries have been held up by rigorous testing in subsequent experiments and add to the knowledge base. Theories get revised based on new evidence and their explanatory power grows. In contrast, with pseudoscience they are not rigorously tested and only add unnecessary complications and confusion to the treatment, which still lacks evidence to support its effectiveness.

2. *"Absence of self-correction"* (p. 7). Proponents of pseudoscience generally will not admit when they are wrong; hence, no self-correction occurs. Practitioners of legitimate science, in contrast, will be transparent about their errors and correct them. Generally, the more time and money a person invests in something, the more difficult it is for that individual to admit when he or she is proven wrong. It is much easier to revert to the kinds of ad hoc hypotheses described in item 1, than to essentially go back to the drawing board and start over, which might mean admitting that years of time and effort were all for naught. Nevertheless, a real scientist knows that errors do, in fact, occur and a scientist who is loyal to scientific values of discovery of what is true and advancing genuine knowledge, above all else, will have the integrity to admit when wrong, whatever the cost of self-correction. One way we in the mental health profession can encourage such an attitude is to reinforce with recognition and praise colleagues who make such admissions, rather than condemning and penalizing them. It is the people who would not admit when they are wrong who ought to incur our social disapproval and ultimate condemnation.

3. *"Evasion of peer review"* (p. 7). Proponents of pseudoscientific practices may rationalize their lack of peer-reviewed publications
by claiming that the scientific community, journal editors, and
reviewers are biased against them and will not accept their sub-
mitted articles for publication. We recognize that the peer-review
system is far from perfect and not all decisions are necessarily
fair. Sometimes studies deserving publication get rejected due to
biases on the part of reviewers and/or editors, and at other times,
highly flawed studies may be accepted for publication. However,
if deserving authors persist and resubmit to other journals, good
studies do eventually get published. Proponents of pseudoscientific approaches tend to blame the system rather than consider that
there may be actual serious flaws in the methodology of studies
they submit.

Recently, there has been more and more emphasis on evidence-
based practice, which has made such excuses and evasion unacceptable. This has brought about a variation in this theme where
trademarked therapies publish their own journals, which contain
only favorable articles and studies, staffed and reviewed almost
exclusively by proponents and yet declare themselves to be "peer
reviewed." Thus, such proponents evade actual peer review by colleagues who have no vested interest in the approach, by publishing what are essentially vanity journals. The lesson to be learned
is that when looking for evidence, be sure to notice which journals
published the studies. If the same journal name keeps coming up,
investigate further and determine whether the journal is owned and
operated by proponents of the therapy. If so, and no other favorable
studies exist, then proponents may be evading genuine peer review
in this manner.

4. *"Emphasis on confirmation and refutation"* (p. 8). It is easy to find
confirmatory evidence for just about anything if one looks for it.
However, the job of the real scientist is, in the words of physicist
Richard Feynman, to bend over backward to prove oneself wrong.
This involves designing rigorous experiments to test and potentially falsify our most cherished notions. Being a real scientific
social worker as opposed to a pseudoscientist means putting first
the learning of the truth that will ultimately best serve our clients,
rather than the evasion of rigorous tests that could falsify claims.

5. *"Reversed burden of proof"* (p. 8). The burden of proof for any claim is on the person who makes the claim. Promoters of pseudoscientific practices tend to reverse this burden. This commonly takes the form of demanding that critics prove that their approaches do not work. Whenever a critic rightfully asks for evidence, the pseudoscientist commonly demands that the critic prove him or her wrong. Such a demand is valid only if the claimant has already produced solid evidence that the approach is effective. It is only at that point that the burden of proof would shift to the critic.

   A more subtle form of this are instances when careful reviews of an intervention are conducted and existing studies are found to be flawed, leading to the conclusion that there is no good evidence to support that intervention. A common retort is the demand that the reviewers provide "balance" by showing flaws in studies that produced negative results. Although this certainly ought to be done, the main point being missed is that if claimants have failed to meet the burden of proof, the approach cannot be deemed effective, no matter how badly flawed the negative studies were. Additionally, the reality of any given situation is not necessarily "balanced." What reviewers of interventions ought to aim for instead is accurate evaluation of the existing evidence.

6. *"Absence of connectivity"* (p. 8). Pseudoscientific approaches commonly claim to be based on entirely new models of the world or paradigms, which have suddenly materialized. *Breakthrough, groundbreaking discovery*, and *paradigm shift* are terms we might often see in advertisements for such interventions, which are said to be completely unlike anything that came before. Although such dramatic shifts may sometimes occur in legitimate science, real scientists first investigate more mundane explanations that may fit current empirically supported models before considering that such a shift has occurred. Moreover, legitimate science demands that high-quality evidence be produced and replicated before even considering that such a paradigm shift may have occurred. The claims for some approaches would, if accepted, mean completely overturning the laws of physics as we know them. Hence, the well-known saying that extraordinary claims require extraordinary evidence applies.

7. *"Overreliance on testimonial and anecdotal evidence"* (p. 9). One need only surf the Internet for a brief period of time to witness countless

examples of this. All too often we can observe even licensed mental health professionals advertising a service or particular intervention that lacks strong research support and, instead, basing claims on testimonials and anecdotes of success. For treatments that already have been demonstrated to have strong research support, anecdotes and testimonials can be used to illustrate what the treatment can accomplish for people. In that case, anecdotes would not be used as evidence, but rather as an illustration of existing evidence. It is always important, however, to accompany such anecdotes and testimonials with an accurate presentation of what the research shows. The problem with using anecdotes and testimonials as evidence is that even if these are honestly reported, the person advertising is going to focus on successes. We rarely, if ever, see testimonials from people who have not gotten the results expected for a particular intervention on a website promoting that intervention. All too often such failures are not acknowledged or explained. Therefore, there is no substitute for well-designed studies published in peer-reviewed journals to provide evidence for the efficacy of a particular intervention.

The problem with an overreliance upon testimonial evidence was noted by Sternberg (1897) in his article titled "Science and Pseudo-Science in Medicine":

> The fact that a considerable proportion of those that are sick from various acute or chronic ailments recover after a time, independently of the use of medicinal agents or methods of treatment, taken in conjunction with this tendency to ascribe recovery to the treatment employed, makes it an easy matter to obtain certificates of cure for any nostrum which an unprincipled money-seeker may see fit to offer to a credulous public. If ten in a thousand of those who have used the alleged remedy believe themselves to have benefited, their certificates will answer all purposes of exploitation and the 990 will not be heard from by the general public. (p. 205)

This observation alone illustrates why control groups are needed to properly evaluate new claims regarding potentially effective treatments.

8. *"Use of obscurantist language"* (p. 9). While legitimate science, of course, has specialized language that is necessary to provide

explanations, pseudoscientific practices tend to use specialized jargon that sounds scientific and technical but does not explain anything. One test would be to ask whether ordinary language would suffice in explaining the existing phenomenon. Does the term actually describe phenomena shown to exist? Does the term ultimately have a referent in reality or is it a term that sounds like a valid concept, but has no basis in fact? For example, one LCSW recently proclaimed in a videotaped audition for the *Oprah* show, "Beliefs have energy stuck in them…by using your own meridian system you can learn how to release the stuck energy and replace your negative beliefs with positive ones" (myown.oprah.com/audition/index.html?request=video_details&response_id=20419&promo_id=1, para. 1). The critically thinking social worker might ask, just what is "stuck energy"? How would you measure that? How would you know if you had it? What exactly gets stuck and where? What is a meridian system? How would that be measured? However, this LCSW offers no way to do that, but only supports her belief by saying that she has done this work successfully with thousands of clients and with herself, an example of item 7.

9. *"Absence of boundary conditions"* (p. 10). Pseudoscientific approaches tend to claim, without evidence, that they can treat a variety of different types of problems. The motto of one such approach sums it up by producing a video that urges people to "try it on everything" (see www.thetappingsolution.com/index2_May.php, para. 1) and proponents literally mean just that. Testimonials for this approach abound on the Internet, claim that it cures a wide variety of different mental and physical conditions (e.g., posttraumatic stress disorder, various phobias, child behavior problems, various aches and pains, constipation, incontinence, cancer, infertility, and multiple sclerosis, just to name a few), and that it even works on animals. Legitimate science, in contrast, proceeds more cautiously, doing rigorous randomized controlled studies on one type of problem at a time. Although it may eventually turn out to be the case that a particular intervention works for multiple types of problems, this is determined through careful testing rather than from random testimonials.

10. *"The mantra of holism"* (p. 10). Unsupported practices can be rationalized by maintaining that they are being used in conjunction with other approaches and yet are not evaluated apart from the

other approaches. This is another way to protect claims from falsification, resulting in not knowing what, if anything, is producing the positive results observed. A recent example of this was a pilot study conducted by a group of LCSWs (Wimmer, Vonk, & Bordnick, 2009) purportedly done on attachment therapy for children. Aside from the fact that no conclusions about its efficacy could be drawn because there was no control group, other major problems with the study were that the children were given a wide variety of different interventions, which came under the broad umbrella called "attachment therapy," including holding therapy, parent education, parent skills training, intensive family therapy, narrative therapy, psychodrama, eye movement desensitization and reprocessing (EMDR), and neurofeedback, and there was no specified standardized protocol as treatment varied from child to child. Thus, even if pre-/postchange did actually occur, we would have no way of knowing which of these therapies, if any, produced the changes.

Although there can often be valid ways to combine various interventions, it is still important that each intervention being used be tested separately to know if it helps, harms, or does not produce any change. If it is claimed that an intervention is helpful, when used in conjunction with other interventions, evidence to that effect needs to be produced.

The aforementioned characteristics are intended to be guidelines. Not all of them apply to every form of pseudoscience. However, the more of these a particular intervention has, the more likely it is to be of concern.

## PSEUDOSCIENCE: A HISTORY LESSON

Pseudoscientific practices are not new. Throughout the existence of mankind, human beings have not wanted to suffer and, thus, have been seeking solutions and answers to the various problems and travails of living. Practices that purport to provide claims of cures to alleviate such suffering have likely existed for as long as human beings have lived on this planet. A panoply of claimed "cures" that were promoted during the 17th through early 20th centuries was documented and described in a 1923 book by an American psychiatrist, James J. Walsh, simply entitled

*Cures.* Although they varied in type, Walsh noted that their appeal transcends history and that such cures are most appealing when human beings are suffering, noting that:

> It is not surprising that men should take up with absolutely ridiculous cures of all kinds, for most of us have not too much reasoning power anyhow, and when we have anything the matter with us most of whatever little we have is likely to vanish. A drowning man will grasp at a straw, but a sick man will grab at the veriest will-o'-the-wisp. When a poor sufferer is told that here is some wonderful new remedy or mode of treatment that has cured others and that he ought to try, especially if he is told by some one who says it has cured him, it would be more than could possibly be expected of human nature if he did not try it. (p. 2)

With the proliferation of cures today on the Internet, it would appear that the only thing that has changed with regard to their appeal is that there are now easier and faster ways to promote them. Human needs and the propensity for vulnerability to the appeal of such cures, especially when they are suffering from a condition that has no genuine cure, have remained very much the same.

Walsh documents a number of different types of claimed cures, including personal healers, drug cures, various devices that have been marketed, mystical cures, and some cures that are so absurd they are humorous, which he called "cures with a punch" (p. 59). One example of such a cure was moss that was scraped from the sculls of criminals who had been hanged and sold during the 17th and 18th centuries as *Usnea* in pharmacies and prescribed by physicians to treat patients who had "wasting or nervous diseases" (p. 65).

A cure that was very popular in the 17th century, later documented by Oliver Wendell Holmes and described by Walsh, was called *Unguentum Armarium* or the weapon ointment. This special ointment, prepared from a proprietary, complicated formula requiring difficult-to-obtain elements, was claimed to work only when the recipe was followed exactly. What made this treatment unusual was that the weapon ointment was not applied directly to a wound; it was instead, applied to the weapon that caused the wound, such as a sword. If the actual weapon could not be obtained, a dummy weapon could be constructed from wood, although there was controversy over whether this was equally effective. The weapon ointment was endorsed by Lord Francis Bacon, now known to be the father of modern scientific experimentation and originator of inductive philosophy. Bacon was initially skeptical, but eventually became convinced that this was a valid treatment. He became convinced in a way similar to how many highly educated people in modern times become convinced of seemingly ridiculous practices—he witnessed the results directly—he saw it with his own eyes; therefore, he came to believe that it must be true. This is exactly how one of us (Pignotti) became convinced of the power of a modern, novel, unsupported therapy known as thought field therapy, only realizing the error years later (Pignotti, 2007).

How could such a highly educated person as Francis Bacon fall for such a ridiculous practice? In an explanation as eloquent as any we have seen, Walsh notes that even Bacon could fall for this because:

> He was quite as capable of being carried away in a matter of this kind as anyone else. His logic was all right but the facts were all wrong. It must not be forgotten that facts are not truths, in spite of the prevalent impression in the matter, unless you have all the facts. When some of the facts are missing it is perfectly impossible to draw conclusions far wide of the truth. (Walsh, 1923, p. 113)

The weapon ointment was used by some of the most highly educated men of that period. Skeptics became convinced by witnessing its seemingly miraculous results firsthand, even under conditions in which the person did not know he or she was being treated; it was said to even work on animals, a point Bacon found compelling, which seemed to rule out positive suggestion. What was not considered, however, due to the fact that this weapon ointment predated germ theory, was the preliminary step to the protocol, which was to carefully clean and bandage the wound, a procedure not commonly done in those days. This is the most likely explanation for the miraculous cures rather than the subsequent application of the special ointment to the weapon. Treatment failures could easily be explained away by claiming that there had been an error in the complicated concoction of the formula.

Although the weapon ointment eventually fell out of favor as a passing fad, the very next generation adopted an equally ridiculous "cure" called the sympathetic powder, which was applied to the blood-stained clothing of wounded people and said to bring about healing. The sympathetic powder became even more popular than the weapon ointment. The formula for the special powder was kept secret until a more altruistic person discovered the formula and made it public. Once again, this powder was used by prominent physicians of the day.

During the 18th century, devices called Perkins Tractors (PT) became very popular, which were invented by Dr. Elisha Perkins (1741 to 1799) of Norwich, CT. Dr. Perkins, a Yale graduate, was the son of a physician who was also a Yale graduate. Dr. Perkins has been described as a 6-foot-tall, robust man who traveled up to 60 miles per day on horseback to make house calls to his patients. Dr. Perkins took 5-minute naps on their couches and claimed that he only got 3 to 4 hours of sleep a night. He was viewed as being an unselfish, sincere, "good-hearted" man and, perhaps, he actually was and was not intentionally conning anyone. Perkins invented the "tractors," a device consisting of two short metallic rods made with a number of different types of metals, believed to have special curative properties. Looking like overly large chopsticks, today PT are nothing more than artifacts that can be seen in museums (although there are some contemporary counterparts still being used).

Perkins made unwarranted extrapolations from the legitimate science of his day, relating to the genuinely scientific, breakthrough discoveries about electricity. For example, primitive batteries were made of alternating layers of dissimilar (e.g., copper and zinc) metal disks. This provided his "tractors" with the superficial appearance of being based on "science." Perkins, considered to be an altruistic person, engaged in charity. Tractors were given to clergy free of charge, and sold to professional people at 5 pounds and to the general public at 10 pounds.

The process of applying the tractors was called tractoration. When one was tractorated, it was crucial that the tractors be drawn downward against a person's body to effect a cure. It was believed that drawing them upward could make the problem worse. Dr. Perkins was seen as an exceptional genius by the people of his day. The spread and popularity of PT went viral (to use a modern term), spreading into Europe, producing many positive testimonials and selling like hotcakes. Perkins's son also became involved and headed up the movement in England, claiming to have published 5,000 successful cases within 3 years. Furthermore, Perkins's son claimed that because those 5,000 cases did not include all successful cases (only about 1 in 300), the number of actual cures was believed to exceed a whopping 1,500,000! Apparently, believers did not adhere to the maxim "The plural of anecdote is not data."

In order to answer the objection raised by the skeptics of the day that the cure was due to positive suggestion, as was the case with the earlier weapon ointment, proponents claimed that animals, such as horses, had successfully been treated with PT. Not everyone, however, was convinced. The skeptic included members of Perkins's own profession. What finally put an end to this fascinating saga is when skeptical physicians made a pair of tractors out of wood, making them appear as if they were metallic by painting them to look like the real thing. The fake tractors produced the same miracle cures and, because the claimed mechanism of action for the treatment was believed to be based on the metal and the same results were obtained with the wooden devices, the claims were falsified. By 1810, the tractors were considered to be completely discredited.

A similar and more famous experiment was conducted by Benjamin Franklin and Antoine Lavoisier that finally refuted and falsified Mesmerism, a very popular practice of the late 18th century that was based on the belief of a life force and universal fluid, perhaps related to magnetism, which, when blocked, could cause a variety of different ailments, including mental health problems. Patients sat in magnetized water or held onto magnetized poles while the healer waved a magnetic wand over the patient. This led to very colorful and dramatic public group demonstrations. Mesmer also dutifully did his share of charity work by tying indigent patients to trees believed to be magnetized. Finally, King Louis XVI commissioned a more systematic investigation, carried out by Franklin and Lavoisier, which employed, as a sham control, treatments that appeared to be Mesmerism but actually did not contain any form of magnetization. When the sham treatments produced the same results, Mesmerism was somewhat discredited, thanks to this early application of a "double-blind" study.

Harvard psychology professor Richard J. McNally (1999) has drawn some interesting historical and sociological parallels between the movement that promoted Mesmerism and a modern novel therapy, EMDR. Both claimed to be breakthrough discoveries of their day, applied to a wide variety of different conditions, and were discovered and promoted by charismatic individuals who had epiphanies while walking in nature. Both developed successful proprietary training courses and formed societies to promote the novel treatments and, although both were financially successful, pro bono charity work was also done. Dramatic emotional experiences were reported by people who attended the training courses and both EMDR and Mesmerism restricted their trainees from teaching the techniques themselves to others without being authorized to do so. Finally, both EMDR and Mesmerism have been the topic of satire. In 1784 in Paris, a musical comedy believed to be a satire of Mesmerism was produced, greatly outraging the proponents of Mesmerism who considered it slanderous. Likewise, a satirical website (sudotherapay.tripod.com) has appeared on the Internet, which features a treatment called Sudotherapy, invented by a Dr. Fatima Shekel. Because the website depicts shifting eyes that follow the image of a cat named Sudo, and because Fatima Shekel has the same initials as EMDR's founder, some EMDR proponents believed this to be a parody of EMDR and were outraged, maintaining that the website was libelous. However, satire is protected under the First Amendment and, thus, no legal action was ever taken. McNally's fascinating historical analysis demonstrates that although the names of the treatments and the media of promotion have changed, there are many characteristics that these historical treatments have in common with current novel therapies.

It is interesting to note that in these historical examples, scientific experimentation often put an end to the usage of particular putative cures, such as PT, whereas today, the tendency is to resort to post hoc (after the fact) explanations to explain away such disconfirmation. To this day, various bracelets and other forms of jewelry are sold to promote health. Whether the gimmick involves putative magnetism, ions, radio waves, or other mechanisms, the fundamental idea is that these things are supposedly based on science. One so-called health bracelet currently available says:

> The metal bracelet receives electricity (similar to a radio wave) traveling in the air. To receive such wave in the air, the bracelet's materials should have a good conduction. Thus, the bracelet is plated with gold or silver. The wave received in the air is converted to electricity by the bracelet and the

current will help in rejuvenating the nervous system. (www
.pyroenergen.com/articles07/health-bracelet.htm)

One can purchase magnetic belts, abdominal ankle and wrist wraps,
rings, and bracelets to improve one's physical and mental health.
YouTube videos tell consumers about how health bracelets align one's
body's bioenergy (see www.qray.com/Benefits.aspx). This is all recy-
cled Mesmerism! Why these scams continue to proliferate is an interesting phenomenon, and one which we explore throughout this book.
Perhaps, the ability we now have to communicate with one another
more quickly and easily through media such as the Internet provides
a more fertile ground for proliferation of such creative, albeit bogus,
explanations.

Essentially, hindsight is 20/20 when it comes to such practices.
When looking at the historical practice of pseudoscience, it is easy for
most of us to be amused and to recognize that what was considered a
miraculous breakthrough treatment by a past generation is seen as an all
too obvious and humorous farce by subsequent generations, who then,
in turn, adopt their own versions. It does not appear that the advent of
modern science has changed very much regarding this phenomenon,
and we draw parallels to treatments we describe in subsequent chapters. This leads to the question of how is it that even highly educated,
intelligent people can be taken in by such practices and convinced that
they are helping themselves and/or others.

## HOW SMART PEOPLE CAN BE FOOLED
## AND WHY WE NEED GOOD RESEARCH

Throughout human history, intelligent and highly educated people
have become convinced that interventions are effective, even when the
interventions lack evidence. We operate on the assumption that most
social workers and other helping professionals enter these professions
with laudable intentions and sincerely believe that they are truly making the best decisions and helping their clients. How is it, then, that
well-intentioned, educated, intelligent people can become involved in
pseudoscientific practices?

One common theme that can be observed in most advertisements
and material on the Internet promoting such approaches is testimonials

and anecdotes, compelling reports of personal experiences people have had with success. People (including the authors!) seem to love to read such success stories and sometimes find them compelling. Mental health professionals who get involved in such practices might have done so following a compelling personal or clinical experience. Skeptics are often answered by believers in these approaches that they need to experience the intervention for themselves and try it out with their clients. Proponents assert that then and only then will they will finally realize how powerful the intervention is. After all, it seems pretty difficult to argue with something somebody saw with his or her own eyes. Doesn't that make the power of the approach self-evident? If thousands of clients have reported great benefits from a treatment, doesn't that mean that there has to be something to it? As the history of the many popular treatments based solely on large numbers of testimonials and anecdotes that have come and gone has shown us, not necessarily.

Advocates for an evidence-based approach to mental health practice challenge such claims that are based only on compelling testimonials and anecdotes. Why are not these compelling personal and clinical experiences enough? The answer to this involves gaining an understanding of how human biases can influence how we interpret what we see with our own eyes. The philosophy of naive realism, first espoused by Francis Bacon, maintains that we gain knowledge directly through direct, firsthand observation. In essence, naive realism is the philosophy that what we see is what we get and that seeing is believing. However, history has shown that Bacon himself came to false conclusions about weapon ointment because of what he witnessed, firsthand. That is, through direct perception of reality, it seemed self-evident to him that the weapon ointment was a highly effective treatment. He witnessed people and even animals having it applied and then miraculously recovering. There were no optical illusions; he saw what he saw. Although optical illusions can and do occur, the main problem with naive realism is not that people are not seeing what they are seeing. The problem is that naive realists believe that what they observe is self-evident and that conclusions can be drawn from it, requiring no further thought or critical consideration of possible alternative explanations.

Direct observation is an excellent starting point, but when this is not followed up with rigorous testing and critical consideration of alternative explanations to control for, it can lead to highly fallacious conclusions that may harm clients or, at the very least, waste their time and money. In sensory-based terms, what Bacon accurately observed was people and animals who were wounded make miraculous recoveries, after having their wounds cleaned and bandaged and having a specially prepared ointment placed on the offending weapon. The error was in the conclusion that the weapon ointment was the cause of the recovery because he saw it with his own eyes. That conclusion involved making an unwarranted interpretive leap that went beyond what we could have known through direct observation and yet naive realists believed that they could do this. What Bacon and the others of his day failed to consider was the possible benefit of cleaning and bandaging the wound.

Today, many clinicians are essentially naive realists, taking their experiences and observations at face value and leaping to unwarranted conclusions about them, failing to think through, consider, and test for alternative explanations. To make causal inferences, we need to design studies that carefully and systematically control for alternative explanations. Through rigorous tests, we can discover, first, whether there is any effect from the treatment at all and, if so, we can do even more rigorous testing to find the mechanism of action—what specific elements in the treatment bring about its beneficial effect.

The main problem with leaping to conclusions based on direct observation is that, as human beings, each of us brings our own biases to those observations. We may think that we are simply describing what we are seeing, but without checking this out through rigorous experiments, we cannot make valid claims about an intervention. Someone who has had a compelling personal experience with a particular intervention, and wishing to confirm it, will begin to seek out other instances of success. As human beings, we tend to want to focus on successes and confirmation of our most compelling experiences and dearly held beliefs. This is known as confirmation bias, and as Paul Meehl points out, no human being, including a clinician, is exempt from the tendency to rely on confirmation bias. We tend to focus on that which confirms our most cherished beliefs and dismiss or explain away evidence that runs contrary to and would disconfirm those beliefs. Examples of this phenomenon will be provided throughout this book.

In contrast, the scientifically oriented practitioner goes against this human tendency by actively seeking out alternative explanations and controlling for them in rigorous experiments. For the scientist, striving to find out the truth about the matter is more important than being right about his or her initial observations. Real scientists are willing to prove themselves wrong, even about their most deeply cherished notions. Pseudoscientists may engage in critical thinking when it comes to the opposing point of view, but when it comes to their own point of view, they look only to show how they are correct, rather than how they may be proven wrong.

Additionally, social psychology experiments have demonstrated the compelling power that commitment and consistency have over the decisions made by people. As human beings, we like to be thought of as consistent (Cialdini, 2009). As we can readily see from political advertisements and elsewhere, people who change their minds about something are commonly accused of "flip flopping" and being weak-minded and wishy-washy. Frequently changing one's mind based on nothing but emotional whim and impulse is not an admirable human quality. However, the distinction between such fickleness and change of one's mind after careful reflection, consideration of alternative explanations, and testing of a previously strongly held notion is often not recognized.

Is commitment and consistency not a good thing? It depends. Quite often it is, if it means staying with what was initially a sound decision and working through conflicts and problems that result in an enduring valued relationship that produces benefit to the parties involved. However, what happens when a person makes a decision based on the facts available at that time, only later to find out new facts that show that he or she was mistaken? A classic example would be involvement in an abusive relationship. A person may stay in such a relationship out of a sense of commitment, trying to make things work out, trying to change someone who is going to continue to be abusive, to his or her own detriment. In that case, putting the value of commitment above all else does not seem to be such a good idea. Most people would readily see that the decision to leave such a relationship would be a wise one. How about a person who commits to the practice of an intervention that seems to work, but ultimately sees that it is not what it was claimed to be? It would not make sense to accuse such a person of being wishy-washy or flip-flopping. However, all too many people make the mistake, in essence, of making commitment their highest value, even when they are involved with something that ultimately is not beneficial to them or the people to whom they provide services. This is particularly the case when a person has invested a great deal of time and/or financial resources.

One of the authors of this book (MGP) has written about her own involvement, empirical testing, and ultimate disillusionment with a form of psychotherapy based on principles now seen to be pseudoscientific and invalid (Pignotti, 2007). The other author (BAT) as a teenager received therapy sessions from an unlicensed and unqualified psychotherapist (but an otherwise lovely elderly woman) who used an electronic device called the Mathison Electropsychometer (how is that for a scientific-sounding name!) to help him through a difficult time in his adolescence. The Electropsychometer was invented in the 1940s by a Californian chiropractor named Volney Mathison (see en.wikipedia .org/wiki/Volney_Mathison). The device is basically a biofeedback device that measures skin resistance. It is harmless and does nothing to the client except provide a powerful placebo effect. The founder of the pseudo-religion called Scientology adopted Mathison's device, changed its name to the E-Meter, and incorporated it into Scientology's (unvalidated) assessment practices, claiming that it could locate "charged" areas of a person's life that need to be addressed. Scientology members are charged large fees for their therapy sessions, where it remains widely used. The device is usually available for purchase on eBay. Thus, both the authors of this book have had personal experiences with what they would later come to term *pseudoscientific practices*, in the name of legitimate therapy.

Human beings can fall into what Anthony Pratkanis has called a *rationalization trap*. This phenomenon is observed in consumers who make a large financial investment in something, which leads them to rationalize their choice and ignore or explain away any evidence showing that the decision, perhaps, was not a wise one. Proprietary training for some pseudoscientific practices can be very expensive. The most advanced level of one novel therapy, called thought field therapy voice technology (TFTVT; to be discussed in later chapters), costs $100,000. People who have had to sell property, take out large loans, or make other financial sacrifices to pay for such training are not likely to want to admit it if they see evidence that it is not what it is claimed to be. Instead, the tendency will be to rationalize their decision by engaging in confirmation bias and explaining away contrary evidence. Although most proprietary training programs do not cost $100,000, many are expensive enough to lead the person into rationalizations that support the superiority of the intervention he or she was trained in. Adding in their investment of time and the social support and reinforcement the new adherent to the novel therapy can receive at the hands of respected and established practitioners of the new treatment, a very powerful convergence of forces can dramatically influence the newly trained psychotherapist.

Such an investment and commitment to a pseudoscientific practice can get further reinforced by associations and societies built up around such an approach where proponents can regularly meet at conferences or through online discussion groups, to discuss all their positive experiences. Typically, discussion of any negative experience is frowned upon and, in some cases, those making serious challenges or criticisms can be expelled from the organization or the online discussion group. For example, one of us (Pignotti) after practicing and teaching thought field therapy (TFT), was expelled from an Internet discussion group and asked to resign from the association after conducting a controlled study that disconfirmed the highly expensive TFTVT and attempting to discuss its findings with colleagues and the inventor (Pignotti, 2005, 2007). Only one other practitioner was persuaded by the findings and discontinued practicing TFTVT. The other practitioners, having made such a large commitment, seem to have fallen into a rationalization trap and explained away the disconfirmatory results, and many, 7 years later, are still practicing TFTVT and other forms of TFT, even though favorable randomized clinical trials for the many conditions and populations for which they make claims have not been published in legitimate peer-reviewed journals.

Although personal experience can be highly compelling, can clinicians learn from experience? Some clinicians claim that what they are doing, even though it is not based on research evidence, is valid because they have had decades of practice experience. However, evidence shows that the ability of clinicians to learn from experience has been greatly overestimated. Thus, although experience undeniably has some value, boasting of having years and years of clinical practice experience, in the absence of basing such practice on evidence, may also amount to years and years of confirmation bias.

Reviewing the literature on the relationship between experience and clinical competence, Garb and Boyle (2014) concluded:

> Although research has often supported the value of training, learning from clinical experience has had less support. Narrative reviews of clinical judgment have concluded that

when clinicians are given identical sets of information, experienced clinicians are no more accurate than less experienced clinicians and graduate students, though they may be better at structuring judgment tasks. (p. 20)

Garb and Boyle go on to describe a more rigorous review, a meta-analysis that was conducted showing that the combined effect of training and experience was positive, but very small (an effect size of only $d = 0.12$), and other results, unlike the narrative reviews, showed that the "the effects of training and experience were not significantly different" and that "having specific training and experience with a judgment task was unrelated to validity" (p. 20).

Garb and Boyle maintain, as we do, that clinicians may choose to use and continue using pseudoscientific practices because it is very difficult to learn from clinical experience. The reason for this is the biases we previously discussed, such as confirmation bias, along with other cognitive factors and heuristics, and shortcuts taken by human beings in an attempt to deal with the large amount of information we are faced with processing in our daily lives. This is particularly true of busy clinicians who, in the field of social work, frequently have large caseloads. Many practitioners, when faced with overwhelming amounts of information, are inclined to take shortcuts.

Additionally, much clinical folklore exists, which, although widely believed, is based on myth rather than on evidence. Lilienfeld, Lynn, Ruscio, and Beyerstein (2010), in their book *50 Great Myths of Popular Psychology*, expose some of these myths that are taken for granted and unquestioned by many mental health professionals and asserted to be true by numerous authorities, yet shown to be false or at least not completely correct. Sometimes what "everybody knows" simply is not so. Some of these myths that are also relevant to social work practice include the following:

#9: Old age is typically associated with increased dissatisfaction and senility. (p. 56)

#10: When dying, people pass through a universal series of psychological stages. (p. 60)

#11: Human memory works like a tape recorder or video camera, and accurately records the events we've experienced. (p. 65)

#18: Most students learn best when teaching styles are matched to their learning styles. (p. 92)

#33: Low self-esteem is a major cause of psychological problems. (p. 162)

#34: Most people who were sexually abused in childhood develop severe personality disturbances in adulthood. (p. 166)

#37: Psychiatric labels cause harm by stigmatizing people. (p. 181)

#38: Only deeply depressed people commit suicide. (p. 186)

#40: Adult children of alcoholics display a distinctive pattern of symptoms. (p. 192)

#41: There has recently been a massive epidemic of infantile autism. (p. 195)

#43: Most mentally ill people are violent. (p. 209)

#47: Expert judgment and intuition are the best means of making clinical decisions. (p. 227)

#48: Abstinence is the only realistic goal for alcoholics. (p. 232)

#49: All effective psychotherapies force people to confront the "root" causes of their problems in childhood. (p. 236)

Some of these myths have become springboards for the development of pseudoscientific practices. For example, a set of therapies that was very popular in the 1980s and 1990s, purported to recover repressed memories of childhood sexual abuse, was based on two of these myths: the mistaken belief that the mind operates as a video recorder and that such memories can be accurately retrieved, fully intact, and the myth that childhood sexual abuse is inevitably responsible for serious problems in adulthood. For instance, women suffering from postpartum depression were told, without basis, that their depression was caused by repressed memories of childhood sexual abuse, and that these memories needed to be recovered and dealt with by a lengthy therapy. A friend of one of the authors, who obtained a PhD in clinical psychology from a highly reputable university, was told by one of her professors that all overweight women had been sexually abused as children. This notion was not based on scientific evidence, and yet it was being taught as if it were an unquestionable fact. The belief in these myths led to a number of false allegations that tore families apart and caused the individuals undergoing such therapy much needless pain and suffering. Thankfully today, there is increasing emphasis on evidence-based mental health practice and such clinical lore that "everybody knows" is being challenged.

## Misuse of Legitimate Research

With the increasing emphasis of research in mental health practice, an additional way in which theories and practices can be made to appear as if they have more evidence than they do is to cite legitimate research, but then make unwarranted generalizations and claims based on that research. For this reason, it is very important to actually check references that are cited in articles and ask questions such as:

- What type of article is being referenced? Is it actual research, a review of research, or an opinion piece?
- If it is research, was it published in a peer-reviewed journal? What were the researchers' conclusions? Were they reasonable and warranted? (Because the peer-review system is far from perfect, it is important to ask these questions, even for peer-reviewed published studies.)
- What were the conclusions of the author citing the research? Did they go beyond conclusions in the original research?
- Is it a review of research, and what type of review was it? Systematic reviews that have specified and transparent methodology (e.g., disclosing inclusion and exclusion criteria and how the search for evidence was conducted in such a way that it could be replicated) are easier to check than narrative reviews that do not specify how they obtained the articles reviewed and are in danger of reflecting the authors' biases.
- If it is an opinion piece, were the opinions given logically coherent and supported by evidence?
- Were the references self-references? There is nothing wrong with self-references, but it is important to see if the references add to the statements made in the original article or if they are essentially repetitions of the same ideas in the original article.

To provide our readers with an example, a psychiatrist who writes mostly narrative (not systematic) reviews of neuroscience and is very popular with some clinical social workers who use his writings to attempt to provide scientific support for theories on trauma and neuro-science that are, in our opinion, tentative and shaky, at best, made the following statement in a medical journal, accompanied by a long string of references (this is just one of a number of passages in his writings that we find problematic in terms of support):

> According to van der Kolk and McFarlane [230] a central fea-ture of PTSD is a loss of the ability to physiologically mod-ulate stress responses which leads to a reduced capacity to utilize bodily signals as guides to action, and this alteration of psychological defence mechanisms is associated with an impairment of personal identity. These deficits are the expres-sion of a malfunctioning orbitofrontal cortical-subcortical sys-tem, the senior executive of the right brain [14,18,29,31,45,56].
> (Schore, 2002, p. 22)

By analyzing the references in this passage we found that the first one [230] was from a book chapter (van der Kolk & McFarlane, 1996) con-taining largely unsubstantiated theories and speculation (see McNally, 2003b for an evidence-based critique on the first author's theories and their inadequate evidence).

The string of references at the end are as follows: [14], [45], and [56] are references to books and book chapters by the same author (Schore); [18], [29], and [31] are all references to similar narrative reviews by the same author from a journal. In other words, this long, impressive-looking string of references at the end of the passage is comprised of self-references, not to actual primary studies reporting databased original research, but to other narrative reviews. Readers may find the impressive-sounding neuroscientific terms in the article too intimidat-ing to actually check out and may just assume that the conclusions being drawn are scientific, but when the substance of these articles is examined, we found very little actual research behind them, cer-tainly not enough to warrant the definitive conclusions that are made that have given this work the reputation of being based on solid sci-ence. This author is frequently referred to as a researcher by clinical social workers who admire his work, yet a PsycINFO and MEDLINE database search has not revealed any research this person has actu-ally conducted, only narrative reviews with sweeping conclusions that appear to far outweigh the actual evidence. This is one of many illustrations we could provide that demonstrates the lesson that we need to examine references provided and not automatically assume that because articles contain scientific jargon, they are based on solid scientific evidence.

This appears to be an example of what Gambrill (2011) refers to as the problem of what she labels "bogus citations," wherein a claim is supported by a citation, which, when reviewed, is simply a prior statement of the same claim, as opposed to solid empirical data backing the claim. In this situation, she states:

> The printed word…serves a ceremonial/ritualistic function similar to the laying on of hands. Citations become like slogans, and like slogans, the more they are repeated, the more they may be influenced. This ritualistic function designed to lend authority to material that does not warrant it, other with the lack of critical appraisal skills on the part of readers (or motivation to use them) help to account for the extent of uncritical reading and propaganda-like material in the professional literature. (Gambrill, 2011, p. 660)

In the chapters that follow, we explore a number of different types of pseudoscientific practices and assessment procedures that are not based on sound evidence and yet make claims that go far beyond the evidence. We hope that the information you gain from these chapters will be of value, not only in avoiding those specific practices we select to discuss, but also in learning how to recognize and challenge pseudoscientific thinking, replacing it with critical thinking and a more evidence-based approach to practice.

## REFERENCES

American Psychiatric Association. (2000). *Diagnostic and statistical manual of mental disorders* (4th ed., text rev.). Washington, DC: Author.

American Psychiatric Association. (2013). *Diagnostic and statistical manual of mental disorders* (5th ed.). Arlington, VA: Author.

Bunge, M. (1998). *Philosophy of science: From problem to theory, volume one (revised edition)*. New Brunswick, NJ: Transaction.

Cialdini, R. B. (2009). *Influence: Science and practice.* Boston, MA: Pearson Education.

Festinger, L. (1985). *A theory of cognitive dissonance.* Stanford, CA: Stanford University Press.

Gambrill, E. (2011). Ethical aspects of outcome studies in social, behavioral and educational interventions. *Research on Social Work Practice, 21,* 654–663.

Garb, H. O., & Boyle, P. A. (2014). Understanding why some clinicians use pseudoscientific methods. In S. O. Lilienfeld, S. J. Lynn, & J. M. Lohr (Eds.), *Science and pseudoscience in clinical psychology* (2nd ed., pp. 19–41). New York, NY: Guilford Press.

Gibbes, J. H. (1925). Quacks and quackery. *The Scientific Monthly, 21,* 533–550.

Lilienfeld, S. O., Lynn, S. J., & Lohr, J. M. (2014). Science and pseudoscience in clinical psychology: Initial thoughts, reflections, and considerations. In S. O. Lilienfeld, S. J. Lynn, & J. M. Lohr (Eds.), *Science and pseudoscience in clinical psychology* (2nd ed., pp. 1–16). New York, NY: Guilford Press.

Lilienfeld, S. O., Lynn, S. J., Ruscio, J., & Beyerstein, B. L. (2010). *50 great myths of popular psychology.* West Sussex, UK: Wiley-Blackwell.

Lilienfeld, S. O., Ritsche, L. A., Lynn, S. J., Cautin, R. L., & Latzman, R. D. (2014). Why ineffective psychotherapies appear to work: A taxonomy of causes of spurious therapeutic effectiveness. *Perspectives on Psychological Science, 9,* 355–387.

McNally, R. J. (1999). EMDR and Mesmerism: A comparative historical analysis. *Journal of Anxiety Disorders, 13,* 225–236.

McNally, R. J. (2003a). The demise of pseudoscience. *The Scientific Review of Mental Health Practice, 2,* 97–101.

McNally, R. J. (2003b). *Remembering trauma.* Cambridge, MA: Harvard University Press.

Mercer, J., Sarner, L., & Rosa, L. (2003). *Attachment therapy on trial: The torture and death of Candace Newmaker.* Westport, CT: Praeger.

Pignotti, M. (2005). Thought field therapy voice technology vs random meridian point sequences: A single-blind controlled experiment. *The Scientific Review of Mental Health Practice, 4,* 38–47.

Pignotti, M. (2007). Thought field therapy: A former insider's experience. *Research on Social Work Practice, 17,* 392–407.

Pignotti, M., & Thyer, B. A. (2012). Novel unsupported and empirically supported therapies: Patterns of usage among licensed clinical social workers. *Behavioural and Cognitive Psychotherapy, 40,* 331–349.

Quantheory. (2011, February 25). Letter to the editor. *The Chronicle Review,* p. B18.

Sagan, C. (1996). *The demon-haunted world: Science as a candle in the dark.* New York, NY: Ballantine Books.

Schore, A. N. (2002). Dysregulation of the right brain: A fundamental mechanism of traumatic attachment and the psychopathogenesis of posttraumatic stress disorder. *The Australian and New Zealand Journal of Psychiatry, 36,* 9–30.

Shermer, M. (2004, June). Death by theory. *Scientific American,* p. 48.

Sternberg, G. M. (1897). Science and pseudo-science in medicine. *Science, 5*(110), 199–206.

van der Kolk, B. A., & McFarlane, A. C. (1996). The black hole of trauma. In B. A. van der Kolk, A. C. McFarlane, & L. Weisaeth (Eds.), *Traumatic stress: The effects of overwhelming experience on mind, body, society* (pp. 3–23). New York, NY: Guilford Press.

Walsh, J. J. (1923). *Cures: The story of cures that fail.* New York, NY: D. Appleton and Company.

Wimmer, J. S., Vonk, M. E., & Bordnick, P. (2009). A preliminary investigation of the effectiveness of attachment therapy for adopted children with reactive attachment disorder. *Child and Adolescent Social Work, 26,* 351–360.

# CHAPTER 2

# Pseudoscience in Clinical Assessment

*The cure for the "pseudo-science of much of our present investigation" (Mary) Richmond claimed, is "more investigation" and a willingness to use "our best brains, time and strength upon [the] delicate task of finding out the right thing to do."*—AGNEW (2004, p. 106)

Clinical social workers make extensive use of a wide array of assessment methods, with this variety of approaches to assessment dictated by the expansive meaning of the term, which has been defined as:

> The process of determining the nature, cause, progression, and prognosis of a problem and the personalities and situations involved therein; the social work function of acquiring an understanding of a problem, what causes it, and what can be changed to minimize or resolve it. (Barker, 2014, p. 29)

Each of these components in turn—nature, cause, progression and prognosis, personalities, and situations—is of itself a complex concept, and widely divergent methods have been developed to address each domain of assessment. Assessing personalities is considerably different from assessing social situations, which is in turn distinctive from arriving at a prognosis or prediction about the likely course of the client and his or her situation. Other definitions of assessment are equally broad in scope, such as:

> Assessment is an ongoing process, in which the client participates, the purpose of which is to understand people in relation to their environment; it is a basis for planning what needs to be done to maintain, improve, or bring about change in the person, the environment, or both. (Coulshed & Orme, 2006, p. 21)

It had been correctly noted that accurate assessment is the foundation of evidence-based practice (Grady & Drisko, 2014). A social worker seeking to learn about various methods of clinical assessment can and should be guided by existing published research addressing the merits of the assessment method in question. Regrettably, our textbooks do not emphasize this enough. One survey of social work assessment texts found that "while the notion of needing to base assessments on research and not just on unsubstantiated assumption is actively encouraged in a few textbooks...others include little or no explicit discussion of research evidence" (Crisp, Anderson, Orme, & Lister, 2006, p. 352). A more recent investigation of the sources of information social workers use when assessing and intervening in cases of interpersonal violence states "explicit research knowledge was not identified as a major influence for exploring these areas" (Forgey, Allen, & Hansen, 2014, p. 58). This makes social work students and practitioners vulnerable to adopting bogus or pseudoscientific assessment methods, of which there are abundant examples, some of which are reviewed later in this chapter. We encourage students and practitioners to evaluate clinical assessment methods according to their scientific merits before adopting them into practice and to discontinue using assessment practices that are scientifically questionable. We believe that this analysis is overdue in social work—a focused critique concerning the reliability and validity of some popular assessment tools may improve future social work assessment.

## THE RELIABILITY AND VALIDITY OF SOCIAL WORK ASSESSMENT

Social work has long known that the reliability of the methods used in assessment is of crucial importance. We note with approval Mary

Richmond's emphasis on the reality and importance of objective facts, such as:

> The word *fact* is not limited to the tangible. Thoughts and events are facts. The question whether a thing be fact or not is the question whether or not it can be affirmed with certainty. The gathering of facts is made difficult by faulty observation, faulty recollection, and by a confusion between the facts themselves and the inferences drawn from them. (Richmond, 1917, p. 63)

and

> No considerable group of social case workers…seem[s] to have grasped the fact that the *reliability* of the evidence on which they base their conclusions should be no less rigidly scrutinized than is that of legal evidence by opposing counsel. (Richmond, 1917, p. 39, emphasis in original)

Some 35 years later, social worker Mary Macdonald similarly stressed this point:

> The essence of research is that the findings relate to *that which is observed, and not the individual observer.* This is the criterion of objectivity, or reliability…In research the burden of proof is on the investigator, and he is expected to show that his results are not the matter of personal whim. (Macdonald, 1953, p. 136, emphasis added)

Stressing the importance of obtaining factual and reliable evidence in social work assessment does not imply that one should ignore the client's subjective experiences, but only that attempting to undertake a solely subjective accounting of the client-in-situation is an incomplete appraisal, at best. Inferences, however, are best kept to a minimum among the most respected approaches to social work assessment. Again turning to Mary Richmond (1917), we find entire chapters devoted to the problems (and possibilities) of making inferences. We believe that social workers need to ask a series of simple questions about any assessment method they propose to use with clients, and one of the most fundamental questions to ask (and to answer) is:

- *Is there good evidence that the assessment method yields reliable results?*
  Reliability refers to the consistency of the results obtained by using the assessment method, and there are different forms of examining reliability. One is called test–retest reliability. If the assessment measure is completed by the client on one occasion, with a particular result obtained, does the measure yield a similar result if the assessment method is properly readministered, and the client or situation has not truly changed? For example, if a social worker uses a structured interview protocol to help determine if a given client meets, or does not meet, formal diagnostic criteria for the condition labeled major depression, and the same clinician assesses the same client again a week later, and the client's affective state has not significantly changed, will the structured interview yield the same conclusion? Test–retest reliability was also noted as important by Richmond when she stated that "Psychologists realize now that tests of memory, like most other mental tests, must be repeated to eliminate accidental factors" (Richmond, 1917, p. 47). Examining test–retest reliability is one way to help control or eliminate the role of "accidental factors" (e.g., maybe the client had insufficient sleep the night before) in the results of an assessment method.
  Another form of reliability is interobserver (or interrater) reliability. If two social workers independently assess the client using a given assessment method, do they arrive at similar results? Interrater reliability pertains to making formal diagnoses, for example, or in directly measuring behavior. One of the authors (BAT) has used dual independent raters to evaluate the use of over-the-shoulder safety belts among children as part of a school-based safety intervention program. By objectively demonstrating that the observers recorded similar observations, we can be more confident that any apparent changes that were observed following intervention really did happen and were not an artifact or spurious. If anatomically correct dolls (ACD) are used by social workers in interviewing small children suspected of having been sexually abused, are the conclusions arrived by two independent pairs of clinicians similar (e.g., yes, abuse occurred, or no, it did not) for a given child? If, with a large group of children, the social workers' agreement is high, then

the use of the dolls can be said to have high interrater agreement. If interrater agreement is too low (e.g., less than 80% agreement), then the method can be said to be sufficiently unreliable and not useful in clinical practice or research. High reliability does not mean that the conclusions are accurate, only that they are consistent, but without consistency in results, no assessment measure can be said to be valid.

If the assessment method involves a pencil and paper scale completed by the client (or by caregivers), another form of reliability may be important, one called internal consistency. If a rapid assessment instrument is supposed to measure one thing, for example, reports of depressed thinking or the client's generalized anxiety, internal consistency can be appraised by correlating the total score of the odd-numbered items with the total score of the even-numbered items, and examining this over a large number of scales completed by different clients. If the correlation is sufficiently high (e.g., greater than 0.80) one may have greater confidence that the scale is consistently measuring that one thing. However, if this measure of split-half reliability is too low (e.g., less than 0.80), then the scale lacks adequate internal consistency and should not be used in practice or research. Another somewhat more complicated measure of internal consistency is called coefficient alpha, and is similarly evaluated, in that an alpha of 0.80 or higher is usually considered necessary for a scale to be clinically useful.

If you are contemplating using a particular method of clinical assessment, determine if considerations such as test–retest reliability, interrater agreement, or internal consistency are important (they usually are). Try and locate information found in published reports describing what has been found related to the reliability of the measure you are considering to use. If it is too low, reassess your intention to use this assessment method.

If the assessment method you are considering to adopt has demonstrated that it is satisfactorily reliable, then the next question to ask is:

- *Is there good evidence that the assessment method yields valid results?*

Validity refers to the extent that a given assessment measure is genuinely assessing what it is said to measure. An assessment measure could be reliable (e.g., your bathroom scale consistently tells you weigh 130 pounds, no matter how many times you get on and off it in the morning) but also invalid (the scale may be consistently off by, say, 5 pounds), in which case you never do learn your "real" true weight. Among the several types of validity are those of face validity (does the measure, at least superficially, appear to assess such and such a factor?); content validity (does the measure do a comprehensive, or at least adequate, job of assessing the construct under consideration?); concurrent validity (does the measure correlate highly with known or accepted measures of the construct supposedly being assessed?); and predictive validity (does knowledge of the results of your assessment now enable you to more accurately predict the client's situation at some point in the future?). For example, as a result of some formal assessment method, can you more accurately estimate the likelihood that a first-time juvenile offender will commit another crime, that a discharged psychiatric patient will need to be rehospitalized, or that a depressed client will try to commit suicide?

Take, for example, a purported measure of parenting skills. You could see if, on the face of it, it really does appear to measure such behaviors. This is a subjective judgment, not a quantitative one. If so, you could then see if it provides a genuinely comprehensive measure of a mother's or father's parenting skills. A parenting skill measure that only assesses the parent's use of say, disciplinary methods, would have less content validity than one that provided an assessment of disciplinary methods as well as ways to support a child's positive behaviors. A self-report scale of client's depression that assesses cognitive, behavioral, and affective states would be seen as having better content validity than one that provided a measure of only one of these dimensions. A scale that asked caregivers to rate only the so-called positive symptoms of schizophrenia displayed by a client has less content validity than one that provided ratings of both positive *and* negative symptoms, if the measure was billed as a comprehensive way to assess the symptomatology of chronic mental illness.

The importance of using social work assessment methods that are valid was noted early on in a 1938 editorial published in the prestigious journal *Social Service Review*, titled "Pseudo-science versus Sound Administrative Procedures." In this article, the author criticized the then recently developed rating system used by the Iowa Old Age Assistance Commission to determine the amount of assistance an elderly person's family might be expected to contribute to the care of the senior. Points were awarded based on the client's age, degree of disability, local agricultural conditions, and familial earnings, and entered into a statistical formula. Because the awarding of points was rather subjective, the author concluded, "This statistical formula, this so-called objectivity which ignored individual family situations and variations from the basic average assumptions is the same kind of pseudo-science as the Pirquet nutritional index, except it is more pseudo and less science. Social work clinicians reject it for the same reasons as the pediatricians rejected the pelidisi" (Anonymous, 1938, p. 502). The Pirquet nutritional index and pelidisi, a supposed measure of nutritional status, were invalid measures of dietary status used at the time. The authors were equating the Iowa Rating Scale used in social welfare eligibility determinations with these invalid dietary measures as equally pseudoscientific, and urged that the former be discontinued. This is an early (and largely ignored) precedent for excluding pseudoscientific assessment methods from social work practice.

- *If the assessment method is theoretically based, is the theory a sensible one supported by adequate empirical evidence?*
  Some, but not all, assessment methods are theoretically based. By theoretically based, we mean that the assessment method is clearly derived from one or more formal psychosocial or other etiological–causal theories. A structured interview designed to assess a client's eligibility to receive certain social or health care benefits (an eligibility determination) could be a clear example of a nontheoretically based assessment method. Some structured interviews used to arrive at diagnostic determinations (e.g., a *Diagnostic and Statistical Manual of Mental Disorders,* Fifth Edition [*DSM-5*] diagnosis) are also atheoretical in the sense that they convey no etiological assumptions as to the nature of the client's presumptive problem. One may use such an interview protocol to determine if a client does or does not meet the formal criteria for a diagnosis of say, panic disorder, as described in the *DSM-5* (American Psychiatric Association [APA], 2013). The series of questions used, as well as the diagnostic criteria found within the *DSM-5,* are generally theoretically neutral, not based on any etiological assumptions (e.g., the problem has a biological or psychosocial or familial etiology), and are more focused on simple descriptive features.

Conversely, a number of clinical assessment methods are clearly derived from one or more theories. Often these are theories of the mind or of intrapersonal dynamics, or sometimes of forces external to the individual. Certain forms of assessment have as their default assumptions the hypothesis that dysfunctional family dynamics underlies psychopathological behavior displayed by individuals. Projective tests such as the ink blot test, wherein clients are asked to describe what they "see" in a standardized series of ink smears, or in the House–Tree–Person test, wherein clients are asked to draw a house, draw a person, and to draw a tree, are clearly derived from psychodynamic theory, as are assessment methods based on the clinician's inferences of what the client says about his or her own dreams. The Myers–Briggs Type Indicator personality inventory is a supposed measure of the human personality based on the psychodynamic psychology of Carl Jung, and a social worker's use of his or her hands to supposedly sense distortions in a client's energy field (EF) is based on various theories of energy psychology. The process called behavioral assessment has as its theoretical position the hypothesis that environmentally based contingencies of reinforcement and/or punishment may be causally responsible for a client's dysfunctional actions.

It is important to ascertain if a given assessment method is clearly derived from one or more formal theories because even if an assessment method does possess adequate reliability and validity, if the underlying theory or the method it is based on is erroneous, then any conclusions, however reliable and valid, drawn from an assessment method based on that theory, are likely invalid. Thus, well-trained clinicians should seek out credible information pertaining to the degree of empirical support behind any theories undergirding a given assessment method. If the evidence seems sufficient, and the method possesses adequate reliability and validity, then the clinician is on firmer grounds for adopting this method in his or her practice. If the evidence is credible but largely negative, that is, the theory has been proven to be incorrect, then the use of any assessment method derived from that theory, even if reliable and valid, is difficult to justify according to the principles of evidence-based practice. If the available evidence is insufficient, or perhaps entirely absent (unhappily not an infrequent occurrence), certainly caution is warranted before enthusiastically adopting the assessment method. We recognize that the absence of evidence is not evidence of absence.

Simply because something has not been researched and supported does not mean it is invalid or unjustifiable, and thus we certainly believe in being open to under-researched practices. But one need not be so open that one's brains fall out! One illustration of being too open-minded follows.

Therapeutic touch (TT) is one example of a theoretical approach to assessment and treatment of mental, emotional, and physical ailments premised on the theory that the human body is surrounded by an invisible EF, unknown and thus far undetectable by conventional science. Distortions or perturbations in this EF supposedly cause human distress and illness. It is claimed that a therapist such as a nurse, social worker, or psychologist can be trained to detect these invisible energy misalignments by moving his or her hands over a client's body, without touching the client. When the therapist intuits or senses a distortion adjacent to a particular point on the client's body, the therapist use his or her hands to "realign" the distorted EF, thus providing relief and restoring health. The therapist can use his or her hands to visualize replacing bad energy with good, while holding the hands motionless over the supposedly affected body part, or perhaps imitate grasping, pushing, or discarding the bad vibrations (Sayre-Adams & Wright, 1995). TT has been around for a long time and has been adopted by some clinical social workers. Earlier variants can be found in the so-called magnetic healers of the 1800s, the work of Mesmer in the 1700s, and even earlier in the oracular healers of ancient Greece. The practice of Reiki or of "aligning the chakras" may be familiar techniques to some readers, and these too are a variation on the theory that TT is based on. The TT literature itself introduces a hodgepodge of mystical concepts to explain how TT works, invoking the Hindu concept of pranic energy, the Chinese theory of Ying-Yang forces and of *qi*, and analogies to the laying on of hands of Christian faith healers.

An important consideration of the validity of TT theory for a clinical social worker to appraise is whether or not these presumptive human EFs can be detected *at all*. If the answer is no, then the whole TT enterprise is founded on a spurious claim. If these EFs cannot be reliably detected, then how could they possibly be therapeutically corrected by a clinical social worker? A search of the literature will find only one well-controlled study investigating whether or not experienced TT practitioners could blindly determine which of their two hands was closest to the investigator's hand (behind a screen, and randomly alternated). The evidence was crystal clear: They could not (Rosa, Rosa, Sarner, & Barrett, 1998). The experimental protocol was agreed to beforehand by the TT practitioners as a fair one. Thus, if experienced therapists could not reliably detect the energies they purport to realign, then the entire theoretical edifice of TT collapses. This is not to say that the method may not possess beneficial effects plausibly attributable to placebo influences and comforting human interaction, only that the approach is not one that the evidence-based practitioner would wish to offer to clients with an implication that anything more than such placebo effects could be expected.

Social workers seeking credible and contemporary information on the reliability and validity of assessment methods for potential use in their practice are advised to consult review articles published in recent issues of high-quality professional journals. Smith-Osborn and Bolton's (2013) article is an example of one such review article, dealing with the topic of assessing resilience; Therrien and Hunsley (2012) focus on measures of anxiety in older adults; and Joiner, Walker, Pettit, Perez, and Cukrowicz (2005) focus on the assessment of depression. The journal *Research on Social Work Practice* regularly publishes articles on the psychometric properties of various scales and assessment measures intended for use in social work practice and is a useful resource to consult.

In Table 2.1, we present a series of factors that may serve as warning signs that a given assessment may be in fact a bogus or pseudoscientific approach to clinical measurement. No single one of these features may be considered damning, but we suggest that the more of these elements that are associated with a given assessment method, the more cautious clinical social workers need to be before devoting extensive time to learning about, or utilizing, that method in their practice. In the next section, we describe selected methods used by some clinical social workers to assess client functioning and change. We have focused on those that generally lack credible evidence that they are either reliable or valid. Some are less widely used than others, but each one *is* being used by professional social workers to assess clients. You may judge for yourself the ethics of such practices. Be warned! Some of what you are about to read may surprise or even shock you.

**TABLE 2.1**
**Some Selected Warning Signs That an Assessment Method May Be Pseudoscientific or Bogus[a]**

- Claims that the assessment method yields exceedingly remarkable and effective results
- Someone making large sums of money from selling the assessment method, providing training in it, or lecturing about it
- Someone receiving significant personal or professional recognition or accolades as an "expert" in the novel training method
- Requiring practitioners being trained in the assessment method to sign pledges of secrecy or promises not to teach others the method
- The use of florid language in making claims, using words such as "unbelievable," "incredible," etc.
- The complaint that the assessment method is being ignored or excluded by the "establishment" or mainstream of the profession
- The use of neologisms, made up words describing the assessment method and how it works
- The inappropriate application of genuine scientific terminology to describe the use or application of the assessment method (e.g., quantum, chaos theory, neurolinguistic programming)
- Failure to conduct research on the method's reliability and validity, and to publish this research in independent peer-reviewed journals
- An overreliance on anecdotal claims and testimonial evidence regarding the assessment method's usefulness
- Overreaching claims—stating that the assessment method is remarkably effective for assessing a wide array of problems, often seemingly unrelated
- The invocation of theological or religious language (e.g., chakras, *qi*, Reiki, prana, angels, spirits of the dead) to describe what the assessment method measures
- Claiming to assess nonreligious but otherwise metaphysical forces or energy fields unknown to science (e.g., auras, bioenergetic fields, meridian points)

[a] No single one of these warning signs is an indictment branding the assessment method as pseudoscientific or bogus, but generally the more of these features characterize a given method, the greater the likelihood that the method is a form of hucksterism, pseudoscience, or extreme naïveté.

# ANATOMICALLY CORRECT DOLLS

Anatomically correct dolls, for example, dolls with secondary sexual characteristics, are sometimes used in clinical assessment to aid in ascertaining if a child has been sexually abused. The use of such dolls would seem to have some face validity, for example, it makes superficial sense, and they are comparatively widely used in the field of child protective services, and within clinical social work in particular (e.g., Faller, 2005). The implications of a false positive (erroneously concluding that a child *had* been sexually abused) or false negative (erroneously concluding that a child *had not* been sexually abused) finding of sexual abuse are enormous, with grave familial ramifications. Despite their widespread use, the available research is not encouraging of a strong reliance on ACD. For example, Cronch, Viljoen, and Hansen (2006) concluded:

> Overall, research in this area indicates that anatomically detailed dolls should be avoided with preschool children, due to the suggestibility and lack of self-representational skills found in this age group. (p. 201)

> Anatomically detailed dolls should be used cautiously, should be avoided with very young children, and should be introduced to obtain further details only after the child has already disclosed. (p. 205; see also Thierry, Lamb, Orbach, & Pipe, 2005, and Aldridge, 1998)

ACDs are not an assessment method to be used casually, and as a strong indicator of abuse (or its absence) among small children. Social workers employ such methods at their peril, as well as that of their clients.

Some readers will recall the McMartin Preschool Trials of the 1980s, when the operators of a preschool in California were accused of sexually abusing the young children they cared for. More than 360 children were diagnosed as having been molested, of which about half had been interviewed by a social worker using ACD. Incredible (but believed) claims were made that the school contained hidden rooms and underground tunnels (there were none) where children witnessed infant sacrifice and adults drinking blood. Satanic rituals were said to be conducted at the school, and animals (a horse!) were supposedly killed in front of the children. Several members of the accused McMartin family remained in jail for years during the investigation. None of the claims of sexual abuse were substantiated, and no one was found guilty of child abuse. All charges were dropped, and years later, one supposed victim or witness recanted his testimony of having been abused saying that he was only saying things he believed his parents wished him to say. This is a striking example of how using a clinical assessment method of ill-founded reliability and validity had a tragic consequence (Eberle & Eberle, 1993).

# APPLIED KINESIOLOGY AND OTHER BIOENERGETIC ASSESSMENT METHODS

## Thought Field Therapy and Applied Kinesiology

Applied kinesiology (AK) was invented by a chiropractor, George Goodheart (1975). AK is a procedure that employs testing of the strength of muscles in a person's body (usually by applying pressure to an outstretched arm) that is claimed to provide feedback about various aspects of bodily or emotional functioning. AK was applied to the treatment of emotional problems by a psychologist, Roger Callahan, who used AK testing in conjunction with a therapy he invented called thought field therapy (TFT; Callahan & Trubo, 2001). TFT employs the supposed stimulation of acupressure meridian points while thinking about an upsetting issue.

Callahan used an AK-based procedure that he calls causal diagnosis or TFTDx to determine a prescribed, individualized sequence of meridian points on the body to be stimulated, usually by finger tapping. Once the correct sequence of body points is assessed, the client (or sometimes the therapist) taps on the indicated spot/spots in particularly structured sequences. It has been claimed that these spots on the body act like the "delete" key on a computer keyboard, to eliminate traumatic memories and other dysfunctions. TFTDx is claimed to have a 95% treatment success rate (Callahan & Trubo, 2001). A more advanced level of TFT is called voice technology (VT), an assessment procedure carried out over the telephone that is claimed to determine specific TFT treatments and said to have a 97% success rate. TFTDx is provided by a number of social workers (Callahan Techniques, n.d.; Pignotti, 2005a, 2007a). TFT was recently recommended to members of the House Veteran Affairs Committee for posttraumatic stress disorder (PTSD) by an licensed clinical social worker (LCSW; Bray, 2007) and variants of TFT have even been taught at a top-ranked school of social work (Pignotti, 2007b). However, a controlled study conducted by a licensed social worker revealed that no differences in treatment outcomes existed between the sequences of tapping points identified by VT and those that were randomly tapped upon (Pignotti, 2005b). Thus, if TFT's supposed degree of success is based on the proper assessment and selection of points on the body to tap, and a randomized controlled trial showed no difference in outcomes between "properly selected" body sites, and randomly chosen ones, then the theoretical foundations of TFT have been shown to be false. Furthermore, there are no existing credible studies that support the efficacy of any form of TFT diagnosis or treatment (Pignotti & Thyer, 2009, 2015). To the extent that TFT "works," it would seem largely on the basis of placebo influences and suggestion. This is also the general conclusion for the apparent efficacy of acupuncture, according to a series of systematic reviews prepared by the Cochrane Collaboration (see www.Cochrane.org). When "real" acupuncture is compared with placebo acupuncture involving random needle placement, generally equivalent results are obtained. This suggests that the theory (i.e., there are invisible EFs undetected thus far by science, largely responsible for human physical and emotional health) behind acupuncture is invalid, and the assessments involved in proper needle placement are invalid.

## Other Energy Therapy Assessment Methods

A number of offshoots of TFT diagnosis and assessment have been developed and are also being practiced by LCSWs. For example, energy diagnostic and treatment methods (EDxTM) employ a method similar to TFTDx, "but more sophisticated in diagnosis" (Philips, n.d., para. 4). There are no published studies to support claims being made for any of these offshoots.

Another form of assessment and treatment involves testing a different proposed energy system of points on the body representing various organs, called the chakras (based on Hindu theology), spiritual nodes of energy said to be located along the groin, spine, and head axis. An LCSW, Susan Wright, has authored a book titled *The Chakras in Shamanic Practice: Eight Stages of Healing and Transformation* (Wright, 2007). Relatedly, a method called Seemorg Matrix™, recently renamed advanced integrative therapy (AIT), was developed by a master's in social work (MSW) (Clinton, 2005) and is described as "an amalgam of approaches from eastern spirituality, western psychology, and psychoneuroimmunology" (p. 1). The client is asked to move his or her hand down what is claimed to be a series of chakras on the body while repeating a verbal phrase connected with a trauma. This is believed to move the trauma through the chakras and produce healing. The main website for AIT claims that it provides "lasting relief from a range of intractable psychological disorders, physical diseases, allergenic symptoms and spiritual impasses" (Seemorg Matrix Work, n.d., para. 2). These extraordinary claims appear to be based primarily on testimonials.

The primary use of testimonials as evidence of a treatment's efficacy has long been known to be problematic. Here, for example, is a quote from an 1897 article titled "Science and Pseudo-science in Medicine":

> The fact that a considerable proportion of those who are sick from various acute or chronic ailments recover after a time, independently of the use of medicinal agents or methods of treatment, taken in connection with this tendency to ascribe recovery to the treatment employed, makes it an easy matter to obtain certificates of cure for any nostrum which an unprincipled money-maker may see fit to offer an incredulous public. If ten in a thousand of those who have used the alleged remedy believe themselves to have been benefited, their certificates will answer all purposes of exploitation and the 990 will not be heard from by the general public. (Sternberg, 1897, p. 205)

Social workers are also liable to be misled because clients who are pleased with the results of their therapy may be more likely to return to the therapist, extolling the benefits of their "treatment" and of the practitioner's expertise. This can, over time, give rise to a biased perception of therapeutic efficacy, even among the most honest and well-intended professionals.

Another energy-based therapy that is claimed to identify and treat allergies and has become popular with some LCSWs is called the Nambudripad allergy elimination technique (NAET; Nambudripad, 2003). NAET testing is carried out through AK while a person is holding small vials that are said to contain the energetic essences of various substances. Once the allergies are identified, treatment is carried out through stimulation of points along the spine. In reality, these vials contain only water, and this method has never been shown to be a reliable or valid method of assessing a client's presumptive sensitivity to environmental toxins.

Leading social work assessment texts uncritically, and usually approvingly, present theoretical content on supposed life energy forces that clinicians are urged to try and assess and modify. For example, we are told in *Social Work Diagnosis in Contemporary Practice* (Turner, 2005), that:

> The flow of qi along the 14 meridians governs the well-being of our internal systems...The *qi* energy is a cosmic force that flows through the human body in a very orderly and logical way. Balance and harmony of the flow of *qi* results in health. The imbalance or disharmony of the flow leads to illness. (Chan, Ho, & Chow, 2005, pp. 460, 462)

These authors go on to discuss how social work clients can be provided with therapies predicated on realigning or healing one's *qi*, treatments such as *qigong, Tai-jiquan, yoga,* acupressure, moxibustion, massage, *qi* meditation, Reiki, hands-on healing, and reflexology. Acupressure is pressing on various points of the body, moxibustion involves holding burning herbs close to these supposed meridian points, and reflexology involves pressing on various points on the bottom of the client's foot, to affect health, including mental well-being. It is disheartening to see how far some professional social workers have drifted from the discipline's person-in-environment approach to assessment and treatment via advocating these untested or demonstrably false approaches.

## PERSONALITY TYPING AND TESTING

### The Enneagram

The Enneagram is a system of nine personality types, developed by Oscar Ichazo and the Chilean psychiatrist, Claudio Naranjo. Opinions about its origin differ. Some say that the Enneagram was influenced by the theological teachings of Gurdjieff's Fourth Way, whereas others maintain that the teachings of the ancient Sufis were influential (Riso, 1990). The nine personality types are said to represent different fixations of the ego that limit a person from developing and realizing his or her full potential as a human being. For example, Type 1 represents a person who has a fixation on perfection, order, and intolerance, whereas Type 8 represents a person who has a fixation on power, aggression, and is being dictatorial. No one type is considered to be superior to any other type and each type has its strengths and its weaknesses.

A search of the PsycINFO database reveals scant evidence of any formal psychometric analysis of the Enneagram. Only one refereed publication was identified that contained preliminary psychometric analyses of the Riso-Hudson Enneagram Type Indicator (RHETI; Newgent, Parr, Newman, & Higgins, 2004). However, these authors did not conduct an exploratory or confirmatory factor analysis, and the reliability (alpha) coefficients produced mixed results, with two types being unacceptably low. Although a number of other Enneagram assessments appear in popular books, it does not appear that they have undergone any peer-reviewed published psychometric analyses.

An Internet search on "Enneagram" and "LCSW" revealed that a number of LCSWs utilize the Enneagram in their practices. One LCSW (Bartlett, 2005) writes on her website that although she was initially skeptical, after investigating it, she decided to study it further because she found "the Enneagram's description of personality styles to be subtle, complex, and useful" (para. 2). After finding it helpful for herself in her own relationship with her husband, she decided to use it professionally in her practice. The decision to use a particular approach in psychotherapy based on personal and clinical experience rather than on empirical evidence is consistent with an international study on more than 4,900 psychotherapists, including social workers (Orlinsky, Botermans, & Ronnestad, 2001). The study demonstrated that clinical and personal experience was a more important influence on the practice of psychotherapy than research, a discouraging finding replicated by many similar studies over the years.

## The Myers–Briggs Type Indicator

The Myers–Briggs Type Indicator (MBTI) is a widely used personality test that is based on the personality theories of Jung (1921/1971). Jung proposed three dimensions comprising the human personality and the developers of the MBTI added a fourth (Myers & Myers, 1995). These dimensions are described as follows:

1. *Introversion* (I) versus *extraversion* (E): Extraverts are said to be energized by interactions with others and the outside world, whereas introverts draw their energy from time spent in solitude.

2. *Sensing* (S) versus *intuition* (N). S types mainly focus on tangible, concrete details, whereas N types tend to focus more on abstract concepts and the big picture (contrary to a popular misconception, the N dimension does *not* mean that this type necessarily disregard tangible evidence in favor of intuitive hunches).

3. *Thinking* versus *feeling*. This dimension pertains to the way in which people make decisions. T types make decisions based on principles of logic and reason, whereas F types make decisions based on personal values.

4. *Judging* versus *perceiving*. This dimension was added to Jung's theory by the developers of the MBTI. J types prefer to schedule and plan their time in advance, whereas P types prefer to live their lives in a more open-ended and unplanned manner.

According to Jung, these personality traits are set at birth and are not expected to change. The types are not intended to be indicative of pathology, but rather are said to be normal, healthy personality differences with no good or bad types.

The MBTI classifies the test taker as one of each of the four types, producing 16 possible type combinations. For example, INTJ would indicate a preference for introversion, intuition, thinking, and judging. The MBTI was developed by Katherine Briggs and her daughter Isabel Briggs Myers. Neither had any formal psychological training. Myers and Briggs developed the MBTI by making notes from library research on index cards and then testing them out on close friends and acquaintances whose type they felt that they already knew and later on classes of college and medical students (Myers & Briggs Foundation, n.d.).

The ability to administer the MBTI is not limited to psychologists. Anyone can take qualification training under the auspices of the Center for Applications of Psychological Type (CAPT) that owns the right to the MBTI, which enables people to purchase and administer the MBTI (CAPT, 2008). The costs of this training are considerable. The initial level of certification takes 4 days and about $1,000 in tuition, exclusive of travel, hotel, and meals, and there are several advanced levels as well. An Internet search on the terms "LCSW" and "MBTI" reveals that a number of LCSWs have taken this qualifying training and use the MBTI in their practice.

The CAPT website claims that the MBTI is "based on well-researched and validated personality theory with proven applications in a variety of fields" (CAPT, para. 1). However, many of the studies published about the

MBTI are in CAPT's own journal, and reviews of the MBTI literature have revealed serious problems with the reliability and validity of the MBTI (Boyle, 1995; Hunsley, Lee, & Wood, 2003; Lorr, 1991; Pittenger, 2005).

If clinical social workers find themselves in agency settings that utilize the MBTI, they should refrain from using the results to provide career advice, based on the lack of sound evidence for the validity of the 16 personality types and the scant evidence for a link between type and job suitability (Pittenger, 2005). To use the MBTI to steer a person away from a career he or she might be interested in, or from managerial positions based on the MBTI type, would do a grave disservice. Closer to home, we find social work educators recommending that the MBTI be used to facilitate social work field education by using it with students, faculty, and field instructors (Moore, Dietz, & Dettlaff, 2004). It was recommended that students and potential field instructors be "matched" by their MBTI in order to promote a more successful internship. We believe that such claims are premature.

## Electronic or Mechanical Assessment Devices

Some practitioners in our field have an affinity for employing gizmos, defined as "a mechanical device or procedure for which the clinical benefit in a specific clinical context is not clearly established" (Leff & Finucane, 2008, p. 1830), and it seems based on the idea that the use of technological devices somehow conveys more of an aura of scientific analysis or of enhanced credibility. There is a love of bells and whistles that many of us share, and adopting gizmos into one's assessment armamentarium may be a psychologically and financially rewarding experience for the social worker, regardless of any enhancements to his or her assessment or diagnostic accuracy. The medical fad of performing crude lobotomies on the mentally ill in the 1950s is an extreme example of what Leff and Finucane (2008) called "Gizmo Idolatry," and clinical social workers have not been immune to engaging in analogous practices. Here are a few examples of social work assessment methods using gizmos:

### Radionics

Radionics is a method that uses a device claimed to be able to diagnose and heal people and animals at a distance (Frank, n.d.). Proponents believe that the equipment broadcasts energy patterns that are similar to those claimed to be contained in homeopathic remedies and that distance assessment and healing can be accomplished by having something from the person's body, such as a lock of hair, in the presence of the machine. Sometimes, radionics practitioners employ pendulums to dowse for a remedy. Proponents claim without basis that it is "very effective in a significant number of cases" (Frank, n.d., para. 2).

A web search on "LCSW" and "radionics" revealed that LCSWs are using these types of devices in practice. One type of radionics device is marketed as the Intergetix-EMDR and is claimed to facilitate eye movement desensitization and reprocessing (EMDR; Intergetix Inc., n.d., para. 7). An LCSW based in Chicago who provided only her first name and middle initial is among the practitioners listed on the company website (Intergetix Inc., n.d.).

## QXCI aka EPFX aka Scio

Another device in the same family as radionics devices is the Quantum Xrroid Consciousness Interface (QXCI), also referred to as the Electrical Physical Feedback Xrroid Equipment and Program (EPFX) or Scio. The QXCI is marketed as a biofeedback device claimed to be able to "detect reactions to things like stress, viruses, deficiencies, allergies, and food sensitivities" (Hamilton, 2006, para. 2). The device is also claimed to:

> give a reasonable and as accurate as is possible measurement of your current energetic levels of vitamins and minerals, bacteria, viruses and hormone levels and it compares all its results to what is a "normal" reading. If it finds an imbalance, in some cases it can energetically help correct the underlying causes of problems such as allergies, food sensitivities, weight gain, digestive problems, insomnia, depression, arthritis, skin problems, headaches and migraines. (para. 4)

Although this device is claimed to be the result of 20 years of research, we have been unable to identify any referred journal publications systematically evaluating its usefulness.

*The Seattle Times* (Berens & Willmsen, 2007) reported that the inventor of the EPFX, who has sold more than 10,000 devices in the United States, was brought up on charge by the Food and Drug Administration (FDA) and indicted for a felony, but fled the United

States and now runs his operation from Hungary. The device is reported to be currently selling for $19,900. The article reported on a number of cancer patients who had allegedly sought treatment from EPFX practitioners, abstained from or delayed standard medical treatment, and died.

A search of the Internet revealed a number of LCSWs that were using QXCI/Scio or EPFX. For example, one LCSW offers a workshop on using the EPFX to help couples in relationships, claiming to "identify and shift the unconscious patterns holding your partnership back from being what you want it to be" (Benoit & Neander, 2008, para. 2). An MSW who uses EPFX in her practice claims that the EPFX will:

1. Measure your total body for its reaction to 8,500 items and treat homeopathically the subtle problematic energetic disturbances

2. Provide a total body electrical massage

3. Detect stress, energetic imbalance, or abnormal energy by finding and shifting its frequency, using the cybernetic biofeedback

4. Explore intricate therapies such as electroacupuncture, scalar, color therapy, NLP [neurolinguistic programming], and so on

5. Increase the conscious-to-unconscious bond to heighten your awareness and take responsibility regarding health and life flow issues (Clements, n.d., para. 8)

One of the authors (BAT) encountered a graduate student who had consulted a MSW (unlicensed, working out of a medical doctor's office), who attached the student to a complicated electrical device, claiming that the device could diagnose her ailments according to the vibrations emitted by her body, and that the device could send back countervibrations to cure her. She was assured that the device was "approved by the FDA." I expressed incredulity that such a device existed (or at least really worked as described) and urged her to keep me posted as to her progress. She experienced no improvements, and discontinued the treatments, no worse off, except somewhat poorer.

It is possible that the device the student encountered is the BICOM (see www.waveworks.com.hk/howitworks.html), which can also be researched by using "BICOM Bioresonance Therapy" as a search term on the Internet. Sadly, one of the authors (BAT) has a former MSW and PhD student who is a distributor for the BICOM device in one of the southern states. The BICOM is a very impressive-looking electronic device, but one of no demonstrable value. A skeptical look at the BICOM device can be found at scepticsbook.com/2010/01/25/zap-there-goes-your-hard-earned-money.

## Putative Allergy and Toxin Detection Devices

A wide variety of other devices claiming to detect allergies are being sold on the Internet. For example, an LCSW based in Connecticut (Radomski, n.d.) advertises a number of devices and methods claimed to diagnose allergies and putative toxins. The website lists three other LCSWs who have been trained in these methods. The cheapest device, which sells for $50, is called the E-Tox Laser (a fancy name for what is essentially a laser pointer) used to supposedly stimulate acupressure points (it does not; there is no credible evidence that acupressure points exist, much less that a laser pointer can "stimulate" them). For $195, one can purchase an advanced laser that has an on–off switch and a wider beam. The most expensive device offered is the Eagle Guardian, which can be purchased for $845. The website claims "It is as if the Guardian provides the body with a clear signal/roadmap to the underlying causes of imbalance— harmful degenerative processes, micro-organisms, parasites, toxins, deficiencies, etc." (para. 2). The practitioners point these low-powered lasers (e.g., pointers) at various places on the client's body (the ubiqui- tous meridians, acupressure points, or other supposed energy nodes), and this is said to realign or fix disturbances in the body's EF.

## Clarity Meter (aka E-Meter)

The Clarity Meter is a device used by some of the advanced-level pro- ponents of traumatic incident reduction (TIR; Gerbode, 1995, 1998), which is an offshoot of Dianetics and Scientology, and is essentially the same as a device used by scientologists called the E-Meter. A web search revealed that practitioners with social work degrees are among the advanced practitioners of TIR. The Clarity Meter machine is essentially a galvanic skin response (GSR) device that measures electrical resistance (e.g., sweat!) when an electrode is placed in contact with the surface of the skin. However, a number of unsubstantiated claims are made for this device. A drop in skin resistance is believed to be an indicator that an emotionally charged area has been identified. Moreover, the website of the developer of the Clarity Meter claims that:

> It is used for discovering and handling suppressed or repressed thoughts, memories, and impressions which impact upon people's behavior and feeling of well-being. The utilization of the Clarity Meter can significantly enhance the speed and effectiveness of many kinds of developmental therapies, regression techniques, and meditation procedures. (Clarity Meter, n.d., para. 3)

Further claims are made that "it surpasses other meters used for simple psychology demonstration purposes and clearing" (para. 4) and that the therapist "uses the data to decide what to do next in the session" (Gerbode, 1998, para. 5). Again these are all unrealistic claims made without credible supportive evidence. Such devices are readily available via websites such as eBay.

## Gentle Wind Project Instruments

A set of instruments that sold from $400 to $20,000 was promoted by an MSW and former LCSW who ran a business called the Gentle Wind Project (GWP). Among the claimed healing instruments sold were "personality cards" that claimed to assess what "GWP-given personality traits have been assigned to him or her by the 'spirit world'" (Bergin & Garvey, 2004, para. 5). The company also offered distance soul readings based on hair samples and one couple reported being introduced to this by a licensed social worker (Bergin, 2008). Two whistle-blowers were sued by GWP for statements made on the Internet, although the charges were eventually dropped at both the state and federal levels. The Attorney General's Office of the state of Maine, where the business was located, sued GWP for false claims, fraud, and improper spending of charitable donations (Johnson, 2006), and the operation was eventually shut down (Associated Press, 2006). However, the owners of GWP have reportedly begun a new, similar business in another state (Nevada) under a different name that continues to sell similar healing instruments ranging from $365 to $6,260 and also offers astrology and readings based on hair samples (Winds of Change, 2008).

## HAIR ANALYSIS

The chemical analysis of a client's hair has some legitimate value, for example, in detecting illegal drug use (e.g., cocaine) some weeks after use. However, a number of social workers offer hair analysis for other, less legitimate, purposes. Typically, a sample of the client's hair is taken from the back of the neck and sent by the social worker to a commercial hair analysis company, which returns back a report of the client's supposed deficiencies, excesses, and imbalances in the client's nutritional state, unknown allergies, or body chemistry. Superficially, this conveys an aura of scientific objectivity, but the reality is that hair analysis is not a medically recommended means of diagnosis or assessment, except for a very limited range of issues, such as past substance abuse. Barrett (2010, pp. 6–7) states that "Hair analysis is worthless for assessing the body's nutritional status or serving as a basis for dietary or supplement recommendations...Should you encounter a practitioner who uses hair analysis for any these purposes, run for the nearest exit and complain to your state attorney general." Despite this, a recent Internet search using "hair analysis" and "LCSW" revealed more than 2000 "hits." Possible malpractice?

## NEUROLINGUISTIC PROGRAMMING

NLP is an approach to psychosocial assessment and treatment developed by Richard Bandler and John Grinder, and derived, in part, from the theories of social worker Virginia Satir. NLP has penetrated the clinical social work literature to a modest extent (e.g., Angell, 2011) despite the frankly hostile attitude its advocates have expressed toward demands of scientific validation of this approach's extraordinary claims. Angell (1996, p. 499) notes that "theoreticians and practitioners of NLP view scientific inquiry to be the antithesis of the subjective systematic client-centered view of their approach" and Clancy and Yorkshire (1989) expressed the NLP view as "We are not scientists, and what we do is not science, so we do not have to offer proof" (p. 26). A review of the evidence that included an examination of 70 papers on NLP (Heap, 1988) found that the claims of proponents to be able to conduct assessments based on eye movements and representational systems (e.g., visual, auditory, kinesthetic) were not supported, and no further evidence to support these theories has materialized since that review was conducted (see also Coe & Scharcoff, 1985; Sharpley, 1987; Tye, 1994). Lack of evidence had not deterred the advocates of NLP from making extravagant claims, such as:

> NLP (Neuro-linguistic Programming) is the Most Powerful technology available to understand the human mind and communication that can shift your Personal and Business Life so you can live your Life by Design rather than Default. (available from http://nlp.org/viewseminar.php?seminarid=405 downloaded on 29 July 2008)
>
> In terms of assessment, a social worker who promoted NLP claimed that "…accurately assessing a client's representation system (visual, auditory, or kinesthetic) can help build rapport during therapy and improve insights into clients' actions. Adverbs, adjectives, and verbs used in speech reveal the client's representation systems." (Zastow, Dotson, & Koch, 1986, p. 29)

See also Zastrow (1990), Gray (2001), and Taylor (2004) for further illustrations of NLP being promoted within social work. Social workers can become licensed practitioners of NLP via attending expensive week-long training workshops and earn approved social work continuing education units (CEUs) by attending lectures on the topic. Dishearteningly, the latest edition of an influential social work treatment book contains an uncritical chapter on the use of NLP to assess and treat clients (Turner, 2011), and clinical social workers can earn continuing education (CE) credits needed for renewing their license, by taking classes on NLP (www.zurinstitute.com/neuro_linguistic_programming_course.html).

## REIKI

A number of LCSWs have incorporated the assessment and treatment method known as Reiki into their practice (see Jackson, 2004, whose work describes it as a rising star in complementary care). Reiki is a Japanese variant of the laying on of hands we previously encountered in TT, described earlier in this chapter, and which may also be found in the approach called polarity therapy. Reiki practitioners are said to be able to assess an invisible EF (called *ki*, not to be confused with the Chinese *qi*) surrounding the human body, to detect disturbance in this flow of energy, and to heal distressed people by realigning these energies with physically touching the clients or by simply hovering their hands over clients. The University of Maryland School of Social Work provided CE workshops in Reiki, taught by a social worker, and Reiki is said to be useful for such varied issues as the labored breathing of dying cancer patients, stress, fatigue, burnout, compassion fatigue, reduce heart rate, lower blood pressure, eliminate pain, alter hormone levels, improve sleep, and decrease agitation. These are remarkable claims. Unfortunately, a systematic review of randomized controlled trials of Reiki showed that it has no effects (Lee, Pittler, & Ernst, 2008). Jackson (2004) describes how one book on Reiki authored by a clinical social worker has sold more than 65,000 copies. We doubt any single edition of any traditional social work textbook has enjoyed such sales. Here is the Facebook page to one MSW who teaches Reiki and is a self-described Reiki master: www.facebook .com/events/539808186062740.

## PERSON-IN-ENVIRONMENT SYSTEM

A person-in-environment (PIE) system represents a uniquely social work effort to describe, classify, and code the problems of clients—in other words, it is an assessment method (Karls & Wandrei, 1992). It is an attempt to come up with a reliable and valid scheme to classify a client's psychosocial functioning factors, "to provide a truly biopsychosocial assessment of a social work client [and]...a tool that allows social workers to systematically conceptualize and describe client's problems in the language of social work" (Williams, Karls, & Wandrei, 1989, p. 1126), truly a useful undertaking, if legitimate. Williams et al. (1989) asserted that PIE would be field tested for its reliability across practitioners, formally tested for its reliability across practice settings at various sites across the United States, and assess its validity. Then, if the validity is acceptable, it would be disseminated as a practice and teaching tool. These noble plans did not come to fruition apparently. In 1994, the National Association of Social Workers began selling the PIE book and manual (Karls & Wandrei, 1994), but our own recent literature search found that *nothing* has apparently been published related to the system's reliability and validity. For our profession's major disciplinary association to promote a system of psychosocial assessment before demonstrating that the system is reliable and valid strikes us as unconscionable. We can better understand how individual social workers succumb to hucksterism by promoting bogus methods of assessment in order to reap financial benefits, but we are considerably less tolerant when the culprit is not an individual but a supposedly reputable professional association. It is long past due for the National Association of Social Workers (NASW) to commission credible research studies on the PIE system and to publish the results in peer-reviewed professional journals. Until these are forthcoming, the unsupported claims made as to the capabilities of the PIE system should be moderated, and the tool should be more accurately described and marketed as an experimental method of unproven value. Nevertheless, despite this lack of evidence, the PIE is being used clinically by social workers (Karpetis, 2013).

## OTHER EXAMPLES

Space does not permit us to more fully describe the plethora of other methods of social work assessment which we believe can be classified as pseudoscientific or bogus. Such methods abound in fields such as developmental disabilities and clinical psychology (Jacobson, Foxx, & Mulick, 2006; Lilienfeld, Lynn, & Lohr, 2003). One, the assessment method called facilitated communication (FC), enjoyed widespread popularity in the 1990s. FC involved being able to help more accurately assess the cognitive abilities of persons with serious intellectual impairments by having a trained "facilitator" hold the disabled person's hand over a keyboard. Amazingly, persons so supported could apparently respond to questions, compose poetry, write essays, and complete advanced academic coursework, without heretofore displaying any knowledge of the alphabet, of the elements of grammar, or of spelling. Sadly, well-controlled studies clearly demonstrated that FC involved unwitting guidance from the "facilitators." When the latter were not aware of the questions, the disabled person's communicative abilities disappeared. In essence, FC was simply an elaborate ouija board phenomenon. Many thousands of professionals, parents, and caregivers received training (at great cost) in FC, falsely raising hopes and subjecting persons with disabilities to hours of tedious sitting hunched over keyboards having their limbs unknowingly manipulated by well-meaning but naive facilitators (Jacobson et al., 2006). FC is still with us, being taught at the Institute on Communication and Inclusion within the College of Education at Syracuse University.

In December 2007, a teenage girl with autism was said to have typed, via having her hand held over a keyboard by a facilitator, allegations that her father had been sexually abusive. A social worker believed these allegations and filed a complaint with the Michigan Department of Human Services. The father was immediately arrested and spent 80 days in jail. There was no initial and immediate objective appraisal of the legitimacy of the allegations obtained via FC although this could have been done within several days of the disclosure, using independent facilitators or blinded investigations. Instead, the father was taken to court. An independent psychologist hired by the family was able to conclusively show that their daughter could not have made the allegations and that, as in so many other cases, the facilitator was the origin of these horrific allegations. In the summer of 2014, the state of Michigan agreed to pay the family $840,000 to drop the case. Here is something the court said:

> The Court also found that XXX [name redacted by the authors], a social worker with the state Department of Human Services who placed the children in foster care, could not claim governmental immunity. The court ruled that "XXX's [name redacted by the authors] actions are especially troubling in this situation given the multiple documented errors in the facilitated statement used as the sole basis for XXX's [name redacted by the authors] recommendation." (Retrieved September 10, 2014, from theddnewsblog.blogspot .com/2013_09_01_archive.html)

If the social worker involved had maintained a suitably critical attitude toward the allegations of sexual abuse, and of FC as a means of assessing an autistic person's possible sexual experiences, much of the injustice associated with case could have been avoided. See search.freep .com/sp?aff=1100&skin=&keywords=Wendrow for a series of articles on this recent case.

## GENOGRAMS AND ECOMAPS

Genograms and ecomaps are widely taught clinical assessment methods found in social work. As an exercise, we encourage the reader to try and locate any published studies on the reliability or validity of such methods. You may be surprised (or perhaps not, after reading this chapter) on what you (cannot) find!

## ARE YOU SERIOUS?

The pseudoscientific assessment methods described in this chapter are regrettably not solely found on the fringe of social work practice (Barth, 2014; Lee, Ng, Leung, & Chan, 2009). In September 2014, we reviewed the CE offerings related to assessment, which were being advertised by the Kripalu Center for Yoga and Health, located in Stockbridge, MA. CE hours are mandated by most states for clinical social workers to renew their license to practice, usually something along the lines of 30 CE every 2 years. CE is deemed important for social workers to remain abreast of current developments. The Kripalu Center website states that:

> SW: Programs have been approved for Category 1 Continuing Education hours for relicensure, in accordance with 258 CMR. Collaborative of NASW and the Boston College and Simmons College Schools of Social Work. (Retrieved September 9, 2014, from http://kripalu.org/cecredits)

In other words, two respected graduate social work programs, located in prestigious universities, and in conjunction with the National Association of Social Workers, collude to approve the Kripalu Center's social work CE courses. Table 2.2 describes some of these programs, their content, and instructors' backgrounds. Look at some of the assessment methods being taught to social workers, for use in their professional practice

- Assessment *qi*, an EF unknown to science, the existence of which whose existence has never been proven, much less demonstrated that practitioners can reliably detect its flow.

**TABLE 2.2**
**Continuing Education Offerings Available at the Kripalu Center for Yoga and Health, as Approved by the National Association of Social Workers, Dealing With the Topic of Assessment Methods**

- *The Wisdom of the Enneagram: Moving Beyond Personality* (12 CE credits)

  Look past the veils of your personality type and habits to enjoy a more direct experience of your authentic self. Enneagram Institute faculty member Michael Naylor views the Enneagram personality types as nine distinct aspects of human nature that can be found in all of us, regardless of our type's dominant orientation. Come explore how these different aspects of yourself manifest personally in your life, enabling you to access deeper inner resources and lasting joy. This workshop features exercises for each type, as well as music, meditations, and practices that help bring your centers of intelligence (thinking, feeling, and instinct) into greater alignment, opening you to the transformative action of Spirit. Learn how to use the "Wake-Up Call" to move your awareness away from the habit of your personality type toward contact with essence and authenticity.

- *Yi Quan Qigong: Develop Health, Balance, and Inner Strength* (8.5 CE)

  Ever wonder why, in spite of the miracles of modern medicine, more than 700,000 Americans practice ancient healing exercises from China? Qigong is among the world's most popular and best-researched methods to improve health and vitality. Discover the secrets of one of the greatest qigong masters in Chinese history, Wang Xiangzhai, equally renowned as a healer, athlete, and spiritual mentor.

- *Primordial Qigong: Healthy Body, Awakened Mind, Unity With the Tao* (23.5 CE)

  Primordial Qigong (Hunyuan Gong) is a revered and comprehensive system of health and longevity exercises from China. It is the legacy of Hu Yaozhen, the Taoist priest and healer who coined the term "medical qigong" and was one of the first to apply qigong in hospitals. Primordial Qigong cleanses the body of impure and stagnant energy and recharges the system with vitality. It teaches you how to harmonize with qi, the life force.

- *Evidence-Based Qigong Certification: Nurturing Mind, Body, and Spirit* (8.5 CE)

  The Chinese word "qi" is identical in meaning to the Sanskrit word "prana." Come deepen your understanding of the spiritual root common to all Eastern energy practices.

- *The Art of Reiki: Reiki 1* (8.5 CE, taught by an MSW)

  Because your body is a constantly changing and renewing energy system, you have the opportunity in every moment to recreate yourself in wholeness. Reiki, a gentle, hands-on healing art of Japanese origin, reconnects you with your ability to heal yourself, others, and animals. It helps to reduce stress, relieve pain, balance emotions, and facilitate personal healing and spiritual growth. Reiki is based on the understanding that all conditions of imbalance are rooted in the human energy field, and it is these underlying.

*(continued)*

**TABLE 2.2** (*continued*)
**Continuing Education Offerings Available at the Kripalu Center for Yoga and Health, as Approved by the National Association of Social Workers, Dealing With the Topic of Assessment Methods**

- *The Art of Reiki: Reiki 2* (8.5 CE, taught by an MSW)

  Expand your healing abilities as you explore how Reiki can reduce stress, relieve pain, balance emotions, and facilitate personal healing and spiritual growth. Based on the understanding that all conditions of imbalance are rooted in the human energy field, Reiki addresses underlying energetic patterns to create wellness and reconnect you with your ability to heal yourself, others, and animals.

  In Reiki 2, you

  - Learn ancient Reiki symbols and how to apply them for additional empowerment
  - Learn to access cellular memory to heal challenging emotional situations
  - Receive the Reiki 2 attunement
  - Learn to offer Reiki to people and situations at a distance

- *Techniques for Mind–Body Integration: Somatic Therapy Training* (28.5 CE)

  Body-based psychotherapy goes quickly to the heart of the issues in our tissues. This training for healers of all stripes gives you a basic foundation for practicing somatic therapy through the dynamics of life-force energy. Learn to unlock the defensive patterns hidden beneath consciousness and free up the vital core energy within. Combining principles and exercises from bioenergetics, core energetics, somatic experiencing, formative psychology, and Anodea Judith's signature Chakra Therapy, this workshop addresses

  - The energetics of charging and discharging
  - The formation and dissolution of body armor
  - Bioenergetic character structures and childhood development
  - Working with trauma and PTSD
  - Balancing the chakras
  - Decoding the language of illness

  Learn how to interpret and dissolve defensive body armor by freeing and balancing the energetic life force that flows through the core. Techniques include bioenergetic exercises in dyads, movement, breath, dance, massage, body reading, and therapeutic demonstrations by the instructor. [Authors' note: The presenter of this training is a self-described Pagan High Priestess.]

- *Medical Intuition Healing Intensive* (8.5 CE)

  "A Medical intuitive is an alternative medicine practitioner who claims to use their self-described intuitive abilities to find the cause of a physical or emotional condition. Other terms for such a person include medical clairvoyant, medical psychic or intuitive counselor" (c.f. http://en.wikipedia.org/wiki/Medical_intuitive)

(*continued*)

**TABLE 2.2** *(continued)*
**Continuing Education Offerings Available at the Kripalu Center for Yoga and Health, as Approved by the National Association of Social Workers, Dealing With the Topic of Assessment Methods**

- *Lightworkers Healing Method Intensive: Angelically Guided Energy Healing* (29.5 CE)

  Be the person your soul wants you to be, and help others do the same, by learning to channel divine healing. The Lightworkers Healing Method is an accessible skill that applies to every arena of life. Physical, mental, emotional, spiritual, financial, and interpersonal issues can all be healed. In this combined Level One–Two intensive, you practice

  ○ Channeling and working with subtle energy
  ○ Creating sacred space in healing sessions and in your life
  ○ Self-care techniques so that healing work strengthens rather than drains you
  ○ Locating and releasing the traumas that cause disease
  ○ Soul-fragment retrieval, healing, and reintegration
  ○ Accessing past lives to heal the deepest, oldest wounds

  Experience the joy of channeling divine guides, angels, and light beings. When you learn to be a vessel for higher dimension healers, miracles happen in your healing practice and in your life. [Authors' note: Here is the self-described mission of the instructor of this course.]

  > "Yes, she heals people just like John of God. But the most amazing thing about her is that she teaches other people to do the same thing. She is creating a WAVE of Esther Hicks/John of God healer-channelers." (Retrieved September 9, 2014, from http://lightworkersmethod.com/LynnMcGonagill.html)

*Source:* All the content in this table is quoted directly from the website of the Kripalu Center for Yoga and Health. Retrieved September 9, 2014, from http://kripalu.org/cecredits

CE, continuing education; PTSD, posttraumatic stress disorder.

- Use of the Enneagram, an assessment method of no demonstrated reliability or validity.
- Teaching the practice of Reiki, healing others through assessing the client's invisible EF, a field, which like *qi*, has never been shown to exist, and a practice that has been shown to be no more effective than placebo therapy.
- Assessing the chakras of clients, yet another form of energy the existence of which cannot be reliably detected, by anyone.
- The use of so-called medical intuition, a fancy phrase for old-fashioned clairvoyance, to diagnose and assess client problems.
- Dream analysis, trying to assess clients' issues on the basis of their reports of their dreams.

- Invoking divine guides and angels (!) (what used to be called having a séance) to assess and heal via channeling the spirits of the dead.

The aforementioned examples are assessment methods being used in social work now—not in the distant past, but *today*. This bogus, mystical, and pseudoscientific content is being sponsored by respected institutions of higher education, organizations supposedly dedicated to discouraging mysticism and quackery, not encouraging it via their official approval. And to see that the weight of the prestigious NASW is also sponsoring these CE offerings is even more dismaying. A simple Google search using the terms "LCSW" and "channeling" will disclose contemporary LCSWs who use these methods, channeling spirits, medical intuition, and past-life regression therapy, in their practice (e.g., www.inneraccess101.com/practitioner_usa.htm). One current MSW has a professional business devoted to the practice of teaching others to supposedly channel spirit beings (www.inneraccess101.com/staff.htm). Here is how another LCSW describes some of the assessment and treatment services she provides:

---

### Channeling

Would you like to receive guidance from Beloved Brother? Beloved Brother offers ancient wisdom teaching and provides answers to your questions. I offer in-person and phone readings. All sessions are recorded for you. Fee: $80.

### Medical Intuition

This Medical Intuition style uses the body's physiology as an entry point. I attend to what the body has to say, show, and reveal. The body itself reports while I record the information that it gives. These messages are then sourced from the original place within the body. From here, it is possible that root causes of the body's conditions can be found. No diagnosis or recommendations are made. After the body scan results are given, you and I can discuss what might be done to gain further knowledge or steps to take in order to set the body in balance. Often scans are helpful

---

*(continued)*

(*continued*)

when brought to your healing team as additional information to be worked with. You do not need to be physically present, as geographical location is not a factor in gathering the body's report of its conditions. Fees:

- Medical intuition body scan: $135 (scan and results over the phone)
- Medical intuition body scan package: $160 (includes the scan results and energy healing session)
- Core mining: $65 (focus in on a key or specific area of the body)

### One Heart Vibrational Healing

Pervasive patterns in people's lives create stagnation on all levels of our being. If stagnation is recognized, it can be transformed. Sessions allow you to address the patterns in your life that are wished to be healed. The healing occurs through a gentle laying on of hands, clairvoyantly tracking the energy, and encouraging its natural flow into higher vibrational frequencies. One heart healing occurs through willingly aligning one's heart and soul with the Heart of The Divine. Fee: $95

### Past Life Regression

Past Life Regression is a technique to further explore the self. During a trance-like state, you will be able to tune into the subconscious to recall memories and experiences of past life times. Fee: $95

*Source:* Retrieved September 9, 2014, from http://casandramay.com/services

So this LCSW can assess you over the telephone, using medical intuition and the channeling of spirit guides. And in doing so, is applying methods taught in CE programs for social workers approved by universities and the NASW itself! If the readers are embarrassed by this state of affairs, so are the authors.

## CONCLUDING REMARKS

We believe that clinical assessment in social work practice is a very important topic. We believe that clients should have the right to be provided with clinical assessment methods that are well supported by credible empirical research as reliable and valid methods (where these assessment methods are known to exist), analogous to prior claims that clients should have the right to be provided with effective psychosocial treatments, where these are known to exist (Myers & Thyer, 1997). The use of unreliable and invalid assessment methods can have serious deleterious consequences. Social workers waste time and energy learning about these approaches and using them. They can then make ill-founded and possibly harmful conclusions about their clients, with corresponding negative effects. Clients can be harmed, least of all by having their time and money wasted, and possibly by being subjected to unwarranted conclusions about themselves ("He is a sexual offender," "She has been abused," "You need anger management training"), and perhaps being provided with inappropriate psychosocial services. The profession is harmed by being associated with pseudoscientific assessment practices, which impair our ability to gain respectability as a legitimate health care profession and to provide genuinely effective services to the public.

We too have faith in the purgative effects of well-crafted scientific studies to help us discriminate the helpful from the bogus, both in terms of assessment methods and in the selection of psychosocial treatments. We believe that our discipline will benefit from the emerging movement known as evidence-based practice and that over time, the specific assessment practices (and those akin to them) we have identified in this chapter will gradually disappear from the landscape of professional social work having been replaced with more genuinely useful ones. We concur with the sense, if not the predictive abilities, of Mattaini and Kirk (1991, p. 263), who stated that "efforts to improve the reliability and validity of social work assessment models are likely to intensify, because reliability and validity are critical to effective practice and professional survival. Many dimensional and contextual systems are available now, but these innovations need more rigorous development and empirical testing in practice settings with clinicians, researchers, and clients."

Some readers may view this chapter as overly critical. We believe that writing as we have is a useful antidote to the excessively uncritical elements within clinical social work. We subscribe to the view of the late Pope Benedict XVI:

> In some circles to speak of truth is seen as controversial or divisive, and consequently best kept in the private sphere. And in truth's place—or better said its absence—an idea has spread which, in giving value to everything indiscriminately, claims to assure freedom and to liberate conscience. This we call relativism. But what purpose has a "freedom" which, in disregarding truth, pursues what is false or wrong? (Pope Benedict XVI, April 19, 2008, retrieved April 22, 2008, from csnblog .wordpress.com/2008/04/19/text-of-pope-at-youth-rally)

We close this chapter with another pertinent quotation from Mary Richmond, least we be seen as professional misanthropes:

> No one will accuse me of disloyalty to the group with which I have been identified so long because I have not hesitated to point out its present weaknesses on the diagnostic side. My task was undertaken because there are weaknesses, but it could not have been pushed forward if many social case workers had not been doing effective and original work, though often under great difficulties. (Richmond, 1917, p. 11)

## NOTE

Portions of this chapter were previously published in Thyer, B. A., & Pignotti, M. (2011). Science and pseudoscience in clinical assessment. In C. Jordan & C. Franklin (Eds.), *Clinical assessment for social workers: Quantitative and qualitative methods* (3rd ed., pp. 163–178). Chicago, IL: Lyceum Books. Reprinted with permission of Lyceum Books.

## REFERENCES

Agnew, E. N. (2004). *From charity to social work: Mary Richmond and the creation of an American profession*. Urbana, IL: University of Illinois Press.

Aldridge, N. C. (1998). Strengths and limitations of forensic child sexual abuse interviews with anatomical dolls: An empirical review. *Journal of Psychopathology and Behavioral Assessment, 20*, 1–41.

American Psychiatric Association. (2013). *Diagnostic and statistical manual of mental disorders* (5th ed.). Washington, DC: Author.

Angell, G. B. (1996). Neurolinguistic programming theory and social work treatment. In F. J. Turner (Ed.), *Social work treatment* (4th ed., pp. 480–502). New York, NY: Free Press.

Angell, G. B. (2011). Neurolinguistic programming theory and social work treatment. In F. J. Turner (Ed.), *Social work treatment* (5th ed., pp. 327–342). New York, NY: Free Press.

Anonymous. (1938). Pseudo-science versus sound administrative procedures. *Social Service Review, 12*, 499–502.

Associated Press. (2006). *Gentle Wind Project drops lawsuit against whistle-blowers.* Retrieved July 9, 2008, from http://www.boston.com/news/local/maine/articles/2006/11/10/gentle_wind_project_drops_lawsuit_against_whistle_blowers/

Barker, R. L. (Ed.). (2014). *The social work dictionary* (6th ed.). Washington, DC: NASW Press.

Barrett, S. (2010). *Commercial hair analysis: A cardinal sign of quackery.* Retrieved February 15, 2011, from http://www.quackwatch.com/01Quackery RelatedTopics/hair.html

Barth, F. D. (2014). *Integrative clinical social work practice: A contemporary perspective.* New York, NY: Springer.

Bartlett, C. (2005). *The Enneagram field guide. Introduction.* Retrieved June 22, 2008, from http://www.insightforchange.com/EnneagramFieldGuide.html

Benoit, V., & Neander, S. E. (2008). *Relationship intention to improve your partnership.* Presentation at a Virtual Conference from the Repatterning Practitioners Association, February 23, 2008. Retrieved June 22, 2008, from http://www.repatterning.org/conferencedetails1.htm#SECTION_B

Berens, M. J., & Willmsen, C. (2007, November 19). How one man's invention is part of a growing worldwide scam that ensnares desperately ill. *The Seattle Times.* Retrieved June 22, 2008, from http://seattletimes.nwsource.com/html/localnews/2004020583_miracle18m2.ht

Bergin, J. (2008). *Inside the Gentle Wind Project: A husband's perspective.* Retrieved July 9, 2008, from http://www.windofchanges.org/Husbandsperspective.html

Bergin, J., & Garvey, J. (2004). *The Gentle Wind Project: Insider stories.* Retrieved July 9, 2008, from http://www.cs.cmu.edu/~dst/Gentle-Wind/documents/GWP-Insiders.pdf

Boyle, G. J. (1995). Myers-Briggs Type Indicator (MBTI): Some psychometric limitations. *Australian Psychologist, 30,* 71–74.

Bray, R. L. (2007). *House Veteran Affairs Committee symposium on PTSD.* Retrieved June 22, 2008, from http://rlbray.com/

Callahan, R. J., & Trubo, R. (2001). *Tapping the healer within.* Chicago, IL: Contemporary Books.

Callahan Techniques. (n.d.). *VT diagnostic support and consultations.* Retrieved June 22, 2008, from http://www.tftrx.com/vt_schenck.html

Center for Applications of Psychological Type. (2008). *The MBTI® Qualifying Program.* Retrieved July 8, 2008, from http://www.capt.org/training-workshops/MBTI-Training-qualifying.htm

Chan, C., Ho, P. S. Y., & Chow, E. (2005). A body-mind-spirit model in health: An eastern approach. In F. J. Turner (Ed.), *Social work diagnosis in contemporary practice* (pp. 456–468). New York, NY: Oxford University Press.

Clancy, F., & Yorkshire, H. (1989, February/March). The Bandler method. *Mother Jones,* pp. 22–28, 63–64.

Clarity Meter. (n.d.). *Website.* Retrieved June 22, 2008, from http://www.clear-ingtech.net/index.html

Clements, M. J. (n.d.). *EPFX = QCXI + SCIO (Biofeedback).* Retrieved June 22, 2008, from http://www.bold-eagle.com/home/epfxqxciscio.html

Clinton, A. (2005). *The theoretical basis of Seemorg Matrix™.* Retrieved June 22, 2008, from http://www.seemorgmatrix.org/ArticlesPDF/Article.4.pdf

Coe, W. C., & Scharcoff, J. A. (1985). An empirical evaluation of the neurolinguistic programming model. *The International Journal of Clinical and Experimental Hypnosis, 33,* 310–318.

Coulshed, V., & Orme, J. (2006). *Social work practice* (4th ed.). Basingstoke: Palgrave Macmillan.

Crisp, B. R., Anderson, M. R., Orme, J., & Lister, P. G. (2006). What can we learn about social work assessment from the textbooks? *Journal of Social Work, 6,* 337–359.

Cronch, L. E., Viljoen, J. L., & Hansen, D. J. (2006). Forensic interviewing in child sexual abuse cases: Current techniques and future directions. *Aggression and Violent Behavior, 11,* 195–207.

Eberle, P., & Eberle, S. (1993). *The abuse of innocence: The McMartin preschool trial.* Buffalo, NY: Prometheus Books.

Faller, K. C. (2005). Anatomical dolls: Their use in assessment of children who may have been sexually abused. *Journal of Child Sexual Abuse, 14*(3), 1–21.

Forgey, M. A., Allen, M., & Hansen, J. (2014). An exploration of the knowledge base used by Irish and U.S. child protection social workers in the assessment of intimate partner violence. *Journal of Evidence-Based Social Work, 11*, 58–72.

Frank, S. (n.d.). *Radionics.* Retrieved from http://infoholix.net/category .php?mId=90

Gerbode, F. A. (1995). *Beyond psychology: An introduction to metapsychology* (3rd ed.). Menlo Park, CA: IRM Press.

Gerbode, F. A. (1998). Biomonitoring as an aid to viewing. *Free Spirit Journal.* Retrieved June 22, 2008, from http://www.clearingtech.net/article2.html

Goodheart, G. (1975). *Applied kinesiology 1975 workshop procedure manual* (11th ed.). Detroit: Author.

Grady, M., & Drisko, J. (2014). Thorough clinical assessment: The hidden foundation of evidence-based practice. *Families in Society, 95*, 5–14.

Gray, R. M. (2001). Addictions and the self: A self-enhancement model for drug treatment in the criminal justice system. *Journal of Social Work Practice in the Addictions, 1*(2), 75–91.

Hamilton, A. (2006). *We hear a lot about energetic medicine—So what is it?* Retrieved June 22, 2008, from http://www.worldwidehealth.com/article .php?id=391&categoryID=61

Heap, M. (1988). *Neurolinguistic programming—An interim verdict.* New York, NY: Croom Helm.

Hunsley, J., Lee, C. M., & Wood, J. M. (2003). Controversial and questionable assessment techniques. In S. O. Lilienfeld, S. J. Lenn, & J. M. Lohr (Eds.), *Science and pseudoscience in clinical psychology* (pp. 39–76). New York, NY: Guilford Press.

Intergetix Inc. (n.d.). *Health navigator systems and related products.* Retrieved June 22, 2008, from http://www.energy-medicine.info/products.html and http://www.energy-medicine.info/practitioner.html

Jackson, K. (2004). Reiki—Rising star in complementary care. *Social Work Today, 4*(3), 28–29.

Jacobson, J. W., Foxx, R. M., & Mulick, J. A. (2006). *Controversial therapies for developmental disabilities: Fad, fashion, and science in professional practice.* Mahwah, NJ: Lawrence Erlbaum.

Johnson, C. (2006). Couple: Maine lawsuit vindicates our claims. *Foster's Sunday Citizen.* Retrieved July 9, 2008, from http://www.windofchanges.org/ Couple_-_Maine_Lawsuit_Vindicates_Our_Claim_-_Fosters_7–23-06.pdf

Joiner, T. E., Walker, R. L., Pettit, J. W., Perez, M., & Cukrowicz, K. C. (2005). Evidence-based assessment of depression in adults. *Psychological Assessment, 17*, 267–277.

Jung, C. G. (1971). *Collected works of C. G. Jung: Vol. 6. Psychological types* (H. G. Baynes, Trans., revised by R. F. C. Hull). Princeton, NJ: Princeton University Press. (Original work published 1921)

Karls, J. M., & Wandrei, K. E. (1992). PIE: A new language for social work. *Social Work, 37*(1), 80–85.

Karls, J. M., & Wandrei, K. E. (Eds.). (1994). *Person-in-environment system: The PIE classification system for social function problems.* Washington, DC: NASW Press.

Karpetis, G. (2013). Employing assessment systems in social work: A practitioners-researchers approach. *Social Work in Mental Health, 11,* 542–562.

Lee, M. Y., Ng, S.-M., Leung, P. P., & Chan, C. L. (2009). *Integrative body-mind-spirit social work: An empirically based approach to assessment and treatment.* New York, NY: Oxford University Press.

Lee, M. S., Pittler, M. H., & Ernst, E. (2008). Effects of Reiki in clinical practice: A systematic review of randomized clinical trials. *International Journal of Clinical Practice, 62,* 947. doi:10.1111/j.1742–1241.2008.01729.x

Leff, B., & Finucane, T. E. (2008). Gizmo idolatry. *JAMA, 299,* 1830–1832.

Lilienfeld, S. O., Lynn, S. J., & Lohr, J. M. (2003). *Science and pseudoscience in clinical psychology.* New York, NY: Guilford Press.

Lorr, M. (1991). An empirical evaluation of the MBTI typology. *Personality and Individual Differences, 12,* 1141–1145.

Macdonald, M. E. (1953). Essentials in the evaluation of social casework. *Journal of Psychiatric Social Work, 22*(3), 135–137.

Mattaini, M. A., & Kirk, S. A. (1991). Assessing assessment in social work. *Social Work, 36,* 260–266.

Moore, L. S., Dietz, T. J., & Dettlaff, A. J. (2004). Using the Myers-Briggs Type Indicator in field instruction supervision. *Journal of Social Work Education, 40,* 337–349.

Myers & Briggs Foundation. (n.d.). *Original research.* Retrieved July 7, 2008, from http://www.myersbriggs.org/my-mbti-personality-type/mbti-basics/original-research.asp

Myers, I. B., & Myers, P. B. (1995). *Gifts differing: Understanding personality type.* New York, NY: Davies-Black Publishing.

Myers, L. L., & Thyer, B. A. (1997). Should social work clients have the right to effective treatment? *Social Work, 42,* 288–298.

Nambudripad, D. S. (2003). *Say goodbye to your allergies.* Buena Park, CA: Author.

Newgent, R. A., Parr, P. E., Newman, I., & Higgins, K. K. (2004). The Riso-Hudson Enneagram type indicator: Estimates of reliability and validity. *Measurement and Evaluation in Counseling and Development, 36,* 226–237.

Orlinsky, D. E., Botermans, J., & Ronnestad, M. H. (2001). Towards an empirically grounded model of psychotherapy training: Four thousand therapists rate influences on their development. *Australian Psychologist. Special Issue: Training in Clinical and Counseling Psychology, 36*, 139–148.

Philips, M. (n.d.). *Dr. Maggie Phillips, Ph.D. referrals and links.* Retrieved June 22, 2008, from http://users.lmi.net/mphillips/links.html

Pignotti, M. (2005a). Thought Field Therapy in the media: A critical analysis of one exemplar. *The Scientific Review of Mental Health Practice, 3*(2), 60–66.

Pignotti, M. (2005b). Thought Field Therapy Voice Technology vs. random meridian point sequences: A single-blind controlled experiment. *The Scientific Review of Mental Health Practice, 4*(1), 38–47.

Pignotti, M. (2007a). Thought Field Therapy: A former insider's experience. *Research on Social Work Practice, 17*, 392–407.

Pignotti, M. (2007b). Questionable interventions taught at top-ranked school of social work. *The Scientific Review of Mental Health Practice, 5*(2), 78–80.

Pignotti, M. G., & Thyer, B. A. (2009). Some comments on *Energy Psychology: A Review of the Evidence*: Premature conclusions based on incomplete evidence? *Psychotherapy, Theory, Research, Practice, Training, 46*, 257–261.

Pignotti, M. G., & Thyer, B. A. (2015). New age and related novel unsupported therapies in mental health practice. In S. O. Lilienfeld, S. J. Lynn, & J. M. Lohr (Eds.), *Science and pseudoscience in clinical psychology* (pp. 191–209). New York, NY: Guilford Press.

Pittenger, D. J. (2005). Cautionary comments regarding the Myers-Briggs type indicator. *Consulting Psychology Journal: Practice and Research, 57*, 210–221.

Radomski, S. (n.d.). *Allergy antidotes.* Retrieved June 22, 2008, from http://www.allergyantidotes.com/OrderProducts.htm and http://www.allergyantidotes.com/Products_files/remedy_makers.htm#EagleGuardian

Richmond, M. (1917). *Social diagnosis.* New York, NY: Russell Sage Foundation.

Riso, D. R. (1990). *Understanding the Enneagram: The practical guide to personality types.* New York, NY: Houghton Mifflin.

Rosa, L., Rosa, E., Sarner, L., & Barrett, S. (1998). A close look at therapeutic touch. *JAMA, 279*, 1005–1010.

Sayre-Adams, J., & Wright, S. G. (1995). *The theory and practice of therapeutic touch.* New York, NY: Churchill-Livingstone.

Seemorg Matrix Work. (n.d.). *Seemorg matrix work: The new transpersonal energy psychotherapy.* Retrieved June 22, 2008, from http://www.seemorgmatrix.org/

Sharpley, C. F. (1987). Research findings on neurolinguistic programming: Nonsupportive data or an untestable theory? *Journal of Counseling Psychology, 34,* 103–107.

Smith-Osborn, A., & Bolton, K. W. (2013). Assessing resilience: A review of measures across the life course. *Journal of Evidence-Based Social Work, 10,* 111–126.

Sternberg, G. M. (1897). Science and pseudo-science in medicine. *Science, 5*(110), 199–206.

Taylor, R. J. (2004). Therapeutic intervention of trauma and stress brought on by divorce. *Journal of Divorce and Remarriage, 41,* 129–135.

Therrien, Z., & Hunsley, J. (2012). Assessment of anxiety in older adults: A systematic review of commonly used measures. *Aging & Mental Health, 16*(1), 1–16.

Thierry, K. L., Lamb, M. E., Orbach, Y., & Pipe, M. E. (2005). Developmental differences in the function and use of anatomical dolls during interviews with alleged sexual abuse victims. *Journal of Consulting and Clinical Psychology, 73,* 1125–1134.

Turner, F. J. (Ed.). (2005). *Social work diagnosis in contemporary practice.* New York, NY: Oxford University Press.

Turner, F. J. (Ed.). (2011). *Social work treatment: Interlocking theoretical approaches.* New York, NY: Oxford University Press.

Tye, M. J. (1994). Neurolinguistic programming: Magic or myth? *Journal of Accelerative Learning & Teaching, 19,* 309–342.

Williams, J. B., Karls, J. M., & Wandrei, K. (1989). The person-in-environment (PIE) system for describing problems of social functioning. *Hospital & Community Psychiatry, 40,* 1125–1127.

Winds of Change. (2008). *Gentle Wind Project morphs to Family Systems Research Group (FSRG).* Retrieved July 9, 2008, from http://www.windofchanges.org/GWPconnections.html

Wright, S. J. (2007). *The chakras in Shamanic practice: Eight stages of healing and transformation.* Rochester, VT: Inner Traditions.

Zastrow, C. (1990). Social workers and salesworkers: Similarities and differences. *Journal of Independent Social Work, 4*(3), 7–16.

Zastow, C., Dotson, V., & Koch, M. (1986). The neuro-linguistic programming treatment approach. *Journal of Independent Social Work, 1*(1), 29–38.

# CHAPTER 3

# Pseudoscience in Treating Children and Adolescents

Because children and adolescents are legally unable to make decisions for themselves and must rely on decisions made for them by adults, young persons are perhaps the most vulnerable population that social workers deal with. Although we believe that helping professionals who work with children are largely well intentioned, many are using interventions that are based largely on testimonials and anecdotes, are often not empirically supported, and have in some cases been shown to cause harm. This is especially the case with interventions aimed at foster and adopted children, a population with whom social workers frequently work. In this chapter, we discuss interventions that are primarily aimed at children and adolescents. Interventions targeting adults that are also used with children are discussed in Chapters 4 and 5.

A tendency exists on the part of some individuals to label the people who have come forward and exposed the abusive nature of these interventions as sensationalistic or to accuse them of exaggeration. However, we assure our readers that as indicated in our references, the material in this chapter is well documented through court records and videotapes of actual treatment sessions, as well as the published works and recorded presentations of the proponents of the interventions we describe. While on one hand some of these interventions are not necessarily harmful and are simply unsupported, other times we will be presenting interventions that are obviously intrinsically harmful and it would not be an exaggeration to consider such approaches as abuse in the name of therapy.

We hope that our readers will take some time to thoughtfully consider the material presented in this chapter. We discuss these interventions and their dangers to demonstrate how even the most well-intentioned social workers can get drawn into practices that can do great damage when practices are based on belief and desperation for answers, even if such answers have no evidence to support them.

## INTERVENTIONS FOR EMOTIONAL AND BEHAVIORAL PROBLEMS DUE TO ALLEGED "ATTACHMENT DISORDERS"

Attributing a child's or adolescent's emotional and behavioral problems to an attachment disorder has become very popular among mental health professionals, including clinical social workers who are often at the forefront of intervention with this population. This is especially the case for children who have been placed in foster care or adopted. Because such children are separated from their birth parents, any problems that they have are frequently attributed to attachment difficulties. Misconceptions about attachment abound and have frequently been the basis for interventions that have not been well tested and have sometimes caused serious harm. A recent survey of nearly 400 licensed clinical social workers (LCSWs) throughout the United States revealed that 26% of respondents reported having practiced some form of attachment therapy (AT; Pignotti & Thyer, 2012). Although the survey did not tell us what exactly was being done in the name of AT, it does show that more than a quarter of the respondents used the term *attachment* to describe what they do.

We wish to begin by correcting some misperceptions and misrepresentations of the position taken by critics of so-called ATs. Frequently, critics of AT have been accused of lumping all such therapies together, maintaining that they are all the same. This is not the position we (or the other critics of AT) take. We recognize that there are a number of different types of therapies that come under this wide umbrella term. Not all are necessarily harmful and not all practitioners do the same thing in their practice with clients. Some therapies have been documented to be harmful or contain techniques that have been shown to be harmful. Others, although not necessarily harmful, base claims on client testimonials and clinical experience rather than on well-designed outcome studies published in peer-reviewed professional journals. Thus, these therapies remain untested and their capacity to help or harm is unknown.

We are not in any way intending to imply that there are associations or linkages between the advocates of the different forms of "attachment" therapies included in this chapter. What these treatments have in common is that they fit the topic of this chapter, which is a discussion of interventions for children that lack empirical support and make claims that go beyond the evidence. We also recognize that not all therapists practicing such methods wish to refer to themselves as "attachment therapists." The approaches we discuss in this section are therapies that in some way utilize various theories relating to the psychological attachment between a child and his or her primary caregiver, usually the biological mother. Nothing that is written in this section should be interpreted to mean that we are applying any labels to anyone who practices the interventions discussed in this section. Our sole purpose is to discuss their content and present the evidence or lack thereof. For example, a behavior analyst may work to promote a child with autistic disorder to develop the social skill of saying "good morning," to maintain eye contact during conversations, or to respond positively in response to a maternal hug. These are efforts to foster one dimension of attachment-related behaviors, but such clinicians operating from the perspective of applied behavior analysis would not label themselves as attachment therapists or as providing AT. We also wish to make perfectly clear that we believe that the general field of attachment theory is a legitimate domain of developmental psychology, and learning about empirically supported principles relating to how normal attachment arises and how tenuous attachments or overly engaged attachments develop can be important areas for clinical social workers to be informed about (Carney & Young, 2012).

For those who understandably might find our lengthy exposure of dangerous and questionable treatments discouraging and daunting, please bear with us because we also present some empirically supported alternatives. We include a discussion of these approaches later in this section, as safer, more empirically supported alternatives to the various forms of AT.

A task force convened by the American Psychological Association and the American Professional Society on the Abuse of Children (APSAC; Chaffin et al., 2006) issued a report reviewing and evaluating techniques that come under a large umbrella of procedures that have come to be known as ATs. At the outset, the report stated that the terms *attachment disorder, attachment problem,* and *attachment therapy,* although increasingly popular in usage, do not have a precise, consensus-based definition, and yet are frequently applied to a population of children who have been maltreated early in life and have become part of the foster care system or were internationally adopted after having spent their early years in large orphanages where neglect was prevalent. The report noted that particular concern has been expressed about:

> A variety of coercive techniques are used, including scheduled holding, binding, rib cage stimulation (e.g., tickling, pinching, knuckling), and/or licking. Children may be held down, may have several adults lie on top of them, or their faces may be held so they can be forced to engage in prolonged eye contact. Sessions may last from 3 to 5 hours, with some sessions reportedly lasting longer. (Chaffin et al., 2006, p. 79)

The purpose of the APSAC task force report was to summarize positions taken by critics and proponents of various ATs and to then make recommendations for assessment and treatment of children who have been described as having attachment disorders. The task force noted that not all attachment-based interventions are controversial and some have evidence to support their efficacy. They noted that "shorter term, more focused and goal-directed interventions" (p. 78) tended to be the most effective and that this was true regardless of the severity of the problems in the family and whether they were carried out for the purpose of prevention or intervention. In contrast, the more broadly focused and extensive interventions were the ones that were shown to do harm. They further noted that the characteristics of effective interventions for attachment problems appear to be similar to the characteristics of many of the other effective interventions for children including a behavioral, goal-directed focus and involving training in parenting skills. Although proponents of the more controversial ATs frequently justify themselves due to their assertion that traditional therapies do not work, the task force concluded that this was not the case. That is, the tried-and-true approaches are often quite effective.

Another major problem noted by the task force was that of assessment and diagnosis. The only officially recognized diagnosis at the time of the task force, the *Diagnostic and Statistical Manual of Mental*

*Disorders,* Fourth Edition, Text Revision (*DSM-IV-TR*) and now the *DSM-5* (American Psychiatric Association, 2013), is the reactive attachment disorder (RAD) and the criteria for RAD do not include many of the symptoms that proponents of controversial ATs (hereafter referred to as AT proponents) attribute to attachment disorder. The *DSM* definition requires that the symptoms must have started prior to age 5 years and emphasizes a child who minimally seeks comfort when distressed and extreme withdrawal and reluctance to initiate any kind of contact. The symptom of indiscriminate friendliness that was in the *DSM-IV-TR* was removed from the *DSM-5* and put into a separate diagnostic category called disinhibited social engagement disorder, which makes the *DSM-5* definition of RAD even more removed from what AT proponents call "attachment disorder."

In contrast, AT proponents attribute a myriad of symptoms to attachment difficulties that have no empirical basis for such an attribution. Some of these supposed symptoms include aggressive behaviors, particularly toward the mother, crazy lying (lying about the obvious), poor eye contact, obsession with violence and bloody imagery, inability to anticipate consequences of behavior, compulsion to be in control and fear of being controlled, dissociation, affect and behavioral disregulation, impulsivity, alterations in consciousness, loss of meaning, somatization, inability to differentiate facial expressions, lack of eye contact with caregivers, discomfort with touch, and shame (Howe, 2003; Hughes, 1999, 2003). Hughes (2003) has suggested that the wide range of symptoms attributed to attachment problems be viewed as a spectrum. However, this view has yet to garner sufficient support to meet the standards for acceptance as a recognized diagnosis.

Nancy Thomas, a self-described parenting coach who wrote a book that is immensely popular with AT proponents, was quoted in an earlier edition of a publication authored by two LCSWs who supported her views (we note that in the current edition of this volume, the chapter we quote from has been omitted):

> Jeffrey Dahmer, Edgar Allen Poe, Hitler, Ted Bundy, Saddam Hussein, and Ted Kaczynski, the Unabomber—what do all of these infamous individuals have in common? All had attachment breaks in their childhood and did not receive therapeutic help. (Thomas, quoted in Forbes & Dziegielewski, 2002, p. 143)

The notion that serial killers and other sociopaths have problems attributed to attachment disorders has no sound basis in research evidence, however intuitive such a conclusion may seem. At best this view can be seen as a hypothesis. Although there is little empirical evidence of a relationship between sociopaths and attachment disorders, this assertion is used to convince parents that if they do not accept the "help" offered by AT proponents their child may grow up to become a serial killer. Although many of the books are more than 20 years old, they are currently being sold on AT websites and, as revealed in numerous message board discussions among proponents, they still subscribe to the unsupported notions contained therein. Magid and McKelvey (1987) maintained that children who do not form normal attachments can become psychopaths as adults, and that even though not all do, most will "suffer from some form of psychological damage" (p. 3). Again, this statement is without any credible evidentiary basis. On the contrary, a recent systematic review of longitudinal studies of internationally adopted children (Pignotti, 2011) showed that although a subset of children continued to have major problems, the majority had only mild problems that went away over time, as the child adjusted to his or her adoptive family. Moreover, not all children with behavioral problems had attachment disorders and not all children with attachment disorders had behavioral problems. In fact, a substantial proportion of children raised in traditional-style orphanages in the United States appear to function quite well as adults, with no apparent adverse sequelae to their earlier institutional living and social environments (Myers & Rittner, 2001). More recently, an international study of five developing countries comparing more than 1,300 orphaned or abandoned children (OAC) raised in an institution with more than 1,400 OAC children living in community settings with more family-like environments, found essentially equivalent health, emotional, and cognitive functions, and physical growth, between the two groups. There was no evidence of poorer well-being as a result of living in an institution (Whetten et al., 2009). This is not to say that institutional care and orphanage care are desirable, only that the common view that children raised in such environments usually suffer irreparable damage in their capacity to form attachments is not supported. Although there can be some relationship, behavioral problems and attachment problems have been shown to be two distinct categories and no causal link has been demonstrated.

The APSAC task force recommendations included:

1. Treatment techniques or attachment parenting techniques involving physical coercion, psychologically or physically enforced holding, physical restraint, physical domination, provoked catharsis, ventilation of rage, age regression, humiliation, withholding or forcing food or water intake, prolonged social isolation, or assuming exaggerated levels of control and domination over a child *are contraindicated because of risk of harm and absence of proven benefit and should not be used* [emphasis added].

2. Prognostications that certain children are destined to become psychopaths or predators should never be made based on early childhood behavior. These beliefs create an atmosphere conducive to overreaction and harsh or abusive treatment. Professionals should speak out against these and similar unfounded conceptualizations of children who are maltreated.

3. Intervention models that portray young children in negative ways, including describing certain groups of young children as pervasively manipulative, cunning, or deceitful, are not conducive to good treatment and may promote abusive practices. In general, child maltreatment professionals should be skeptical of treatments that describe children in pejorative terms or that advocate aggressive techniques for breaking down children's defenses. (Chaffin et al., 2006, p. 86)

Nevertheless, controversial attachment-based therapies remain popular with some clinical social workers, and this next section will be devoted to describing the ones of most concern.

## CANDACE NEWMAKER: NOT JUST A "REBIRTHING THERAPY" DEATH

In 2000, a 10-year-old adopted child, Candace Newmaker, died while undergoing 2-week AT intensive in Colorado at the hands of two master's of social work (MSW)-level social workers, Connell Watkins and Julie Ponder. This ultimately fatal session, the AT intensive, and the trial of the therapists that followed have been described in detail (Mercer, Sarner, & Rosa, 2003) as well as in numerous media reports, court records, and the Colorado State Licensing Board's outline of charges against Watkins and Ponder.

Watkins and Ponder were both found guilty of reckless child abuse resulting in death, sentenced to 16-year prison terms and are permanently banned by the State of Colorado from ever practicing again. Candace was killed during a therapy session that employed a technique known as rebirthing that involved the child assuming a fetal position and wrapping her in a flannel blanket from head to toe. Her wrapped body was surrounded by more than a dozen pillows to simulate a "womblike" experience. She was urged to struggle out of the cocoon of pillows and blankets in order to be "reborn." The session involved Watkins, Ponder, and two adult assistants placing a total of 673 pounds of their weight on the child, pressing heavily against her. Although Candace repeatedly protested that she could not breathe and was going to die, the therapists ignored her pleas at least 34 times (this session was videotaped) because they believed she was just being manipulative, and taunted her instead of releasing the child. After 50 minutes, Candace became quiet and still, and 20 minutes later, when her therapists, after deeming her a "quitter," unwrapped her from the blankets, they discovered that she was no longer breathing and her face was blue. By the time the paramedics arrived, they were able to restart her heart, but her pupils were already fixed and dilated. She was rushed to the hospital, where she died the following morning of cerebral edema. The entire session and those of other sessions that occurred during her therapy intensive had been videotaped and were presented to the jury as evidence at the trial.

One of the primary misconceptions about Candace's death is that it was a "rebirthing therapy" death when, in actuality, what led to Candace's death was the range of practices of the therapists and their theoretical system, which led them to ignore her pleas that she could not breathe. Watkins and Ponder subscribed to the myth that children with "attachment disorder" were manipulative and thus did not take her seriously. It was their unquestioning acceptance of the major assumptions behind the invalidated attachment theories that led skeptic Michael Shermer to, we believe accurately, describe her death as a "death by theory" (Shermer, 2004).

In addition to the rebirthing session, 10 additional hours of videotape of Candace's previous therapy during that same intensive were played to the jury at the Watkins and Ponder trial. These sessions consisted of holding therapy (HT). In one 2-hour session, Candace had her face grabbed for forced eye contact 90 times, her head was shaken 309 times, and the therapists screamed at her 68 times, just inches away from her face. In another session, Candace's mother, who was obese, laid on her for an hour and 42 minutes and licked her face 21 times. Additionally, Candace's long hair was cut off and she was required to sit motionless for up to 30 minutes at a time.

Clearly, it would be no exaggeration to conclude that based on these videotapes, Candace's last days of life consisted in torture, all in the name of therapy with Connell Watkins, an unlicensed MSW, in charge and another unlicensed MSW, Julie Ponder, in charge of the final rebirthing session. The practice of such therapies is not limited to unlicensed MSWs, as we illustrate in the following sections.

## RESTRAINTS FOR SAFETY VERSUS THERAPY OR BEHAVIOR CONTROL

At the heart of many of the criticisms of attachment-based therapies is the use of restraints, either for alleged safety purposes or as therapy. The APSAC task force report issued a qualifying statement that their prohibition is not meant to include restraints that are used for safety purposes. However, the task force did not appear to investigate or discuss which types of safety restraints have empirical support for their safety and efficacy, and this has been the topic of much recent attention and debate. Recent reviews investigating this topic are mixed. However, it is important to clarify that although controversy exists on the use of safety restraints, there is no controversy and widespread consensus that restraints should be used only for safety and not as therapy. Although some reviews have concluded that very little information about the use of safety restraints is based on actual research evidence (Mohr, Petti, & Mohr, 2003), others have concluded that some forms of restraints are indeed dangerous whereas other forms of restraints are relatively safe, when the benefits of eliminating an immediate threat to physical safety are weighed against the risks (Winston, Fleisig, & Winston, 2009). While many people might assume that these procedures, because they are done in institutions such as hospitals that are associated with science, are often carried out by people wearing white lab coats, and have been well tested, this is not necessarily always the case and, at times, their use may be based on authority rather than on evidence. Most alarmingly, a review of the deaths that occurred due to the use of restraints found that although the restraints were used "correctly" in the vast majority of the deaths, even under highly supervised conditions, this did not prevent death:

> When scholars reviewed 63 cases of asphyxia death following restraint use in individuals ranging in age from 26 weeks to 98 years, they found that restraints had been properly applied in 57 cases (16). This finding suggests that *restraints pose an inherent danger to patients even when proper techniques are used.* [emphasis added] Although fatal positional asphyxia has been documented in adults, it has not been documented in children. However, it is probable that small size alone is a significant factor increasing children's susceptibility to death by this mechanism. (Mohr et al., 2003, p. 3)

If even the "correct" use of physical restraints did not prevent death, then we ought to be very concerned about restraints that are being recommended for use at home, unsupervised, by parents who are not professionals. Fatal position asphyxia refers to the facedown, prone restraint position, especially if weight is being placed on the child's torso. In such a position, a person's abdomen may be restricted, which can prevent breathing and cause asphyxiation. Obese and/or severely agitated people are particularly at risk. Given that the restraints are frequently used on children because they are out of control and agitated, this is of particular concern. The same review also reports harmful psychological aftereffects from such procedures:

> Likewise, children and adolescents who had been restrained during psychiatric hospitalization reported nightmares, intrusive thoughts, and avoidance responses resulting from their restraint experiences, as well as marked startle responses associated with being held in benign and nonthreatening situations. They also reported painful memories and fearfulness at seeing or hearing others being restrained and a mistrust of mental health professionals (6). Five years later,

they continued to experience intrusive thoughts, recurrent nightmares, avoidance behaviours, startle responses, and mistrust. (Mohr et al., 2003, p. 5)

According to a review published in the *American Journal of Orthopsychiatry*, the theories behind such therapies that employ restraints have virtually no empirical evidence to support them. With regard to the underlying theories related to restraints:

> None of the theories has been subjected to careful and systematic empirical evaluation. To be sure, there is a need for research to assess the propounded theoretical models to determine which are sound and which need to be revised.... Such assumptions need to be carefully examined and revised on the basis of empirical observations. Moreover, there is a paucity of high-quality, methodologically sound research to inform clinical practice. (Day, 2002, p. 274)

The lack of evidence revealed in numerous recent reviews would seem to challenge the notion that many methods of restraints that are accepted by some clinicians, even when carried out for safety practices, are not based on science. Their usage appears to be based more on clinical lore than it does on scientific evidence. Because of the well-documented dangers inherent in facedown prone restraints even under highly supervised conditions, as of June 2010, they have been banned in institutional settings in 10 states, and lobbying efforts are underway in a number of other states to have them banned. However, controversy exists whether prone restraints should be banned entirely. In states such as Florida where prone restraints have not been banned entirely, some have argued (Winston et al., 2009) that not all prone restraints are dangerous and have recommended their continued usage, provided that they are used: (a) only for threats to immediate safety and never as therapy or discipline; (b) only where less restrictive restraints are not possible; (c) only where de-escalation techniques have been tried and failed or were not possible; (d) no weight is placed on the torso of the individual being restrained, not even straddling the person's torso; and (e) prone restraints are to be used only by individuals who have been properly trained to use them. For this reason, Winston et al. did not provide diagrams in their training materials; so the information could not be passed on to those unqualified to use their recommended method. The emphasis in their methods is on prevention of a crisis occurring, necessitating restraints in the first place, by learning to recognize and act upon early warning signs using empirically supported behavioral techniques.

Nevertheless, a number of practices involving the use of restraints in the name of therapy (to promote child compliance) for reasons of discipline (not safety) are currently being recommended by mental health professionals, including clinical social workers. The use of restraints for behavior control has a long history. Note that, unlike some ATs, the purpose here is not to provoke the child into a rage for the purpose of reliving past trauma and attempt to create attachment, but rather, to control a child who is already exhibiting out of control and possibly dangerous behavior, although some therapists may use restraints for both purposes. When criticized, some proponents of restraints will insist that they are being only used for safety purposes. However, a more careful examination of the writings of some individuals also includes a rationale to show the child who is in charge, namely, the parents, with the ultimate goal of having a child who obeys the therapist and the parents without question.

An early example of restraints as a means of behavior control is provided by the renowned icon of hypnotherapy, Milton Erickson (1962). In one of Erickson's publications entitled "The Identification of a Secure Reality" (1962) he presents a case of a mother with a child who had serious behavior problems that she had been unable to change. Erickson advised the mother to forcibly hold down the child for an extended period of time and to place her full weight on the child. Although the mother initially protested that she weighed 150 pounds and that this would be too much for the child, Erickson wrote that he "educated" her and convinced her to use this method. He describes how the mother carried out his detailed instructions:

> His mother merely smiled at him, seized him, and threw him quickly to the floor on his stomach and sat her full weight upon him. When he yelled at her to get off, she replied mildly that she had already eaten breakfast and she

had nothing to do except try to think about ways to change his behavior. However, she pointed out that she was certain she did not know any way, therefore it would all be up to him (p. 296).

Erickson then went on to describe how the mother continued to put her weight on the boy, who was in what we now know to be the very dangerous facedown, prone position, for 5 hours, in spite of his yelling, screaming, shouting profanities, and promises to be "good." After time passed, he pleaded to be allowed to go to the bathroom and the mother responded that she had not finished her thinking and continued to restrain him, although hours later, she did allow him a brief bathroom break. During the hours the boy was restrained, the mother made a telephone call, drank coffee, ate fruit and sandwiches, and read a book. After 5 hours had passed, the boy finally surrendered and stated that he would do whatever she wanted him to do. The mother continued to restrain him for an additional hour and finally let him up. When the boy asked for something to eat, the mother refused because lunchtime had already passed and she also refused him dinner because dinner was supposed to be eaten after breakfast and lunch and because he had missed those meals, he would have no dinner. In other words, the boy was deprived of food for an entire day and given only water to drink. The next morning, he was only allowed to eat oatmeal (which he also had for lunch) while the rest of the family enjoyed a breakfast of pancakes and sausages.

At the conclusion of the article, Erickson stated that the boy had become unquestioningly obedient of her and would do whatever she wanted him to do. Clearly, unquestioning obedience as a goal, even with children, violates the social work value of self-determination. Although dealing with a child's destructive, out-of-control behavior effectively is a laudable goal, unquestioning obedience of authority figures, even when they are highly abusive, is not. This was not an isolated case, as Erickson also stated "Over the years, there have been a number of comparable instances, some almost identical" (p. 303). Today, Erickson is a highly revered figure among clinical social workers and perusal of the website of the Erickson Foundation (www.erickson-foundation.org) reveals that many LCSWs are actively involved and supportive of his methods.

The methods described by attachment parenting coach, Nancy Thomas, bear a remarkable resemblance to those described by Erickson. In a workshop and online training program, Thomas advised:

> I have had instances where a kid is so out of control that they refuse to stay. When that happens, I will sit on the child. I have had to do this with dogs as well, and they are generally more dangerous with their teeth and claws than children. . . . I pick a good book and read while I sit on a child and that really seems to upset them because they feel that I should be miserable like they are. (Bonding & Attachment Workshop , n.d.)

Another example of a proposed home-based intervention that includes the use of facedown-prone hold, restraining the child purportedly for safety and behavior control, is described in a self-published book as a therapeutic hold (Federici, 2003). A diagram of the hold is included in the book (p. 111) and instructions are given for performing the hold. Although the author does caution that only parents who are properly trained should use this technique, we question whether this is sufficient. The advice given to consult a therapist with experience with disturbed children in a state hospital is also not sufficient in our opinion, because the fact that someone was employed in such a facility does not necessarily mean that he or she is properly trained, much less qualified, to train nonprofessionals who might then be using the hold under unsupervised conditions. Experts on prone restraint (Winston et al., 2009) have indicated that inadvertently placing too much pressure on the torso can result in asphyxiation and even trained professionals have to be very cautious and limit the time performing such holds. Moreover, properly trained professionals are trained in the latest behaviorally based de-escalation techniques, so that they can do everything possible to prevent having to do the hold in the first place. That said, we need to stress that any use of prone holds at all is very controversial, as some states have banned the procedure altogether in hospitals and/ or school settings.

# HOLDING THERAPY

HT, also known as therapeutic holding or cradling, may or may not involve forcible restraint of a child. Early forms of HT were derived from psychologist Robert Zaslow's rage reduction therapy known as the Z-process (Zaslow & Menta, 1975). Although HT and other AT proponents frequently pay lip service to the highly regarded psycho-analytically derived attachment theories of John Bowlby, HT, especially in its early forms as practiced throughout the 1970s, 1980s, and 1990s, appears to have been more influenced by Zaslow's rage reduction (Zaslow & Menta, 1975), which in turn was influenced by a number of other therapies that were popular around that time that encouraged the venting of emotion, particularly rage as being therapeutic (e.g., primal therapy, bioenergetics). Zaslow originally designed his Z-process to target autistic children. His theory was that children who have been severely neglected and/or abused failed to form attachments and thus will not make eye contact and connect with people and will have autistic symptoms. Zaslow believed such children to have repressed rage toward adult authorities in their life and act this out through a variety of behavior problems. His treatment involved provoking the child into a rage and forcing eye contact with the child, which he believed (without basis) would eventually break the child down and bring about attachment.

In 1972, Zaslow's license was revoked by the state of California. However, in the late 1970s, psychiatrist Foster Cline, who was one of the founders of the Attachment Center at Evergreen (ACE), located in Evergreen, Colorado, adopted Zaslow's methods for use with children believed to have attachment disorders. Cline describes a typical session:

> I lay the child across my lap so that his head is on my left with his body stretching out to the right. The child's head is cradled in my left arm. I may hold the child's left arm up and around the top of his head...One way or another, the child's legs have to be restrained so that they cannot kick the therapist or other furniture in the room. This may take other people or sometimes we can restrain their legs with one of our own.

With my free right hand I can also open the child's eyelids, to force eye contact, or close his mouth when I don't like what he is saying…the therapist controls the placement and quantity of tactile stimulation with his free right hand, varying it from a fun little "spider" burrowing into the navel or subclavicular space, to a somewhat abrasive, rubbing stimulation of the rib cage…All of this varied, high-intensity stimulation is necessary to break up the child's habitually rigid and stereotyped responses. (Cline, 1979, pp. 171–172)

Photographs of Cline are shown (p. 182) in the book, *High Risk Children Without a Conscience* (Magid & McKelvey, 1987). Cline is shown poking a child's ribs in order to provoke the child, who is in a supine position, into a rage while being held down by three other adults. It was reported that the child was screaming that he hated the therapist. This highly invasive therapy was justified by the notion that if these children were not treated aggressively, they would grow up to be sociopaths who lacked a conscience. There is no scientific evidence, however, to support this notion, nor is there evidence to support the efficacy of such a treatment. This book also contains a foreword by then Congresswoman Patricia Schroeder, who is now a highly revered figure in some skeptic circles and was even a keynote speaker at a recent Cochrane Collaboration conference for work unrelated to this topic. Nevertheless, in her foreword, Schroeder made statements that were completely lacking in scientific support (although such support was claimed), such as the notion that mothers who work outside the home will create attachment problems that will cause irreversible damage to their children, some of whom may become sociopathic criminals as adults who lack a conscience. Schroeder stated in her foreword that, to attempt to remedy this situation, she introduced the Family and Medical Leave Act (FMLA). Schroeder stated, regarding mothers who work outside the home, even though they may need to do so:

We must all face reality. What we are doing now has caused irreversible damage to some of our children. Response must come from many places including the home, workplace, schools and the government. At the federal level I have introduced the Family and Medical Leave Act. With it we hope to establish a minimum labor standard dealing with leave policy at the time of the birth, adoption or serious illness of a child. (Schroeder in Magid & McKelvey, 1987, Foreword, no page number indicated)

There is no empirical evidence, however, to support the notion that lack of conscience and subsequent serious behavior problems in a child is a consequence of having a mother who works outside the home or even from abuse or neglect at the hands of one's parents. To date, Schroeder has not, to the best of our knowledge, publicly recanted any of the notions she outlined in her foreword, even after the matter was brought to her attention. Although there are, of course, other good reasons for a new parent to take time off of a job to care for a relative, this is an example of how a social policy can be based upon fear mongering and notions that have no basis in scientific fact and why it is so important to have macro-level evidence-based practice, which will be discussed at greater length in a later chapter.

In 1993, a death occurred at ACE, Colorado. Thirteen-year-old Andrea Swenson died of an overdose of aspirin, after being left alone in the therapeutic foster home that was part of the ACE program. The therapists were not disciplined, but there was a lawsuit, which was settled out of court (Auge, 2000). However, Cline was later disciplined by his state board for another incident at ACE and, in 1996, he voluntarily surrendered his license and has become a "parenting advisor." With Jim Fay, Cline codeveloped a related treatment method called love and logic (L&L). L&L, although widely advertised, has no evidence to support its efficacy other than consumer satisfaction surveys published on the website (www.loveandlogic.com).

In 2010, the state of Colorado permanently revoked the license of Neil Feinberg, LCSW. Feinberg was formerly a therapist for ACE and has described Connell Watkins as his mentor while she was a clinical director at ACE. After a lengthy series of charges and stipulations beginning in 1985 for practicing similar therapies, his license was finally permanently revoked. The documents resulting in the revocation of Feinberg's license can be found at the Colorado Department of Regulatory Agencies website: doraimage.state.co.us/LibertyIMS::/sidGE5uR055yiWN2816/Cmd%3D%24%244A63C58JHiCNfhx9o%3Bon5v%3D%23wGH and doing a search on "Feinberg." The final series of charges consisted of three complaints. One of the complaints alleged that he had used a licking technique on an 8-year-old child while resting his elbows on top of him. Videotapes were made of his work. In one 1993 videotape of his work at ACE, he is shown in a HT session saying to a child "I'll yell at you! I'll piss you off! I'll spit on you! I'll lick your goddamned face! But I'm not going to hurt you." A video of Feinberg practicing his techniques can be viewed at www .childrenintherapy.org

Another form of HT, also originally developed for autistic children and later applied to children believed to have attachment problems, was developed by psychiatrist Martha Welch (1989). At least two LCSWs who have been proponents of various forms of holding and ATs reportedly studied directly under Welch. Welch's methods have also been known as compression therapy, direct synchronous bonding (DSB), and prolonged parent–child embrace (PPCE). Welch recommends that parents evoke anger in defiant children by holding them tightly and to calmly respond to any screaming, spitting, swearing, biting, or attempts to free themselves. Welch believed that, eventually, if parents persisted, the child would cease fighting and become relaxed and tired, during which the mother could comfort the child and bonding could begin.

These abusive methods are frighteningly akin to the physical restraints and bindings used near the end of the 18th century by British physicians to treat "the madness of King George," depicted in a 1994 film of that name. A medical doctor, called in to treat the King's increasingly erratic speech and behavior, decides that treatment would consist of subjecting His Majesty to prolonged periods of physical restraint. On release, any deviation from normal behavior would be instantly met with a renewed period of restraint imposed on the King. The doctor dispassionately recites his "prescription" to the staff, for example, "If he swears or indulges in meaningless discourse, His Majesty must be restrained." At one point, the impassioned King exclaims, "I am the King of England!" to which the doctor replies "No sir! You are the *patient!*" Thereupon, the King is bound in a chair and gagged. A video clip depicting this dramatic first use of forcible restraint on the King can be found on YouTube. In terms of learning theory, HT is simply the use of positive punishment, presenting an aversive situation to a child contingent on the child's display of an undesirable behavior, including simple noncompliance with any parental demand. By using brute physical force to restrain a child and only releasing the child after a period of obedience, and repeating this process so that the punishment is essentially unavoidable, noncompliance is reduced, after which obedience is rewarded (with decent food, etc.).

Social workers can be at the forefront of advocating on behalf of young people by protesting the application of abusive and restrictive therapies involving physical restraint, preventing their initial application, and working toward their discontinuance when encountered. Take a contemporary version of HT called packing therapy:

> This alleged therapy consists of wrapping the patients (wearing only underclothes or naked in the case of young children) several times a week during weeks or months in towels soaked in cold water (10C to 14C). The individual is wrapped with blankets to help the body warm up in a process lasting 45 minutes, during which time the child or adolescent is accompanied by two to four staff persons. The alleged goal of this technique, as defined by proponents of this therapy, is to "allow the child to rid him- or herself progressively of its pathological defense mechanisms against archaic anxieties," by achieving a "greater perception and integration of the body and a growing sense of containment." (Amaral et al., 2011, p. 191)

The only word for such an intervention is abuse; it is akin to treatments provided 200 years ago for those deemed insane. One would hope that a social worker coming across such an intervention would rapidly and forcefully intervene, and not stand idly aside as others took responsibility for this harmful practice.

We find it repugnant that the use of physical restraint is in any way construed as a form of therapy, a position not uncommonly found in the social work and broader child treatment literature (e.g., Howe & Fearnley, 1999, 2003; Steckley, 2012). And within this literature there is all too frequently an absence of initially recommending a less restrictive psychosocial intervention intended to promote healthy child–parent attachment, even though a number of empirically supported alternatives exist (e.g., O'Connor, Matias, Futh, Tantam, & Scott, 2013).

## THERAPEUTIC PARENTING

Another practice that comes under the umbrella of ATs is known as therapeutic parenting (TP). Sometimes TP is carried out by individuals who are not the child's legal parents, individuals known as therapeutic foster parents. This term, however, is a generic one, and most therapeutic foster parents have no involvement with the specialized treatment under discussion here called TP. Candace Newmaker resided in such a setting in Colorado during her therapy intensive, just prior to her death. In such homes, the children are subjected to strict discipline, lengthy manual labor, and austere living conditions. Parents are also instructed to carry out such practices with the child, when he or she returns home.

One of the top proponents of TP, Nancy Thomas, is a self-described professional therapeutic parent who holds no mental health credentials, but reports training with a number of other attachment "experts" who are or were once licensed mental health professionals, including Neil Feinberg, who as we stated earlier, had his LCSW permanently revoked in 2010 (see Nancy Thomas's website www.attachment.org/pages_nancy. php). Her guide for TP (Thomas, 1997) is widely used by LCSWs who practice attachment-related therapies and a number of LCSWs are listed on her website as referrals. Examples of recommendations from the guide, which as of 2010, she is still promoting on her website are as follows:

> In the beginning, rewards and bonuses should be food, clothing or necessities. (p. 121)

> In the beginning, your child should learn to ask for everything. They must ask to go to the bathroom, to get a drink of water, EVERYTHING. When it starts to feel like they must ask to breathe, you are on the right track...it is the child's job to make the parents happy with the child. (p. 52)

> Your child must realize that going to school is a privilege. (p. 66)

> When given directions it is unacceptable for the child to ask "why?" or "what?" NEVER answer these questions. (p. 37)

> [regarding car manners]...distraction needs to be dealt with....A mature enough child in good weather might need

to walk home. It is safest to follow at a distance in the car. Or the child could do push-ups on the side of the road until the specified amount is done correctly. (p. 41)

Additionally, Thomas has made the unsupported claim that "AT and HT are the only therapies that have proven to be effective with attachment disordered children" (p. 21). As our earlier review indicates, no such evidence exists.

## SURVIVORS OF ATs

Some young adults who describe themselves as survivors of various ATs told their stories on a website entitled "A Search for Survivors" and indicated that the trauma from these approaches has stayed with them well into adulthood and in some cases alienated them from their parents. For instance, one survivor reported she was being treated at a university-based anxiety clinic for posttraumatic stress disorder to deal with her childhood experiences in HT (Mercer, 2012) and another has reported that she has persistent nightmares and intrusive memories of her childhood experiences with HT that she received when she was only 4 years old. The website is no longer in existence because the survivor who ran it was subjected to harassment by HT proponents and threatened with legal action that would have compromised the individual's anonymity. Reports from some of the survivors, however, still exist on www .childrenintherapy.org/victims/victims.html

Although these reports are obviously anecdotal in nature, given that this form of therapy has a lack of randomized controlled trials (RCTs) to support its safety and efficacy and given that as social workers our first ethical duty is to do no harm, we need to give serious consideration to such reports. Moreover, given some of the descriptions of what went on in such sessions, it may be considered unethical to do research on such methods that are so obviously physically and emotionally abusive, although research could be conducted on the less extreme forms of HT.

Since the death of Candace Newmaker, even though it was not directly due to HT, the abusive nature of this therapy was brought out through videotapes shown at the trial of her therapists. Although the tapes were ultimately sealed, the brutality of these approaches was publicized. As a result of the deservedly bad publicity during the early

2000s, what appears and is purported to be a kinder, gentler, form of HT was developed (Howe & Fearnley, 2003). In this form of HT, the procedure is fully explained to the child and the child's consent is said to be obtained, although legally, the notion that a child can provide consent is not accurate, as minor children are only capable of providing assent. Moreover, it is difficult to know what kind of social pressures are brought to bear to obtain such "consent." The newer form of HT does not directly attempt to provoke the child into a rage through invasive, coercive methods. According to its proponents, this form of HT "is aimed at emotionally recreating the close proximity that elicits and facilitates both verbal and nonverbal communication, interaction and experiences between the protective, loving caregiver and child" (Howe & Fearnley, 2003, p. 381). The goal is to create an attachment bond that the child presumably did not form or formed incompletely and to help the child feel safe to express a variety of different feelings such as sadness and anger, as well as to bring up past traumas, presumably so that they can be resolved. Although this approach is not as obviously intrinsically physically harmful and assaultive as the older forms of HT, it still lacks evidence to support its efficacy.

Even though this newer approach does not appear to be physically dangerous, due to the fact that no RCTs have been carried out we cannot know whether this treatment does more harm than good in terms of the conditions it is designed to treat. There is evidence that facilitation of venting of some emotions, such as anger, can actually make them worse. Additionally, there are numerous problems of recovering memories of trauma that are discussed in Chapter 4.

The extent to which the earlier form of rage reduction HT is still being practiced is unknown. Some reports, such as a study based on child and worker self-reports, published in the *British Journal of Social Work* (Sudbery, Shardlow, & Huntington, 2010), do not make it clear exactly what form of HT was carried out. Although the website of the treatment facility where the study was carried out depicts the newer form of HT, the article, which contained no clear description of the intervention, could be mistakenly construed as an endorsement for the harsher forms of HT even if it was not.

Some social workers and others applying for grants are avoiding using the term HT altogether because they fear they will be denied funding for research. In a conference sponsored by the Association for Treatment and Training in the Attachment of Children (ATTACh), an LCSW who was then a doctoral student in social work (Wimmer, 2004), described how a Georgia attachment organization was able to obtain 3 years worth of grant funding from the state of Georgia from 2000 through 2003 for AT for children who had been given a diagnosis of RAD. In her conference talk, Wimmer emphasized the importance of gaining credibility with state officials before applying for such a grant. She noted that when the organization in Georgia had applied for funding, they purposely avoided using the term HT and instead used the term *cradling*, due to the bad publicity that HT had recently received. She stated that "they knew that if they put the word 'Holding' in there, the state would have apoplexy. The Attorney General or someone would pull the whole program, so they were wise enough not to do that" (Wimmer, 2004, 49:45). This would seem to indicate a lack of transparency on the part of those applying for funding, which makes it more difficult to identify when questionable interventions are being proposed.

Although in a later report by social workers (Wimmer, Vonk, & Bordnick, 2009) it was denied that the earlier, more invasive, coercive forms of HT were employed in the Georgia intervention, the model this same article reported using was one directed by Dr. William Goble, who was a leading proponent of the older, more invasive forms of HT described previously. Goble was the therapist who, in 1999, had diagnosed Candace Newmaker with attachment disorder without ever having examined her, based on an unvalidated assessment procedure carried out at long distance with her adoptive mother. Goble then recommended a 2-week intensive AT and referred Candace's adoptive mother to Connell Watkins, the unlicensed MSW who was in charge of delivering what was later shown in court, via 10 hours of videotape, to be a highly aggressive, invasive, and abusive intervention. The same year of Candace's death, 2000, the year that the grant funding in Georgia began, a model said to have been developed and directed by Gobble was used in the Georgia-funded project. Although a later report denied that they had employed the coercive forms of HT, Goble, as recently as 1999 at an ATTACh conference, which occurred less than a year prior to Candace's death, defended the more controversial forms of HT, maintaining that neither he nor Connell Watkins had ever had a child die or be injured by it, and he claimed (while laughter in the audience could be heard) that when a child protested "I can't breathe" that this was just a manipulative strategy on the part of the child (Gobble, 1999).

The intervention with the children in Georgia also involved eye movement desensitization and reprocessing (EMDR) and neurofeedback (NFB), approaches that are discussed later in this book. Based on a later publication (Wimmer et al., 2009), which reported an uncontrolled, pre-/post-treatment study on this multifaceted intervention, a number of different therapies were involved and no uniform protocol was specified. In addition to the fact that the research design precluded drawing any conclusions about the efficacy of the intervention being tested in this study, if there had been positive effects, it would have been impossible to know which part of the intervention was responsible.

## REPARENTING

Another technique under the umbrella of AT is called reparenting. Reparenting has also been used apart from AT and has its roots in transactional analysis (TA), although TA has since disavowed this practice. Reparenting was developed by Schiff (1970), a psychiatric social worker. During the 1960s, Schiff had schizophrenic patients reside with her and her husband in her home and claimed to have reparented and cured some of them although no formal studies have ever shown this to be the case. Schiff believed that psychotic conditions such as schizophrenia, rather than being neurologically based disorders, were caused by bad parenting, a notion that has since been highly discredited.

Although initially used with adults, reparenting methods are now commonly used with adopted and foster children and adolescents, which will be the focus of the present discussion. There are two issues involved with reparenting that need to be addressed: (a) Can a person actually be regressed to an earlier age? and (b) are therapeutic methods that use age regression and supposedly reprocess missed or inadequate developmental stages be helpful to clients? That is, can we really redo a person's missed developmental stages to his or her benefit? Contrary to popular clinical lore, neither of these notions has empirical support.

Age regression is used in reparenting and other forms of therapy as well, such as the attempt to recover memories of trauma, which is discussed in a later chapter. Age regression is commonly induced by hypnosis, but not all such interventions involve formal hypnotic induction. Controversy exists as to whether age regression is real or role-playing. By role-playing, we do not mean that the person is intentionally being deceptive. People entering into such processes as well as their therapists are usually sincerely convinced that this is an authentic phenomenon, but is it?

Research on age regression has shown that people who are age regressed can display what they believe to be the developmental characteristics of the age to which they are regressed, even if those beliefs are false and run contrary to actual expected developmental patterns (Nash, 1987). This demonstrates that people may not literally regress to a past developmental stage but, rather, are acting in accordance with the belief that they are doing so and raises serious doubts regarding the reality of age regression. One of the authors of this book (BAT) recalled participating in a hypnosis-training program as a teenager. He was supposedly hypnotized while standing in front of a class of several dozen adult students, and asked to write his name on a blackboard. He did this. The hypnotist then gave him the suggestion that Bruce was now 12 years old and to write his name again. Lo and behold, the signature changed, to a looser, more childlike script. He was further "regressed" to age 6 years, and asked to write his name again, and now he wrote his name in clumsy block letters! To an outside observer it appeared as if Bruce had regressed psychologically to a much earlier age. In reality, Bruce was feeling the powerful social psychological pressures to comply with what was requested of him by the hypnotist, and at no point did he feel any younger or lose his awareness of being 16 years old. It was all subtle role-playing, although afterward he asserted to the others in class that yes indeed, he had regressed. The concept of hypnosis as a unique psychological state, which can permit unusual phenomena to be displayed is clearly an incorrect one, a view that has largely been superceded by the view that hypnosis is more akin to role-playing or acting, in response to social influences (Barber, 1999; Johnson & Barber, 1978; Spanos & Barber, 1974).

The notion that a person can redo earlier developmental stages and make up for their earlier lack is known as recapitulation. Proponents of recapitulation believe that earlier deficits in childhood developmental stages can be made up for by essentially redoing parenting at a later age by what is said to be regressing the child, adolescent, or adult, back to an infantile state and engaging in actions such as cradling, bottle feeding, feeding sweets, having the person wear diapers, speaking baby talk, and having the therapist take complete control of the person's physical needs. The goal is to go back and reprocess the missed developmental stages, resulting in a better outcome where secure attachment is achieved. Rebirthing is another technique used as recapitulation.

There is no evidence that the goal of successfully redoing past missed or poorly negotiated developmental stages has ever been achieved through such interventions. Infant and child development occurs over a period of years and involves complex patterns of interaction and trans-actions between a parent and child, rather than a one-way, linear rela-tionship of a parent doing something to a child. Empirically supported treatments with children that have been shown through well-designed research to work, demonstrate that intervening with and training the parent is critical to successful treatment. In fact, successful intervention can be conducted with biological parents in the first place (Barth et al., 2005) that may get a family through a crisis and might make some of the foster placements and adoptions unnecessary. Even though there is no empirical support for the notions behind reparenting, this has not stopped a number of people from practicing these methods, sometimes to the detriment of the clients involved who may have otherwise been helped with existing empirically supported interventions.

## WILDERNESS THERAPY

Wilderness therapy (WT), also known as outdoor behavioral health care (OBH) is an intervention that typically targets adolescents with behavioral and emotional problems as well as substance abuse issues. These programs are sometimes presented as an alternative to punitive measures for youth who have committed offenses that have brought them into the juvenile justice system. In WT programs, adolescents are encouraged to participate in outdoor physical activities such as lengthy hikes and activities that involve some perceived form of physical risk such as a ropes course. Additionally, such programs are designed to encourage group cohesiveness with peers, become emotionally vulner-able, and share personal feelings and experiences with group members. The theoretical rationale for such programs varies, with some propo-nents describing this intervention as behavioral, others as experiential, and some describing it as attachment based.

WT is considered to be an intervention that is widely accepted by social workers and solid empirical and theoretical support is claimed (Reamer, 2006). Reamer contends that the main problem with WT lies in cases where it has been incorrectly carried out. Although it may be popular and widely accepted by social workers, we disagree that it has solid empirical support. A database search of PsycINFO and Social Work Abstracts revealed only one RCT (Elrod & Minor, 1992) with a small number of participants ($N$ = 42). That study revealed no significant differences in criminal offenses posttreatment although participants in the treatment group were significantly less likely to commit status offenses although even there, the actual difference is not very great (45% in WT group vs. 61% in the comparison group). The authors concluded:

> The findings of this study indicate that an intervention like Project Explore, consisting of an outdoor experiential component, youth social skills training, and parent skills training, is no more effective in reducing offense than probation services that allow caseworkers regular and meaningful contacts with clients. (p. 258)

The authors went on to note that based on the study limitations, conclusions should not be drawn that this approach is ineffective. However, more research is needed and to date, no further RCTs have been conducted. The remaining outcome studies were comparative evaluations without randomized assignment, qualitative studies, case studies, and pre-/posttreatment studies that had no control group (Clem, Prost, & Thyer, 2015). Such studies, even when samples are large, are not sufficient to warrant the claim that WT has solid research to support it. When interventions do not have replicated, well-designed RCTs to support their efficacy with clearly specified steps for carrying them out (protocols), claims about whether they are being carried out correctly (treatment fidelity) become moot because there is no evidence that carrying out the treatment correctly results in a safe, efficacious treatment. Regardless of its claimed theoretical basis, WT needs to be tested with RCTs for safety and efficacy before claims can be made about its efficacy.

Children can be placed in WT programs based on participating in a "Wagon Train" experience, trekking cross country on horseback or riding in covered wagons or stage coaches, herding cattle, and living in teepees, often at taxpayers' expense! (see www.vq.com/extraordinary-experiences and www.ncjrs.gov/App/Publications/abstract.aspx?ID=62694). Although some studies that examined WT yielded promising results, which, if any, forms of WT are efficacious have yet to be determined. On the downside, there have been a number of casualties from WT, which are described in the next section.

## BOOT CAMPS

Some programs identifying themselves as WT have militaristic boot camp atmospheres, although not all WT programs do. Proponents of WT have pointed out that this is an invalid association, as there is a difference in the theoretical approach of WT and boot camps with the former being based on a model of experiential education and the latter based on a military and disciplinary model. Some programs appear to combine the two models.

In 2007, the United States Government Accountability Office (GAO) issued a report on WT (Kutz & O'Connell, 2007) that examined wilderness programs, boot camps, and other programs for troubled youth. The GAO's investigation focused on the operation of American-owned and operated treatment facilities between 1990 and 2007. They reported uncovering thousands of allegations of abuse, some resulting in deaths, at residential treatment facilities such as boot camps, wilderness programs, and other residential facilities that targeted troubled youth for treatment. They were unable to find any agency or website that officially collected complaints, so the exact number of complaints is unknown. However, because there are no specific reporting requirements for such incidents, examination of voluntarily reported incidents from the National Child Abuse and Neglect Data System (NCANDS) database, operated by the U.S. Department of Health and Human Services revealed that in the year 2005 alone, there were 1,619 staff from 33 states reported to have been involved in incidents of abuse in such residential programs, although such allegations do not constitute proof that abuse actually did occur in all cases.

In 2006, a 14-year-old boy in Florida was admitted to a boot camp in Panama City. After admission, he was immediately forced to participate in a vigorous physical training regimen. He collapsed, saying he could not continue. Guards were caught on videotape covering his mouth and forcing him to breathe ammonia fumes through his nose, in an effort to force him to continue to run. Martin was repeatedly "taken down," had the eight adult staff press on painful pressure points, and was repeatedly hit and tightly gripped on his limbs. While he was not "beaten" to death, his beating was clearly visible on the videotape. The actual cause of death was suffocation via ammonia inhalation, forced on him by the guards as punishment for not exercising enough. His crimes were stealing his grandmother's car, curfew violation, and taking some candies.

Before Martin's death, the state had received more than 180 complaints about excessive force being used at the Panama City Boot Camp. After his death, the state closed down its five juvenile boot camps (holding 130 youth) and replaced them with a therapeutic model that prohibited physical intervention against juvenile inmates. Martin's family received a settlement of $2.4 million. Too little, too late (see en.wikipedia .org/wiki/Martin_Anderson_death_controversy).

The GAO examined in detail 10 closed civil or criminal cases that occurred between 1990 and 2004 where a youth had died while in such a facility. In these cases, they found untrained staff, inadequate nourishment, reckless or negligent practices, and/or ineffective management, deemed as contributors to these deaths. The cases involved death from dehydration, heat stroke, or brain injuries that occurred while hiking, suicide, or a severed artery to the neck after being restrained in a face-down position for 45 minutes. They noted that because there was no standard definition for "boot camp" or "WT," individual programs vary and not all are necessarily harmful.

Additionally, some of the facilities investigated by the GAO, in efforts to boost enrollment, misrepresented their services to parents, claiming to have services that they were not qualified to deliver and, in some cases, to have credentials that they did not in fact possess. To date, there is no evidence other than testimonials and anecdotes that boot camps are an effective intervention and there is much documentation that they have frequently caused physical harm. Emotional harm is also a strong possibility that needs to be further investigated.

## EMPIRICALLY SUPPORTED ALTERNATIVES TO QUESTIONABLE INTERVENTIONS FOR BEHAVIORAL AND SO-CALLED ATTACHMENT PROBLEMS

What we have presented thus far appears to be quite grim and may be discouraging to people who are seeking help for their children. Such parents often turn to these questionable treatment approaches because they are offered by people who claim to be experts and do not know where else to turn. The good news is that, as stated in the APSAC report discussed earlier, well-supported, humane, behavioral approaches do exist that have been shown to be effective for serious behavioral problems. Such approaches can often make the use of any kind of physical restraint unnecessary by preventing situations that would pose an imminent danger in the first place. Current guidelines such as those laid out for schools in the Keeping All Students Safe Act of 2010 (HR 4247) require that the use of restraints should be used only for the time period where imminent danger exists, must cease immediately if the child or adolescent backs down, and prone restraints must never be used.

A recent risk management guide on restraints and seclusion has been issued by the National Association of State Mental Health Program Directors (NASMHPD; Haimowitz, Urff, & Huckshorn, 2006), which is available at www.nasmhpd.org. The report states that a clear consensus among health professionals has been reached that restraints should be used only for safety and as a measure of last resort. No mention is made of any legitimate use for restraints as therapy or to show a child who is in charge. The report recommends that in the exercise of professional judgment, the following points be taken into consideration:

1. Each use of restraint or seclusion poses an inherent danger, both physical and psychological, to the individual who is subject to the interventions and, frequently, to the staff who administer them.

2. The decision to use restraint or seclusion nearly always is arbitrary, idiosyncratic, and generally avoidable.

3. Many inexpensive and effective alternatives to restraint and seclusion have been developed and successfully implemented across a broad range of mental health facility types. (p. i)

The NASMHPD report states that although effective, successful implementation of such alternatives requires personnel to be willing to "examine basic assumptions and change long-standing behaviors, especially with respect to coercion and conflict which characterize much of the mental health delivery system today" (p. 17).

Donat (2005) points out that a number of effective alternatives to reduce the use of restraint and seclusion exist that are based on behavioral science that are underused. For example, token economy and contingency management programs have been shown to be successful in reducing patient violence that might lead to restraints and seclusion in institutional settings (Donat, 2003). Social worker Stephen Wong (Liberman & Wong, 1985) was an earlier pioneer in developing ethical practice guidelines for the use of restraints and other restrictive procedures as a tool for enhancing patient safety and sometimes, under very carefully monitored conditions, integrated into a behavioral treatment plan. Wong was also an early critic of therapeutic holding (Wong, Rolph, Martinez-Diaz, & Thorne-Henderson, 1990) where he pointed out that such holds can in some cases have a paradoxical effect and worsen the symptoms such as aggression that they were designed to treat. A number of highly regarded, transparent, and effective staff training programs are available to provide instruction in safe methods of physical restraint (Winston et al., 2009), all of which emphasize prevention of unsafe behaviors on the part of clients before problems arise, and using reinforcing techniques to promote more effective methods to communicate than being aggressive. See, as one example, the safety care training provided by QBS, Incorporated (qbscompanies.com/site). In any case, the use of restraint is never justified as a means of exacting compliance or obedience from a child or adolescent, as a form of punishment, or as a convenience for staff, only as means of ensuring safety. Some credible organizations, such as the Florida Association for Behavior Analysis, have prepared position papers on the appropriate use of methods of restraint (e.g., fabaworld.org/pdf/FABA-Statement-Use-of-Restraint-Seclusion-Fl-Schools-draft02.pdf), and these have clear relevance to the use of so-called HTs. It is particularly disturbing to see a variant of HT recently described in a leading social work journal as a legitimate form of therapy (Sudbery et al., 2010). It should be noted that the judicious use of restrictive procedures such as temporarily holding a client for reasons of safety will likely never be completely done away with in caring for out-of-control individuals at risk for injuring themselves or others (Liberman, 2006; Lutzker, 1996). However, physical restraints of any kind should never be part of any kind of treatment plan. There are many ways in which an agitated individual can be "talked down" without having to resort to physical restraints and those must be tried first. There is a considerable ethical and empirical literature on the use of restrictive procedures to control unsafe behavior (see, e.g., the special section on seclusion and restraint found in the September

2005 issue of the journal *Psychiatric Services*). However, the advocates of HTs seem completely unaware of this highly relevant material.

## UNSUPPORTED TREATMENTS FOR ATTENTION DEFICIT HYPERACTIVITY DISORDER AND LEARNING DISABILITIES

Attention deficit hyperactivity disorder (ADHD) is characterized by persistently high levels of inattention, impulsivity, and hyperactivity. Attention deficit disorder without hyperactivity can also be diagnosed according to *DSM-5* (American Psychiatric Association, 2013). Prevalence of ADHD among school-aged children ranges from 5% (Polanczyk & Rohde, 2007) to as high as 11% (Wolraich et al., 2012). According to the *DSM*, there is no single test that can be used to diagnose ADHD. The *DSM* also notes that diagnosis in children younger than 4 or 5 years old is problematic due to the behavioral variability inherent among toddlers and preschool-aged children. Given that, to date, there are no standardized assessments to definitively detect ADHD, the diagnosis is typically made based on behavioral indicators directly observed in the child or reported by parents and/or teachers, although some psychologists supplement this with assessment procedures, even though they lack sufficient reliability and validity, in and of themselves, to serve as a diagnostic tool. Given that there are no standardized tests to diagnose ADHD, the possibility of misdiagnosis may be quite high, especially because some of the symptoms might be, at times, observed in children who do not meet the criteria for the disorder. Nevertheless, ADHD is one of the most common conditions for which children are referred to mental health clinics (Aupont et al., 2013).

Empirically supported treatments for ADHD include psychostimulant medications and behavior analysis (Hinshaw, Klein, & Abikoff, 2007) or a combination, although medications are not claimed to be a cure and beneficial effects cease when the child stops taking the medication. Because many parents are averse to having their child on such medications and there are side effects that can be legitimate cause for concern, and behavior analysis, while shown to be effective, might not completely deal with the symptoms for all children, alternative treatments with less or no empirical support for ADHD are appealing and quite common.

# DIETARY AND SUPPLEMENT INTERVENTIONS

Even though LCSWs as social workers are not qualified to give dietary health care advice, a survey of 321 clinical social workers (Henderson, 2000) revealed that 45% of those surveyed considered themselves to have moderate knowledge of dietary supplements and nutritional alternatives and nearly a quarter of social workers had referred clients to others for alternative diets.

The belief that a child's hyperactivity can be caused by excess sugar intake, although without any empirical basis, is widespread. Additionally, many proponents of alternative diets believe that food allergies can cause hyperactivity. Although this could be true in rare cases, alternative methods to test for food and other forms of allergies are common. One such technique, known as applied kinesiology, developed by a chiropractor, involves having the person hold a homeopathic vial said to contain the energetic essence of a substance (it actually contains plain water) and then testing muscle strength, with and without the vial. Typically, the client is asked to extend his or her arm out rigidly and to resist the clinician's effort to push the arm down. This is repeated when holding the vial of water. If the person's muscles test weaker while holding the homeopathic vial, that person is said to be allergic to the substance whose "essence" is said to reside in the vial. The client is then told to avoid that substance (e.g., wheat, rice, shellfish) or the person is offered an unsubstantiated treatment for the allergy that usually involves the stimulation of points on the spine or elsewhere on the body. These bogus treatments are often quite costly.

One LCSW (see www.allergyantidotes.com) who is also a naturopath, offers a system called allergy antidotes that targets ADHD and a number of other conditions. This approach involves testing for allergies through the use of muscle testing and then treating them by stimulating alleged meridian points on the body. More details on this assessment procedure are provided in Chapter 2 and the treatment is described in more detail in the section on developmental disabilities.

An Internet search of "food allergy," "ADHD," and "LCSW" reveals a number of LCSWs promoting food allergy diagnosis and treatment for ADHD, although most appear to be providing referrals rather than directly attempting to use such treatments.

## NEUROFEEDBACK

NFB is an intervention that involves hooking a person up to an EEG machine and having the individual play a game where he or she is rewarded for producing desired brain waves, as reflected in meter readings, light displays, or sounds. We will describe this intervention in more detail in our chapter on developmental disabilities. Earlier reviews (Lohr, Meunier, Parker, & Kline, 2001) have determined that NFB for ADHD lacked sufficient support to meet the American Psychological Association's criteria to be classified as empirically supported and yet proponents have heavily marketed this intervention and made claims that it is effective. More recently, however, a number of RCTs and quasi-experimental outcome studies with favorable results have been conducted that warrant a reevaluation of NFB (Williams, 2010). Nevertheless, a more recent double-blind study (Arnold et al., 2013) was conducted that employed sham controls (which the studies in the Williams, 2010, review did not), where one group got the actual reinforcement of the correct brainwaves and the sham control group did not get those brainwaves reinforced. The blinding process was tested and determined that it worked (parents could not tell the difference between the real and sham NFB). The results were that although both the NFB and the sham showed large significant improvements as measured by parental report, there were no differences between the NFB group and the sham control group. The authors noted the study limitations of small sample size and the fact that a different method was used for adjusting brainwaves than was normally used. However, this was a post hoc conclusion on the part of the authors and the lack of difference in treatment and sham groups calls into question whether the basis for NFB is valid. This study needs to be repeated with a larger sample and the usual methods used to determine whether the null results still occur.

Additionally, claims have been made regarding NFB for a wide variety of different conditions that have very little support such as autism, posttraumatic stress disorder and other anxiety disorders, depression, addiction, and a variety of different physical conditions such as brain injuries. Although we applaud the efforts of NFB proponents in conducting RCTs on NFB for ADHD, we also need to note that making claims for other conditions for which it has not been supported is an example of *lack of boundary conditions*, one of the characteristics of a pseudoscience we discussed in Chapter 1.

## INTERVENTIONS FOR CHILDREN WITH DEVELOPMENTAL DISABILITIES

A number of pseudoscientific interventions exist that target children with developmental disabilities including autism. These interventions, which also target adults, are discussed in our chapter devoted entirely to this topic.

## REFERENCES

Amaral, D., Rogers, S. J., Baron-Cohen, S., Bourgeron, T., Caffo, E., Fombonne, E.,...van der Gaag, R. J. (2011). Against Le packing: A consensus statement. *Journal of the American Academy of Child and Adolescent Psychiatry, 50,* 191–192.

American Psychiatric Association. (2013). *Diagnostic and statistical manual of mental disorders* (5th ed.). Arlington, VA: Author.

Arnold, L. E., Lofthouse, N., Hersch, S., Pan, X., Hurt, E., Bates, B.,...Grantier, C. (2013). EEG neurofeedback for ADHD: Double-blind sham-controlled randomized pilot feasibility trial. *Journal of Attention Disorders, 17,* 410–419.

Attachment Center at Evergreen. (1993). *Bonding and attachment therapy.* Evergreen, CO: Author.

Auge, K. (2000). *Alternative therapies not so new in Evergreen.* Retrieved August 19, 2010, from http://extras.denverpost.com/news/news0617d.htm

Aupont, O., Doerfler, L., Connor, D. F., Stille, C., Tisminetzky, M., & McLaughlin, T. J. (2013). A collaborative care model to improve access to pediatric mental health services. *Administration and Policy in Mental Health, 40,* 264–273.

Barber, T. X. (1999). Hypnosis: A mature view. *Contemporary Hypnosis, 16,* 123–127.

Barth, R. P., Landsverk, J., Chamberlain, P., Reid, J. B., Rolls, J. A., Hurlburt, M. S.,...Kohl, P. L. (2005). Parent-training programs in child welfare services: Planning for a more evidence-based approach to serving biological parents. *Research on Social Work Practice, 15,* 353–371.

Bonding & Attachment Workshop. (n.d.). Chatsworth, CA: Foster Care & Adoptive Community, Online Training Program, 2 parts.

Carney, M. M., & Young, P. M. (2012). Attachment theory. In B. A. Thyer, C. N. Dulmus, & K. M. Sowers (Eds.), *Human behavior in the social environment: Theories for social work practice* (pp. 165–192). New York, NY: Wiley.

Chaffin, M., Hanson, R., Saunders, B. E., Nichols, T., Barnett, D., Zeanah, C.,...Miller-Perrin, C. (2006). Report of the APSAC Task Force on attachment therapy, reactive attachment disorder, and attachment problems. *Child Maltreatment, 11*(1), 76–89.

Clem, J. M., Prost, S. G., & Thyer, B. A. (2015). Does wilderness therapy reduce recidivism in delinquent adolescents? A narrative review. *Journal of Adolescent and Family Health, 7*(1), Article 2. Retrieved from http://scholar.utc.edu/jafh/vol7/iss1/2

Cline, F. (1979). *Understanding and treating the severely disturbed child*. Evergreen, CO: Youth Behavior Program.

Day, D. M. (2002). Examining the therapeutic utility of restraints and seclusion with children and youth: The role of theory and research in practice. *The American Journal of Orthopsychiatry, 72*, 266–278.

Donat, D. C. (2002). Employing behavioral methods to improve the context of care in a psychiatric hospital: Reducing hospital reliance on seclusion and restraint. *Cognitive and Behavioral Practice, 9*, 28–37.

Donat, D. C. (2003). An analysis of successful efforts to reduce the use of seclusion and restraint at a public psychiatric hospital. *Psychiatric Services, 54*, 1119–1123.

Donat, D. C. (2005). Encouraging alternatives to seclusion, restraint, and reliance on PRN drugs in a public psychiatric hospital. *Psychiatric Services, 56*, 1105–1108.

Elrod, H. P., & Minor, K. I. (1992). Second wave evaluation of a multi-faceted intervention for juvenile court probationers. *International Journal of Offender Therapy and Comparative Criminology, 36*, 247–262.

Erickson, M. H. (1962). The identification of a secure reality. *Family Process, 1*, 294–303.

Federici, R. S. (2003). *Help for the hopeless child: A guide for families*. Alexandria, VA: Dr. Ronald Federici and Associates.

Forbes, H. T., & Dziegielewski, S. F. (2002). Reactive attachment disorder. In S. F. Dziegielewski (Ed.), *DSM-IV-TR in action* (pp. 143–168). New York, NY: John Wiley.

Gobble, W. (1999). *Children with reactive attachment disorder: An introduction to diagnosis, parenting and treatment*. Annual Conference, Association for Treatment and Training in the Attachment of Children (ATTACh). September 30–October 2, Alexandria, VA.

Haimowitz, S., Urff, J., & Huckshorn, K. A. (2006, September). *Restraint and seclusion: A risk management guide*. Alexandria, VA: National Association of State Mental Health Program Directors.

Henderson, L. (2000). The knowledge and use of alternative therapeutic techniques by social work practitioners: A descriptive study. *Social Work in Health Care, 30,* 55–71.

Hinshaw, S. P., Klein, R. G., & Abikoff, H. B. (2007). Childhood attention-deficit/hyperactivity disorder: Nonpharmacological treatments and their combination with medication. In P. E. Nathan & J. M. Gorman (Eds.), *A guide to treatments that work* (pp. 3–27). New York, NY: Oxford University Press.

Howe, D. (2003). Attachment disorders: Disinhibited attachment behaviours and secure base distortions with special reference to adopted children. *Attachment & Human Development, 5,* 265–270.

Howe, D., & Fearnley, S. (1999). Disorders of attachment and attachment therapy. *Adoption & Fostering, 23,* 19–30.

Howe, D., & Fearnley, S. (2003). Disorders of attachment in adopted and foster children: Recognition and treatment. *Clinical Child Psychology and Psychiatry, 8,* 369–387.

Hughes, D. A. (1999). Adopting children with attachment problems. *Child Welfare, 78,* 541–560.

Hughes, D. A. (2003). Psychological interventions for the spectrum of attachment disorders and intrafamilial trauma. *Attachment & Human Development, 5,* 271–277.

Johnson, R. F., & Barber, T. X. (1978). Hypnosis, suggestions, and warts: An experimental investigation implicating the importance of "believed-in efficacy." *The American Journal of Clinical Hypnosis, 20,* 165–174.

Kutz, G. D., & O'Connell, A. (2007). *Residential treatment programs: Concerns regarding abuse and death in certain programs for troubled youth.* Washington, D.C.: U.S. Government Accountability Office.

Liberman, R. P. (2006). Elimination of seclusion and restraint: A reasonable goal? *Psychiatric Services, 57,* 576; author reply 576–576; author reply 578.

Liberman, R. P., & Wong, S. E. (1985). Behavior analysis and therapy and restrictive procedures. In K. Tardiff (Chair), *Seclusion and restraint: The psychiatric uses* (pp. 29–36). Report of the American Psychiatric Association Task Force on the Psychiatric Uses of Seclusion and Restraint. Washington, DC: American Psychiatric Association.

Lohr, J., Meunier, S. A., Parker, L. M., & Kline, J. P. (2001). Neurotherapy does not qualify as an empirically supported behavioral treatment for psychological disorders. *The Behavior Therapist, 24*(5), 97–104.

Lutzker, J. R. (1996). Timeout from emotion; time for science. *Child and Family Behavior Therapy, 18,* 29–34.

Magid, K., & McKelvey, C. A. (1987). *High risk children without a conscience.* New York, NY: Bantam Books.

Mercer, J. (2012). Reply to Sudbery, Shardlow and Harrington: Holding therapy. *British Journal of Social Work, 42,* 556–559.

Mercer, J., Sarner, L., & Rosa, L. (2003). *Attachment therapy on trial: The torture and death of Candace Newmaker.* Westport, CT: Praeger/Greenwood.

Mohr, W. K., Petti, T. A., & Mohr, B. D. (2003). Adverse effects associated with physical restraint. *Canadian Journal of Psychiatry, 48,* 330–337.

Myers, L. L., & Rittner, B. (2001). Adult psychosocial funding of children raised in an orphanage. *Residential Treatment for Children and Youth, 18*(4), 3–21.

Nash, M. R. (1987). What, if anything, is regressed about hypnotic age regression? A review of the empirical literature. *Psychological Bulletin, 102,* 42–52.

O'Connor, T. G., Matias, C., Futh, A., Tantam, G., & Scott, S. (2013). Social learning theory parenting intervention promotes attachment-based caregiving in young children: Randomized clinical trial. *Journal of Clinical Child and Adolescent Psychology, 42,* 358–370.

Pignotti, M. (2011). Reactive attachment disorder and international adoption: A systematic research synthesis. *The Scientific Review of Mental Health Practice, 8,* 30–49.

Pignotti, M., & Thyer, B. A. (2012). Novel unsupported and empirically supported therapies: Patterns of usage among licensed clinical social workers. *Behavioural and Cognitive Psychotherapy, 40,* 331–349.

Polanczyk, G., & Rohde, L. A. (2007). Epidemiology of attention-deficit/hyperactivity disorder across the lifespan. *Current Opinion in Psychiatry, 20,* 386–392.

Reamer, F. (2006). Nontraditional and unorthodox interventions in social work: Ethical and legal implications. *Families in Society, 87,* 191–197.

Schiff, J. (1970). *All my children.* Philadelphia, PA: M. Evans and Company.

Shermer, M. (2004). Death by theory. *Scientific American, June,* p. 48.

Spanos, N. P., & Barber, T. X. (1974). Toward a convergence in hypnosis research. *The American Psychologist, 29,* 500–511.

Steckley, L. (2012). Touch, physical restraint and therapeutic containment in residential child care. *British Journal of Social Work, 42,* 537–555.

Sudbery, J., Shardlow, S. M., & Huntington, A. E. (2010). To have and to hold: Questions about a therapeutic service for children. *British Journal of Social Work, 40,* 1534–1552.

Thomas, N. (1997). *When love is not enough: A guide to parenting children with RAD— reactive attachment disorder.* Glenwood Springs, CO: Families by Design.

Welch, M. (1989). *Holding time.* New York, NY: Fireside.

Whetten, K., Ostermann, J., Whetten, R. A., Pence, B. W., O'Donnell, K., Messer, L. C., & Thielman, N. M.; Positive Outcomes for Orphans (POFO) Research Team. (2009). A comparison of the wellbeing of orphans and abandoned children ages 6-12 in institutional and community-based care settings in 5 less wealthy nations. *PLoS One, 4*(12), e8169.

Williams, J. M. (2010). Does neurofeedback help reduce attention-deficit hyperactivity disorder? *Journal of Neurotherapy, 14*, 261–279.

Wimmer, J. S. (2004). *Georgia's program of attachment therapy for adopted children with special needs.* Annual Conference, Association for Treatment and Training in the Attachment of Children (ATTACh), October 3–6, Richmond, VA.

Wimmer, J. S., Vonk, M. E., & Bordnick, P. (2009). A preliminary investigation of the effectiveness of attachment therapy for adopted children with reactive attachment disorder. *Child and Adolescent Social Work Journal, 26*, 351–360.

Winston, M., Fleisig, M., & Winston, L. (2009). *The premature call for a ban on prone restraint: A detailed analysis of the issues and evidence.* Sunrise, FL: The Professional Crisis Management Association.

Wolraich, M. L., McKeown, R. E., Visser, S. N., Bard, D., Cuffe, S., Neas, B.,...Danielson, M. (2014). The prevalence of ADHD: Its diagnosis and treatment in four school districts across two states. *Journal of Attention Disorders, 18*, 563–575.

Wong, S. E., Rolph, B., Martinez-Diaz, J., & Thorne-Henderson, M. (1990). How therapeutic is therapeutic holding? *Journal of Psychosocial Nursing and Mental Health Services, 28*(11), 24–28.

Zaslow, R., & Menta, M. (1975). *The psychology of the A-process: Attachment and activity.* San Jose, CA: San Jose State University Press.

# CHAPTER 4

# Pseudoscience in Treating Adults Who Experienced Trauma

The large number of pseudoscientific interventions used with adults precludes our covering each one in this book. Therefore, rather than make these next two chapters encyclopedic in nature and attempt to cover each and every questionable treatment, we will present a discussion of what appears to be the most widely used interventions by social workers and/or interventions that were developed by social workers. The results of our own survey of 365 licensed clinical social workers (LCSWs) throughout the United States revealed that those who reported a specialization in trauma, posttraumatic stress disorder (PTSD), or grief–loss were more than three times as likely to use a novel unsupported treatment than those who did not report such a specialty (Pignotti & Thyer, 2012). Of the 136 participants who reported a specialization in trauma, nearly 87% had reported using at least one such unsupported therapy within the past year. Some of these interventions are simply unsupported, whereas others have been shown to actually do harm (Lilienfeld, 2007). We will therefore be devoting this entire chapter to a discussion of various pseudoscientific interventions used for trauma and/or PTSD. Some of these interventions also use the belief that trauma is at the root of all or most emotional difficulties and diagnoses to address a variety of different diagnoses and types of problems. The chapter that follows discusses pseudoscientific interventions that target a wide array of different conditions using something other than the trauma model, but may also include treatment of trauma, among other conditions. We conclude with an overview on what are known as power therapies and the culture their proponents have created.

# INTERVENTIONS FOR TRAUMA AND/OR PTSD

## What Is Trauma?

Discussing the nature of trauma is important because, as we later illustrate, misconceptions about trauma can form the basis for a number of pseudoscientific interventions. The entire definition of what constitutes a traumatic event has been a hotly debated issue that continues to be under consideration with each new edition of the *Diagnostic and Statistical Manual of Mental Disorders* (*DSM*); so we begin there, because what is considered a trauma can obviously have a major impact on whether a trauma model is chosen for intervention. What constitutes trauma as far as a diagnosis of PTSD is concerned? The latest edition of the *DSM* (*DSM-5*; American Psychiatric Association, 2013) changed the classification of PTSD from an anxiety disorder as in the *DSM-IV-TR* to a new category in *DSM-5* called trauma and stressor-related disorders. The criteria for the traumatic event have also been made somewhat more stringent. As with *DSM-IV-TR*, the person must have experienced, witnessed, or been confronted with an event that involved actual or threatened death or serious injury, but *DSM-5* specifies that exposure to details of the event *cannot* be solely through media (e.g., repeatedly watching a traumatic event on TV news) unless that media exposure was work related. The *DSM-5* also specifies sexual assault. As with the *DSM-IV-TR*, the event must have caused clinically significant distress or impairment of functioning in life, such as have an impact on the person's social relationships, work, or other areas of life. This is a change from the *DSM-IV-TR*, which described the individual's response as fear, helplessness, and horror due to the lack of evidence that these symptoms reliably predicted the onset of PTSD. Instead, the *DSM-5* focuses on behavioral symptoms such as reexperiencing and avoidance. Instead of three, there are now four clusters of symptoms: reexperiencing, avoidance, negative cognitions and mood, and arousal. The *DSM-5* also eliminated the previous distinction made in the *DSM-IV-TR* between acute and chronic PTSD.

Although the *DSM-5* criteria specify that only events described earlier can qualify for a diagnosis of PTSD, clinicians have been faced with a number of people who experienced events that they felt were traumatic and met the diagnostic criteria for PTSD in every other way, and yet did not meet part 1 of Criterion A. For example, some people who have experienced divorce, confidence schemes or fraud, sexual harassment in the workplace, cult involvement, work-related stress, job loss, racism (Thyer & Lankton, 2012), and a number of other events that although seriously disturbing, did not involve any threats of death or serious injury to oneself or others, have reported full-blown symptoms of PTSD.

There are also events that are commonly placed into the trauma model, even though they were not experienced as traumatic at the time of the event (which precludes a PTSD diagnosis) and only later, when the person grasped the full meaning of the event, did they become interpreted as a trauma. Examples of this include sexual abuse that did not include physical force (e.g., penetration) and/or violence (Clancy, 2009) and people who were in abusive group situations such as cults, who may have even regarded the experience as positive at the time of their involvement, only later to come to recognize that they had been deceived and manipulated. In naming these examples, we in no way intend to minimize the pain and suffering of people who have been through such experiences. Our point is that they do not meet the *DSM-5* Criterion A definition for trauma, which requires that the event be experienced as traumatic *at the time* and thus would not qualify for a diagnosis of PTSD, even if all the other criteria were met.

Recent research has found that it is not uncommon for people who did not experience an event that most people would experience as traumatic, to nevertheless have full-blown symptoms of PTSD. For example, Clancy (2009) describes a woman who accidentally ran over a grasshopper with her lawnmower and subsequently developed all the symptoms of PTSD, or a person watches a horror movie and experiences long-term, intrusive, distressing flashbacks of the movie that persist for months or even years. A number of recent studies have supported this notion, that people who do not meet Criterion A can nevertheless experience PTSD symptoms that are just as strong or even stronger than people who experienced events that did meet Criterion A (Long et al., 2008).

As a result of such reports, some people have argued for a broadening of Criterion A, whereas others have objected that this is bracket creep that would defeat the purpose of the PTSD diagnosis. That is, if the PTSD diagnosis were to be redefined as anyone's subjective experience of any event, then a traumatic event could no longer be presumed to be the cause of the symptoms. Such a diagnosis could also become a self-fulfilling prophecy and some treatments for trauma have resulted in increasing rather than decreasing distressing symptoms.

On the other hand, supporters of broadening the definition have argued that if such people are suffering and their functioning is impaired, the inability to diagnose them with PTSD might prevent them from qualifying for insurance coverage for treatment. Worse yet, victim blaming may occur. The PTSD diagnosis has been supported by some activists because the cause of the symptoms is attributed to the traumatic event, rather than to any pathology that lies within the victim himself or herself. As Herman (who has advocated for a new diagnosis of complex PTSD, which, to date, has not been accepted by any *DSM* committee) puts it:

> The lack of an accurate and comprehensive diagnostic concept has serious consequences for treatment, because the connection between the patient's present symptoms and the traumatic experience is frequently lost…they may collect a pharmacopeia of remedies: one for headaches, another for insomnia, another for anxiety, another for depression. None of these tends to work very well, since the underlying issues of trauma are not addressed. (Herman, 1992, pp. 118–119)

However, the question remains, to what extent trauma truly is the underlying cause of the person's problems. There are people with histories of horrifying childhood abuse that meet Criterion A in every way, who are relatively symptom free in their adult lives, and yet there are people who experienced little, if any, childhood abuse who are highly symptomatic. The research on PTSD makes it quite clear that although the severity of the traumatic event is indeed positively related to PTSD, it is not a direct, dose–response relationship. In other words, there are other risk factors that can make people more likely to develop PTSD, such as female gender, lack of social support, a history of other trauma, other existing diagnoses, and perhaps the most controversial of all, the finding that a higher IQ is a protective factor against PTSD. Note that this does not mean that no one with a high IQ ever develops PTSD, as there are other factors that could make such a person vulnerable. However, the mere suggestion that IQ is related to PTSD, although this has been found in more than one well-designed study, has been a cause for outcry among those who feel that such identification blames the victims.

If there are other risk factors that make one vulnerable to PTSD, that would be considered a politically inconvenient truth. Although such findings may be politically inconvenient, as social workers and clinicians, we need to consider what will be of most benefit to the client. If well-designed studies show that there are other risk factors for PTSD than trauma, is ignoring these in the best interest of the client? We do not think so. As Harvard psychologist Richard J. McNally puts it, "Ultimately, the best form of advocacy is a commitment to pursuing the truth about trauma, wherever it may lead us" (McNally, 2003, p. 285).

If someone does have multiple risk factors for the development of PTSD, it does not mean that we need to blame them, any more than we would want to blame anyone for any diagnosis they might incur. Additionally, the presence of such risk factors does not make the deeds of the perpetrators any less reprehensible, nor should this mean that the perpetrators should not be held accountable. We can continue to advocate for our clients and see that perpetrators are brought to justice, regardless of whether clients had preexisting vulnerabilities. However, the arguments are well taken against the *DSM* categories of the past such as masochistic or self-defeating personality disorder that had no empirical basis and additionally had sexist connotations. We now examine some specific approaches for treating trauma and its aftermath.

## Psychological Debriefing and Critical Incident Stress Debriefing/Critical Incident Stress Management

Although the terms *psychological debriefing* (PD) and *critical incident stress debriefing* (CISD) are often used interchangeably, CISD is actually a subcategory of PD. PD can be defined as a form of intervention administered to people in the immediate aftermath (within about 3 days) of a traumatic event that has the goal of relieving distress and preventing more long-term effects such as the development of PTSD (Devilly, Gist, & Cotton, 2006). PD approaches employ "ventilation/catharsis, normalization of distress, and psycho-education regarding presumed symptoms" (Devilly et al., 2006, p. 320). CISD is a proprietary form of PD, developed by Mitchell (1983) and has been widely disseminated to first responders to disasters as well as mental health professionals specializing in trauma through trade magazines, conferences, and seminars.

Although designed as a group-based intervention, CISD has also been administered one-on-one to individuals.

Critical incident stress management (CISM), which was developed in response to the widespread criticism of CISD, includes a wider range of techniques that include education on psychological responses to trauma; acute care to individuals, groups, families, and organizations; and interventions and services that are provided after the traumatic incident. CISD is sometimes used within this framework to describe the specific seven-phase intervention with small groups, usually administered within 2 to 3 days after a traumatic event. However, the fact remains that no evidence exists that CISM has in any way improved the outcomes of CISD and both remain lacking in support for prevention of PTSD (Fawzy & Gray, 2007). Additionally, Fawzy and Gray point out that much confusion exists as to which components are necessary and sufficient for CISM, which makes it difficult, if not impossible, to test for efficacy. McNally, Bryant, and Ehlers (2003) concluded that CISM is an administrative framework rather than an intervention.

A number of meta-analyses and reviews, including those sponsored by the Cochrane Collaboration (Rose, Bisson, Churchill, & Wessely, 2002; Rose, Bisson, & Wessely, 2005), have concluded that CISD and/or PD either make the subsequent development of PTSD *more likely* or *make no difference* (Devilly et al., 2006; McNally, Bryant & Ehlers, 2003; van Emmerick, Kamphuis, Hulsbosch, & Emmelkamp, 2002). As a result, CISD has been categorized as a potentially harmful treatment (Lilienfeld, 2007).

Proponents of CISD (e.g., Everly, Flannery, & Mitchell, 2000) have argued that the poor results were due to poor treatment fidelity and that when CISD is done correctly, it works well. However, they have failed to meet the burden of proof with well-designed, replicated randomized controlled studies, that doing CISD correctly produces favorable results. As Rosen (1999) has pointed out, treatment fidelity can only be legitimately discussed after it has been established that doing a particular intervention correctly produces the desired results. With CISD, this is not the case. Everly et al. argued against using control groups because that would be withholding assistance, which would be unethical. However, because it has not been established that CISD truly helps people or even does no harm, this argument is circular and begs the very question that the research is attempting to answer.

According to the *DSM-5*, PTSD cannot be diagnosed until 4 weeks after a traumatic event. Contrary to the assertions made by CISD proponents, performing randomized controlled trials (RCTs) is particularly important when it comes to any interventions administered in the early aftermath of trauma that claim to reduce rates of PTSD. The majority of people who experience a traumatic event, although a high percentage initially experience a variety of forms of psychological distress in its immediate aftermath, recover on their own and do not go on to develop PTSD (Breslau, 2009). In other words, the symptoms remit without any kind of intervention, and when left to their own devices, most people recover on their own. Even among the minority meeting the criteria for PTSD 4 weeks after a trauma, 50% improve in 3 months with no treatment, and what used to be called *chronic PTSD* (eliminated in *DSM-5*), defined as symptoms persisting after 6 months, is even less common (Yehuda & McFarlane, 1995). Time and time again, what the evidence shows is that resiliency is the norm, not the exception. To control for such natural remission, RCTs comparing CISD to no treatment are critical to perform. Simple pre- and posttests would predictably reveal dramatic changes in symptoms that may have nothing to do with the intervention, because we know that these symptoms remit in the majority of people who do not receive any intervention. What we need to know is whether the CISD group has even more improvement than a group that was not treated, who nevertheless improved and all indications are, based on the reviews cited earlier, that it does not.

Contrary to the results of the independently conducted reviews, the developers of CISD/CISM (Everly, Flannery, & Eyler, 2002) conducted a meta-analysis of CISM that reported highly favorable results. However, this meta-analysis contained serious flaws. No inclusion criteria for the studies were specified. Six of the eight studies reviewed were studies authored by directors of the International Critical Incident Stress Foundation (ICISF) and at least two were published in a journal owned by ICISF. In studies where interventions are administered by enthusiastic practitioners, allegiance effects can occur. In other reviews, studies adduced in support of CISM (Everly et al., 2000) were criticized (Devilly et al., 2006) for being comprised of presentations made at proprietary conferences, government reports that did not contain any actual data, or reports unavailable for inspection. Additionally, the few published studies were not RCTs and contained major methodological flaws and again, some of these studies were published in the proprietary ICISF journal. Ironically, some of the studies adduced in support of CISD (e.g., Chemtob, Thomas, Law, & Cremniter, 1997) did not follow the protocol deemed by proponents to be so necessary for success. The lesson to be learned here for clinicians who are seeking out evidence for the interventions they use is to note the source of the reviews and make sure to seek out high-quality reviews of the evidence, such as those conducted by independent reviewers on behalf of the Cochrane and Campbell Collaborations, organizations that have clearly specified protocols and standards for systematic reviews.

In spite of the overwhelming evidence against CISD and CISM, it is still widely used among LCSWs (Pignotti & Thyer, 2012). The International Critical Incident Stress Foundation (ICISF), according to its website (www.icisf.org), continues to defend its methods and offer proprietary trainings to first responders and mental health professionals who specialize in trauma and a number of persons with LCSWs and master's in social work (MSWs) are listed on their faculty.

It is important to make a distinction between CISD- and CBT-based early interventions for trauma, which are aimed only at those people who present with clinical symptoms, request therapeutic assistance, and have been shown to be helpful. In contrast, CISD is intended to be administered to *every* person who has experienced a particular traumatic event and it has not been uncommon for fire and police departments and the military to hire CISD teams and make attendance mandatory for anyone who has experienced a particular trauma. Given its lack of evidence, this not only represents a colossal waste of time and resources and intrudes on the right of individuals to self-determination but also is of serious concern, given the possibility that such interventions could do more harm than good for some of the participants who were forced to attend and presumably not informed of its lack of evidentiary support.

Why do some clinicians continue to believe in and practice such a highly discredited model? Reviewers of the CISD/CISM approach (Gist & Devilly, 2010) have surmised that it is because of the well-intentioned sense of urgency mental health practitioners have to do something aggressive to help relieve the emotional suffering of those who are struck by disaster. However, as Gist and Devilly have noted, what the best evidence shows is that because only a minority develop PTSD following a disaster, most symptoms go away on their own and that aggressive interventions, such as debriefing, can actually harm repressors of symptoms, and the principle of less is more applies.

Additionally, given the popularity and pervasiveness of the CISD/CISM model, some people are under the false impression that there are no alternatives, when in fact, community-based responses at the macro level and psychological first aid (PFA) are interventions that have been shown to be effective (see Gist & Devilly, 2010, for a full review and description). Such interventions utilize existing community supports in a culturally competent manner, identify those who have requested psychological assistance, and use empirically supported brief screening tools such as the Trauma Screening Questionnaire (TSQ; Brewin et al., 2002) to identify those in the minority who may need professional care. Those in need of professional help can then be referred to qualified, competent mental health professionals who can administer empirically supported approaches such as trauma-focused cognitive behavioral therapy (Ehlers & Clark, 2003). Recent studies of selected behavioral and cognitive therapies aimed at the prevention of the development of PTSD among recently traumatized persons have demonstrated their effectiveness. We recommend the Jerusalem Trauma Outreach and Prevention study as one such positive report, and also note that this randomized experimental study was coauthored by a social worker (Glaltzer-Levy et al., 2013).

Time and time again, dire predictions about mass PTSD casualties have failed to materialize (Sommers & Satel, 2005). A prime example is that following the 9/11 attacks it was predicted that one in four residents of New York City would develop diagnosable long-term PTSD. However, later epidemiologic studies showed (Galea et al., 2003) that 4 weeks after the attacks, only 7.5% were determined to have probable PTSD and after 6 months, only 0.6% showed probable PTSD. That is, 92% of those said to have been likely to be diagnosed with PTSD were not, in fact, diagnosable 6 months following the attacks.

There is also an element of vested financial interests that contribute to the persistence of the CISD/CISM model, because entire businesses and careers have been built upon this model. Additionally, based on discussions we have had with proponents of these methods, the reason they give is that the results they have witnessed through their firsthand clinical experience have been highly compelling to them. We know from a number of surveys of clinicians, that they value their firsthand, clinical and personal experience over research findings and this appears to be the case with CISD. The problem is that, as discussed in Chapter 1, experience is accompanied by all of our preconceived ideas and biases, including confirmation bias, the tendency to focus on that which confirms our beliefs (in this case, the workability of CISD), and explain away that which conflicts. Although providers of CISD might well have received positive feedback from participants, it is all too easy to focus on those successes and explain away failures. Moreover, a self-reported positive feeling about the experience and gratitude toward the debriefers does not necessarily mean that those participants are less likely to develop PTSD. They may well have been among the majority of people who experience trauma who have a natural remission of symptoms without any intervention, or it is possible that despite their positive feelings about the group experience, it did not actually prevent their development of PTSD.

Additionally, when people are involved in a group situation where everyone is perceived to be feeling positive about an intervention, demand characteristics may prevent people who have less-than-positive feelings from saying so. There are too many variables that are not controlled and can lead to faulty conclusions about clinical experience. The only way to control for other possible explanations and find out if the intervention is truly effective in doing what it claims (in this case, preventing PTSD) is to perform well-designed RCTs that replicate the findings—preferably administered by people who do not have a vested interest in the intervention and the CISD/CISM model. This has been done and the verdict (admittedly provisional, capable of being changed) is in—CISD/CISM does not work.

## Interventions That Address Memory of Traumatic Events

We now shift our focus to interventions that involve traumatic events that occurred in the past, rather than its immediate aftermath. Such interventions are used by clinicians, not only to treat PTSD but also to address dissociative disorders or even other symptoms such as anxiety, depression, eating disorders, relationship difficulties, and a number of other problems a client may present with, if the therapist subscribes to the belief that childhood trauma is at the root of most problems, as many do. Nevertheless, a number of misconceptions exist about trauma and memory recovery that, although believed by many clinicians, have no empirical basis.

The most basic misconception that is at the root of many questionable interventions for trauma is the notion that human memory operates like a video recorder and that people, especially if they are under hypnosis or put through some other process in a therapy session such as guided visualization, can retrieve accurate memories from their past. This notion has been falsified by a large body of memory research (see McNally, 2003, for a review) that demonstrates that memory is reconstructive and what we remember can often be far from accurate. There is also a misconception that if someone recovers a memory that is accompanied by strong emotions and even physiological responses such as increased heart rate, then the memory must be true. However, McNally points out that laboratory experiments have shown that people who believe in the highly unlikely event that they have been abducted by unidentified flying objects can produce physiological and emotional responses that are just as strong as those of a comparison group of survivors of verifiable events, such as war trauma. A number of therapies exist that purport to cure a wide range of conditions by recovery of traumatic memories of early childhood, the birth experience, prenatal events, alleged past-life events, satanic ritual abuse, and abduction by space aliens.

Social worker Tim Stocks (1998, 1999) published thorough reviews of the empirical evidence (and lack thereof) of the validity of the concept of supposed recovered memories, of the possibility of recovering suppressed or forgotten memories using recovered memory therapies, and of the failure of recovered memory therapy to produce therapeutic changes in clients exposed to such treatments. Among the techniques and therapies used in recovered memory therapy were "bodywork," hypnosis, dream interpretation, the analysis of flashbacks, journaling, guided imagery, truth serum, survivors groups, and the disputation of client doubts. His conclusions:

> A review of the literature on recovered memory techniques supports the conclusion that such techniques do not reliably recover valid memories. Although each of the techniques may lead to recovery of accurate memories, they can also result in the recovery of distorted or wholly constructed memories (Stocks, 1998, p. 431) . . . there are no procedures that have been demonstrated to reliably distinguish confabulations from accurate memories (p. 431) . . . the available evidence indicates that individuals in recovered memory therapy are more likely to deteriorate than improve . . . there is no evidence that the benefits of recovered memory therapy outweigh its risks.

This raises serious questions about the appropriateness of memory recovery work in therapy. (p. 432)

We now turn to a discussion of some of the more specific approaches to the treatment of trauma.

## Primal Therapy

Primal therapy (PT) was developed by Arthur Janov (1970), who holds a MSW from the University of California, Los Angeles, along with a PhD in clinical psychology from Claremont College. PT also has many offshoots, and some of these offshoots also incorporate reparenting techniques (discussed in Chapter 3). Widely popular in the 1970s and 1980s, PT continues to this day and is currently being promoted through Janov's website (www.primaltherapy.com). PT and its offshoots are based on the unsupported notion that a wide variety of emotional problems are caused by various so-called primal experiences that occurred in early childhood, infancy, during birth, or prenatally where emotional needs were not met (e.g., a mother not responding to a crying infant). Although PT apparently has no peer-reviewed published controlled studies to support its efficacy, on the current PT website, Janov claims (see www.primaltherapy.com/what-is-primal-therapy.php):

> Painful things happen to nearly all of us early in life that get imprinted in all our systems which carry the memory forward making our lives miserable. It is the cause of depression, phobias, panic and anxiety attacks and a whole host of symptoms that add to the misery. We have found a way into those early emotional archives and have learned to have access to those memories, to dredge them up from the unconscious, allowing us to re-experience them in the present, integrate them and no longer be driven by the unconscious. For the first time in the history of psychology there is a way to access feelings, hidden away, in a safe way and thus to reduce human suffering. It is, in essence, the first science of psychotherapy. (Janov, 2010, para. 1)

This description implies that Janov subscribes to the discredited notion that memory operates as a video recorder and that if we can access these "imprints" from our "emotional archives" through his techniques, human suffering will be effectively reduced. Although no randomized controlled studies have been conducted and published in peer-reviewed journals on PT, a number of highly effective empirically supported approaches exist to address the conditions he names that do not in any way involve dredging up and reliving past experiences.

Janov subscribes to the theory (as do many other trauma therapy methods) that traumatic memories are repressed and that when people uncover the memories through his methods and fully experience the feelings involved, they will be healed. On the contrary, recent research on memory has found that evidence for repression is lacking and that trauma is very well remembered, more so than ordinary events (McNally, 2003). Although exposure therapy for PTSD has been shown to be highly effective, there is no evidence that Janov's methods, for which he makes unique claims, are effective for PTSD. With regard to the other conditions, he claims that PT will successfully address conditions such as depression, phobias, and panic attacks, and there is no evidence that these conditions are caused by primal early childhood, birth, or prenatal experiences.

Janov believes that failure of the parents to meet certain basic human needs in the early life of a human being is responsible for a wide variety of mental and physical problems. His theory bears similarities to Zaslow's theories, discussed in Chapter 3, who believed that a child's behavior problems and rage are caused by unmet needs in infancy and that fully venting and feeling the rage and emotional pain will bring about a resolution and healing. Janov further believes that the pain from these unmet needs is so great that we block it off by suppressing deep breathing, and thus, engaging in deep breathing is part of his treatment. According to Janov, each experience of needs not being met is added to a primal pool of unmet needs and the cumulative results are the cause of various emotional and physical difficulties in adulthood. He does not believe that these experiences need to be traumatic in the sense of the *DSM-5* Criterion A definition. He provides the examples of parents forcing their children to consistently say "please" and "thank you," not being held when they need to be, or being told not to complain when they are unhappy, as ways in which such damage can occur and all of these common experiences are ones that are addressed in PT. Because it is likely that most of us can remember having some of these experiences, this makes us all candidates for PT promotions.

Proprietary training in PT, as described on Janov's website (www .primaltherapy.com/training-program-primal-center.php), requires a minimum of 5 years of what is described as intensive training at Janov's center with sessions videotaped and monitored by Janov and/or his wife. The training costs $4,500 for the first year, $3,500 for the second and third years, and trainees are themselves required to undergo PT for which they must pay. Applicants are required to fill out a detailed questionnaire that asks highly personal questions. The application asks for details about a person's birth, prior history of various emotional and physical problems, the last time he or she cried, and sexual "preferences," as well as any treatment he or she had. A special package deal of $10,450 is offered for the training and therapy.

Patients of Janov's center (www.primaltherapy.com/becoming-a-patient.php) begin with a 3-week, on-site intensive where they are required to spend the 3 weeks alone (when not in session), and it is recommended that they not work, make phone calls, snack, or take any kind of drugs other than prescriptions. After the 3 weeks, they are urged to continue with follow-up therapy, the length of which can vary, but the website states that patients should expect to stay for an average of 1 year for therapy at Janov's center. The therapy consists of individual and group sessions, and for patients unable to stay the entire length of time, telephone and video therapy via Skype is also offered. After a period of time, patients are encouraged to find a buddy to work with.

Keep in mind that this considerable investment of both time and money is based on a treatment, which, to date, claims to be scientific but lacks even minimal scientific evidence for its efficacy. For an excellent and thorough critical analysis of PT, we recommend the website by a former primal therapist who is now a doctoral psychology candidate, entitled "Debunking Primal Therapy" (debunkingprimaltherapy .com).

## Traumatic Incident Reduction

Traumatic incident reduction (TIR) is an intervention used primarily for people who suffer from the aftereffects of trauma and is also used to address a number of other conditions. In our own survey, nearly 10% of our respondents reported having used TIR within the past year, about the same percentage that reported using exposure therapy for PTSD, and according to the TIR website, a number of the practitioners listed hold LCSWs (www.tir.org). Although TIR can be considered a form of exposure therapy, proponents make claims of superiority to conventionally accepted forms of therapy. TIR has also been used in conjunction with CISM, an intervention we previously discussed.

TIR was developed by psychiatrist Frank Gerbode (1995). Gerbode, after graduating from Yale University and completing a residency at Stanford, by his own report, spent 13 years (from 1971 to 1984) as a member of the Scientology and Dianetics organizations. Dianetics was invented by science fiction writer L. Ron Hubbard who, in 1950, published a bestselling book, *Dianetics: The Modern Science of Mental Health* (Hubbard, 1950), a book that made a number of bold mental health claims that have not been scientifically tested, regarding the elimination of trauma and other mental and physical problems (see Atack, 1990, for a full history). As a point of clarification, although many of the techniques of TIR are the same or similar to Scientology and Dianetics, TIR is not in any way connected with the Scientology organization, nor is it practiced by active scientologists. Unlike Scientology, TIR is an open system with no secret techniques, no harsh organizational practices, and is far less expensive. Moreover, TIR has no requirement that people reexperience past lives or deal with alleged disembodied spiritual entities, although Gerbode (1995) does not preclude these concepts from his work and one of the authors (MGP) has been in contact with TIR proponents who have frequently delved into purported past lives. Additionally, TIR makes no claims that people who do their technique will develop the kind of extraordinary powers claimed by advanced levels of Scientology.

That being said, TIR and Dianetics/Scientology do have some striking similarities. Gerbode (1995) stated that he left Scientology due to differences he had with abusive organizational practices, although he still found much of value in its therapeutic techniques. He noted, "Despite our parting of the ways...it would be wrong not to acknowledge the wealth of information I have found in the Scientology materials...the wealth of practical and theoretical data accumulated through the actions and interactions of this group is extraordinary" (pp. xviii–xix). He also noted, "Many people have advised me not to mention this episode in my life because the idea of Scientology conjures up disreputable images in the public mind" (p. xviii).

A number of writers (Atack, 1990; Corydon & Hubbard, R.D. [note that this author is L. Ron Hubbard's son], 1987; Miller, 1987) have documented similarities between Scientology/Dianetics and parts of earlier theories and philosophies (e.g., Sigmund Freud, Alfred Korzybski, Carl Rogers). L. Ron Hubbard himself acknowledged that Freud was an influence (Corydon & Hubbard, 1987) but also claimed that Dianetics went beyond Freud's approach of just talking about problems.

When Gerbode trained in Dianetics in the 1970s, scientologists were teaching it in standardized courses as a scripted procedure known as Routine 3R (R3R; Hubbard, 1963). Other than minor wording changes, the procedures of R3R and TIR (as outlined in a TIR textbook by French & Harris [1999]) are essentially the same. Both employ scripted procedures that the therapist is expected to follow verbatim, where the person is asked to: (a) identify a trauma or unwanted feeling they are interested in dealing with; (b) identify the date and duration; (c) follow instructions to mentally go to that incident, close his or her eyes, and describe what he or she is aware of; (d) go silently through the experience to the end; (e) recount to the therapist what happened; and (f) follow instructions to go through the experience a second time and recount what happened. After that, the person is asked if the incident seems to be getting lighter or heavier. If lighter, the incident is gone through again. If the experience seems heavier, the person is asked if there is an earlier, similar experience or, if not, if the current one began earlier. The earlier experiences are dealt with in the same manner until the person reaches an end point, which consists of an insight about the experience, awareness of decisions made or an intention formed at the time of the incident, the client having attention on the present instead of the past, and appears happy and relaxed. (Additionally, in Dianetics and sometimes in TIR, if a galvanic skill response device known as the electrodermometer or E-Meter is used, the needle should have a floating appearance believed to indicate the absence of emotional charge.) The person is then asked about experiences on three other causal directions, known as flows: the person causing the trauma or feeling to someone else; others causing others to have the trauma; and the person causing the trauma to self. The steps outlined earlier are employed on these flows.

Gerbode (1995) described TIR as being part of a larger discipline of what he refers to as metapsychology. He defines metapsychology as:

> The study of the person and her abilities, the origin, structure, and function of the mind, and the relationship between

person, mind, and physical universe. It is the discipline that unifies mental and physical experience; it seeks to discover the rules that apply to both. (p. 6)

Gerbode made it clear that TIR and metapsychology are inductive approaches. He maintained, "The basic data and observations needed to understand the subject have always been available to us—as our own experiences" (p. 7) and that TIR comes from these alleged data and observations. Gerbode (1990) also claimed that metapsychology is not committed to any particular theory but, rather, is a pragmatic method, an unbelief system that operates through direct experience. He further recommended that the reader make his or her own confirmatory observations to verify metapsychology, which illustrates his emphasis on confirmation rather than on refutation.

Similar to a number of other innovators of novel therapies, Gerbode considers TIR a paradigm shift. He has claimed that the field of psychology has been "pre-paradigmatic for long enough ... [Metapsychology proposes] a long-overdue paradigm—one that is sufficiently based on intersubjectively agreed-upon observations to be a crystallization point for the formation of a new science: metapsychology" (Gerbode, 1995, p. 7).

TIR refers to its procedure as viewing (Gerbode, 1995) because the process instructs the person to view experiences as if they were viewing a movie, which again, implies the view of memory operating as a video recorder that one can simply play back. TIR has two forms: basic and thematic. Basic TIR (not the same usage of the word as the basic incident in a chain) has the person reexperience a single traumatic experience, using the scripted process described earlier. Thematic TIR uses the same process to guide the person through reexperiencing a chain of similar experiences, going earlier and earlier until he or she reaches the basic and experiences the end point consisting of emotional relief and an insight, often about the intention formed at the time of the trauma.

In addition to Hubbard's dianetic theories (often downplayed or not mentioned in the TIR literature), TIR proponents have attempted to relate TIR to other more-recognized theories and maintained that it came mainly from Sigmund Freud and Carl Rogers (Moore, 2005). Bisbey (1995) listed re-evaluation co-counseling ([RC]; Jackins, 1970) as an influence on the development of TIR (RC is also an early offshoot of Dianetics).

Gerbode (2004) described TIR as being different from conventional trauma approaches that rely on either the theory of catharsis or coping. He used the Freudian term *anamnesis* to describe what occurs in TIR, noting that anamnesis (defined as recovery of repressed memories) is required for full resolution of a trauma. Gerbode also referred to a practice Freud engaged in (before he began doing free association) where he directed patients to deal with chains of similar traumatic events in reverse chronological order. The assumption inherent in the theory of anamnesis, that the mind operates as a video recorder and has the ability to recover and replay repressed memories, has been falsified by modern memory research (for a review, see McNally, 2003). Moreover, the evidence for repression and forgetting of trauma is weak and when critically reviewed, the bulk of the evidence indicates that unless there is physical brain damage or the memory occurred at a very early age, memory for traumatic events is well remembered and stronger than for ordinary events (for a review, see McNally, 2003).

TIR proponents (Moore, 2005) cited the work of Carl Rogers as related to TIR. The TIR facilitator follows rules for facilitation that forbid any sort of interpretation or evaluation of the client on the therapist's part. This, however, is also part of a set of Scientology guidelines called the Auditors Code (Hubbard, 1968), and the rules of facilitation bear a number of similarities to Scientology's code.

TIR has also been associated with cognitive behavioral theories (Bisbey, 1995). More recently, TIR proponents have connected it with the increasingly popular mindfulness-based cognitive behavioral approaches (Whitfield, 2006). It appears that since Gerbode discouraged connecting TIR to any particular theory, as noted previously, proponents have felt free to relate it to a number of theories associated with popular psychotherapeutic interventions.

TIR proponents state that its basic 3- to 4-day training is sufficient to qualify a person to practice TIR (see www.tir.org for a full description). In the United States, the training is advertised as costing $695 (see tir-woct18.eventbrite.com) and is often conducted by unlicensed individuals and open to all, regardless of professional degrees or licensure. Thus, a person with no mental health credentials or previous experience could take this training and subsequently could hang out a shingle and practice TIR, although a number of licensed individuals including LCSWs also teach and practice TIR.

TIR proponents make a number of claims about the efficacy of this therapy. TIR's main website states, "It is highly effective in eliminating the negative effects of past traumatic incidents" (from www.tir .org/faq.html). A promotional advertisement for a basic training in TIR states, "TIR simply pulls PTSD and most anxiety and panic disorders out by their roots. Literally. Not in 30-plus years of practice have I used a more remarkably effective clinical procedure" (Robert H. Moore, PhD, quoted on www.psychotherapyontario.org/site/index. cfm?DSP=Section&ID=44). Various promotions on the Internet have made a number of other similar claims and can be found by a Google search on "traumatic incident reduction."

TIR proponents say that it differs from exposure-based therapies in the following ways (French & Harris, 1999):

1. An indeterminate length of session that continues until an end point is reached

2. Specialized communication drills claimed to improve the quality of the intervention (French & Harris, 1999), which are similar to the training routines done by scientologists

3. A prescribed series of steps for the procedure that does not allow the therapist to interpret for the client

To date, there is apparently only one peer-reviewed published RCT on TIR, conducted by a doctoral student in social work (Valentine & Smith, 2001). The sample consisted of 123 female inmates at the Tallahassee Federal Correction Institute who reported suffering from a traumatic event. Because the researchers compared TIR to a wait-list control rather than to another intervention, reviewers (Lohr, Devilly, Lilienfeld, & Olatunji, 2006) noted that the research design, which lacked a comparison group with an active treatment, failed to control for therapist enthusiasm, allegiance, and placebo effects. Hence, there were no grounds to claim that the effects were due to any specific attribute of TIR rather than to a nonspecific effect from the therapeutic relationship. In addition, the therapists could have inadvertently conveyed positive expectations for improvement in the protocol for preparing participants for the treatment. The therapists reportedly told participants: "I will just help you to see it [the trauma] until you feel better about it" (Valentine, 1997, p. 110).

Additionally, an unpublished RCT was conducted on TIR for a doctoral dissertation (Bisbey, 1995) where TIR was compared to direct therapeutic exposure (DTE) and a wait-list control group. Participants in both the TIR and DTE groups showed more improvement on scales for PTSD than those of the control group, and the TIR group showed significantly more improvement than the DTE group at both post-test and follow-up. However, this study was never published in a peer-reviewed journal, and the author was one of the therapists and a proponent of TIR. Two of the other three therapists were also TIR proponents.

In evaluating novel therapies, the principle of Occam's Razor (that the simplest adequate explanation that fits the facts is more likely to be the correct one) is helpful to keep in mind. In the case of TIR, when Occam's Razor is applied, the simplest adequate explanation is that the positive results are due to the well-tested mechanism of exposure. To date, there is no solid evidence that there are any features unique to TIR that would make it more effective, much less the paradigm shift it is claimed to be.

## Hypnosis and Other Suggestive Techniques for Memory Recovery of Childhood Sexual and Other Forms of Abuse

We wish to preface our remarks in this section with the statement that we recognize that childhood sexual abuse is a very real, serious problem that pervades every socioeconomic level. Well-designed epidemiological studies that employed random sampling methods with representative populations found that approximately 45 million Americans (1 in 10 men and 1 in 5 women) reported having had a sexual experience with an adult as a child (Finkelhor, Hotaling, Lewis, & Smith, 1990; Vogeltanz et al., 1999). This section is in no way intended to minimize the reality of sexual abuse, to which the feminist movement and others have brought well-deserved attention, but rather to examine some of the claims and therapies lacking in empirical support used to recover memories of childhood sexual abuse that may result in the creation of false memories that have led to the accusation of innocent people and have done some clients more harm than good.

A heated controversy erupted in the 1990s over the use of hypnosis and other suggestive techniques for the purpose of what were believed to be repressed memories of childhood sexual abuse. Although many clinicians balk at using the term *recovered memory therapy* and few now describe what they do in that way, techniques used for memory recovery can include asking leading questions, age regression, guided visualization, past-life regression, symptom interpretation, dream interpretation, physical symptom interpretation (body memories), and bibliotherapy. Proponents of these methods believe that wholesale repression of multiple incidents of traumatic experience occurs, although current research shows that trauma is actually well remembered (McNally, 2003). Although evidence exists that people might not think about experiences of sexual abuse for a period of time, especially if they were not traumatic at the time of the experience, there is very little compelling evidence to support the notion that these memories were repressed. Although people might assume that this controversy is outdated, recent legal cases have shown that the controversy has continued well into the new millennium. In a recent amicus curiae (friends of the court) brief, McNally noted:

> The notion that traumatic events can be repressed and later recovered is the most pernicious bit of folklore ever to infect psychology and psychiatry. It has provided the theoretical basis for "recovered memory therapy"—the worst catastrophe to befall the mental health field since the lobotomy era. (McNally, 2006, para. 9)

In addition to recovering alleged memories of childhood sexual abuse, such therapies often involved recovery of memories that involved alleged satanic ritual abuse where parents were believed to have been involved in an organized satanic cult that performed rituals of human sacrifice, cannibalism, secret satanic societies, and a number of other highly unlikely events that the alleged participants were supposedly induced to forget. The cure, it was claimed, was a lengthy therapy that involved recovering memories of all that happened. Some of these therapies were later found to do more harm than good (Lilienfeld, 2007), producing serious psychiatric decompensation, suicidal depression, and isolation from family members who were believed to be responsible.

Although isolated cases of satanic ritual abuse have been documented, there is no evidence of repressed memories in such cases, nor that the individuals involved were part of any kind of highly organized cult. For example, one documented case (Weir & Wheatcroft, 1995) involved four adults who employed occult rituals and paraphernalia to sexually abuse teenage children who provided detailed accounts to authorities and had not repressed their memories of the events. These adults did not act as part of any kind of organized satanic conspiracy and a thorough investigation by a Federal Bureau of Investigation (FBI) agent who had once believed in the possible existence of such abuse (Lanning, 1991) has not turned up any evidence of the existence of such practices on the consistent, organized level of a satanic cult. However, to believers, this lack of evidence is not convincing as a conspiracy of silence is believed to exist. Essentially, believers have recreated a nonfalsifiable proposition, because in their eyes, any evidence that runs contrary to beliefs is further evidence of a cover-up conspiracy.

Additionally, some of the survivors of sexual and/or satanic ritual abuse were also believed to have multiple personality disorder (MPD; now referred to as dissociative identity disorder [DID]). Some clients were believed to have literally hundreds, sometimes even thousands, of personalities, referred to as alters. Although DID is included in the current *DSM-5* and there is virtually no controversy that it exists, controversy does exist as to its cause. There are several competing models of its etiology (causation; Lilienfeld & Lynn, 2014). The sociocognitive model (SCM) maintains that DID is a socially constructed disorder. Although its symptoms are very real and distressing to the client, the symptoms were iatrogenic (created and suggested either by a therapist who sincerely believed in the existence of such alters or by the widespread media attention DID has received through books and movies such as *Sybil* and, more recently, the popular television series *The United States of Tara*). More recently, in her book *Sybil Exposed*, journalist Debbie Nathan (2011) discovered documentation of the case on which *Sybil* was based that provided evidence that a number of Sybil's psychiatrist's assertions were fabricated and that the psychiatrist had used highly suggestive techniques and administered a drug, sodium pentothal, to get Sybil's "alters" to manifest.

In contrast, the posttraumatic model (PTM) maintains that DID is caused by severe childhood trauma where the child finds the experience so unbearable that he or she has to create an alternate identity to cope. Proponents of the PTM cite studies that show that more than 90% of people diagnosed with DID have a history of childhood trauma (Gleaves, 1996). However, the problem that has been pointed out with such studies is that the memories of the participants were usually recovered in therapy for DID and consisted of retrospective self-reports from patients who were largely uncorroborated (Kihlstrom, 2005). Another approach is the operant model, which suggests that a client's display of the different behavioral repertoires labeled as personalities is shaped and maintained by the reinforcers that follow the display and shifting of these so-called personalities. Kohlenberg (1973) tested this hypothesis by taking baseline rates of the amount of time a hospitalized client with purported MPD displayed each of three distinct personalities (e.g., behavioral repertoires). Following baselines, one personality (the one identified as the normative one) was selectively reinforced, and the amount of time the patient remained in this selected personality dramatically increased. Then, the staff ceased providing social reinforcement to the client when the previously selected personality was displayed, and the occurrence of this persona dramatically declined. This suggests, but does not prove, that social reinforcement contingencies play an important role in the display of supposedly different "personalities, perhaps their development, and certainly their maintenance." See also Aldridge-Morris's (1989) book *Multiple Personality: An Exercise in Deception.*

In addition to influencing psychology and psychiatry, this "folklore" referred to in McNally's amicus curiae brief also impacted the social work profession. Clinical social workers were very much at the forefront of the recovered memory movement and some, such as E. Sue Blume, LCSW, were prominent activist proponents of therapy aimed at recovery of such alleged memories that were believed to be the cause of a wide variety of symptoms. If readers are wondering why we are discussing what some may regard as ancient history, this is not the case. As of September 2010, Blume's website, www.esueblume.com, still mentioned and promoted her book, *Secret Survivors* (Blume, 1990), and there is no statement that she has changed her mind about the material it contains. Although it is not clear whether she still practices all the methods recommended in her book, she continues to promote the book and has not, to the best of our knowledge, retracted any of the statements and continues to maintain a private practice with stated specialties that include incest recovery and dissociation including DID.

Blume maintained that "Amnesia or 'blocking' is the most common feature of Post-Incest Syndrome...*perhaps half of all incest survivors do not remember that the abuse occurred*" (p. 81). Thus, she used lists of symptoms as indicators of whether a person was repressing a memory of childhood incest. She began her book with a 34-item checklist appearing before the title page, indicating that if people identified with many of these characteristics, they could be incest survivors. This checklist and other similar popular checklists have not been properly studied for reliability and validity. Blume's checklist included items such as fear of being alone in the dark, wearing baggy clothing, gastrointestinal problems, eating disorders, phobias, trust issues, and many other symptoms that could have many alternative explanations. Although this particular checklist appeared in a book, the advent of the Internet appears to increase the popularity of a variety of different symptom checklists, few of which have been properly tested for reliability and validity. Such checklists can be compelling to people who are seeking explanations for various difficulties they are having in their lives. However, such unvalidated checklists can mislead people into self-diagnosis that can be highly damaging, especially if it leads them to enter lengthy and expensive therapy with a practitioner of unvalidated methods, which may result in worsening of a problem that could have been effectively addressed using empirically supported methods.

In later writings, Blume (1995) compared anyone who was skeptical of the validity of recovered memories to Holocaust deniers. Naturally, because people do not like being compared to Holocaust deniers, this induced some people to be reluctant to question the unvalidated material being presented as unquestioned fact in such writings. Additionally, skeptics of recovered memory therapies have been accused of being antifeminist. For example, when social psychologist Carol Tavris was critical of such therapies and the unfounded claims about memory and trauma that accompany them, she reported having received a number of irate letters from mental health professionals noting that "One feminist psychiatrist accused me of writing a 'malicious screed' while another clinician, representing the consensus of the letter writers, said that my essay placed me 'directly on the side of the molesters, rapists, pedophiles and other misogynists'" (Tavris, 2003, p. xv). However, it is our position, as well as Tavris's, that perpetuating notions that have been shown to be false do feminism more harm than good, as they trivialize the very real widespread sexual abuse that has been documented to exist, as we pointed out earlier.

A number of prominent legal cases revolved around the issue of recovered memories of sexual abuse. Although there were a number of cases in the early 1990s where adults who recovered memories of childhood sexual abuse in therapy sued their parents or other alleged perpetrators, by the mid-1990s the tide had begun to turn and a number of court decisions ruled that memories of sexual abuse that had been recovered in therapy in the absence of corroborating evidence were not considered valid evidence and thus were to be excluded from testimony (Pope & Hudson, 1995).

Additionally, a number of former clients who had recovered memories in therapy of sexual and satanic ritual abuse and who later came to the conclusion that the memories were not valid, sued their former therapists, and prevailed in court decisions. For example, in Appleton, Wisconsin, Nadean Cool sued her psychiatrist and in 1997 was awarded $2.4 million (Loftus, 1997). Cool's psychiatrist had diagnosed her as having DID with more than 120 personalities, and through hypnosis and other suggestive techniques, recovered alleged memories of having been in a satanic cult, eating babies, having sex with animals, and being forced to watch the murder of her 8-year-old friend. He also performed 5-hour-long exorcisms on her. Also in 1997, in Houston, Texas, Lynn Carl sued and won a $5.8 million judgment against her therapist who had diagnosed her as having 500 multiple personalities and convinced her that she had been abused in a satanic cult (Smith, 1997). Ms. Carl's children were also affected as she had them committed to a hospital based on the belief that they too had been abused in the alleged satanic cult.

Third-party lawsuits against therapists were also brought by parents of clients who had falsely accused them of sexual abuse due to memories they had recovered in therapy. One such case in New Hampshire, *Hungerford v. Jones*, involved a social worker, Susan Jones, who had used guided imagery and visualization techniques that she had learned in a weekend workshop with no other expertise in the area, with a client to recover memories of sexual abuse (Applebaum, 2001). Jones encouraged the client to cut off all contact with her father and to file a criminal complaint against him. The father's criminal case was dismissed and he sued the therapist. This resulted in a ruling against the therapist, which was upheld by the New Hampshire Supreme Court.

Although the numerous court cases of the 1990s and early 2000s have no doubt made clinicians more reluctant to openly practice recovered memory therapies, perusal of the Internet shows some evidence that at the very least, a minority of clinicians are continuing to practice such questionable techniques, including treatment of allegedly large numbers of multiple personalities. One of us (Pignotti) has also received communication from former patients who were recently involved in such therapy, who feel they were greatly harmed, including therapy from LCSWs.

One very recent lawsuit that showed this type of therapy is continuing at least in some treatment centers involved four former patients of an eating disorder treatment center suing the treatment center and one of its lead therapists. The lawsuits occurred between November 2011 and December 2012 (Nasseff, 2011; Taylor, 2012; Thompson, 2012; Travers, 2012) and the defendants were alleged to have implanted false memories of trauma related to child sexual abuse and satanic ritual abuse, as well as DID diagnoses and the implantation of multiple personalities. The plaintiffs alleged that the defendants used hypnosis to create false memories of abuse and instill in them the belief that they were at the time of their hospitalization current members of a satanic cult.

One of the main therapies employed by Castlewood was the parts work therapy known as internal family systems (IFS; Schwartz, 1995), a therapy which proposes that people who have been traumatized over a period of time develop "parts" or "subpersonalities" in order to cope. IFS addresses not only people diagnosed with DID but also claims that these "parts" play a role in other trauma-related disorders and problems as well. In a paper posted on Castlewood's website that contains no publication citation (Schwartz, Schwartz, & Galperin, n.d.), the authors state that "Unfortunately, no well-constructed outcome studies testing the IFS model and methods have been completed" and they maintain that "the best evidence of IFS is from empirical observations in the clinician's office" (pp. 7–8). The authors maintain that "Until the results of these studies are in, skeptical clinicians are left to test these assertions within their own practices" (p. 8). Apparently, the authors do not understand the dangers of such "tests" in which paying therapy clients are being used as guinea pigs, often without having given informed consent for a treatment that is highly experimental. In spite of this lack of evidence, IFS markets provide expensive training to mental health professionals. According to brochures on the main IFS website (see www.selfleadership.org), the training consists of three levels, which together cost $7,400, not including such additional expenses as travel, lodging, and textbooks and offers annual conferences.

People who have been involved in groups thought of as destructive cults and feel they need help to recover from a bad experience may seek help from a therapist with a stated expertise in destructive cults. They might, ironically, end up with a therapist who offers parts work, because one of the theories offered is that a person in a cult develops a pseudo-personality of the ideal cult member, suppressing the real "self." One self-proclaimed "cult expert" with a background in neurolinguistic programming and IFS, stated that "members of mind control cults suffer from a dissociative disorder that causes them to vacillate between an authentic identity and a cult identity" (Hassan, 2000, p. 176) and more recently has claimed to be an expert in human trafficking and applied his untested model to its victims. Such assertions have never been subjected to empirical tests or published in peer-reviewed journals.

Hence, those who consider themselves to be victims of destructive cults might be going from the frying pan into the fire when they enlist the services of certain self-proclaimed cult experts. There is also no evidence that getting therapy from a "cult" expert produces superior results to getting therapy from other therapists, yet some have been known to charge fees as high as $8,000 per day for their intensive therapy services. If having been in a cult is considered trauma (although much of it does not fit the *DSM* criteria for trauma, although some might), then self-proclaimed cult trauma experts appear to be unaware of the large body of literature on resiliency discussed previously. Surveys were conducted showing high rates of symptoms reported by former cult members. However, such surveys are obtained from samples of individuals who had already been exposed to beliefs from the "cult recovery" community and additionally, because standardized assessments for problems such as anxiety, depression, dissociative states, and PTSD were typically not conducted in these studies, there is no way to know whether the self-reported symptoms met the criteria for a diagnosis or were symptoms that are felt by most people but were pathologized and exaggerated by "cult experts," many of whom make their living working with such people. Not surveyed are the many people who leave groups typically considered cults and, after an initial period of adjustment and mourning the losses associated with leaving, went on to live normal, healthy productive lives free of such pathology that some "cult experts" believe nearly all ex-cult members have unless they get their specialized services.

## Past-Life Regression Therapy

Although not as common as therapy to recover memories of abuse, therapies used to recover alleged memories of past lives, believed to be the cause of a number of different emotional and physical problems are widely promoted on the Internet. A search of the Internet on "past-life regression" and "LCSW" reveals that a number of LCSWs offer this therapy (see, e.g., www.cardinalcenterforhealing.com, www.rosanewechsler .com, www.maryfrench.com, www.selfgrowth.com/experts/batya_ wininger). A number of such practitioners state that they were trained by Dr. Brian Weiss, a psychiatrist who authored a number of popular books on past-life regression (see www.brianweiss.com for details) and has appeared on a number of popular media programs such as *Oprah*. Weiss also sells a deck of 50 healing cards, offered through amazon.com for $12.44. Weiss offers trainings open to professionals and nonprofessionals described on his website www.brianweiss.com/protrain.html

These trainings are invaluable opportunities to:

- Learn past-life therapy techniques while having the opportunity to explore your own past lives
- Retrieve and release memories from childhood and prior lives in order to find more peace, joy, and health in the present
- Establish ways of building healthy relationships, enhancing creativity, and finding greater satisfaction in life
- Gain confidence in applying these techniques with your patients (para. 2)

You will explore:

- Regressions: into childhood, infancy, in utero, past lives
- Metaphors and symbols
- Hypnosis training and other deepening techniques
- Psychospiritual therapies
- Past-life regression therapy
- The mind–body connection (para. 3)

These 5-day trainings, offered through the Omega Institute by Dr. Weiss and his wife, Carole K. Weiss, MSW (see eomega.org/omega/ workshops/b23bef1bc2b121523aedbaef22cf7c9b) cost $950, and Dr. Weiss states that about half the group consists of mental health professionals. On a video at the aforementioned website describing the workshop, Dr. Weiss claims that participants will learn techniques that cure various psychological and physical symptoms.

Unrelated to Weiss, a professional association for past-life regression founded in 1980 also exists (see www.iarrt.org/join.html) that provides certification for past-life regression practitioners, publishes a *Journal of Regression Therapy* and a newsletter, and holds an annual conference. The association also announced that it is conducting a study on the effectiveness of past-life regression therapy and invites people to participate via its website (www.iarrt.org/downloads/PastLifeRegression_Post-SessionSurvey.pdf). However, this so-called post-session survey appears to be more of a consumer satisfaction survey, and the results could not be legitimately used to claim efficacy of this therapy because there was no control group and no standardized assessment measures were used.

A study was conducted at Harvard's psychology department by two researchers who do not themselves practice or believe in past-life regression (Meyersburg & McNally, 2011). A group of 40 nonpsychotic people who reported having had past-life memories were compared to a group of 35 people who had no such memories. The group that said they recalled past lives reported lower levels of death distress and greater meaning in their lives than the group that did not recall any past lives, and the more vivid the reported memories and the higher the certainty level of the reality of the experience, the lower the level of death distress. Although this study did not test whether such a therapy is effective for those with the types of psychological and physical problems past-life regression claims to successfully treat that we discussed earlier, this study might provide some insight into the reasons why people may find this sort of intervention attractive. Another study reported that people with past-life memories scored higher on measures of absorption and magical ideation (Meyersburg, Bogdan, Gallo, & McNally, 2009). However, these authors were quick to point out that a high score on absorption and magical ideation does not signify psychopathology and earlier research has shown that people with such beliefs did not show evidence of psychopathology on standard measures (Spanos, Menary, Gabora, DuBreuil, & Dewhirst, 1991).

However, harm from past-life regression has also been reported. Israel's Health Ministry made the decision to ban government-certified hypnotherapists from using reincarnation hypnosis after they received complaints from individuals who said they suffered serious emotional damage from the practice (Even, 2009). One of the cases was a 23-year-old man being treated for depression who, following the recall of a purported past-life death, suffered from panic attacks imagining he was stuck in a coffin. Although past-life recall in and of itself is not an indicator of psychopathology, people with preexisting problems who seek such therapy might be harmed and, for some people, the therapy may do the opposite of what was claimed.

## Eye Movement Desensitization and Reprocessing

Eye movement desensitization and reprocessing (EMDR; Shapiro, 1995) is an intervention that exposes a client to a traumatic memory while employing bilateral eye movements, hand tapping, or auditory stimulation in each ear. Most commonly, bilateral, saccadic (side-to-side) eye movements are employed where the client is instructed to follow the therapist's finger or a wand that moves from side to side. Shapiro proposes her accelerated information processing theory as an explanation for how it works, which she described as follows:

> The valences of the neural receptors (synaptic potential) of the respective neuro networks, which separately store various information plateaus and levels of adaptive information, are represented by the letters Z through A. It is hypothesized that the high-valence target network (Z) cannot link up with the more adaptive information, which is stored in networks with a lower valence. That is, the synaptic potential is different for each level of affect held in the various neuro networks.... The theory is that when the processing system is catalyzed in EMDR, the valence of the receptors is shifted downward so that they are capable of linking with the receptors of the neuro networks with progressively lower valences. (Shapiro, 1995, pp. 317–318)

If readers are finding this description difficult to follow, take comfort in the fact that so do we! From our point of view, we consider this description to be an eloquent example of obscurant jargon, one of the hallmark indicators of pseudoscience we discussed in Chapter 1. A more comprehensible explanation is presented on the EMDR Association's website (www.emdr.com/theory.htm):

> When a traumatic or very negative event occurs, information processing may be incomplete, perhaps because strong negative feelings or dissociation interfere with information processing. This prevents the forging of connections with more adaptive information that is held in other memory networks. For example, a rape survivor may "know" that rapists are responsible for their crimes, but this information does not connect with her feeling that she is to blame for the attack. The memory is then dysfunctionally stored without appropriate associative connections and with many elements still unprocessed. When the individual thinks about the trauma, or when the memory is triggered by similar situations, the person may feel like she is reliving it, or may experience strong emotions and physical sensations. A prime example is the intrusive thoughts, emotional disturbance, and negative self-referencing beliefs of posttraumatic stress disorder (PTSD). (para. 3)

However, a large body of recent memory research on trauma has failed to support the notion that there are any special mechanisms for the processing and storage of traumatic memory (McNally, 2003). Interestingly enough, contrary to popular belief among many trauma therapists, the notion that fragmented, unprocessed memories are at the root of PTSD has been brought into question. Studies that have shown people with PTSD are no more likely to have such fragmented, unprocessed memories than people who do not have PTSD (Gaerts, 2010). It turns out that the earlier studies adduced in support of memory fragmentation in people with PTSD had not compared such people to a control group of people without PTSD. On the contrary, some studies have even shown that traumatic memories are well processed and are integrated into the person's system of autobiographical memories. Bernsten, Willert, and Rubin (2003) have suggested that such memories, because they are so well integrated, have become vivid reference points and landmarks in a person's memory and, thus, highly salient to the individual. This is just the opposite of what most clinicians believe to be the case about trauma and, thus, all these efforts to integrate and process trauma may be all for naught. Bernstein et al. found that such reference points differentiated individuals with PTSD from those who did not have PTSD. This calls into question not only the theory on which EMDR is based, but other trauma theories as well.

What sets EMDR apart from most approaches considered to be pseudoscientific is that a number of RCTs have been conducted on EMDR, leading it to be listed as an empirically supported treatment for PTSD by the Division 12 of the American Psychological Association, because it meets that group's criteria of having at least two randomized controlled studies with positive results. Nevertheless, to date, given that there is no evidence that anything unique to EMDR is responsible for the positive outcomes in comparing it to no treatment (Devilly, 2002) and the florid manner in which it has been marketed (Herbert et al., 2000), we are including it in this book. Moreover, systematic reviews for some client groups, such as combat veterans (Albright & Thyer, 2010), have revealed that the evidence for EMDR falls short of labeling it as an empirically supported treatment for that specific form of PTSD.

Because EMDR does employ elements of exposure, the principle of Occam's Razor that the simplest adequate explanation that fits the facts is usually the correct one, would lead us to conclude that where EMDR has been shown to be effective, it is the element of exposure that is responsible for the positive outcomes, rather than Shapiro's accelerated information processing model. A recent review published by proponents of EMDR frankly acknowledge that "EMDR's mechanism of action remains unspecified" (Gunter & Bdoner, 2009, p. 161). This, however, is not quite true. Shapiro has published widely on what she specifically says is EMDR's mechanism of action—Gunter and Bodner's (2009) cautiously wordier statement simply reflects that Shapiro's supposed mechanisms have been tested and shown to be invalid. At present, the present authors judge Hembree and Foa's (2003, p. 191) conclusion to be legitimate: "The hypothesis that the benefit of EMDR is due to nonspecific treatment effects or to the imaginal exposure aspect of the procedure cannot be ruled out."

EMDR is used for a variety of conditions other than PTSD. There is very little empirical support for such conditions, and even for research directly related to PTSD, reviews are mixed. A review of PTSD research conducted by the Institute of Medicine (2007) found studies on all treatments except for prolonged exposure lacked sufficient evidence to be classified as efficacious, and thus they did not classify EMDR as efficacious. EMDR is also frequently used to treat a wide variety of conditions other than PTSD for which there is very little, if any, empirical evidence. In our own survey of LCSWs (Pignotti & Thyer, 2012), we found that although exposure therapy for PTSD has more empirical support than EMDR, a considerably higher percentage of our respondents used EMDR (16.1%) than exposure therapy for PTSD (9.5%). Additionally, almost as many of our participants used EMDR for conditions other than PTSD (14.7%).

Another way in which EMDR qualifies as a pseudoscience is the manner in which it was developed and marketed (Herbert et al., 2000). EMDR was invented by psychologist Francine Shapiro and the story of her discovery (Shapiro, 1995) is often repeated. Shapiro was taking a walk in the woods one day in 1987 and while focusing on disturbing thoughts, she noticed that while her eyes were moving from side to side looking at surroundings, her anxiety had lessened. She began trying eye movements with her clients while they focused on distressing experiences, which ultimately led to her development of EMDR. Although Shapiro has strongly encouraged that EMDR be studied, which is laudable, from the beginning extraordinary claims have been made about EMDR that go beyond the evidence. EMDR has been portrayed as a paradigm shift (Shapiro, 1995) and heralded as a breakthrough therapy. Widespread promotion of EMDR in the media has occurred. For example, in 1994, ABC's *20/20* did a segment on EMDR where claims were made that EMDR worked where conventional approaches had failed, which were based on nothing more than clinical anecdotes. Herbert et al. (2000) noted:

> The majority of the story focused on three clinical anecdotes of trauma victims successfully cured by EMDR, as well as an interview with Francine Shapiro discussing her discovery of the technique. The only hint of critical comment was two sentences totaling 15 seconds in an 11-minute story. The show's host briefly noted that there were critics of the treatment who questioned its validity. This skepticism, however, was immediately dismissed by the host: "But don't try telling this to Eric... [the client]." No airtime was allotted to critics of EMDR, despite the fact that a leading critic was interviewed extensively on camera, and spent several hours reviewing the

scientific evidence concerning the technique with the show's producers. (Herbert et al., 2000, p. 955)

Additionally, EMDR proponents have come up with ad hoc hypotheses to explain away unfavorable results that do not support its theory, which is one of the hallmark indicators of a pseudoscience (see our discussion in Chapter 1). For example, when no difference was found in a dismantling study designed to control for eye movements, between eye movements and a control procedure of fixed eyes focusing on a dot, Shapiro attempted to explain this away by giving a complicated explanation as to how even the fixed eye condition could not rule out bilaterality (Pitman et al., 1996). This type of post hoc explanation renders her theory unfalsifiable and thus places it outside the realm of science, because to qualify as scientific, a theory must be falsifiable. More ways in which EMDR has been said to use social influence strategies that are consistent with those used by other forms of pseudoscience (Herbert et al., 2000) are discussed in the next chapter.

## REFERENCES

Albright, D. L., & Thyer, B. A. (2010). Does EMDR reduce post-traumatic stress disorder sympomatology in combat veterans? *Behavioral Interventions, 25,* 1–19.

Aldridge-Morris, R. (1989). *Multiple personality disorder: An exercise in deception.* East Sussex, England: Lawrence Erlbaum.

American Psychiatric Association. (2013). *Diagnostic and statistical manual of mental disorders* (5th ed.). Arlington, VA: Author.

Applebaum, P. S. (2001). Law & psychiatry: Third-party suits against therapists in recovered memory cases. *Psychiatric Services, 52,* 27–28.

Atack, J. (1990). *A piece of blue sky.* Secaucus, NJ: Lyle Stuart.

Bernsten, D., Willert, M., & Rubin, D. C. (2003). Splintered memories or vivid landmarks? Qualities and organization of traumatic memories with and without PTSD. *Applied Cognitive Psychology, 17,* 675–693.

Bisbey, L. B. (1995). No longer a victim: A treatment outcome study of crime victims with post-traumatic stress disorder [Doctoral dissertation]. California School of Professional Psychology, San Diego, CA. *Dissertation Abstracts International: Section B: The Sciences and Engineering, 56*(3-B), 1692.

Blume, E. S. (1990). *Secret survivors: Uncovering incest and its aftereffects in women.* New York, NY: Ballantine Books.

Blume, E. S. (1995). The ownership of truth. *Journal of Psychohistory, 23,* 131–140.

Breslau, N. (2009). The epidemiology of trauma, PTSD, and other posttrauma disorders. *Trauma, Violence and Abuse, 10,* 198–210.

Brewin, C. R., Rose, S., Andrews, B., Green, J., Tata, P., McEverly, C., & Foa, E. B. (2002). Brief screening instrument for posttraumatic stress disorder. *British Journal of Psychiatry, 181,* 158–162.

Chemtob, C. M., Thomas, S., Law, W., & Cremniter, D. (1997). Postdisaster psychosocial intervention: A field study of the impact of debriefing on psychological distress. *American Journal of Psychiatry, 154,* 415–417.

Clancy, S. (2009). *The trauma myth.* New York, NY: Basic Books.

Corydon, B., & Hubbard, R. D. (1987). *L. Ron Hubbard: Messiah or madman.* Secaucus, NJ: Lyle Stuart.

Devilly, G. J. (2002). Eye movement desensitization and reprocessing: A chronology of its development and scientific standing. *The Scientific Review of Mental Health Practice, 1,* 113–138.

Devilly, G. J., Gist, R., & Cotton, P. (2006). Ready! Fire! Aim! The status of psychological debriefing and therapeutic interventions: In the work place and after disasters. *Review of General Psychology, 10,* 318–345.

Ehlers, A., & Clark, D. (2003). Early psychological interventions for adult survivors of trauma: A review. *Biological Psychiatry, 9,* 817–826.

Even, D. (2009, July 24). Health Ministry to hypnotists: Stop helping clients explore past lives. Retrieved from http://www.haaretz.com/hasen/spages/1102563.html

Everly, G. S., Flannery, R. B., & Eyler, V. A. (2002). Critical incident stress management (CISM): A statistical review of the literature. *Psychiatric Quarterly, 73,* 171–182.

Everly, G. S., Flannery, R. B., & Mitchell, J. T. (2000). Critical incident stress management (CISM): A review of the literature. *Aggression and Violent Behavior, 5,* 23–40.

Fawzy, T. I., & Gray, M. J. (2007). From CISD to CISM: Same song, different verse? *The Scientific Review of Mental Health Practice, 5,* 31–43.

Finkelhor, D., Hotaling, G., Lewis, I. A., & Smith, C. (1990). Sexual abuse in a national survey of adult men and women: Prevalence, characteristics and risk factors. *Child Abuse and Neglect, 14,* 19–28.

French, G., & Harris, C. (1999). *Traumatic incident reduction.* Boca Raton, FL: CRC Press.

Gaerts, E. (2010). Posttraumatic memory. In G. M. Rosen & B. C. Frueh (Eds.), *Clinician's guide to posttraumatic stress disorder* (pp. 77–95). Hoboken, NJ: John Wiley.

Galea, S., Vlahov, D., Resnick, H., Ahern, J., Susser, E., Gold, J., . . . & Kilpatrick, D. (2003). Trends of probable post-traumatic stress disorder in New York City after the September 11 terrorist attacks. *American Journal of Epidemiology, 158*, 514–524.

Gerbode, F. A. (1990). Metapsychology: The un-belief system. *Institute for Metapsychology Newsletter (online article)*. Retrieved September 12, 2010, from http://www.healing-arts.org/tir/unbelief.htm

Gerbode, F. A. (1995). *Beyond psychology: An introduction to metapsychology* (3rd ed.). Menlo Park, CA: IRM Press.

Gerbode, F. A. (2004). Critical issues in trauma resolution. In V. R. Volkman (Ed.), *Beyond trauma: Conversations on traumatic incident reduction.* Ann Arbor, MI: Loving Healing Press.

Gist, R., & Devilly, G. J. (2010). Early intervention in the aftermath of trauma. In G. M. Rosen & B. C. Frueh (Eds.), *Clinician's guide to posttraumatic stress disorder* (pp 153–176). Hoboken, NJ: John Wiley.

Glaltzer-Levy, I. R., Ankri, Y., Freedman, S., Israeli-Shalev, Y., Roitman, P., Gilad, M., & Shalev, A. Y. (2013). Early PTSD symptom trajectories: Persistence, recovery, and response to treatment: Results from the Jerusalem Trauma Outreach and Prevention Study (J-TOPS). *PLOS ONE, 8*, e70084. doi:10.1371/annotation/0af0b6c6-ac23–4fe9-a692-f5c30a3a30b3

Gleaves, D. H. (1996). The sociocognitive model of dissociative identity disorder: A reexamination of the evidence. *Psychological Bulletin, 120*, 42–59.

Gunter, R. W., & Bodner, G. E. (2009). EMDR works... But how? Recent progress in the search for treatment mechanisms. *Journal of EMDR Practice and Research, 3*, 161–168.

Hassan, S. (2000). *Releasing the bonds: Empowering people to think for themselves.* Somerville, MA: Freedom of Mind Press.

Hembree, E. A., & Foa, E. B. (2003). Interventions for trauma-related emptional disturbances in adult victims of crime. *Journal of Traumatic Stress, 16*, 187–199.

Herbert, J. D., Lilienfeld, S. O., Lohr, J. M., Montgomery, R. W., O'Donohue, W. T., Rosen, G. M., & Tolin, D. F. (2000). Science and pseudoscience in the development of eye movement desensitization and reprocessing: Implications for clinical psychology. *Clinical Psychology Review, 20*, 945–971.

Herman, J. L. (1992). *Trauma and recovery.* New York, NY: Basic Books.

Hubbard, L. R. (1950). *Dianetics: The modern science of mental health.* Los Angeles, CA: Bridge Publications.

Hubbard, L. R. (1963). *Hubbard Communications Office Bulletin 24 June, 1963, Routine 3, Engram Running by Chains, Bulletin 3.* East Grinstead, Sussex, England: Author.

Hubbard, L. R. (1968). *Hubbard Communications Office Bulletin 14 October 1968, Revised 19 June, 1980, The Auditor's Code.* East Grinstead, Sussex, England: Author.

Institute of Medicine. (2007). *Treatment of posttraumatic stress disorder: An assessment of the evidence.* Washington, DC: The National Academies Press.

Jackins, H. (1970). *Fundamentals of co-counseling manual.* Seattle, WA: Rational Island.

Janov, A. (1970). *The primal scream.* New York, NY: Dell.

Kihlstrom, J. F. (2005). Dissociative disorders. *Annual Review of Clinical Psychiatry, 1,* 227–253.

Kohlenberg, R. (1973). Behavioristic approach to multiple personality: A case study. *Behavior Therapy, 4,* 137–140.

Lanning, K. V. (1991). Ritual abuse: A law enforcement view or perspective. *Child Abuse and Neglect, 15,* 171–173.

Lilienfeld, S. O. (2007). Psychological treatments that cause harm. *Perspectives on Psychological Science, 2,* 53–70.

Lilienfeld, S. O., & Lynn, S. J. (2014). Dissociative identity disorder: A contemporary scientific perspective. In S. O. Lilienfeld, S. J. Lynn, & J. M. Lohr (Eds.), *Science and pseudoscience in clinical psychology* (2nd ed., pp. 113–152). New York, NY: Guilford Press.

Loftus, E. F. (1997). Creating false memories. *Scientific American, 277,* 70–75.

Lohr, J. M., Devilly, G. J., Lilienfeld, S. O., & Olatunji, B. O. (2006). First do no harm, and then do some good: Science and professional responsibility in the response to disaster and trauma. *The Behavior Therapist, 29,* 131–135.

Long, M. E., Elhai, J. D., Schweinle, A., Gray, M. J., Grubaugh, A. L., & Frueh, B. C. (2008). Posttraumatic stress disorder diagnostic rates and symptom severity between Criterion A1 and non-Criterion A1 stressors. *Journal of Anxiety Disorders, 22,* 167–178.

McNally, R. J. (2003). *Remembering trauma.* Cambridge, MA: Harvard University Press.

McNally, R. J. (2006). Amicus curiae brief in *Taus v. Loftus,* Supreme Court of California. Retrieved September 16, 2010, from http://www.religioustolerance.org/rmtmcnally.htm

McNally, R. J., Bryant, R. A., & Ehlers, A. (2003). Does early psychological intervention promote recovery from posttraumatic stress? *Psychological Science in the Public Interest, 4*, 45–79.

Meyersburg, C. A., Bogdan, R., Gallo, D. A., & McNally, R. J. (2009). False memory propensity in people reporting recovered memories of past lives. *Journal of Abnormal Psychology, 118*, 399–404.

Meyersburg, C. A., & McNally, R. J. (2011). Reduced death distress and greater meaning in life among individuals reporting past life memory. *Personality and Individual Differences, 50*, 1218–1221.

Miller, R. (1987). *Barefaced messiah: The true story of L. Ron Hubbard.* New York, NY: Henry Holt.

Mitchell, J. T. (1983). When disaster strikes . . . The critical incident stress debriefing process. *Journal of Emergency Services, 8*, 36–39.

Moore, R. H. (2005). Psychological foundations for TIR. In V. R. Volkman (Ed.), *Traumatic incident reduction: Research and practice* (pp. 15–21). Ann Arbor, MI: Loving Healing Press.

Nasseff v. Castlewood Treatment Center, LLC and Mark Schwartz, Sc.D. (2011). Retrieved from https://www.courts.mo.gov/casenet/base/welcome.do

Nathan, D. (2011). *Sybil exposed.* New York, NY: Free Press.

Pignotti, M., & Thyer, B. A. (2012). Novel and empirically supported therapies: Patterns of usage among licensed clinical social workers. *Behavioural and Cognitive Psychotherapy, 40*, 331–349.

Pitman, R. K., Orr, S. P., Altman, B., Longpre, R. E., Poiré, R. E., & Macklin, M. L. (1996). Emotional processing during eye movement desensitization and reprocessing (EMDR) therapy of Vietnam veterans with post-traumatic stress disorder. *Comprehensive Psychiatry, 37*, 419–429.

Pope, H. G., & Hudson, J. I. (1995). Can memories of childhood sexual abuse be repressed? *Psychological Medicine, 25*, 121–126.

Rose, S., Bisson, B., & Wessely, S. (2005). A systematic review of brief psychological interventions ("debriefing") for the treatment of immediate trauma related symptoms and the prevention of post-traumatic stress disorder. *The Cochrane Collaboration* (database online). Updated issue 3. Hoboken, NJ: John Wiley.

Rose, S., Bisson, J., Churchill, R., & Wessely, S. (2002). *Psychological debriefing for the prevention of post traumatic stress disorder (PTSD).* Cochrane Database of Systematic Reviews, Issue 2. doi:10.1002/14651858.CD000560

Rosen, G. (1999). Treatment fidelity and research on eye movement desensitization and reprocessing (EMDR). *Journal of Anxiety Disorders, 13*, 173–184.

Schwartz, R. (1995). *Internal family systems therapy.* New York, NY: Guilford Press.

Schwartz, R., Schwartz, M., & Galperin, L. (n.d.). The internal family system model: Systematically-based individual psychotherapy for complex traumatic stress disorders. Retrieved December 23, 2012, from http://www .castlewoodtc.com/wp-content/uploads/2011/07/courtois_ctsd.pdf

Shapiro, F. (1995). *Eye movement desensitization and reprocessing: Basic protocols, principles, and procedures.* New York, NY: Guilford Press.

Smith, M. (1997). Jury Awards $5.8 Million in Satanic Memories Case. *Houston Chronicle,* Houston, TX, August 15.

Sommers, C. H., & Satel, S. (2005). September 11, 2001: The mental health crisis that wasn't. In C. H. Sommers & S. Satel (Eds.), *One nation under therapy* (pp. 177–214). New York, NY: St. Martin's Press.

Spanos, N. P., Menary, E., Gabora, N. J., DuBreuil, S. C., & Dewhirst, B. (1991). Secondary identity enactments during hypnotic past-life regression: A sociocognitive perspective. *Journal of Personality and Social Psychology, 61,* 308–320.

Stocks, J. T. (1998). Recovered memory therapy: A dubious practice technique. *Social Work, 43,* 423–436.

Stocks, J. T. (1999). Recovered memory therapy: Responses to all. *Social Work, 44,* 491–499.

Tavris, C. (2003). Foreword: The widening scientists-practitioner gap. In S. O. Lilienfeld, S. J. Lynn, & J. M. Lohr (Eds.), *Science and pseudoscience in clinical psychology* (pp. ix–xviii). New York, NY: Guilford Press.

Taylor v. Castlewood Treatment Center, LLC. (2012). Retrieved from https://www.courts.mo.gov/casenet/base/welcome.do

Thompson v. Castlewood Treatment Center, LLC and Mark Schwartz, Sc.D. (2012). Retrieved from https://www.courts.mo.gov/casenet/base/welcome.do

Thyer, B. A., & Lankton, A. (2012). Racism-induced trauma. In C. F. Figley (Ed.), *Encyclopedia of trauma.* Thousand Oaks, CA: Sage.

Travers v. Castlewood Treatment Center, LLC. (2012). Retrieved from https://www.courts.mo.gov/casenet/base/welcome.do

Valentine, P. V. (1997). Traumatic incident reduction: Brief treatment of trauma-related symptoms in incarcerated females [Doctoral dissertation]. Florida State University, Tallahassee, FL. *Dissertation Abstracts International, A: The Humanities and Social Sciences, 58*(3), 1098-A.

Valentine, P. V., & Smith, T. E. (2001). Evaluating traumatic incident reduction therapy with female inmates: A randomized, controlled clinical trial. *Research on Social Work Practice, 11,* 40–53.

van Emmerick, A. A. P., Kamphuis, J. H., Hulsbosch, A. M., & Emmelkamp, P. M. G. (2002). Single session debriefing after psychological trauma: A meta-analysis. *Lancet, 360,* 766–771.

Vogeltanz, N. D., Wilsnack, S. C., Harris, T. R., Wilsnack, R. W., Wonderlich, S. A., & Kristjanson, A. F. (1999). Prevalence and risk factors for childhood sexual abuse in women: National survey findings. *Child Abuse & Neglect, 23,* 579–592.

Whitfield, H. J. (2006). Towards case-specific applications of mindfulness-based cognitive-behavioural therapies: A mindfulness-based rational emotive behavioural therapy. *Counselling Psychology Quarterly, 19,* 205–217.

Weir, I. K., & Wheatcroft, M. S. (1995). Allegation of children's involvement in ritual sexual abuse: Clinical experience of 20 cases. *Child Abuse and Neglect, 19,* 491–505.

Yehuda, R., & McFarlane, A. C. (1995). Conflict between current knowledge about posttraumatic stress disorder and its original conceptual basis. *American Journal of Psychiatry, 152,* 1705–1713.

# CHAPTER 5

# Other Pseudoscientific Interventions for Adults

In the previous chapter, we discussed a number of interventions based on the belief pervasive among many mental health professionals that trauma, loosely defined, is the basis for a variety of different disorders. We will now turn our attention to interventions that are based on other beliefs about causes of problems and that address a wide variety of different types of emotional and physical problems that can include but are not limited to trauma.

## THOUGHT FIELD THERAPY AND ITS OFFSHOOTS

Thought field therapy (TFT) is said to be part of a larger discipline called energy psychology (Feinstein, 2008). However, with the exception of some preexisting practices, such as therapeutic touch and Reiki, most contemporary therapies coming under this heading are offshoots of TFT. TFT was invented by psychologist Roger Callahan and involves finger tapping and occasionally other forms of stimulation of specified sequences of supposed meridian points (the same points used in acupuncture) while thinking about a specified problem or unwanted emotion. Callahan reports (Callahan & Trubo, 2001) that he discovered TFT, which he originally called Callahan Techniques, after he learned about a chiropractic muscle testing technique called applied kinesiology (Walther, 1988) from one of his psychiatrist colleagues in the late 1970s. Callahan became fascinated by observing that if he thought about something distressing while his colleague pushed down on his outstretched arm, he was unable to resist and his arm would go down. On the other hand, if he thought about something neutral or positive, his colleague was unable to push his arm down and he was able to keep the muscle strong. This motivated him to take a 100-hour course in applied kinesiology, where he also began learning about acupressure points that are allegedly located throughout the body. Prior to his interest in all this, having received a PhD in clinical psychology from Syracuse University, he had a fairly conventional background and had been practicing since the 1950s as a licensed clinical psychologist. He considered his main orientation to be cognitive behavioral therapy, having studied under Albert Ellis what was then called rational therapy (now called rational emotive behavior therapy [REBT]). Callahan ran an institute for rational therapy in Detroit in the early 1960s as well as having taught psychology at Eastern Michigan University.

Callahan had a large private practice in Beverly Hills during the late 1970s and early 1980s. In 1980, he was treating a woman in her 40s named Mary who had a severe, lifelong phobia of water (Callahan, 1997a). He reports that he had been treating her with systematic desensitization, hypnosis, and any other technique he knew of at the time that he hoped might help. However, he had made little progress with her. In spite of having tried a variety of different techniques, including ones with a high degree of empirical support and considered state-of-the art in 1980, such as systematic desensitization, she was only able to dangle her feet in his swimming pool while remaining terrified of the water. Mary had indicated that every time she thought of water she got a terrible feeling in the pit of her stomach. Finally, applying what he had learned from the chiropractors, he decided to test her stomach meridian and he found it to be supposedly out of balance. Then, on a whim, he added something to what he had been taught, by asking Mary to tap with her fingers, under her eye, which is allegedly the end point to the stomach meridian. After tapping under her eye, Mary reported to Callahan that her fear of the water was completely gone and began running out to Callahan's pool. Callahan, skeptical at first and concerned that she could not swim, ran after her, and attempted to stop her, but she reassured him she realized she could not swim and would not do anything foolish. From that point on, Callahan and Mary herself on a video (Callahan, 1997b) 17 years later, both report that her phobia of water was suddenly and completely gone, never to recur. After that,

Callahan began experimenting with this technique with other clients and using it not only for phobias, but also a variety of other conditions, adding various treatment points and sequences that he derived through muscle testing of various points. He came up with formulas of tapping points for various conditions that he called algorithms. A more complete description of his algorithms and the various levels of TFT is available in his book, *Tapping the Healer Within* (Callahan & Trubo, 2001).

Callahan's theory, which he induced and developed many years after his initial discoveries when he began reading about quantum physics and felt he was highly influenced by the writings of physicists such as David Bohm (Callahan & Callahan, 2000), is that perturbations (disturbances) in what he calls a thought field containing active information (a concept he borrowed from quantum physics) are the root cause of all emotional and many physical problems. Callahan defines a thought field as "an imaginary scaffold upon which one may project or imagine causal entities such as perturbations" (p. 290). The so-called perturbations are believed to manifest in an energy field and correspond to specific acupressure meridian points on the body and tapping on those points unblocks the flow of energy, also known as *qi*, vital life energy (Callahan & Trubo, 2001).

The problem is that there has never been any scientific evidence for the existence of such a meridian system. TFT proponents also boast that it is based on a 6,000-year-old "meridian" system. Although the notion that because something is ancient it is valid is a fallacy, there is an additional problem with the notion that the meridian system is ancient that recently has been called into question by scholars of Chinese studies in a historical analysis (Imrie, Ramey, Buell, Ernst, & Basser, 2001), who demonstrated that the usage of the term *qi* by the ancient Chinese was unrelated to a proposed energy or "meridian" system. *Meridian* was a term coined by the Frenchman Georges Souliét de Morant in 1939, who also erroneously equated ancient *qi* with meridians (Imrie, Ramey, Buell, Ernst, & Basser, 2003–2004). This historical analysis makes a compelling case that the claims that a so-called meridian system that existed as far back as 8,000 BCE are in error. The earliest evidence for acupuncture dates back to the mid-second century BCE and even that evidence is highly ambiguous.

TFT currently offers multiple levels of training through Callahan Techniques, Ltd. (see www.rogercallahan.com for full descriptions). The most basic level, delivered in one- to two-weekend workshops, trains people in the algorithms (i.e., places and ways to tap the body). The more advanced levels train people in a technique he calls causal diagnosis that teaches people how to muscle test to determine more custom-made, individualized sequences of tapping points. A special TFT boot-camp training that combines the algorithm level with basic TFT diagnosis is offered for $497. The most advanced level is called voice technology (VT), a proprietary treatment delivered over the telephone, which costs $100,000 and requires trainees to sign nondisclosure agreements not to reveal its trade secret (Pignotti, 2007). There is also now a lower level of VT advertised on the Callahan website, which he calls optimal health that costs $5,000. Additionally, Callahan himself during his lifetime offered private VT treatment, which cost a minimum of $3,000 for 5 hours. Following Callahan's death in 2013, his wife Joanne, who now runs Callahan Techniques according to the TFT website rogercallahan.com, offers telephone sessions at the rate of $297 for a half hour, with a special offer for discounted sessions at $197 for a half hour, far more than what most licensed mental health professionals charge. Joanne Callahan holds a master's degree in business administration and possesses no mental health licensure or credentials and yet she claims to offer help for a wide variety of psychological and physical problems, although she is very careful about the language she uses to stay within the boundaries of the law.

Emotional freedom technique (EFT) is the leading offshoot of TFT and was developed by a student of Callahan (Craig, 1997). EFT also employs tapping on supposed meridian points, with the main difference being that EFT proponents do not believe that any specified sequence of tapping points is needed for the tapping to be effective. Training in EFT is considerably less expensive than TFT, with a free manual offered on its website www.emofree.com, and it appears to have a higher number of proponents among licensed clinical social workers (LCSWs), according to our own survey (Pignotti & Thyer, 2012). Although efficacy cannot be claimed for either TFT or EFT, there is evidence to support the notion that sequence of tapping points makes no difference in outcome. One of us (Pignotti, 2005) conducted a single-blind controlled study in which participants were randomly assigned to an advanced TFT technique called VT, which prescribes specified sequences versus a control group of participants who were instructed to tap on randomly assigned points and there was no difference in self-reported decreases in subjective distress level. This is important because Callahan during his lifetime charged (and his wife currently charges) extraordinarily high fees on the basis that this proprietary method produces results that are superior to simply tapping on all the points, as prescribed by EFT. As mentioned, those who train in VT, which is a trade secret, must sign a confidentiality agreement not to disclose the secret of VT.

TFT and its offshoots are not only on shaky theoretical ground, but they also lack empirical evidence to support their many claims for curing a wide variety of conditions. One website for EFT even offers a video called *Try It on Everything* (see www.thetappingsolution.com). Perusal of the Internet reveals that leading proponents have claimed success treating a wide variety of conditions, including phobias, panic attacks, posttraumatic stress disorder (PTSD), depression, obsessive-compulsive disorder, children's behavioral problems, chronic pain, nasal stuffiness, pregnancy complications, multiple sclerosis, cancer, atrial fibrillation, other cardiac problems, constipation, and irritable bowel syndrome. Similar to the claims made by proponents of weapon ointment and Perkins Tractors that we discussed in Chapter 1, proponents claim that the results are not placebo because they have successfully treated infants, animals, and even fish. Accounts related to the treatment of these and a number of other conditions can be found at www.emofree.com or www .rogercallahan.com

Callahan made it very clear that he considers TFT to be a hard science, stating that:

> As I have made more discoveries over the last two decades, my success rate has been gradually increasing and getting very close to perfection. This work is now on a par with hard science, physics and chemistry. We are no longer floundering in the wispy world of social science. (Callahan & Callahan, 2000, p. 164)

A number of TFT's top proponents are LCSWs and, like Callahan, make similar grandiose claims about TFT. For example, long-time TFT therapist and trainer Robert L. Bray, an LCSW who has also taught as an adjunct associate professor of social work at San Diego State University, quoted in an interview for *Social Work Today*, stated:

> "We're not talking about a new theory. We're talking about a completely new way of conceptualizing the human being.

TFT is a total paradigm shift." Bray and his peers liken the therapy to the same revolution in thought that saw the discovery of antibiotics usher forth a dawning age in medical practice. (Robb quoting Bray, 2003, p. 21)

One might wonder how Callahan and other proponents can claim that TFT is a science when no independently replicated well-designed, randomized controlled studies exist to support the many claims it makes. However, more recently, TFT proponents, in order to attempt to gain mainstream acceptance, have been engaged in an effort to begin to conduct randomized controlled trials (RCTs) in very limited areas in studies funded by TFT organizations. Callahan has maintained that controlled studies are unnecessary to prove that TFT is efficacious. Callahan et al. were invited to present what they considered to be their best research evidence for TFT in a special issue of the *Journal of Clinical Psychology* (Beutler, 2001). The articles were not peer reviewed and, instead, had critiques published alongside each article. The critiques (Herbert & Gaudiano, 2001; Lohr, 2001; McNally, 2001) noted, among many other problems, a lack of a control or even a comparison group. In response to criticisms, Callahan, repeating his assertion that TFT is hard science, stated:

In light of the findings discussed in this series of articles, clinical psychologists must consider what conditions or circumstances obviate the need for a control group. I propose that for any treatment with a 75% success rate or above, a control group is not required to know something is taking place. (Callahan, 2001, p. 1256)

We disagree. Why do we need well-designed RCTs that use valid assessment measures, even in cases where there is at least a 75% success rate? This question is well worth taking the time to explore, given that many clinical social workers who select interventions based on clinical experience rather than on evidence from RCTs may share Callahan's belief. There are a number of reasons. First of all, we need to consider how "success rate" is assessed and defined. Callahan's primary definition of treatment success is an immediate and complete reduction in self-reported subjective units of distress (SUD; Wolpe, 1969), without doing any follow-up (Callahan & Callahan, 2000; Callahan & Trubo, 2001). No

standardized assessment measures are employed pretreatment to determine whether the individual actually had the condition being treated,
and no standardized assessment measures were administered following
the treatment. Another major problem with Callahan's "success rate" is
that only cases considered to be successful were selected for Callahan's
report in the journal in the first place (McNally, 2001); hence, of course,
he had a very high "success rate!"

Moreover, Wolpe's SUD scale was intended to be used to measure
process, but was not intended to be used as an ultimate outcome measure (Lohr, 2001). Subjective reports can be too easily influenced, and this
is especially the case with the repeated measures taken with TFT, typically before treatment and then after each sequence of tapping points is
performed. Constantly asking a person to report his or her level of distress can introduce expectancy into the self-report of the client. This is
evident in some of the audiotapes of Callahan treating his own clients.
For example, in one audiotape (Callahan, 1994) made publicly available,
Callahan is treating a woman via the radio who reported she was diagnosed with depression and who felt that conventional treatments had
not helped her. Following employing the tapping sequence, the woman
reported that her distress level was unchanged. Callahan questioned
her report, asking her whether she was sure, and it is evident from listening to the tape that he talked her into reporting a lowered distress
level by repeatedly questioning her initial reports. This tape provides a
vivid illustration of the power, not of TFT, but of demand characteristics
in influencing a client's self-report.

Another reason why TFT proponents believe they have such a high
success rate is their use of ad hoc explanations to explain away treatment failures (see Chapter 1). Callahan defines cure as an immediate
complete relief from subjective distress, regardless of how long that
effect lasts. If a person's report of complete relief of distress does not
hold up over time or if the person does not respond to a treatment at all,
he insists that this is always due to the person having come into contact
with a toxin, something the person ingested or inhaled that undid the
effect of the treatment (Callahan & Callahan, 2000). A toxin can be an
ordinarily healthy, commonly eaten food. If a person does not respond
to the treatment, clothing and anything in the immediate environment
are tested as potential toxins. Toxicity testing, in TFT, has *nothing* to do
with legitimate medical or environmental screening for allergens or
toxic substances. On one training audiotape (Callahan, 1998), during a

VT session where a client failed to respond to a treatment for his pain from an injury, Callahan's testing of the client's clothing resulted in the client, who was in a room by himself, needing to remove all of his clothing, piece by piece, while Callahan repeatedly asked him for his SUD level. Of course, such repeated requests can result in demand characteristics inducing expectancy in the client, who in this case was completely naked, or an exhausted or bored client may feel compelled to report a lowered SUD level just to get the session to end. Toxins are tested through muscle testing or VT, and neither method has undergone proper testing for reliability or validity.

Randomized controlled studies, particularly studies that compare TFT to a placebo or ideally a sham treatment, are needed to control for no specific treatment effects, demand characteristics, and placebo effects. Comparing TFT to a no-treatment control group can control for a phenomenon such as change due to the passage of time and regression to the mean (extreme states tend to normalize), but cannot control for the demand characteristics of the situation or placebo effect. More recently, another series of uncontrolled case reports was published (Sakai, Connolly, & Oas, 2010) in a proprietary journal owned by proponents of critical incident stress debriefing (CISD; discussed in the previous chapter). Participants were Rwandans who were suffering from the aftereffects of trauma. It is unstated in the report (but true) that the study was funded by the Association for TFT (ATFT) although the therapist or authors did disclose that they practiced and trained people in TFT. The report presents a series of 50 case studies. Interestingly, the therapists employed a within-subject's control condition of diaphragmatic breathing and progressive relaxation, but chose not to report those data, claiming that this design was improvised at the last minute and inadequate for such a report. Essentially, what they present are, once again, uncontrolled case reports. A description of the TFT intervention with a 15-year-old girl, who at the age of 3 years had witnessed her father's brutal murder and reported having flashbacks every day for the past 12 years, is indicative that the benefit obtained may have been due to the TFT therapists doing what is essentially exposure therapy:

> As we added tapping on the specific acupuncture points to her telling of the story, her heart-wrenching sobbing and depressed affect suddenly transformed into smiles...Then I directed her back to the feelings when she thought about

what happened in the church...The girl started crying again as she remembered seeing other people being killed...We continued to work through each of the traumatic events using the same tapping protocol. She cried upon re-experiencing each of the horrors she witnessed while hiding outside with another young child. After about 15 or 20 minutes focusing and treating the intense disturbing affect brought up by this and a number of other scenes, she started laughing. (Sakai et al., 2010, p. 50)

The description states that she was seen over the next 2 days while these traumatic events were worked on, and in the follow-up description, the authors indicated that participants continued to treat themselves, tapping whenever they were triggered. This indicates that the initial therapy did not permanently eliminate the trauma and that what they were doing amounted to self-exposure, the results likely having nothing to do with tapping and everything to do with exposure. Clearly, this is not the elimination of a trauma within a few minutes that is claimed by TFT proponents and, applying Occam's Razor, the results obtained can be more simply adequately explained by the empirically supported principle of exposure. Additionally, by the authors' own admission, the relaxation and controlled breathing sessions became confounding variables in the study, rather than the controls they had originally been intended to be, because the original design using these as comparison conditions was not executed, nor were the results of these comparison conditions reported.

Videos posted on the ATFT website showing 400 Rwandan orphans singing to welcome the therapists make it evident how well received and highly revered the TFT therapists were by the Rwandan community, which would have included those they trained (see www.atft-foundation.org/previous-projects/project-rwanda.html). Although the well-meaning TFT proponents who presented this video found it moving, this presents a strong possibility of contagion of enthusiasm for the treatment that may well have influenced results. Even though it could well be argued that such participation would be in keeping with cultural traditions and hence appropriate, it also may influence study results. For this reason, as one TFT critic of an earlier study conducted in Kosovo suggested (Rosner, 2001), TFT would be better tested first in the country and culture where it was developed and marketed, the United

States of America, before it is taken to the scenes of various disasters in other countries where performing well-designed controlled clinical trials is all but impossible.

A controlled study with a no-treatment, wait-list control group (treated with TFT 2 weeks later) and treatment was carried out by Rwandan therapists trained by ATFT therapists was published in this same proprietary journal (Connolly & Sakai, 2011). What would have been a better design, which was not employed, was if the Rwandan therapists had been trained to use both actual TFT points and sham TFT points, and not told which were which. The sequences could then have been employed on a control group who did not know what the correct points were supposed to be, thus producing a double-blind experiment. However, such an experiment has yet to be conducted. The closest to such an experiment have been two experiments, one with VT (Pignotti, 2005) that employed sham sequences and produced no difference between treatment and control groups, and an independent experiment using TFT (Waite & Holder, 2003) that compared groups that tapped on sham points, tapped on a doll, and used real EFT points and found no differences. In other words, doing TFT on a *doll* in the presence of the client produced the same modest positive effects as actually tapping on the client's body. It strains credulity beyond belief to contend that TFT meridian points, tapping, algorithms, and toxicity testing have any scientific legitimacy. Thus far, we have no reason to conclude that the positive effects of TFT or EFT have anything to do with the treatments themselves.

In spite of the considerable problems with the claims of tapping therapies, a psychologist who runs a business related to these therapies managed to publish a second more extensive review in a major American Psychological Association (APA) journal where he identified 18 randomized controlled trials for tapping therapies (Feinstein, 2012). This review contained the same weaknesses that we have previously noted. Of the 18 studies, 10 employed only a wait-list or no-treatment control group, and the remainder employed control conditions of relaxation, diaphragmatic breathing, an inspirational talk by a coach, and supportive therapy, none of which control for what they claim to be the reason for its effectiveness, tapping on energy meridian points on the body. The only study where EFT was compared to an empirically supported treatment was one that employed cognitive behavioral therapy (CBT) for test anxiety, but because there were only five participants in each group, this would severely limit the ability to do adequate statistical analysis. Some of the studies included by Feinstein were "in press" and impossible to submit to an independent review or critique. This review reiterates our earlier conclusion that methodologically sound controlled study that compares a tapping therapy to a control group that employs shamtapping points has yet to yield positive results.

## NEUROLINGUISTIC PROGRAMMING

Neurolinguistic programming (NLP) was developed in the 1970s by John Grinder, a linguist, and Richard Bandler, a computer programmer and mathematician. NLP is based on modeling (Bandler & Grinder, 1979). Modeling, in NLP terms, means to find people who are excellent at whatever it is that one wants to model and then study the structure of how they are able to do what they do. Bandler and Grinder, who were initially interested in studying people who were considered excellent communicators and therapists, studied the work of Milton Erickson, known as the grandfather of hypnosis, Fritz Perls, the founder of gestalt therapy, and Virginia Satir, who was a well-known clinical social worker and family therapist.

While observing the work of Satir, Bandler and Grinder noticed that she was especially good at gaining rapport, empathizing, and effectively communicating with her clients; they also noticed that as she achieved rapport with her clients, she matched their body language, as well as their usage of language. For example, if the client was using visual terms, she would use visual terms and if the client was using auditory terms, she would use auditory terms. Bandler and Grinder (1975, 1976) theorized that each person had a primary representational system that was visual, auditory, or kinesthetic. For example, visual people would use mostly visual language, for instance, *I see what you mean*, while auditory people would tend to say *I hear you*, and a kinesthetic person would say *That feels right to me*. NLP proponents believe that matching the most used sensory representational system will enable a person to gain good rapport with an individual. They applied this technique to psychotherapy, as well as to other professions such as sales and to personal areas such as the ability to attract members of the opposite sex. Any area where it is advantageous to gain influence over another is one where it is said that NLP may be used. Additionally, Bandler and

Grinder claimed to have found an association between eye movements and representational systems. A typical visual person, they claim, looks up and to the left when remembering an event, an auditory person would move eyes from side to side, whereas a kinesthetic person would look down and to the right.

NLP is frequently described as a pragmatic system, and most proponents have make claims on the basis of informal experimentation and their own experience rather than on well-designed research. However, as NLP became more popular, some research was conducted and reviews of such research have concluded that there is no scientific basis for its theories about representational systems and eye movements (Heap, 1988; Sharpley, 1987). Sharpley noted that NLP proponents had attempted to explain these negative results away by maintaining that the researchers did not properly understand NLP. Sharpley's response was:

> The basic tenets of NLP have failed to be reliably verified in almost 86% of the controlled studies, and it is difficult to accept that none of these 38 studies (i.e., those with nonsupportive, partial, or mixed results) were performed by persons with a satisfactory understanding of NLP (or at least enough of an understanding to perform the various procedures that were evaluated). If it is true that there are data in the clinical files of proponents of NLP that support it in a way different from the experimental data reviewed, then these need to be published and examined according to the traditional methodological yardsticks of experimental and evaluative literature. (Sharpley, 1987, p. 105)

In the more than 20 years that have elapsed since the aforementioned article, to date there is no convincing empirical evidence on the efficacy of NLP. This is perhaps not surprising if you consider the position of one chapter devoted to NLP that appeared in a very influential social work treatment textbook (Angell, 1996, p. 499)—"Theoreticians and practitioners of NLP view scientific inquiry to be the antithesis of the subjective systematic client-centered view of their approach." NLP has also penetrated the social work journal literature (Zastrow, Dotson, & Koch, 1986) and a Google search of "NLP" and "LCSW" reveals a large number of social work practitioners making use of this approach. NLP is also uncritically included in the latest edition of *The Social Work*

*Dictionary* (Barker, 2014, p. 290), published by the National Association of Social Workers, which lends an aura of legitimacy to this pseudoscientific approach.

Bandler, Grinder, and other proponents of NLP have developed such a wide array of techniques of various kinds that it is difficult to evaluate NLP as one, unitary intervention. Some of the techniques may work, not because of any property unique to NLP, but because of properties they have in common with empirically supported therapies such as exposure therapy or CBT. In the 1990s, one particularly popular NLP technique called visual–kinesthetic dissociation (VKD) became the focus of an investigation of four novel therapies for trauma that came to be known as power therapies (Carbonell & Figley, 1999). We now turn to a discussion of these so-called power therapies, and the social influence processes and culture that surround them.

## THE CULTURE OF POWER THERAPIES

The term *power therapy* is said (Devilly, 2005) to have originated on an Internet list server where novel unsupported interventions for trauma were being discussed and promoted. Four novel therapies (which are also used for many conditions other than trauma) in particular were selected for study by Carbonell and Figley (1999). The four therapies, all of which we have discussed previously in this or the previous chapter, are eye movement desensitization and reprocessing (EMDR), TFT, traumatic incident reduction (TIR), and VKD. VKD, an NLP technique, is basically a form of imaginal exposure whereby the person is instructed to visualize a traumatic experience as if the person is in a movie theater, watching himself or herself, watching the movie of the trauma as if it were on a movie screen. After viewing the trauma from that perspective, the person is then instructed to reassociate to the experience and view the experience from a variety of different perspectives, which is believed to be therapeutic. The study of these four therapies, however, was not designed to be a comparison study or an outcome study and, thus, it could not provide adequate empirical support for any of these approaches.

The term *power therapy* has since been more broadly used to include a number of different, novel, unsupported therapies, the proponents of which make extravagant, unsupported claims of being superior to existing supported interventions (Devilly, 2005). Devilly and others have pointed out that the factors that they do have in common that could explain the success reported are imaginal and real-life gradual exposure, along with a cognitive component, all elements of empirically supported therapies for trauma. To date, there is no reason to believe that there is anything especially powerful or unique about any of these power therapies that would warrant the claims being made.

If there are such mundane explanations for these power therapies, one may wonder how is it, then, that they appear to be so compelling and exciting to so many mental health professionals. What would motivate an intelligent, well-educated person to invest so much time and money in learning such practices while possibly neglecting empirically supported practices? What makes them seem so special? Just what is all the fuss about? This may best be explained in terms of social influence processes. What these so-called power therapies do provide us with is examples of how pseudoscientific approaches are developed and promoted and the culture of highly enthusiastic and zealous proponents that has developed around them.

Understanding how power therapies can be related to the nine social influence strategies outlined by Pratkanis (1995) can greatly help us to understand how these cultures came to be. Herbert et al. (2000) and Devilly (2005) have discussed these strategies in relation to these power therapies. Pratkanis outlined nine such characteristics that we discuss, which culminate in the development and marketing of a pseudoscience that results in seducing and attracting even some highly intelligent and well-meaning people. These include (a) phantom goals; (b) rationalization trap; (c) source credibility and sincerity; (d) creating a granfalloon; (e) use of self-generated persuasion; (f) construction of vivid appeals; (g) the use of prepersuasion; (h) the use of heuristics (mental shortcuts taken by human beings) and commonplaces (beliefs that society widely holds); and (i) attacking critics with innuendo and *ad hominem* if all else fails. We will examine each one of these and how it is used in the promotion of power therapies.

1. *Phantom goals* are goals that most people would view as highly desirable yet have not been attained thus far. For example, the complete elimination of all aftereffects of trauma for all people suffering from PTSD would be a phantom goal. Shapiro's early claims included a 100% success rate for EMDR (Shapiro, 1989). Callahan, too, makes

claims of very high success rates of up to 97% for his most advanced level, VT, for the complete elimination and cure of a wide variety of different types of problems (Callahan & Callahan, 2000). TFT proponents have recently extended this to a goal of eliminating suffering worldwide, by traveling internationally to the scenes of various disasters or poverty-stricken countries such as Africa and claiming to eliminate not only emotional distress but also to successfully treat physical conditions such as malaria by using TFT (Spiegel, 2006). The goal of complete elimination of all human suffering worldwide is obviously a very compelling one to many social workers.

2. *Rationalization trap* is a very frequently used marketing tactic in the promotion of a number of pseudoscientific approaches where the practitioner makes a fast commitment to and investment in an approach and, thereafter, in the interest of consistency and the minimization of cognitive dissonance, explains away any conflicting evidence, thus rationalizing maintaining the commitment. Because changing their minds can lead people to be viewed by others as wishy-washy, people are compelled to stay with their commitments, even when there are sound reasons to change their minds. Practitioners who invest in EMDR's or TFT's proprietary trainings may fall prey to rationalization traps. One of us (Pignotti, 2007) has described a personal experience of how this happened. When I first tried TFT and witnessed what I believed at the time were very powerful results that I attributed to the treatment itself, I made some very public postings that went out to hundreds of mental health professionals on the Internet. I quickly gained Callahan's favor, invested a great deal of time and financial resources in training to the highest level, and came to be considered one of the top proponents of TFT. At that point, having such a public profile, I was in a position where it was very difficult for me to consider any contradictory information and, thus, as many TFT proponents do, I rationalized and explained it away, all the while being unaware that I was doing so. I had conducted a controlled study on VT, but in discussing the results with Callahan, had initially explained these results away as well. There came a time, however, when the contradictions became so numerous and obvious to me that I was unable to ignore them any longer, and because I was fortunate to get my hands on some information that explained these sorts of dynamics in relation to pseudoscience (Lilienfeld, Lynn, & Lohr, 2003), I was finally able

to realize my errors and publish the results of my study (Pignotti, 2005).

3. *Source credibility and sincerity* have to do with the creation of a charismatic guru who is often regarded as the scientific genius who made the alleged breakthrough discoveries being marketed. Repeated public assertions are made in promotions and, in modern times, on the Internet that the person is regarded as an internationally acclaimed or leading expert or researcher in his or her field. The term *expert* is bandied about quite a bit on the Internet. Unlike genuine experts, such gurus often claim to be researchers yet have no studies published in peer-reviewed journals and *internationally acclaimed* can mean that they have followers in foreign countries rather than any substantial achievements. Arguments from authority (e.g., I am an expert and you are not) are often made that lack substance. The advocates of pseudoscientific or bogus therapies often claim academic credentials that they exaggerate or simply lack. Advertisements for Richard Bandler's speaking tours and one book said that he had a PhD (which he did not). Francine Shapiro's PhD is from a now-defunct graduate program, the Professional School of Psychological Studies (San Diego, CA), which was never recognized by any federal accreditation organization and the PhD program itself was not accredited by the APA.

   Such gurus are often described by followers as humanitarians and organizations are set up that do "humanitarian" work by delivering pro bono therapy to impoverished people or people who have been victims of disasters. This way, if anyone accuses them of being in it only for the money, they can point to their "humanitarian" efforts and even accuse critics of being against helping orphans, starving people, or whoever is the focus of such efforts. One of us (MGP) was accused on the Internet of being against helping orphans because I had criticized a certain therapist who claimed to have a highly effective intervention for his lack of evidence. My response to such an accusation was that there was no evidence that his intervention did, in fact, help orphans. For all we knew, it may be harming orphans. The image of the charismatic therapy guru as a humanitarian has historical precedents as well. Franz Mesmer also offered pro bono services to poor people, tying them to allegedly specially magnetized trees (McNally, 1999).

4. *The creation of a granfalloon*, a term coined by Vonnegut (cited in Herbert et al., 2000), which means a creation of a meaningless but proud association among human beings. The creation of a granfalloon is essentially a new social identity in which the member can take pride. Joining such an association and taking on such an identity can appeal to a person's need to feel special and part of an elite organization. We can readily observe that a number of the approaches we discussed, including EMDR, TIR, NLP, and TFT, have their own associations along with their own training and certification programs consisting of levels that allow them to use various titles. Participants who complete the various levels receive impressive-looking certificates that they can frame and put on the walls of their offices alongside their diplomas (if they have any), and the people trained to the highest levels have special status within the organization and may be regarded with awe. Such organizations typically restrict anyone other than officially approved trainers from teaching the material, leading to the ability to make exclusive claims. Although some legitimate organizations also have certifications and training standards, the difference is that pseudoscientific organizations make such designations when there is no scientific basis to assume that an "approved" use of the method would be superior to an "unapproved" use.

5. *Use of self-generated persuasion* is considered to be one of the most powerful tactics (Pratkanis, 1995) used in advertising and also in the promotion of pseudoscientific practices. This tactic is used in the creation of multilevel marketing businesses, such as Amway or Mary Kay, where the consumer becomes the salesperson. Although not multilevel organizations, clients of many of the interventions we have been discussing may become motivated to train to become practitioners. For example, one of the top proponents of TIR has written two enthusiastic testimonials on how it had worked for her as a patient, when ordinary exposure therapy had reportedly not worked as well (Bisbey, 1990, 2005). Following that, she went to graduate school, got a PhD, and did her dissertation on a favorable outcome study that compared TIR to exposure therapy, although this was never published in a peer-reviewed journal. In NLP trainings, participants work in small groups and learn the various techniques by doing them on one another, which often leads to positive experiences that convince the participants to get further involved. Similarly, when people are

trained in Scientology, they are paired up with another person and apply the techniques to one another and part of the course completion process, always writing a success story.

6. *Construction of vivid appeals,* especially in the form of testimonials and success stories, is very commonly used in the promotion of pseudoscientific practices and examples that can easily be obtained within minutes by surfing the Internet. A few vivid appeals can have much more persuasive power than examining statistical evidence, which is often viewed as dry and boring. For example, a TFT blog tfttraumarelief.wordpress.com contains numerous videos and written accounts containing vivid testimonials and anecdotes on everything from treating Haitian earthquake survivors, Mexican flood victims, Rwandan orphans, survivors of genocide, 9/11 survivors, a cougar-attack victim, fireworks burn injuries, to the treatment of celebrity Whoopi Goldberg for her fear of flying and even the treatment of a sick dog.

7. *Prepersuasion* is a way of setting things up, so regardless of what transpires, the favored intervention always comes out on top. Pratkanis (1995) outlined three steps for accomplishing this. The first step is that the people doing the promoting are the ones to frame and establish the nature of the issue. There is a saying in politics that the person who frames the issue wins the debate and so it is with anything one wishes to promote. For example, if an intervention wants a humanitarian image, they can talk about how they are helping orphans and the issue becomes about altruism rather than about whether the intervention itself has any evidence to support its efficacy. The second step is to set expectations. Pratkanis (1995) used the example of subliminal tapes, half of which were labeled as subliminal and half of which were not and how they were labeled determined the subjects' reports of improvement. Similarly, homeopathic remedies, if one believes in them, can have effects on people, depending on how they are labeled. The third step is for the promoter to be the one to specify which criteria are used in making decisions. For example, by Callahan defining cure as an immediate self-reported complete elimination of subjective distress, regardless of how long the effects last, this enables him to claim many "cures" that would not normally have been considered such.

8. *Taking advantage of heuristics and commonplaces.* Heuristics are simple rules that we can use as shortcuts. Given the large amounts of information we, as human beings, have to deal with on a day-to-day basis it is only natural for us to be attracted to using heuristics. One commonly used heuristic is the scarcity heuristic. We tend to believe that if something is rare, it is valuable. A common advertising ploy used in the promotion of pseudoscience and elsewhere is when advertising a seminar or workshop, state that space is very limited and filling up fast, so do not delay, register *now*! Another heuristic is the bandwagon or consensus heuristic, the tendency to believe that whatever the majority believes is correct. One way this can be accomplished is having introductory lectures for newcomers highly populated with people who are already true believers, giving the impression that large numbers of people find what is being promoted highly compelling. There is a phenomenon on the Internet known as sock puppetry, where it is not even necessary to recruit many individuals to provide endorsements. One person can post under multiple identities, known as sock puppets, giving the impression that large numbers of people agree when really it is only one person's opinion.

   A commonplace is a widely held belief that is, nevertheless, false or not completely true. For example, many alternative medical approaches are promoted based on the widely held assumption that something natural is always good for you, ignoring the fact that there are poisons, such as arsenic, that are completely natural. The mental health profession has many commonplaces, such as the common myths that we discussed in Chapter 1.

9. *Engage in attacks on critics with innuendo and ad hominem.* If all else fails and critics persist, engage in *ad hominem* attacks on critics. *Ad hominem* means attacking the person rather than addressing the issue. There are numerous examples of this and, with the advent of the Internet, such attacks can go viral (multiply and spread very quickly). This is something with which both of the present authors have had personal experience. After one of us (MGP) began engaging in criticism of various attachment therapies, proponents, in retaliation, began an all-out smear campaign on the Internet that at times has included both of us. I have been called a quack, a kook, a cultist, a terrorist, a criminal, a religious bigot, a prostitute, and

many other highly undesirable names, simply because I chose to criticize and expose abuses done in the name of certain attachment therapies. Author and Harvard psychologist and researcher Susan Clancy, who wrote a book (Clancy, 2009) that provided scientific evidence regarding incest survivors that flew in the face of beliefs that were commonplace among certain self-proclaimed trauma specialists, was unjustifiably attacked as being a pedophile on the amazon.com review page of her book. Earlier similar attacks on Clancy for her research got so virulent that she stated in one interview aired on WNYC in New York (available on YouTube: www.youtube.com/watch?v=Y-hQNBXqjaI) that she ended up deciding to leave the United States and move to Nicaragua, where she currently is faculty in a Harvard-based program, to get away from the constant harassment to which she has been subjected. Clearly, exposing and criticizing pseudoscience or conducting research that results in findings that threaten a pseudoscientist's vested interest can come with a price for the critic. However, we are of the opinion that the price of not criticizing pseudoscientific practices is even higher, especially for the people our profession is trying to help.

## SEXUAL ORIENTATION CHANGE EFFORTS FOR GAYS AND LESBIANS

Finally, we would be remiss if we did not include an area where the social work profession has, commendably, been at the forefront of exposing and strongly condemning bogus, harmful practices directed toward lesbians, gays, and bisexual individuals in an effort to change their sexual orientation. The National Association of Social Workers (NASW) has issued a position statement (NASW, 2000) clearly condemning the practices of reparative or conversion therapies as being in violation of the NASW *Code of Ethics*, as these are harmful practices and amount to discrimination based on sexual orientation. Its statement also points out that although such interventions are claimed to be scientific, they are not, because studies adduced in support of these approaches had serious methodological flaws, such as lack of a control group, very small sample sizes of less than 15 per treatment group, and biased samples. This indicates that such therapies fit the classic definition of pseudoscience.

More recently, following controversy, such therapies have been described with the broader term, sexual orientation change efforts (SOCE). An APA task force on appropriate therapeutic responses to sexual orientation (2009) conducted a systematic review of the literature on SOCE and concluded that these practices are unlikely to be successful and are potentially harmful. Nevertheless, some individuals with religious views that forbid gay and lesbian people from engaging in same-sex relationships attempt to either change their sexual orientation or have them live a life of complete celibacy that their religion may demand.

Although we, as social workers, are ethically obligated to respect both a person's sexual orientation and refrain from discrimination against their religious views, we also need to refrain from engaging in any intervention that has been shown to be ineffective, particularly one that could potentially do more harm than good. The APA Task Force reviewed studies that found that aversive conditioning used as SOCE (including inducing nausea, vomiting, administration of electric shocks, and other painful methods, paired with the individual's arousal to same-sex stimuli) unsurprisingly was particularly harmful with negative side effects of depression, suicidality, anxiety, and loss of sexual feeling and had high dropout rates. Even with nonaversive SOCE, there were individuals who reported that they felt they have been harmed. Over the last 10 years, individuals who sought SOCE were predominantly men who belong to conservative religions that forbid the practice of same-sex relationships.

Recently, a survey was conducted on the SOCE of 1,612 current or former members of one such conservative religious tradition, the Church of Jesus Christ of Latter Day Saints (LDS), who identified as gay, lesbian, or bisexual (Dehlin, Galliher, Bradshaw, Hyde, & Crowell, 2014b). Based on self-reported outcomes of such efforts, while a few participants reported reduction of depression and anxiety and acceptance of same-sex attractions, the overwhelming majority reported that actual efforts to change sexual orientation were ineffective or damaging. When quality of life was measured with standardized assessment, those who had been excommunicated or resigned from the church and were living in a gay- or lesbian-committed relationship reported a significantly greater quality of life, higher level of self-esteem and lower levels of internalized homophobia, sexual identity distress, and depression than those who remained affiliated and reported that they were active in the church and were attempting to live celibate or in a mixed-orientation (heterosexual) marriage (Dehlin, Galliher, Bradshaw, & Crowell, 2014a). Therefore, even though there are benefits to religious affiliation, for this sample, the harm produced by SOCE or refraining altogether from engaging in a relationship outweighed these benefits. Although this was a survey rather than an outcome study, these results with a large sample support earlier evidence that SOCE is ineffective and can even be harmful.

Although some of the more extreme organizations that have employed painful aversive conditioning methods to change sexual orientation have recently shut down, some of the newer organizations that appear to be less radical still encourage those who seek their assistance to live celibate, attempt to live in a heterosexual marriage, or even explicitly attempt SOCE, but are more subtle about saying so, due to controversy. They also continue to deny the existing evidence of the biological origin of same-sex attraction and believe homosexuality is a choice of lifestyle.

Although our own survey (Pignotti & Thyer, 2012) showed that less than 1% of our LCSW participants reported using reparative therapy, in areas with a greater concentration with fundamentalist religious traditions, the percentage may be higher and even a low percentage could represent perhaps hundreds of licensed mental health professionals who are still using these methods. Often, such organizations claim that they achieve desired results, through the use of testimonials and success stories, with scant empirical evidence that these approaches do no harm and are effective.

We have covered a great deal of territory in this chapter and these are but a few of the many pseudoscientific approaches currently being promoted. It would take several volumes to cover them all, but we have tried to select interventions widely used by social workers that serve as exemplars for the many being promoted. We hope that our descriptions of these interventions along with the means by which they are promoted and cultures of pseudoscience are established will be helpful to our readers in learning to recognize a questionable intervention when they see one promoted.

# REFERENCES

American Psychological Association Task Force on Appropriate Therapeutic Responses to Sexual Orientation. (2009). *Report of the task force on appropriate therapeutic responses to sexual orientation*. Washington, DC: Author.

Angell, G. B. (1996). Neurolinguistic programming theory and social work treatment. In F. J. Turner (Ed.), *Social work treatment* (4th ed., pp. 480–502). New York, NY: Free Press.

Bandler, R., & Grinder, J. (1975). *The structure of magic I*. Palo Alto, CA: Science and Behavior Books.

Bandler, R., & Grinder, J. (1976). *The structure of magic II*. Palo Alto, CA: Science and Behavior Books.

Bandler, R., & Grinder, J. (1979). *Frogs into princes*. Moab, UT: Real People Press.

Barker, R. L. (Ed.) (2014). *The social work dictionary*. Washington, DC: NASW Press.

Beutler, L. (2001). Editor's introduction. *Journal of Clinical Psychology, 57*, 1149–1151.

Bisbey, L. B. (1990). A psychologist looks at metapsychology. *Newsletter of the Institute for Research in Metapsychology, 3*(4).

Bisbey, L. B. (2005). From psychology to metapsychology: A clinician's journey. In V. R. Volkman (Ed.), *Traumatic incident reduction: Research and practice* (pp. 31–42). Ann Arbor, MI: Loving Healing Press.

Callahan, R. J. (1994). *Treating depression* [Audiotape]. La Quinta, CA: TFT Training Center.

Callahan, R. J. (1997a). The case of Mary: The first TFT case. *Traumatology, 3*, 30–37.

Callahan, R. J. (1997b). *Videotape: Introduction to TFT*. La Quinta, CA: TFT Training Center.

Callahan, R. J. (1998). *Supervisory session: Recalcitrant pain, toxins, apex (depression with algorithm) for professional use only* [Audiotape]. La Quinta, CA: TFT Training Center.

Callahan, R. J. (2001). Thought field therapy: Response to our critics and a scrutiny of some old ideas of social science. *Journal of Clinical Psychology, 57*, 1251–1260.

Callahan, R. J., & Callahan, J. (2000). *Stop the nightmares of trauma*. Chapel Hill, NC: Professional Press.

Callahan, R. J., & Trubo, R. (2001). *Tapping the healer within*. Chicago, IL: Contemporary Books.

Carbonell, J. L., & Figley, C. (1999). A systematic clinical demonstration of promising PTSD treatment approaches. *Traumatology, 5*, 32–48.

Clancy, S. (2009). *The trauma myth*. New York, NY: Basic Books.

Connolly, S., & Sakai, C. (2011). Brief trauma intervention with Rwandan genocide-survivors using thought field therapy. *International Journal of Emergency Mental Health, 13*, 161–172.

Craig, G. (1997) *EFT: Emotional freedom techniques: A universal aid to healing*. Retrieved September 22, 2010, from http://www.eftuniverse.com/

Dehlin, J. P., Galliher, R. V., Bradshaw, W. S., & Crowell, K. A. (2014a, April 25). Psychosocial correlates of religious approaches to same-sex attraction: A mormon perspective. *Journal of Gay & Lesbian Mental Health.* Advance online publication. Retrieved from http://dx.doi.org/10.1080/1 9359705.2014.912970

Dehlin, J. P., Galliher, R. V., Bradshaw, W. S., Hyde, D. C., & Crowell, K. A. (2014b, March 17). Sexual orientation change efforts among current or former LDS Church members. *Journal of Counseling Psychology.* Advance online publication. Retrieved from http://dx.doi.org/10.1037/cou0000011

Devilly, G. J. (2005). Power therapies and possible threats to the science of psychology and psychiatry. *The Australian and New Zealand Journal of Psychiatry, 39,* 437–445.

Feinstein, D. (2008). Energy psychology: A review of the preliminary evidence. *Psychotherapy, 45,* 199–213.

Feinstein, D. (2012). Acupoint stimulation in treating psychological disorders: Evidence of efficacy. *Review of General Psychology, 16,* 364–380.

Heap, M. (1988). Neurolinguistic programming: An interim verdict. In M. Heap (Ed.) *Hypnosis: Current clinical, experimental and forensic practices* (pp. 268–280). London: Croom Helm.

Herbert, J. D., & Gaudiano, B. A. (2001). The search for the holy grail: Heart rate variability and thought field therapy. *Journal of Clinical Psychology, 57,* 1207–1214.

Herbert, J. D., Lilienfeld, S. O., Lohr, J. M., Montgomery, R. W., O'Donohue, W. T., Rosen, G. M., & Tolin, D. F. (2000). Science and pseudoscience in the development of eye movement desensitization and reprocessing: Implications for clinical psychology. *Clinical Psychology Review, 20,* 945–971.

Imrie, R., Ramey, D., Buell, P., Ernst, E., & Basser, S. (2001). Veterinary acupuncture and historical scholarship: Claims for the antiquity of acupuncture. *Scientific Review of Alternative Medicine, 5,* 133–139.

Imrie, R., Ramey, D., Buell, P., Ernst, E., & Basser, S. (2003–2004). Veterinary acupuncture and historical scholarship: The traditions of acupuncture and TCM. *Scientific Review of Alternative Medicine, 7*(2).

Lilienfeld, S. O., Lynn, S. J., & Lohr, J. M. (2003). *Science and pseudoscience in clinical psychology.* New York, NY: Guilford Press.

Lohr, J. M. (2001). Sakai et al. is not an adequate demonstration of TFT effectiveness. *Journal of Clinical Psychology, 57,* 1229–1235.

McNally, R. J. (1999). EMDR and Mesmerism: A comparative historical analysis. *Journal of Anxiety Disorders, 13,* 225–236.

McNally, R. J. (2001). Tertullian's motto and Callahan's method. *Journal of Clinical Psychology, 57,* 1171–1174; discussion 1251.

National Association of Social Workers. (2000). *Position statement: Reparative or conversion therapies for lesbians and gay men.* Washington, DC: Author.

Pignotti, M. (2005). Thought field therapy voice technology vs. random meridian point sequences: A single-blind controlled experiment. *The Scientific Review of Mental Health Practice, 4,* 38–47.

Pignotti, M. (2007). Thought field therapy: A former insider's experience. *Research on Social Work Practice, 17,* 392–407.

Pignotti, M., & Thyer, B. A. (2012). Novel unsupported and empirically supported therapies: Patterns of usage among licensed clinical social workers. *Behavioural and Cognitive Psychotherapy, 40,* 331–349.

Pratkanis, A. R. (1995). How to sell a pseudoscience. *Skeptical Inquirer, 19,* 19–25.

Robb, M. (2003, December issue). Thought field therapy at your fingertips. *Social Work Today,* 20–23.

Rosner, R. (2001). Between search and research: How to find your way around? Review of the article "Thought Field Therapy—Soothing the bad moments of Kosovo." *Journal of Clinical Psychology, 57,* 1241–1244.

Sakai, C. E., Connolly, S. M., & Oas, P. (2010). Treatment of PTSD in Rwandan child genocide survivors using thought field therapy. *International Journal of Emergency Mental Health, 12*(1), 41–49.

Shapiro, F. (1989). Efficacy of the eye movement desensitization procedure in the treatment of traumatic memories. *Journal of Traumatic Stress, 2,* 199–223.

Sharpley, C. F. (1987). Research findings on neuro-linguistic programming: Nonsupportive data or an untestable theory. *Journal of Counseling Psychology, 34,* 103–107.

Spiegel, A. (2006, March 29). *Unorthodox therapy raises concern in New Orleans* [Radio broadcast]. On *All Things Considered,* National Public Radio.

Waite, W. L., & Holder, M. D. (2003). Assessment of the emotional freedom technique: An alternative treatment for fear. *Scientific Review of Mental Health Practice, 2*(2), 20–26.

Walther, D. (1988). *Applied kinesiology: Synopsis.* Pueblo, CO: Systems DC.

Wolpe, J. (1969). *The practice of behavior therapy.* New York, NY: Pergamon Press.

Zastrow, C., Dotson, V., & Koch, M. (1986). The neuro-linguistic programming treatment approach. *Journal of Independent Social Work, 1*(1), 29–38.

# CHAPTER 6

# Pseudoscience in Developmental Disabilities

Professional social work has a long history of service to persons with developmental disabilities and their families, with service spanning, believe it or not, three centuries (see Adams, 1963; Bruno, 1936; Hesselschwerdt, Sherman, Smith, & Sterling, 1957; Hiebert-Murphy, Trute, & Wright, 2008; Richmond, 1917; Robinson, 1928; Thyer & Kropf, 1995; Warner, 1898; Warner, Queen, & Harper, 1930). Social workers provide a wide array of services, including case coordination, eligibility determinations, family counseling and therapy, genetic counseling, the provision of supportive individual and group therapy to caregivers, information and referral, and direct clinical services, either as individual practitioners or as a member of an interprofessional team (Levy, 1995). At the more macro end of practice, social workers advocate for social policies to support persons with developmental disabilities and their families.

Social workers' input into clinical services imposes a particular responsibility, given our discipline's ethical standards (National Association of Social Workers [NASW], 1996), which mandate that we "should base practice on recognized knowledge, including empirically based knowledge" (p. 22) and "should critically examine and keep current with emerging knowledge relevant to social work and fully use evaluation and research evidence in their professional practice" (p. 25). The NASW *Code of Ethics* also asserts that we need to consult with colleagues who are incompetent and assist them in taking remedial action. If they do not, we are obligated to take actions through appropriate channels to address the incompetence (Standard 2.10—Incompetence of Colleagues, p. 18). As sound research has demonstrated that selected psychosocial interventions seem to be reasonably effective, and that certain other interventions either have little to no empirical evidence that they actually help clients with a disability or may actually engender harm to these persons, the ethical standards enumerated earlier take on a heightened salience (Barlow, 2010; Lilienfeld, 2007; Rhule, 2005).

Other disciplines such as psychiatry (Schechtman, 2007); pediatrics (American Academy of Pediatrics Committee on Children with Disabilities, 1998); speech–language pathology (Gravel, 1994); and psychology (Jacobson, Foxx, & Mulick, 2005) have expressed concern about the use of scientifically unsupported therapies in the treatment of individuals with developmental disabilities, but we are unaware of similar caveats directed to the social work profession, hence the present chapter. Such cautions are overdue for several reasons. One is the apparent proliferation of unsupported, frankly bogus and, in some instances, demonstrably harmful therapies provided by social workers to persons with disabilities and their families. Autistic disorder and other developmental disabilities seemingly lend themselves toward the creation and adoption of pseudoscientific assessment methods and interventions. There are several possible reasons for this, such as:

> Parents are typically highly motivated to attempt any promising treatment, rendering them vulnerable to promising "cures." The unremarkable physical appearance of autistic children may contribute to the proliferation of pseudoscientific treatments and theories of etiology. Autistic children typically appear entirely normal; in fact, many of these children are strikingly attractive...The normal appearance of autistic children may lead parents, caretakers, and teachers to become convinced that there must be a completely "normal" or "intact" child lurking inside the normal exterior...the course can vary considerably among individuals...there is a great deal of variability in response to treatments...persons with autism sometime show apparently spontaneous developmental gains or symptom improvement in a particular area for unidentified reasons. If any intervention has recently been implemented, such improvement can be erroneously attributed to the treatment, even when the treatment

is actually ineffective. In sum, autism's pervasive impact on development and functioning, heterogeneity with respect to course and treatment response, and current lack of curative treatments render the disorder fertile ground for quackery. (Herbert, Sharp, & Gaudiano, 2002, p. 24)

A second, more positive rationale to discuss pseudoscience in the context of social work with persons who experience developmental disabilities is the emergence in the past two decades of a number of psychosocial interventions of credible effectiveness in helping persons with these conditions, interventions that have not yet widely penetrated social work education and practice. The existence of demonstrable useful interventions makes warnings about ineffective therapies all the more pertinent. A third, less laudable, reason is to try and curtail another possibly shameful period of professional social work, akin to that of the complaisance of social workers with the eugenically based euthanasia programs of Nazi Germany before and after World War II (Kunstreich, 2003), and our discipline's embrace of eugenically inspired sterilization and institutionalization programs established in Europe and the United States in the early part of the 20th century (Hauss & Ziegler, 2008; LaPan & Platt, 2005). We believe that one reason why unsupported assessment methods and treatments are adopted by professional social workers is our discipline's general lack of training in critical thinking, and in particular, learning to recognize the characteristics of pseudoscientific theories and therapies. Prior chapters in this book reviewed some of these characteristics, and in this chapter, we describe a number of assessment methods and interventions currently being provided by social workers within the field of developmental disabilities, which we believe are unsupported, pseudoscientific, or more simply bogus.

A recent survey of licensed clinical social workers (LCSWs; Pignotti & Thyer, 2009a) revealed that three quarters of respondents reported having used at least one novel therapy that lacked evidential support and yet made unsupported claims, within the past year. Numerous examples of such practices by LCSWs can be found on the Internet, accompanied by unsupported claims, and this includes practices involving developmentally disabled individuals. However, social workers are not alone in this regard. A survey of teachers serving children with autism spectrum disorders (ASDs) in the state of Georgia (Hess, Morrier, Heflin, & Ivey, 2008) found that interventions with limited support, such as "floor time," "relational development intervention," "cartooning," and "power cards," could be found within that state's educational system, and interventions clearly "not recommended" and possibly dangerous such as "facilitated communication" and "holding therapy" were also being provided. A recent national survey of special educators found that "some practices with little empirical support... are reportedly used with some frequency, and special education teachers reported using ineffective approaches... as frequently as they did those approaches with a strong research base" (Burns & Ysseldyke, 2009, p. 3). Such interventions are widely provided to children with ASDs and other developmental disabilities, even though "most treatments have not been adequately studies and do not have evidence to support their use" (Levy & Hyman, 2008, p. 803). See also the survey of physicians conducted by Golnik and Ireland (2009) on the widespread use of complementary and alternative medicines (CAM) with this population. Subsequently, we describe a number of bogus or pseudoscientific therapies provided primarily to individuals with autism, but we could have included examples from a much wider array of disabilities because the provision of ineffective treatments is pervasive in the human services.

## PSEUDOSCIENTIFIC OR HARMFUL PRACTICES FOR AUTISM

Interventions being promoted for ASDs that lack scientific support and yet make bold claims are very common (Herbert et al., 2002; Jacobson et al., 2005). Herbert et al. (2002) noted a number of possible reasons for the vulnerability of this diagnosis to such approaches. First, such a diagnosis, typically diagnosed in the preschool years, is understandably often devastating and highly upsetting news for parents and such a diagnosis has an impact on all areas of a child's life. Because the etiology of autism is unknown and there is no cure, this renders parents vulnerable to those who make unsupported claims of a cure, thus providing them with the hope that modern science cannot yet offer.

Second, Herbert et al. (2002) note that the normal physical appearance of autistic children could lead parents and other caretakers to conclude that "there must be a completely 'normal,' 'intact' child lurking inside the normal exterior" (p. 24). This may leave them vulnerable to interventions such as facilitated communication (FC), which will be discussed subsequently. Finally, the ASDs are heterogeneous. That is, they present a wide variety of different symptoms and different degrees of severity, and there can also be a high degree of variability in the way individuals within the autism spectrum respond to various treatments. Also, individuals can experience spontaneous improvements not attributable to any particular intervention. If such an improvement occurs following an intervention, however, it is easy to incorrectly assume that the treatment was responsible. All of these factors can make ASD a fertile breeding ground for proponents of pseudoscientific interventions to step in and offer hope for a much desired cure.

## EEG Biofeedback or Neurofeedback for Autism

EEG biofeedback, also known as neurofeedback (NFB), is an intervention that is practiced by a number of health and mental health professionals, including LCSWs. NFB is a form of biofeedback where the person is hooked up to an EEG machine that measures the brain waves (Robbins, 2008). The electrodes can be placed on various areas of a person's scalp, depending on which part of the brain one intends to train. However, there is no actual evidence that where the electrodes are placed makes any difference in outcome. The person, while hooked up to the EEG, plays a game on the computer where he or she is rewarded with points and entertaining visual effects (e.g., a spaceship surging forward) for producing certain brain-wave patterns (e.g., those relating to focused attention or to being relaxed).

NFB was first used for neurologic conditions such as epilepsy and later its use was expanded to include children and adults with attention deficit hyperactivity disorder (ADHD; Robbins, 2008). Still later, applications were expanded to a variety of other problems, including autism. Much of the research published on NFB has been in the *Journal of Neurotherapy*, a journal that is operated by the proponents of this approach. One study published in this journal was a pilot study with a quasiexperimental design (e.g., nonrandom assignment to condition), of 12 children who received NFB and a comparison group of 12 children who did not, which showed a 25% improvement in autism symptoms, compared with only 3% improvement in the comparison group (Jarusiewicz, 2002). Another weak study was an uncontrolled pilot investigation (Scolnick, 2005) on 10 adolescent boys diagnosed with Asperger's syndrome. Half of the boys dropped out before study completion and the other half showed improved behavior, based on reports of parents and teachers. However, as the author notes, other factors such as maturation cannot be ruled out as causes of improvement in this study. Kouijzer, deMoor, Gerrits, Buitelaar, and van Schie (2009) report 12-month follow-up results of a randomized controlled trial (RCT) involving 14 children with ASD, with seven receiving real NFB and seven assigned to a waiting-list condition. Improvements in social behavior and some elements of cognitive functioning were observed in the NFB group, relative to the waiting-list group. The small sample size makes it difficult to generalize these results, but this study does illustrate good-faith efforts to empirically examine the potential efficacy of NFB in the area of autism services.

More recent studies have not improved the evidentiary or clinical rationale for providing NFB for persons with autistic spectrum disorders, ADHD, or other developmental disabilities. One review (Holtman et al., 2011) titled "Neurofeedback in Autism Spectrum Disorders" bluntly concluded that "the existing evidence does not support the use of neurofeedback in the treatment of ASD" (p. 986). Another concluded that "the safety of NF treatment has not been thoroughly investigated in youth or adults" (Hurt, Arnold, & Lofthouse, 2014). A well-controlled randomized trial found that "no statistically significant reductions of symptoms of ASD were observed...EEG biofeedback seems to be an applicable tool to regulate EEG activity and has specific effects on cognitive flexibility, but it did not result in significant reductions of ASD" (Kouijzer, van Schie, Gerrits, Buitelaar, & de Moor, 2013, p. 17).

In spite of the scant evidence for the efficacy of NFB for autism, promotion in the form of uncontrolled case reports and testimonials is widespread on the Internet, accompanied by explanations that have little, if any, scientific support. For instance, one video (EEG Spectrum, 2009) shows a practitioner of NFB claiming that autism is a condition in which the right brain does not learn in the first year of life how to calm itself down and one that can be remedied by teaching the child to calm the right brain through NFB. On this same video, a parent makes a very telling statement that there is no medical model for autism and that NFB "fills that hole." A simple Google search by the reader using "LCSW" and "neurofeedback" will disclose the many social work practitioners using this therapy for persons with ASDs and other development disabilities. This is way ahead of the evidence curve, hence not currently a recommended practice, and qualifies as a pseudoscientific intervention.

The potential for NFB to ultimately demonstrate its clinical efficacy is illustrated by a recent RCT of this intervention (Gevensleben et al., 2009), which did obtain promising results for children ($N = 59$), compared to a control condition ($N = 35$), with ADHD. Independent replication of such effects is eagerly awaited, but until these are forthcoming, social workers and other providers of services to persons with autism and other developmental disabilities should be aware of the weak amount of evidence supporting this intervention with such youth.

## Autism and Other Developmental Disabilities Among Adopted Children

Longitudinal studies have been conducted on internationally adopted children (Rutter, Kreppner, & O'Connor, 2001; Rutter et al., 2007) who were subjected to conditions of severe neglect and deprivation early in life. A subset of these children initially exhibited developmental delays and disability, and some have exhibited symptoms that resembled those of autism, particularly if they were adopted late, meaning that they had spent the first 2 or more years of their lives in orphanages where they were severely deprived and neglected. Nevertheless, an intervention where some of the children were randomized into a group that received improved care (Smyke, Dumitrescu, & Zeanah, 2002) showed that great progress could be made, just by moving the child to an environment where he or she received more individualized attention and caregiving.

Moreover, although a small subset of the children continued to have problems, developmental catch-up has been observed to occur over time in many children with initial problems (Rutter, O'Connor, & English and Romanian Adoptees Study Team, 2004) resulting in considerable improvement without any particular intervention other than the fact of having been adopted. Although attachment problems have sometimes been believed to be the source of a number of developmental problems among late adoptees, Rutter and O'Connor found no association between disorganized attachment problems and cognitive impairment. Unlike typical autism in children who were not subjected to such conditions of neglect and deprivation, the autistic symptoms exhibited when a child was first adopted tended to abate on their own with the passage of time—again, without any particular intervention. Rutter and O'Connor further noted that the problems among these adopted children were not irreversible for the majority of this population.

However, the writings of certain clinicians who work with populations of internationally adopted children give a different impression. One such clinician is psychologist Ronald Federici, who has an individual with an LCSW on his staff who presents with him and has promoted an intervention (Federici, 2003) for older adopted children that lacks empirical support. In an article posted on his website that is currently accessible on the Internet (Federici, 1999) although he notes the possibility of maternal biological and genetic factors as well, he views these children's problems largely as attachment problems with a neurodevelopmental basis.

Federici (1999) has urged that such children receive "immediate and aggressive neuropsychological and neurodevelopmental evaluations for all children, particularly the older, postinstitutionalized child" (para. 4) rather than adopting a wait-and-see attitude. He characterizes these children's problems as a "neuropsychologically-based attachment disorder" (para. 12), and further claims that many of the children have developed autistic-like symptoms that exist, along with mental retardation, due to the developmental delays. Regarding the autistic-like symptoms (which he refers to as institutional autism), his theory is that:

> As a child's memory of the few positive experiences of life gradually fades away, he or she may regress to the most infantile (safe) stages of development. This regression can ultimately lead to a very infantile and autistic state in which the child exhibits an emotionally detached and preoccupied personality structure and presentation which is virtually indistinguishable from classic autism. (para. 18)

Federici further notes that these children do not appear to look their age, and it is often difficult to distinguish their gender.

More recent evidence has examined the well-being of orphaned and abandoned children raised in a traditional orphanage, with similar children raised in residential family settings. This well-designed study used a random sampling methodology to assess cognitive functioning, emotion, physical health, growth, and behavior among 1,357 institution-living children and 1,480 children living in more normal community homes. These authors concluded that "this study does not support the hypothesis that institutional care is systematically associated with poorer wellbeing than community care for OAC (orphaned and abandoned children) aged 6–12" (Whetten et al., 2009, p. e8169). This is not to say that orphanage care is desirable, only that there should not be any default assumption that children raised in institutional environments are necessarily damaged relative to being possibly raised in community settings.

To help the postinstitutionalized child, Federici recommends what he describes as an innovative treatment for older adopted children who present with "a pattern of cognitive and emotional delays as a result of extended institutionalization with questionable, co-morbid brain dysfunction" (para. 30). He claims to have "developed a therapeutic family program which has been found to be highly effective but yet controversial in comparison to more traditional family therapy approaches" (para. 35).

Federici outlines this family program in detail in his self-published book (Federici, 2003). The program, which is recommended for use after other more traditional approaches have failed, is carried out in the child's home with the child's family and has three phases. During the first phase, which is to last at least 4 to 8 weeks, the child must remain within 3 feet of a parent at all times during the waking hours. Federici recommends to "keep [the child] home from school, if necessary" (p. 103) and that the child be involved only with the parents and that "your child is not allowed to have any type of extraneous distractions such as television, radio, video games or time with other friends or siblings" (p. 104). He notes "I like to compare it to boot camp" (p. 104).

The most controversial part of the program is the "therapeutic holds" he recommends. He notes that the purpose of these holds is not the same as those used by proponents of holding therapy, which take a calm child and seek to evoke rage, which he believes retraumatizes the child and hence he does not recommend. Federici recommends two types of holds in this phase. The Sequence 1 hold is "designed for safety and security and should be instituted when a child is actively out of control or unmanageable" (p. 109). The sequence hold is not restricted to times when a child is a physical danger to himself or herself; it can be used any time a child is disobedient or verbally out of control as well. In other words, holding is used as a punitive disciplinary technique to exact compliance from the child, not a method used to ensure the child's safety. For example, in a demonstration of this on a television episode of *Dateline NBC*, where Federici appeared and featured the family of an adopted child, this hold was initiated after the mother asked the child to go to the bathroom and the child had responded that he did not have to go to the bathroom. The restraint was initiated, even though the child was sitting on the bed with his mother and, although defiant, did not appear to be presenting any kind of immediate physical threat at the time the restraint was initiated. Some of the restraints displayed on this video were said to have lasted for hours. A diagram of the holding technique is provided in Federici (1999, p. 111) that shows both parents sitting or laying on top of the child and the instructions state, "it is very important for the child to lie face down during the therapeutic hold to prevent spitting, biting or direct eye contact" (p. 112). Federici recommends that these holds be videotaped because "viewing the tape step-by-step during later role playing is extremely helpful and serves as a powerful intervention" (p. 113). Although no known deaths have occurred specific to Federici's intervention, the potential for harm from the use of this prone restraint technique is well documented, and deaths have occurred even when used under strictly supervised conditions and done "correctly" (Mohr, Petti, & Mohr, 2003). Although Federici claims that this hold has been used in some residential programs, we were unable to find any evidence for the safety and efficacy of such an approach. The use of such holds has been controversial in the so-called therapeutic boarding schools, residential settings, and boot camps, as well as where serious harm has been documented well (Szalavitz, 2006).

The Sequence 2 hold is claimed to be a more gentle hold to promote reconnection with the parent, although again, there is a lack of evidence other than testimonials, that it accomplishes this. Also part of Phase 1 is the assignment of the child to do "hard labor" so that the child can "re-learn the concept of hard work, commitment and task completion" (p. 117). Phase 1 also includes role-plays, behavioral rehearsal, mutual storytelling, and therapeutic games. The remaining two phases, while the child is still being strictly supervised, involve giving the child increasing choices and time spent apart from the family and also employs token and point systems. Although the token and point systems of this intervention do have empirical support, the more aggressive aspects of this intervention do not, and although Federici has claimed that he aims for an 80% improvement rate, to date there is no research in the form of randomized controlled studies to support that this does indeed occur, that this intervention is better than no intervention at all, or even that the program is safe and does no harm. Given the description and diagrams of the Sequence 1 hold, there is cause for concern regarding the lack of testing of this intervention.

This intervention strikes us as similar in intent and procedure to the harsh restraining techniques depicted in the 1994 film titled *The Madness of King George* (see www.youtube.com/watch?v=fgZvg7SR_DE). In it, the behaviorally disruptive King George III is told by his physician "Very well, if Your Majesty will not behave, he must be restrained." The King is then grabbed by attendants, tightly bound into a high-backed chair, and gagged, while the physician recites the list of offenses that will result in his being so restrained, including being rude, complaining and cursing, not having an appetite, and so on. After some time under restraint, during which the King appeared calm, he was released. On the smallest infraction of noncompliance, disobedience, or abberant behavior, the King was unceremoniously picked up and rebound to the chair for a prolonged period of time. Verbal outbursts resulted in gagging. This process was repeated for days. Soon the King acted more normally while unbound, with the doctor controlling the King's initial appearance of a potentially odd behavior via the doctor by gently clearing his throat and giving the King a meaningful glance as a warning sign.

There are certainly circumstances where restraint is needed to ensure the child's safety and its use requires considerable expertise and training. Resources are available for this purpose (see www.qbscompanies.com/site/index.php?option=com_content&view=article&id=53&Itemid=56), but the use of such restrictive techniques to promote simple unquestioning obedience is inappropriate and possibly unethical. Moreover, recent programs to reduce the use of seclusion and restraint and ideally eliminate such practices altogether, such as the Substance Abuse and Mental Health Services Administration's (SAMHSA's) initiative, have shown that restraints are much less frequently needed for safety than most people may realize; when triggers are identified, clients learn what calms them down, staff learn sensitivity to individuals with a history of trauma and abuse, de-escalation techniques are used, and other empirically supported behavioral approaches are implemented

(SAMHSA, 2005). SAMHSA also found that contrary to the popular belief that restraints promote safety, when restraints were reduced and alternatives implemented to prevent their necessity, incidents of violence and harm actually went down.

## "Energy" Therapies

Energy therapies are therapies that theorize that a system of subtle energy exists surrounding the human body and that healing can occur when this system is stimulated in various ways (e.g., acupuncture needles, finger tapping, stroking, touching). Such stimulation is believed to result in balancing and/or removing blocks from the system, resulting in healing from a variety of different ailments, including mental health problems (Callahan & Trubo, 2001; Feinstein, 2008). It is claimed that tapping on specific bodily points functions in a manner analogous to hitting the "delete" key on a computer's keyboard, causing a software program to disappear. Nevertheless, there has not been any convincing scientific evidence that such an energy system exists or that it is the mechanism of action for any success reported with such therapies (Pignotti & Thyer, 2009b).

Two of the most popular energy therapies are thought field therapy (TFT; Callahan & Trubo, 2001) and its offshoot, emotional freedom technique (EFT; Craig, 1997). TFT and EFT, which are carried out by finger tapping on specific purported acupressure points, have made claims to cure or help a wide variety of different types of problems, including developmental disabilities. For example, two LCSWs trained in TFT and EFT (Radomski & Altaffer, 2009) have developed a treatment described called *Ask and Receive*, which is specifically designed to treat people with autism. Radomski and Altaffer believe that:

> The primary cause of autism is an environmental/toxic insult to a genetically sensitive individual occurring between conception and three years of age. There are a large number of potential environmental causes ranging from viruses, bacteria, physical trauma, toxic exposure or profound allergic response which can act together or individually to provide the original insult to the brain of a sensitive individual. (Radomski & Altaffer, 2009, para. 3)

Additionally, the EFT website (www.emofree.com) contains a number of anecdotes, claiming profound changes in autism, using EFT. For example, one of the many testimonials claims in its title, "Mom doing EFT for autistic son yields enormous changes in one month" (Craig, n.d., para. 1). A videotaped testimonial on TFT on a TFT blog claimed that this procedure relieved an autistic boy's fear of water (Cowley, 2009).

A recent national survey of LCSWs in the United States (Pignotti & Thyer, 2009a) revealed that 5.9% of respondents reported having used EFT in the past year and 2.4% reported having used TFT. Although these are not very large percentages and the sample might not necessarily be representative of all LCSWs, these still could potentially represent hundreds of LCSWs using TFT or EFT in their practices, techniques lacking any credible evidence that they help clients. Again a Google search using "LCSW" and "TFT" or "EFT" quickly reveals the surprising extent to which clinical social workers are advertising the provision of energy therapies in their practice.

## Animal-Assisted Therapies

Animal-assisted therapies are therapies that use nonhuman animals, where the client being treated interacts with an animal, via a facilitator. Two of the most popular animal-assisted therapies that are being used on individuals with autism, Asperger's syndrome, or other developmental disabilities are dolphin-assisted therapy (DAT) and equine-assisted psychotherapy (EAP), also known as equine-assisted therapy. A search on the Internet using these terms reveals that a number of LCSWs are involved with delivering these approaches.

According to Lynn Thomas, LCSW, who is a cofounder of the Equine Assisted Growth and Learning Association (EAGALA), EAP is believed to work because:

> Horses react to our body language. This gives incredible and immediate feedback to what people are communicating nonverbally. Participants learn that if they want to change the horse's behavior, they have to change their own behaviors, thoughts, and feelings. It is powerful because it is more than just talking, it is doing! (Thomas, 2002, para. 5)

However, no empirical evidence is offered to support this theory, nor did a database search on relevant terms in relation to autism or developmental disabilities reveal any randomized clinical trials published in peer-reviewed journals that support claims being made for the efficacy of EAP. For example, one LCSW (Smith, n.d.) claims that "EAP is a powerful and effective approach that has an incredible impact on individuals, youths, families and groups" (Smith, n.d., para. 4). Another website (Equine Therapy for Children with Asperger's and Autism, n.d.), promoting EAP and also bovine-, canine-, and elephant-assisted therapies for people with autism and Asperger's syndrome claims that these approaches can help children be calmer, more focused, improve motor skills, and improve their social interaction. Again, no empirical evidence is offered to support these claims.

DAT, an approach where children and sometimes adults, swim and interact with dolphins, has also become very popular as an intervention for individuals with autism and other developmental disabilities. Claims have been made (Nathanson, 1998; Nathanson, deCastro, Friend, & McMahon, 1997) that DAT on children with severe disabilities increases attention span and motivation and improves language skills, does so better and more rapidly than conventional therapies, and that the results hold up over time. Nevertheless, reviews of the studies conducted on DAT (Marino & Lilienfeld, 1998, 2007) have concluded that the empirical evidence does not support the claims being made, due to the serious methodological flaws and threats to internal and external validity found in the existing literature. Marino and Lilienfeld also point out that evidence exists for injuries sustained during DAT as well as the risk of infections and parasitism, which raise serious concerns about the safety of this approach, for both the human's and the dolphin's welfare.

The University of Denver Graduate School of Social Work hosts an Institute for Human–Animal Connection, and offers a certificate in animal-assisted social work (see www.du.edu/socialwork/programs/msw/concentration/certprograms/aaswcertificate.html). Articles have been written (e.g., Tedeschi, Fitchett, & Molidor, 2005) about integrating content on animal-assisted therapy within the social work curriculum, again, without credible data that these interventions yield significant benefits to persons with disabilities. Now the absence of evidence (that animal-assisted therapy is helpful) is not equivalent to concluding that there is evidence of absence (inferring that it is not helpful). But we believe that unusual claims require unusual evidence and it is incumbent upon the promoters of animal-assisted treatment to empirically demonstrate the effectiveness of their techniques, preferably prior to providing them to the fee-paying public. Our concerns about animal-assisted therapy do not extend to more plausible collaborations between the field of social work and veterinary science. The University of Tennessee Colleges of Social Work and Veterinary Medicine offer a specialization in veterinary social work. The focus is on helping clients make decisions about euthanizing their pets, providing grief counseling to bereaved pet owners, and using companion animals to provide stress reduction and support to clients (for prisoners, persons experiencing posttraumatic stress disorder, the perpetrators of violence, nursing home residents, etc., see utcvmfs1 .vet.utk.edu/VSW/Default.aspx). However, there are no exaggerated claims regarding the ability of animal-assisted therapies to produce curative or even significant lasting improvements in intelligence, social skills, or behavioral dysfunctions among persons with developmental disabilities. This seems to us a more legitimate and professional approach to the integration of animals within social work practice.

## Electroconvulsive Therapy

Electroconvulsive therapy (ECT) involves briefly passing a powerful electric current through a person's brain, a current applied through external electrodes usually attached to the forehead. ECT is often provided through facilities that make use of interprofessional treatment teams, including social workers. One of the authors (BAT) assisted in a session of ECT while he was serving in the U.S. Army, and the technique has been recommended in at least one article appearing in the social work literature (Katz, 1992). A number of articles have been published describing its use in treating individuals with developmental disabilities. One case study reported on a 69-year-old woman with mental retardation who received ECT due to her continuous screaming, described as a problem because it caused "considerable distress to other residents and staff" (Snowdon, Meehan, & Halpin, 1994, p. 1). Following ECT, the continuous screaming was markedly diminished. On the other side of the vocalization spectrum, ECT was provided to a 16-year-old girl who suffered from autistic disorder and catatonia (e.g., a *lack* of speech). In this case, a regimen of ECT was followed by an *increase* in speech (Wachtel,

Kahng, Dhossche, Cascella, & Reti, 2008). An 8-year-old boy who met the *Diagnostic and Statistical Manual of Mental Disorders* (*DSM-IV-TR* edition; American Psychiatric Association, 2000) criteria for autistic disorder received 15 sessions of ECT in an attempt to reduce his self-injurious behavior (head banging; Wachtel et al., 2009), with a reported reduction in head banging from about 109 times per hour to about 19. One recent article concluded that "multiple published reports demonstrate the safety and efficacy of ECT in pediatric patients with a wide range of psychopathology. ECT has also been successfully used in youth with autism and other neurodevelopmental disabilities who present with catatonic deterioration" (Wachtel, Dhossche, & Kellner, 2011, p. 395). The evidence for this assertion? In this article, it consisted of two brief case vignettes, which had been previously published. Now, the problems involved in relying on anecdotal evidence have been previously noted in this book, and it seems ludicrous to make such far-reaching conclusions and recommendations on such slender evidentiary reeds, particularly when the treatment, ECT, is of such an extreme nature. We cannot help but note that this article by Wachtel et al. (2011) appeared in *Medical Hypotheses*, a nonblind peer-reviewed journal known for its commitment to publish radical ideas likely to be rejected by more conventional journals. Still, when nonresearch-minded clinicians, parents, or caregivers come across such "evidence," these assertions may be uncritically accepted as having appeared in a "medical" journal, and thus inferred to be legitimate.

It is distressing to see ECT for persons with developmental disabilities such as ASD continuing to be promoted within the professional literature (Dhossche & Wachtel, 2004, 2013; Mazzone, Postorino, Valeri, & Vicari, 2014; Wachtel & Dhossche, 2012, 2013; Wachtel & Shorter, 2013). Although the use of ECT on persons with dysthymic disorder (DD) is not widespread, social workers could find themselves in the position of having some influence on such treatment decisions. In particular, they could appropriately insist on having a thorough review of the evidence of the effectiveness of this treatment prior to it being implemented, this of course being a significant component of the process of evidence-based practice. Second, social workers could work to ensure that other less intrusive or aversive psychosocial treatments are given legitimate trials prior to ECT being implemented. For example, catatonia and inappropriate vocalizations have often been found to respond very well to positive behavioral interventions (e.g., Fuller, 1949; Underwood, Figueroa, Thyer, & Nzechoa, 1989; Underwood & Thyer, 1990). Given the possible negative sequelae to ECT, such as memory loss and brain damage, it would certainly seem incumbent on health care providers to offer their clients with a developmental disability less aversive treatments with a stronger empirical foundation. A further proactive role that social workers could provide is to insist that any course of ECT provided to a client with a developmental disability be delivered in the context of a single-case research design, wherein a baseline of valid data on the behavioral measures of interest, anticipated to be impacted by the ECT, is collected prior to beginning ECT, with such measures being conducted daily through the ECT regimen and thereafter. This practice of empirically evaluating treatment outcomes is also an important component of evidence-based practice and one which social workers could take the lead in providing.

## Mercury, Autism, and the Antivaccination Movement

In 1998, the prestigious journal *The Lancet* published a study claiming that autism was caused by providing small children with a common series of vaccinations used to prevent measles, mumps, and rubella (MMR; Wakefield et al., 1998). Specifically, it was contended that a mercury-based preservative used in such vaccines (and now no longer used) caused autistic disorder. This initial article generated considerable controversy and much concern among parent groups, including those with children with a serious developmental disability, as well as parents in general. A flurry of follow-up articles claimed to support this hypothesis, and others did not, and Dr. Wakefield and his research were the focus of a *60 Minutes* television program segment in the United States. Regrettably, a strong antivaccination movement has arisen that significantly impacted the proportion of children receiving the MMR and other vaccines (e.g., safeminds.org), resulting in measles and other preventable childhood diseases making a comeback among British and North American children and being responsible for a number of deaths. Recently, a British medical panel concluded that Dr. Wakefield had significant financial and scientific conflicts in completing his original article (e.g., his work was paid for by lawyers for parents seeking to sue vaccine makers; and he himself had patented a measles vaccine that could be used in lieu of the MMR vaccination regimen, had it been withdrawn; his study had not been approved by a human subjects board). This led *The Lancet* to retract his article (The Editors, 2010) completely, a very rare action. In addition, a 2012 Cochrane Collaboration systematic review on the role of vaccines and autism found no credible evidence that the former causes the latter (Demicheli, Rivetti, Debalini, & Di Pietrantonj, 2012). Social workers are often in a position to influence parents to obtain recommended vaccinations for their children (Copeland, 1996), and the failure to vaccinate children clearly places them at risk of contracting serious and sometimes deadly illnesses. It is important that social workers be accurately informed as to the evidence, and lack thereof, relating to childhood vaccinations and autism, so that they can share this information with parents and aid them in making medically accurate decisions about the health care regimens provided to their children. Wray et al. (2009) provide an example of an RCT evaluating vaccine safety messages provided to patients, and finding that such information promoted more accurate beliefs about vaccine safety and effectiveness. This study is notable in that one author is affiliated with a prestigious school of social work.

## Facilitated Communication

FC is a technique aimed at helping nonverbal/nonwriting persons with autistic disorder and other intellectual disabilities communicate in writing. The method consists of having a "facilitator" sit next to the client, and hold or support the client's wrist, while the client's hand is suspended over a keyboard. The keyboard may be an electronic device or a simple panel with letters of the alphabet printed on it. The theory behind FC is that many persons with a developmental disability have otherwise normal brains, but are locked in bodies that do not allow them to normally express themselves. Having a facilitator "support" the client's hand is said to enable the client to somehow accurately point to letters in sequence, and spell out words and sentences, thus effectively establishing communication. This is said to occur among persons with disabilities previously not known to have learned the alphabet, spelling, the elements of grammar, or to talk, a truly remarkable claim! FC was introduced into the United States in the early 1990s (it originated in Australia years earlier), and rapidly became a popular method of teaching persons with developmental disabilities because of the apparently strikingly positive results it achieved in enabling the nonverbal to communicate, and display previously unknown intellectual skills.

FC workshops trained literally thousands of human service professions (including social workers), parents, and caregivers in this technique. A FC Institute was established at Syracuse University, a newsletter emerged, and a large number of professional journal and popular magazine articles extolled the remarkable successes this method had. Many behavioral scientists were disturbed at the rapid proliferation of FC, given the lack of controlled evidence that it really "worked." Further troubles emerged when some persons with a disability, communicating through their facilitator, alleged horrific experiences of physical and sexual abuse at the hands of their parents and other caregivers. This raised the issue within the legal and child protective service systems of the legitimacy of the FC-elicited writings, and soon a series of single-subject and then large group design outcome studies employed the obvious technique of testing FC by having the client and facilitator observe stimuli (pictures, small objects) and then ask the client to identify what was seen. Sometimes, the facilitator saw what the client saw, and sometimes they saw different things. Bottom line—in almost every case, it was shown that clients were *not* capable of accurately writing when the facilitator did not know what the client had seen. In other words, FC was simply an elaborate version of the ouija board effect, wherein the facilitator was (usually unwittingly) guiding the responses/writing of the client. A typical outcome of controlled investigation of FC is reported in Montee, Miltenberger, and Wittrock (1995, p. 1): "The results showed that the clients typed the correct answer only when the facilitator had access to the same information, never typed the correct information when the facilitator had no information or false information, and typed the picture or activity presented to the facilitator when it was different from the one experienced by the client."

Jacobson, Mulick, and Schwartz (1995) provide an excellent overview of the rise and relative fall of FC, portraying it as a textbook case of pseudoscience and antiscience infiltrating the human services, and experimental studies since that time have continued to support the hypothesis that the communications displayed in FC originate not with the client but with the facilitator (Mostert, 2001). In 1994, the American Psychological Association adopted a resolution on FC concluding that "facilitated communication is a controversial and unproved communicative procedure with no scientifically demonstrated support for its efficacy" (American Psychological Association, 1994, p. 1). A similar position from the American Academy of Pediatrics Committee on Children with Disabilities (1998, p. 1) reads "currently available information does not support the claims of proponents that these treatments (auditory integration training and facilitated communication for Autism) are efficacious. Their use does not appear warranted at this time, except within research protocols." This position was reaffirmed in February 2010. Nevertheless, FC continues to be promoted and training in it is provided to human service professionals, parents, and caregivers of individuals with developmental disabilities, primarily in the United States, via the Institute for Communication and Inclusion hosted by the College of Education at Syracuse University.

The earlier chapter in this book dealing with assessment described the more recent trials of a family whose father was accused of sexually abusing his teenage daughter who had autism. The social worker believed the allegations obtained from the facilitator, leading to the father's arrest, jail time pending investigation, and eventual release when it was shown that the facilitator was originating the girl's communications. The family has settled out of court for a settlement of more than $800,000. A stiff price for the county to pay the cost of an insufficiently critical attitude toward abuse allegations was obtained via this unsupported method. Simply by having a new facilitator unfamiliar with the abuse allegations to conduct the investigation could have disclosed whether or not the girl's charges were continued using a different person to help her type.

## Social Stories

Social stories are a seemingly benign intervention intended to teach social skills to children with autism and other developmental disabilities. The technique involves a therapist, parent, teacher, or caregiver sitting down with the child and helping the child describe an upcoming everyday social situation. The situation is described from the child's point of view and involves the verbal (and then behavioral) rehearsal of social interactions the child is expected to encounter. These stories are written by the therapist in the first person, in the present tense, and from the child's perspective. When completed, it is written out and placed in a booklet format. The therapist reads the story to the child several times and helps the child role-play the situation. The story should match the child's vocabulary and comprehension level. An example might be:

When we go to school

There will be many other kids there.

I will not know most of them.

They may look at me.

But that is OK.

Mom will help me meet them.

I will say hello.

Social stories are said to be most useful with children with basic language skills, and it is said that using these will help reduce anxiety and problematic behaviors, and increase social skills. This approach has been around for almost two decades (Gray & Garand, 1993). Wang and Spillane (2009) carefully examined all well-designed outcome studies on social skill interventions intended for children with autism, and social stories were among those approaches reviewed. They found a total of six such studies on social stories and all used multiple-baseline single-system designs with small numbers of participants. Social stories did not meet their criteria for being labeled an evidence-based intervention, and they concluded that "the effectiveness of Social Stories as an intervention for improving social skills is questionable" (Wang & Spillane, 2009, p. 318). Somewhat more positively, Kokina and Kem (2010) concluded, based on a comprehensive review of the empirical research on this approach, that "while Social Stories has low to questionable overall effectiveness, they were more effective when addressing inappropriate behaviors than when teaching social skills" (p. 812). This conclusion was based solely on a published single-subject studies.

Social stories would seem to be loosely based on well-established behavioral principles, establishing a relationship with a child, role modeling, verbal and behavioral rehearsal, shaping, social reinforcement for correct responding, and so on. However, its behavioral foundations seem largely unacknowledged by its proponents. Video modeling was determined by Wang and Spillane (2009) to have stronger evidentiary grounds as being highly effective in teaching social skills to children with autism. This approach uses videotapes to demonstrate desired and socially appropriate behaviors to the child with autism, with ample opportunity for rehearsal and praise to be provided. Some variants make videotapes of the child himself or herself displaying approximations of the desired social skills to demonstrate improvements and to compare the child's performance with that displayed on the training tape. See Boudreau and D'Entremont (2010) for another example of this approach with good results, evaluated using single-system designs. Leaf, Oppenheim-Leaf, Sheldon, and Sherman (2012) present experimental single-subject data for six children with autism, finding that social stories were considerably *less* effective than a simpler teaching interaction procedure. A review article (Styles, 2011) titled "Social Stories: Does the Research Evidence Support the Popularity?" found "Several areas of significant weakness in the body of literature which…need to be addressed through further research before EPs (educational psychologists) can recommend Social Stories as a stand alone intervention strategy in the confidence that it represents evidence-based practice" (p. 415).

## Psychoanalytic Theories

Psychoanalytic theories for autistic disorder are most commonly associated with the work of Bruno Bettelheim, who asserted that autism was caused by the infant's experiences with emotionally unavailable caregivers, the iconic "Refrigerator Mother." This etiological theory leads to a recommended treatment, the so-called parentectomy, consisting of removing the child from the home and placing him or her in institutional care, such as Bettelheim's Orthogenic School, in Chicago. The high cure rates claimed by Bettelheim (85%!) through treatment at his Orthogenic School failed to be substantiated, and stories of how children were physically abused there emerged after Bettelheim's death. Currently, most approaches to helping children with autistic disorder involved providing the families with the support and training needed to maintain the child in the home, not in institutional care, and using applied behavior analysis (ABA) as the treatment method. One contemporary psychoanalyst agreed that "intensive psychoanalysis is an inappropriate first-line treatment for autism" (Solms, 2013).

## Hyperbaric Oxygen Therapy

Hyperbaric oxygen therapy (HBOT) is based on the etiological hypothesis that the brains of persons with autistic disorder fail to receive enough oxygen due to diminished blood flow. Stemming from this unproven theory is HBOT, which involves placing the person with autism or another developmental disability in an expensive hyperbaric chamber, wherein the person breathes pressured air, which may or may not be enriched with oxygen. This added pressure is said to enhance blood and oxygen flow to the brain, resulting in improvements in intellect, social responsiveness, and behavioral problems (Rossignol, 2006; Rossignol & Rossignol, 2006). A recently published RCT assigned youths aged 2 to 14 years (mean of 6 years) with a diagnosis of AD to either real HBOT ($N = 18$) or to placebo HBOT ($N = 16$). This study used a double-blind condition wherein neither the youth nor the caregivers or study participants knew if they were receiving real HBOT or placebo HBOT, with placebo sessions in the hyperbaric chamber lasting the same amount of time as real HBOT (80 sessions within 15 weeks). Supplemental oxygen was provided in the real HBOT condition. Outcome measures were reliable and valid, and assessed social skills, cognition, parental stress levels, intelligence, bizarre and stereotypic actions, aggression, self-injury, and so on. What were the results? "No significant differences between the HBOT and placebo groups were found on any of the outcome measures...therefore HBOT at this dosage is not recommended for the treatment of ASD symptoms" (Granpeesheh et al., 2010). This is pretty damning, and consistent with the only other RCT conducted on HBOT (Rossignol et al., 2009). Yet, as Granpeesheh et al. (2010, p. 268) note, "Hyperbaric oxygen therapy (HBOT) is a commonly used treatment for ASD that has been increasing in prevalence in recent years." One recent national survey of the parents of children with ASDs ($N = 248$) found that 2% had used HBOT with their children (Christon, Macintosh, & Myers, 2010). Bent, Bertoglio, Ashwood, Nemeth, and Hendren (2012) reported on an open trial, uncontrolled evaluation of HBOT involving 10 children who received 80 sessions of the treatment. Improvements on a clinician-rated scale were observed, but as the authors noted the lack of a control group limited the ability to conclude that the HBOT caused these improvements, or if they were due to other factors, such as passage of time, clinician bias, placebo, or expectancy effects. A recent review article on the effects of HBOT on persons with autistic disorder by Dunleavy and Thyer (2014) concluded, "It is premature to call HBOT an effective treatment for Autism and ASD. Individuals clinically treated with HBOT outside the context of a RCT should have the effects of the therapy evaluated using rigorous single-subject designs" (p. 1).

The original reports proposing HBOT as a therapy for ASD and other developmental disabilities were published in a journal called *Medical Hypotheses*. Unlike most professional journals, this periodical does not use a blind peer-review process to screen its submissions, and it deliberately seeks cutting-edge content to appear within its pages, radical ideas that might be rejected by more conventional journals. Although it is good to encourage novel and speculative ideas, proposing brain oxygen deprivation as an etiology of ASD, and the promulgation of HBOT as a proposed therapy, have resulted in hundreds, perhaps thousands, of parents arranging for this now-tested and found to be ineffective treatment to be provided to their children. It is very expensive, and a judge in Florida ruled that Medicaid should not pay for it, because it is an experimental treatment (Miller, 2008). Lerman et al. (2008) indicate that HBOT treatment costs about $15,000 per person. The total national costs of HBOT to children, families, and caregivers are impossible to accurately calculate, but the study by Granpeesheh et al. (2010) effectively illustrates a major value of negative studies, in that a widely used treatment has been shown to *not* work. This is good to know, and social workers providing services to families with developmentally disabled children should be familiar with the evidentiary foundations (or lack thereof) of HBOT and other CAM so as to be in a better position to recommend (or not) possible courses of intervention.

The conclusion that HBOT is ineffective is, of course, like most scientific findings, a provisional one. Newer studies could emerge to overturn this negative finding. Such is the nature of scientific advances. We advocate a more cautious approach, however, to bridge the chasm between the promiscuous proliferation of unproven therapies and a radical skeptical view that nothing ever works. This middle ground is exemplified by the work of Lerman et al. (2008) who conducted three single-subject studies on children with autism. The baseline measurement of problem behaviors, academic performance, and communication skills was concurrently made for each child. Stable baselines were obtained and then HBOT was provided to one child after 20 days, and measures of the children's behavior continued on all three youth. The second child had HBOT initiated after 40 days, and therapy was begun on the third child after 60 days. It was hypothesized that if HBOT was genuinely effective, the first child would improve after receiving HBOT, and the second and third would remain unchanged, until they too began HBOT. In fact, there was no clear effect of HBOT for any of the youth, thus failing to support the hypothesis that HBOT would be an effective treatment for children with autism. Using single-system designs is an excellent way to test, at a relatively low cost compared to large-scale RCTs, potentially effective treatments. Failures to find positive effects with these small-scale studies could indicate that investigation should not be pursued, whereas positive results would suggest that larger scale group design experiments are worthwhile.

## MORE PROMISING APPROACHES

The psychosocial approaches to assessment and treatment we have described earlier, which some social workers are providing to persons with developmental disabilities and their families, are characterized by their relative lack of a sound theoretical foundation and a paucity of empirical support above the level of individual anecdotal claims. Moreover, some of these approaches make grandiose claims as to the scope and magnitude of their effectiveness, and some actively resist or disparage efforts to empirically evaluate their usefulness. In contrast to these approaches, the reader is encouraged to become familiar with alternative approaches that can be variously labeled as empirically sup- ported or evidence based. One of the more credible sources of infor- mation consists of systematic reviews commissioned by the Cochrane Collaboration (www.cochrane.org). On this web-based library, one can read completed reviews on topics such as *Auditory Integration Training and Other Sound Therapies for Autism Spectrum Disorder, Parent-Mediated Early Intervention for Young Children With Autism Spectrum Disorders,* or *Vaccines for Measles, Mumps and Rubella in Children.* Another recom- mended website is the What Works Clearinghouse, supported by the U.S. Department of Education (www.whatworks.edu.gov).

Among print resources (but frequently available online via university libraries) that can be very useful are Campbell, Herzinger, and James's (2008) chapter titled "Evidence-Based Therapies for Autistic Disorder and Pervasive Developmental Disorders"; Rogers and Vismara's (2008)

"Evidence-Based Comprehensive Treatments for Early Autism"; Pelham and Fabiano's (2008) "Evidence-Based Psychosocial Treatments for Attention-Deficit/Hyperactivity Disorder"; Yamamoto and Shibuya's (2009) "Evidence Based Supports for Persons With Developmental Disabilities: Contributions of Applied Behavioral Analysis"; Carr, Severtson, and Lepper's (2008) "Noncontingent Reinforcement Is an Empirically Supported Treatment for Problem Behavior Exhibited by Individuals With Developmental Disabilities"; Gustafsson et al.'s (2009) "Effects of Psychosocial Intervention for People With Intellectual Disabilities and Mental Health Problems: A Survey of Systematic Reviews"; and Koegel, Robinson, and Koegel's (2009) "Empirically Supported Intervention Practices for Autism Spectrum Disorders in School and Community Settings: Issues and Practices."

The approach known as ABA is one of the best supported theoretical and practice orientations in terms of being able to effectively assist young people with autism and their families. A recent comprehensive meta-analysis by Virues-Ortega (2010, p. 387) of 22 well-designed studies found that "results suggested that long-term, comprehensive ABA intervention leads to (positive) medium to large effects in terms of intellectual functioning, language development, acquisition of daily living skills and social functioning in children with autism." Parent training in behavior management and educational skill, either as a stand-alone intervention or as a component of early intensive behavior analytic intervention, also seems reasonably well supported as one effective approach to help improve the lives of young children and adults with autism and other developmental disabilities (Matson, Mahan, & Matson, 2009).

Fortunately, the field seems receptive to change along these lines. A recent study of attitudes toward adoption of evidence-based practice (EBP) conducted among early intervention providers found generally favorable views toward EBP, with the more experienced professionals reporting greater congruence between what they did in practice and the principles of EBP (Stahmer & Aarons, 2009). Parents, teachers, and administrators have also been found to strongly endorse the principles of EBP, when it comes to the topic of serving clients with autism and their families (Callahan, Henson, & Cowan, 2008). Thus, it may be that there will be less than anticipated resistance toward adopting a more empirically supported approach to services with the developmental disabilities community.

Obviously, there is much to offer social workers who wish to adopt the process model of evidence-based practice in their work with persons with developmental disabilities and their families. Acquiring skills in empirically supported treatments is one positive step. It is also important to be able to identify and inform potential clients about the lack of empirical support behind a very wide array of other psychosocial interventions. Both of these steps are consistent with professional ethical standards and we hope that this article contributes toward this process.

## NOTE

Portions of this chapter previously appeared in Thyer, B. A., & Pignotti, M. (2010). Science and pseudoscience in developmental disabilities: Guidelines for social workers. *Journal of Social Work in Disability and Rehabilitation, 9*, 110–129. Reprinted with the permission of Taylor & Francis, Publishers.

## REFERENCES

Adams, M. (1963). *The mentally subnormal: The social casework approach.* London, England: William Heinemann Medical Books.

American Academy of Pediatrics Committee on Children with Disabilities. (1998). Auditory integration training and facilitated communication. *Pediatrics, 102,* 431–433.

American Psychiatric Association. (2000). *Diagnostic and statistical manual of mental disorders* (4th ed., text rev.). Washington, DC: Author.

American Psychological Association. (1994). *Resolution on facilitated communication.* Retrieved February 15, 2010, from http://www.apa.org/divisions/div33/fcpolicy.html

Barlow, D. H. (2010). Negative effects from psychological treatments: A perspective. *American Psychologist, 65,* 13–20.

Bent, S., Bertoglio, K., Ashwood, P., Nemeth, E., & Hendren, R. L. (2012). Brief report: Hyperbaric oxygen therapy (HBOT) in children with autism spectrum disorders: A clinical trial. *Journal of Autism and Developmental Disorders, 42,* 1127–1132.

Boudreau, E., & D'Entremont, B. (2010). Improving the pretend play skills of preschoolers with autism spectrum disorders: The effects of video modeling. *Journal of Developmental and Physical Disabilities, 22,* 415–431.

Bruno, F. (1936). *The theory of social work.* New York, NY: D.C. Heath.

Burns, M. K., & Ysseldyke, J. E. (2009). Reported prevalence of evidence-based instructional practices in special education. *Journal of Special Education, 43,* 3–11.

Callahan, K., Henson, R. K., & Cowan, A. K. (2008). Social validation of evidence-based practices in autism by parents, teachers and administrators. *Journal of Autism and Developmental Disorders, 38,* 678–692.

Callahan, R. J., & Trubo, R. (2001). *Tapping the healer within.* Chicago, IL: Contemporary Books.

Campbell, J. M., Herzinger, C. V., & James, C. L. (2008). Evidence-based therapies for autistic disorder and pervasive developmental disorders. In R. G. Steele, D. T. Elkin, & M. C. Roberts (Eds.), *Handbook of evidence-based therapies for children and adolescents* (pp. 373–388). New York, NY: Springer.

Carr, J. E., Severtson, J. M., & Lepper, T. L. (2008). Noncontingent reinforcement is an empirically supported treatment for problem behavior exhibited by individuals with developmental disabilities. *Research in Developmental Disabilities, 30,* 44–57.

Christon, L. M., Macintosh, V. H., & Myers, B. J. (2010). Use of complementary and alternative medicine (CAM) treatments by parents of children with autism spectrum disorders. *Research in Autism Spectrum Disorders, 4,* 249–259.

Copeland, V. C. (1996). Immunization among African American children: Implications for social work. *Health and Social Work, 21,* 105–114.

Cowley, M. (2009). *TFT relieves autistic boy's terror of water.* Retrieved February 1, 2010, from http://tfttraumarelief.wordpress.com/2009/08/12/tft-relieves-autistic-boys-terror-of-water/

Craig, G. (1997). *EFT: Emotional freedom techniques: A universal aid to healing.* Retrieved February 16, 2010, from http://www.emofree.com/download-eftmanual.asp

Craig, G. (n.d.). *Mom doing EFT for autistic son yields enormous changes in one month.* Retrieved February 1, 2010, from http://www.emofree.com/Articles2/autism-improvement-lewis.htm

Demicheli, V., Rivetti, A., Debalini, M. G., & Di Pietrantonj, C. (2012). Vaccines for measles, mumps and rubella in children. *Cochrane Database of Systematic Reviews 2012,* Issue 2. Article No. CD004407. doi:10.1002/14651858.CD004407.pub3

Dhossche, D. M., & Stanfill, S. (2004). Could ECT be effective in autism? *Medical Hypotheses, 63,* 371–376.

Dhossche, D. M., & Wachtel, L. E. (2013). ECT for catatonia in autism. In N. Ghaziuddin & G. Walter (Eds.), *Electroconvulsive therapy in children and adolescents* (pp. 217–246). New York, NY: Oxford University Press.

Dunleavy, D. J., & Thyer, B. A. (2014). Is hyperbaric oxygen therapy an effective treatment for autism: A review. *Journal of Adolescent and Family Health, 6*(1), Article 5. Retrieved from http://scholar.utc.edu/jafh/

EEG Spectrum. (2009). *Neurofeedback and autism.* Retrieved January 2, 2010, from http://www.eeginfo.com/neurofeedback-videos-media.htm

Equine Therapy for Children with Asperger's and Autism. (n.d.). Retrieved February 15, 2010, from http://www.equine-therapy-programs.com/aspergers.html

Federici, R. S. (1999). *Neuropsychological evaluation and rehabilitation for the post institutionalized child.* Paper presented at the Conference for Children and Residential Care, Stockholm, Sweden. Retrieved January 3, 2010, from http://www.drfederici.com/post_child.htm

Federici, R. S. (2003). *Help for the hopeless child.* Alexandria, VA: Ronald S. Federici and Associates.

Feinstein, D. (2008). Energy psychology: A review of the preliminary evidence. *Psychotherapy: Research, Practice, Training, 45,* 199–213.

Fuller, P. R. (1949). Operant conditioning of a vegetative human organism. *American Journal of Psychology, 62,* 587–590.

Gevensleben, H., Holl, B., Albriech, B., Vogel, C., Schlamp, D., Kratz, O.,...Heinrich, H. (2009). Is neurofeedback an efficious treatment for ADHD: A randomized controlled clinical trial. *Journal of Child Psychology and Psychiatry, 50,* 780–789.

Golnik, A. E., & Ireland, M. (2009). Complementary alternative medicine for children with autism: A physician survey. *Journal of Autism and Developmental Disorders, 39,* 996–1005.

Granpeesheh, D., Tarbox, J., Dixon, D. R., Wilke, A. E., Allen, M. S., & Bradstreet, J. (2010). Randomized trial of hyperbaric oxygen therapy for children with autism. *Research in Autism Spectrum Disorders, 4,* 268–275.

Gravel, J. (1994). Auditory integration training: Placing the burden of proof. *American Journal of Speech-Language Pathology, 3*(2), 25–29.

Gray, C. A., & Garand, J. D. (1993). Social stories: Improving responses of students with autism with accurate social information. *Focus on Autistic Behavior, 8,* 1–10.

Gustafsson, C., Ojehagen, A., Hansson, L., Sandlund, M., Nystrom, M., Glad, J.,...Fredriksson, M. (2009). Effects of psychosocial intervention for people with intellectual disabilities and mental health problems: A survey of systematic reviews. *Research on Social Work Practice, 19*, 281–290.

Hauss, G., & Ziegler, B. (2008). City welfare in the sway of eugenics: A Swiss case study. *British Journal of Social Work, 38*, 751–770.

Herbert, J. D., Sharp, I. R., & Gaudiano, B. A. (2002). Separating fact from fiction in the etiology and treatment of autism. *The Scientific Review of Mental Health Practice, 1*, 23–43.

Hess, K. L., Morrier, M. J., Heflin, L. J., & Ivey, M. L. (2008). Autism treatment survey: Services received by children with autism spectrum disorders in public school classrooms. *Journal of Autism and Developmental Disorders, 38*, 961–971.

Hesselschwerdt, P., Sherman, H., Smith, S., & Sterling, M. (1957). Some basic considerations in social work with the mentally retarded. *American Journal of Mental Deficiency, 62*, 131–136.

Hiebert-Murphy, D., Trute, B., & Wright, A. (2008). Patterns of entry to community-based services with children with developmental disabilities: Implications for social work practice. *Child and Family Social Work, 13*, 423–432.

Holtman, M., Steiner, S., Hohmann, S., Poustka, L., Banaschewski, T., & Bolte, S. (2011). Neurofeedback in autism spectrum disorders. *Developmental Medicine and Child Neurology, 53*, 986–993.

Hurt, E., Arnold, L. E., & Lofthouse, N. (2014). Quantitative EEG neurofeedback for the treatment of pediatric attention-deficit/hyperactivity disorder, autism spectrum disorders, learning disorders, and epilepsy. *Child and Adolescent Psychiatric Clinics of North America, 23*, 465–486.

Jacobson, J. W., Foxx, R. M., & Mulick, J. A. (2005). *Controversial therapies for developmental disabilities: Fad, fashion, and science in professional practice.* Mahwah, NJ: Lawrence Erlbaum.

Jacobson, J. W., Mulick, J. A., & Schwartz, A. A. (1995). A history of facilitated communication: Science, pseudoscience, and antiscience. *American Psychologist, 50*, 750–765.

Jarusiewicz, B. (2002). Efficacy of neurofeedback for children in the autism spectrum: A pilot study. *Journal of Neurotherapy, 6*, 39–49.

Katz, G. (1992). Electroconvulsive-therapy from a social work perspective. *Social Work in Health Care, 16*(4), 55–68.

Koegel, L. K., Robinson, S., & Koegel, R. L. (2009). Empirically supported intervention practices for autism spectrum disorders in school and community settings: Issues and practices. In W. Sailor, G. Dunlop, G. Sugai, &

R. Horner (Eds.), *Handbook of positive behavior support* (pp. 149–176). New York, NY: Springer.

Kokina, A., & Kem, L. (2010). Social story interventions for children with autism spectrum disorders: A meta-analysis. *Journal of Autism and Developmental Disorders, 40*, 812–826.

Kouijzer, M., deMoor, J. M. H., Gerrits, B. J. L., Buitelaar, J. K., & van Schie, H. T. (2009). Long-term effects of neurofeedback in autism. *Research in Autism Spectrum Disorders, 3*, 496–501.

Kouijzer, M. E., van Schie, H., Gerrits, B. J., Buitelaar, J. K., & de Moor, J. M. (2013). Is EEG-biofeedback an effective treatment in autism spectrum disorders? A randomized controlled trial. *Applied Psychophysiology and Biofeedback, 38*, 17–28.

Kunstreich, T. (2003). Social welfare in Nazi Germany: Selection and exclusion. *Journal of Progressive Human Services, 14*(2), 23–52.

LaPan, A., & Platt, T. (2005). "To stem the tide of degeneracy": The eugenic impulse in social work. In S. A. Kirk (Ed.), *Mental disorders in the social environment: Critical perspectives* (pp. 139–164). New York, NY: Columbia University Press.

Leaf, J. B., Oppenheim-Leaf, N., Sheldon, J. B., & Sherman, J. A. (2012). Comparing the teaching interaction procedure to social stories for people with autism. *Journal of Applied Behavior Analysis, 45*, 281–298.

Lerman, D. C., Sansbury, T., Hovanetz, A., Wolever, E., Garcia, A., O'Brien, E., & Adedipe, H. (2008). Using behavior analysis to examine the outcomes of unproven therapies: An evaluation of hyperbaric oxygen therapy for children with autism. *Behavior Analysis in Practice, 1*, 50–58.

Levy, J. M. (1995). Social work. In B. A. Thyer & N. P. Kropf (Eds.), *Developmental disabilities: A handbook for interdisciplinary practice* (pp. 187–201). Cambridge, MA: Brookline Books.

Levy, S. E., & Hyman, S. L. (2008). Complementary and alternative medicine treatments for children with autism spectrum disorders. *Child and Adolescent Psychiatric Clinics of North America, 17*, 803–820.

Lilienfeld, S. O. (2007). Psychological treatments that cause harm. *Perspectives on Psychological Science, 2*, 53–70.

Marino, L., & Lilienfeld, S. (1998). Dolphin-assisted therapy: Flawed data, flawed conclusions. *Anthrozoos, 11*, 194–200.

Marino, L., & Lilienfeld, S. (2007). Dolphin-assisted therapy: More flawed data and more flawed conclusions. *Anthrozoos, 20*, 243–249.

Matson, M. L., Mahan, S., & Matson, J. L. (2009). Parent training: A review of methods for children with autism spectrum disorders. *Research in Autism Spectrum Disorders, 3*, 868–875.

Mazzone, L., Postorino, V., Valeri, G., & Vicari, S. (2014). Catatonia in patients with autism: Prevalence and management. *CNS Drugs, 26*, 205–216.

Miller, C. M. (2008, July 10). Boy's treatment case dealt blow. *The Miami Herald.* Retrieved June 17, 2009, from http://www.miamiherald.com

Mohr, W. K., Petti, T. A., & Mohr, B. D. (2003). Adverse effects associated with physical restraint. *Canadian Journal of Psychiatry, 48*, 330–337.

Montee, B. B., Miltenberger, R. G., & Wittrock, D. (1995). An experimental analysis of facilitated communication. *Journal of Applied Behavior Analysis, 28*, 189–200.

Mostert, M. P. (2001). Facilitated communication since 1995: A review of published studies. *Journal of Autism and Developmental Disorders, 31*, 287–313.

Nathanson, D. E. (1998). Long-term effectiveness of dolphin-assisted therapy for children with severe disabilities. *Antrozoos, 10*, 22–32.

Nathanson, D. E., deCastro, D., Friend, H., & McMahon, M. (1997). Effectiveness of short-term dolphin-assisted therapy for children with severe disabilities. *Antrozoos, 10*, 90–100.

National Association of Social Workers. (1996). *Code of ethics.* Washington, DC: NASW Press.

Pelham, W. E., & Fabiano, G. A. (2008). Evidence-based psychosocial treatments for attention-deficit/hyperactivity disorder. *Journal of Child Clinical and Adolescent Psychology, 37*, 184–214.

Pignotti, M., & Thyer, B. A. (2009a). The use of novel unsupported and empirically supported therapies by licensed clinical social workers. *Social Work Research, 33*, 5–17.

Pignotti, M., & Thyer, B. A. (2009b). Some comments on energy psychology: A review of the evidence: Premature conclusions based on incomplete evidence? *Psychotherapy Theory, Research, Training, Practice, 46*, 257–261.

Radomski, S., & Altaffer, T. (2009). *Treating autism spectrum disorders with energy psychology.* Retrieved February 1, 2010, from http://theamt.com/treating_autism_spectrum_disorders_with_energy_psychology.htm

Rhule, D. (2005). Take care to do no harm: Harmful interventions for youth problem behavior. *Professional Psychology: Research and Practice, 36*, 618–625.

Richmond, M. (1917). *Social diagnosis.* Philadelphia, PA: Russell Sage Foundation.

Robbins, J. (2008). *A symphony in the brain: The evolution of new brain wave biofeedback.* New York, NY: Grove Press.

Robinson, B. B. (1928). Problems of the community management of the non-institutionalized feeble-minded and delinquent. *National Conference of Social Work, 28*, 367–372.

Rogers, S. J., & Vismara, L. A. (2008). Evidence-based comprehensive treatments for early autism. *Journal of Clinical Child and Adolescent Psychology, 37,* 8–38.

Rossignol, D. A. (2006). Hyperbaric oxygen therapy might improve certain pathophysiological findings in autism. *Medical Hypotheses, 68,* 1208–1227.

Rossignol, D. A., & Rossignol, L. W. (2006). Hyperbaric oxygen therapy may improve symptoms in autistic children. *Medical Hypotheses, 67,* 216–228.

Rossignol, D. A., Rossignol, L. W., Smith, S., Schneider, C., Logerquist, S., Usman, A., ... Mumper, E. (2009). Hyperbaric treatment for children with autism: A multicenter, randomized, double-blind, controlled trial. *BMC Pediatrics, 9,* 21. doi:910.1186/1471-2431-7-36.

Rutter, M. L., Colvert, E., Kreppner, J., Beckett, C., Castle, J., Groothues, C., ... Sonuga-Barke, E. J. (2007). Early adolescent outcomes for institutionally-deprived and non-deprived adoptees. I: Disinhibited attachment. *Journal of Child Psychology and Psychiatry, 48,* 17–30.

Rutter, M. L., Kreppner, J. M., & O'Connor, T. G. (2001). Specificity and heterogeneity in children's responses to profound institutional privation. *British Journal of Psychiatry, 179,* 97–103.

Rutter, M. L., O'Connor, T. G., & English and Romanian Adoptees Study Team. (2004). Are there biological programming effects for psychological development? Findings from a study of Romanian adoptees. *Developmental Psychology, 40,* 81–94.

Schechtman, M. A. (2007). Scientifically unsupported therapies in the treatment of young children with autism spectrum disorders. *Psychiatric Annals, 37,* 639–645.

Scolnick, B. (2005). Effects of electroencephalogram biofeedback with Asperger's syndrome. *International Journal of Rehabilitative Research, 28,* 159–163.

Smith, D. (n.d.). *What is equine-assisted psychotherapy (EAP)?* Retrieved February 15, 2010, from http://equi-journey.webs.com/whatiseap.htm

Smyke, A. T., Dumitrescu, A., & Zeanah, C. H. (2002). Attachment disturbances in young children. I: The continuum of caretaking casualty. *Journal of the American Academy of Child & Adolescent Psychiatry, 41,* 972–982.

Snowdon, J., Meehan, T., & Halpin, R. (1994). Continuous screaming controlled by electroconvulsive-therapy: A case-study. *International Journal of Geriatric Psychiatry, 9,* 929–932.

Solms, M. (2013). Justifying psychoanalysis. *British Journal of Psychiatry, 203,* 389.

Stahmer, A. C., & Aarons, G. A. (2009). Attitudes towards adoption of evidence-based practices: A comparison of autism early intervention providers and children's mental health providers. *Psychological Services, 6,* 223–234.

Styles, A. (2011). Social stories: Does the research evidence support the popularity? *Educational Psychology in Practice, 27,* 415–436.

Substance and Mental Health Services Administration (SAMHSA). (2005). *Roadmap to seclusion and restraint free mental health services.* DHHS Publication No. (SMA) 05–4055. Rockville, MD: Center for Mental Health Services, Substance Abuse and Mental Health Services Administration.

Szalavitz, M. (2006). *Help at any cost: How the troubled teen industry cons parents and hurts kids.* New York, NY: Riverhead Books.

Tedeschi, P., Fitchett, J., & Molidor, C. E. (2005). The incorporation of animal-assisted interventions in social work education. *Journal of Family Social Work, 9*(4), 59–77.

The Editors. (2010). Retraction-Ileal-lymphoid-nodular hyperplasia, non-specific colitis, and pervasive developmental disorder in children. *The Lancet, 375,* 445.

Thomas, L. (2002). *Horse-play can be therapeutic: Equine-assisted psychotherapy.* Retrieved February 15, 2010, from http://www.strugglingteens.com/opinion/horseplay.html

Thyer, B. A., & Kropf, N. P. (Eds.). (1995). *Developmental disabilities: A handbook for interdisciplinary practice.* Cambridge, MA: Brookline Books.

Underwood, L. A., Figueroa, R. G., Thyer, B. A., & Nzechoa, A. (1989). Interruption and DRI in the treatment of self-injurious behavior among mentally retarded and autistic self-restrainers. *Behavior Modification, 13,* 471–481.

Underwood, L. A., & Thyer, B. A. (1990). Social work practice with the mentally retarded: Reducing self-injurious behavior using nonaversive methods. *Arete, 15,* 14–23.

Virues-Ortega, J. (2010). Applied behavior analytic intervention for autism in early childhood: Meta-analysis, meta-regression and dose-response meta-analysis of multiple outcomes. *Clinical Psychology Review, 30,* 387–399.

Wachtel, L. E., Contrucci-Kuhn, S. A., Griffin, M., Thompson, A., Dhossche, D. M., & Reti, I. M. (2009). ECT for self-injury in an autistic boy. *European Child and Adolescent Psychiatry, 18,* 458–463.

Wachtel, L. E., & Dhossche, D. M. (2012). Challenges for electroconvulsive therapy for catatonia in youth with intellectual disabilities: Another tomato effect? *Journal of ECT, 28,* 151–153.

Wachtel, L. E., & Dhossche, D. M. (2013). ECT for self-injurious behavior. In N. Ghaziuddin & G. Walter (Eds.), *Electroconvulsive therapy in children and adolescents* (pp. 247–280). New York, NY: Oxford University Press.

Wachtel, L. E., Dhossche, D. M., & Kellner, C. H. (2011). When is electroconvulsive therapy appropriate for children and adolescents? *Medical Hypotheses, 76,* 395–399.

Wachtel, L. E., Kahng, S., Dhossche, D. M., Cascella, N., & Reti, I. M. (2008). ECT for catatonia in an autistic girl. *American Journal of Psychiatry, 165,* 329–330.

Wachtel, L. E., & Shorter, E. (2013). Self-injurious behavior in children: A treatable catatonic syndrome. *Australian & New Zealand Journal of Psychiatry, 47,* 1113–1115.

Wakefield, A. J., Murch, S. H., Anthony, A., Linnell, J., Casson, D. M., Malik, M.,...Walker-Smith, J. A. (1998). Ileal-lymphoid-nodular hyperplasia, non-specific colitis, and pervasive developmental disorder in children. *The Lancet, 351,* 637–641.

Wang, P., & Spillane, A. (2009). Evidence-based social skills interventions for children with autism: A meta-analysis. *Education and Training in Developmental Disabilities, 44,* 318–342.

Warner, A. G. (1898). *American charities* (revised edition). New York, NY: Thomas Y. Crowell.

Warner, A. G., Queen, S. A., & Harper, E. B. (1930). *American charities and social work* (4th ed.). New York, NY: Thomas Y. Crowell.

Whetten, K., Ostermann, J., Whetten, R. A., Pence, B. W., O'Donnell, K., Messer, L. C.,...the Positive Outcomes for Orphans Research Team. (2009). A comparison of the wellbeing of orphans and abandoned children ages 6–12 in institutional and community-based care settings in 5 less wealthy nations. *PLoS One, 4*(12), e8169.

Wray, R. J., Buskirk, T. D., Jupka, K., Lapka, C., Jacobsen, H., Pakpahan, R.,...Wortley, P. (2009). Influenza vaccination concerns among older Blacks: A randomized controlled trial. *American Journal of Preventive Medicine, 36,* 429–434.

Yamamoto, J., & Shibuya, N. (2009). Evidence based supports for persons with developmental disabilities: Contributions of applied behavioral analysis. *Japanese Journal of Behavior Analysis, 23,* 46–70.

# CHAPTER 7

# Pseudoscience in Social Work Education and Training

*So we really ought to look into theories that don't work, and science that isn't science.*—CARL SAGAN

When individual social workers, social work organizations, social work academic programs, and social work–affiliated clinics and therapy centers make unusual claims as to an ability to cure, to deliver a treatment that is superior to existing empirically supported therapies, to provide amelioration of distress, or to provide education and training that is said to teach effective practice skills, we believe that such claims are open to public discussion and critical analysis. In this chapter, we refer to specific individual practitioners, social work organizations, and academic programs that we believe have made pseudoscientific claims through some public forum. These venues include websites, advertising brochures, newsletters, journal articles, and books. We do not intend to mock or to personally impugn any individual, agency, or educational program. Although some of the claims we present will seem laughable, we urge the reader to keep in mind that these claims are being presented to the public; to potential and existing clients; and individuals suffering serious impairment in their ability to function due to a mental disorder, behavioral disturbance, or problem in interpersonal functioning. Their problems are real and deserve real (i.e., effective) professional services, not interventions that primarily rely on placebo influences for their apparent effectiveness.

It is tempting to smile when we read about Tong Ren therapy, invented by Tom Tam. The reader will recall the practice of acupuncture, which traditionally involves inserting very thin needles into specific places under the skin, places said to be the location of energy nodes or meridians through which *qi* flows. Moving beyond the mere insertion of needles, other variations involve twirling or rotating the needles, or applying small amounts of electricity through them. Other acupuncture practitioners do away with those pesky needles and simply press against the acupuncture points (acupressure), or hold small burning bundles of herbs close to the meridians (moxibustion) on the body. Tong Ren therapy takes the process a bit further. The client is provided with a 10-inch tall plastic human doll with the traditional acupuncture points outlined on it. The client is then given a small hammer with tiny magnets embedded at the tip of the hammer face, and told to tap the *doll's (!)* acupuncture points. This is said to produce healing in the client's body.

A video of a group of clients engaging in Tong Ren therapy can be found online (see www.youtube.com/watch?v=yHJPPbtdcRk), and the obvious ludicrousness of the "treatment" may bring a smile to one's lips. But then we read a testimonial provided by one licensed clinical social worker (LCSW):

> We, at the Boston Living Center, have had the pleasure of working with Ken Hadden throughout the past year as a Tong Ren Practitioner. Ken has facilitated 30 sessions serving over 200 individuals living with HIV/AIDS at the center. The Boston Living Center is New England's largest community and resource center for people living with HIV/AIDS. The mission is to foster the wellness of all HIV positive people and respond to the changing needs of the HIV/AIDS community...Holistics are one of the most utilized and valued services at the center. Ken expanded our Holistics program to include Tong Ren in 2009. (Retrieved November 6, 2014, from www.amazinghealings.org/Testimonials.html)

We are aware of the point made by philosopher Roger Scruton that "The consolation of imaginary things in not imaginary consolation," but we do contend that it is not a correct professional practice for social workers to promote imaginary (i.e., largely based on placebo influences) interventions for clients with serious conditions. We believe that persons with HIV/AIDS do not deserve the consolation of imaginary things; they deserve to be provided with access to the best available empirically supported therapies, whether they consist of medical interventions to prolong life, or psychosocial interventions to alleviate depression, reduce stress and anxiety, or improve overall morale. At their core, Tong Ren and similar bogus treatments are *not* funny. When provided by professional social workers, there may be malpractice. Regrettably, some major social work organizations deliberately, inadvertently, via slackness, or overall ineptitude, promote pseudoscientific practices within the discipline. We review some of these in this chapter.

# NATIONAL ASSOCIATION OF SOCIAL WORKERS

Social work education and training are a very large enterprise within the United States, Canada, and abroad. In the United States, the major professional membership organization open to individuals is the National Association of Social Workers (NASW), with some 130,000 members. Most NASW members (about 92%) have the master's of social work (MSW) degree, a smaller proportion the bachelor of social work (BSW) degree (about 3%), and another proportion possesses the doctoral degree as their most advanced credential (roughly 4%). The NASW is composed of more than 50 state and territorial chapters, and has some specialty practice sections focusing on particular areas of practice (e.g., child welfare, mental health, private practice). The NASW was formed in 1955 by the voluntary amalgamation of six existing social work organizations in order to better present a unified voice for the profession. It has assets of more than $83 million and rents upscale office space a few blocks from the U.S. Capitol in Washington, DC. More than 85% of the NASW membership comprises women and about 90% are White. The largest area of practice by its members are clinical services in mental health (more than 30%), followed by child welfare, hospital social work, family practice, and a myriad of other areas. Social workers are the largest providers of mental health counseling and psychotherapy services, being greater in number than psychologists and psychiatrists combined. According to Weissman et al. (2006), in 1998, there were about 35,000 psychiatrists,

73,000 psychologists, and 192,000 social workers providing mental health care in the United States. These services are important, as are the psychosocial problems they attempt to redress.

NASW has no formal professional education remit, except for some role in approving and providing continuing educational courses, which most states require for licensure renewal for social workers. It acts largely as a professional guild, with some advocacy, policy lobbying, publishing several journals, supporting specialty practice sections, offering awards, sporadically holding regional meetings, producing several brochures and informational pamphlets, supporting a number of practice credentials, and writing a very influential *Code of Ethics* (*COE*; NASW, 2006).

## COUNCIL ON SOCIAL WORK EDUCATION

The Council on Social Work Education (CSWE, www.cswe.org) is America's largest group of social work educators, with about 3,000 individual academic members, as well as more than 450 academic programs offering the BSW degree and about 200 MSW programs. Its largest initiative is the development of professional accrediting standards for BSW and MSW programs, the initial accrediting of such programs, and their periodic (every 8 years or so) reaccreditation–reaffirmation. The CSWE was founded in 1952 and is recognized by the National Council on Higher Education Accreditation (CHEA) as the sole accrediting body for professional social work in the United States. The CSWE sponsors an annual convention, publishes the *Journal of Social Work Education*, develops educational policies and standards, supports the professional development of social work academics, and, perhaps most importantly, has had its role verified by most state social work licensing boards that stipulate that anyone seeking licensure as a social worker must have received his or her degree from a program accredited by the CSWE. Doctoral education in social work is not accredited by the CSWE or any other organization, although the CSWE does have a newly developed Council on Doctoral Education. Most doctoral programs in social work are academic research PhDs, not professional practice degrees such as the BSW and MSW. Academic degrees are typically not subject to accreditation, whereas professional practice degrees (e.g., social work, nursing, law, medicine, business) are usually accredited. There are a very few doctorate in social work (DSW) degrees that have a focus on practice, but as of yet, no accreditation mechanism exists for them.

The CSWE operationalizes its accrediting standards via a document called the *Educational Policy and Accreditation Standards* (EPAS; CSWE, 2008), available on the organization's website (see www.cswe .org), and through a comprehensive *Handbook of Social Work Accreditation Policies and Procedures*, also available on its website. The extent to which pseudoscience in social work education is permitted or discouraged is largely determined by the accreditation standards found within the EPAS document. The CSWE charges substantial annual fees to its constituent member programs, as well as additional assessments for a program to be initially accredited or to have a program's accreditation reaffirmed. Once accredited, BSW programs pay up to $4,000 or more in annual dues, MSW programs pay up to $6,000 or more annually, and programs offering both the BSW and MSW degrees pay up to $8,000 or more each year (dues are indexed by the number of annual graduates). In addition, individuals who join the CSWE as full members pay $195 annual dues assessment. The organization's assets are in excess of $6 million.

The EPAS addresses, indirectly, pseudoscience in social work education through several standards. Among these are:

*Educational Policy 2.1.3—Apply critical thinking to inform and communicate professional judgments*

Social workers are knowledgeable about the principles of logic, scientific inquiry, and reasoned discernment. They use critical thinking augmented by creativity and curiosity.... Social workers

- distinguish, appraise, and integrate multiple sources of knowledge, including research-based knowledge and practice wisdom.
- analyze models of assessment, prevention, intervention, and evaluation;...

*Educational Policy 2.1.6—Engage in research-informed practice and practice-informed research*

Social workers use practice experience to inform research, employ evidence-based interventions, evaluate their own practice, and use research findings to improve practice, policy, and social service delivery. Social workers comprehend quantitative and qualitative

research and understand scientific and ethical approaches to build knowledge. Social workers
- use practice experience to inform scientific inquiry and
- use research evidence to inform practice

*Educational Policy 2.1.10(a)–(d)—Engage, assess, intervene, and evaluate with individuals, families, groups, organizations, and communities*

...Practice knowledge includes identifying, analyzing, and implementing evidence-based interventions designed to help achieve client goals; using research and technological advances; evaluating program outcomes; and practice effectiveness....(CSWE, 2008)

Although these standards are fine as far as they go, they may not go far enough. For example, Standard 2.1.3 seems to equate research-based knowledge *and* practice wisdom. The problem with this is that while scientific research provides a method to arrive at generally valid conclusions, and to settle disagreements among conflicting data, usually by more research, practice wisdom offers no such systematic way to advance credible knowledge. It has been practice wisdom for several thousand years that the laying on of hands—whether by Greek magnets, the healing powers of a King's royal touch, Mesmer's gestures, Callahan's thought field therapy finger tapping, or other variations on the theme—have been believed by some to possess legitimate therapeutic value. Well, these things do not, except through nonspecific (albeit sometimes impressive) placebo influences. Practice wisdom offers no way out of errors. Scientific research does offer a way to separate false beliefs from valid ones, which is one reason why research is given preferential (although not exclusive) value in evidence-based practice.

There is also the problem of translating mandated educational content into practice. For example, Baker, Stephens, and Hitchcock (2010) surveyed 134 social workers employed in differing practice settings regarding their use of various methods to evaluate their own practice. What they found was dismaying. Almost 20% of the MSWs reported that they did not receive any formal education during their graduate studies on evaluating practice outcomes. Only 6% said that they had used single-subject designs, about 4% said that they used group designs, and 24% said that they used goal attainment scaling methods to evaluate outcomes. The most common "evaluation activities" by social workers consisted of gathering basic statistics on client characteristics and numbers served (75% said they did this) or by using client satisfaction surveys (which are not a legitimate replacement for evaluating outcomes in terms of client functioning), used by about 56%. The most appropriate method to evaluate the outcomes of practice with individual clients involves single-subject studies, and of programs, simple pre- and quasiexperimental designs. These appear to be rarely done in practice, despite their widespread application and appropriateness to social work (Bloom, Fischer, & Orme, 2009; Kazi, 1998; Thyer & Myers, 2007).

We can compare these social work accreditation standards with some relevant analogous standards found within those established by the American Psychological Association (2007, emphasis added):

- ...all students can acquire and demonstrate substantial understanding and competence in the following areas:...Diagnosing or defining problems through psychological assessment and measurement and formulating and implementing intervention strategies *(including training in empirically supported procedures)*...(p. 7)

Psychologists who provide clinical supervision to graduate students in psychology must themselves be licensed to practice psychology (something academic social work has strenuously objected to), and the American Psychological Association further states that they are (2007, emphasis added):

- ...responsible for reviewing with the interns *the relevant scientific and empirical bases for the professional services* delivered by the interns...(p. 16)

These would not, on the face of it, appear to be radical standards for social work to adapt and adopt, but they would certainly strengthen our students' education.

The analogous standards used within the discipline of psychiatry to train its residents are also informative to review. Here are some that are relevant to grounding psychiatric training on scientific literacy and research (italics added):

- IV.A.5.a).(3).(e) applying supportive, psychodynamic, and cognitive behavioral psychotherapies to both brief and long-term individual practice, as well as to assuring exposure to family, couples, group and other individual *evidence-based psychotherapies;*

- IV.A.5.b).(3).(i).(ii) All residents must be educated in research literacy. Research literacy is the ability to critically appraise and understand the relevant research literature and to apply research findings appropriately to clinical practice. *The concepts and process of Evidence Based Clinical Practice include skill development in question formulation, information searching, critical appraisal, and medical decision-making, thus providing the structure for teaching research literacy to psychiatry residents.* The program must promote an atmosphere of scholarly inquiry, including the access to ongoing research activity in psychiatry. Residents must be taught the design and interpretation of data.
- IV.A.5.c) Practice-based Learning and Improvement. Residents must demonstrate the ability to investigate and evaluate their care of patients, to *appraise and assimilate scientific evidence,* and to continuously improve patient care based on constant self-evaluation and lifelong learning.
- IV.B.2.a) Residents will have instruction in research methods in the clinical, biological, and behavioral sciences related to psychiatry, *including techniques to appraise the professional and scientific literature and to apply evidence based findings to patient care.*
- V.C.3. In its evaluation of residency programs, the Review Committee will take into consideration the information provided by the American Board of Psychiatry and Neurology regarding *resident performance on the certifying examinations* during the most recent five years. The expectation is that *the rate of those passing the examination on their first attempt is 50%* and that 70% of those who complete the program will take the certifying examination. (Accreditation Council on Graduate Medical Education [ACGME], 2007)

Several points are noteworthy to make. First, the process of evidence-based practice and the principle of selecting interventions at least in part on the basis of the scientific literature are supposedly integral to psychiatric training. The ability to locate, critically appraise, and translate into clinical practice research studies is also clearly articulated and outlined in language much stronger than that found within the social work accreditation standards.

Bledsoe et al. (2007) reported on a national survey of MSW programs, a study that investigated the extent to which these programs provided training in each of a number of psychotherapies that have been identified in the literature as being empirically supported. A total of 21% of the MSW programs said they provided training in cognitive behavioral therapy, a research-supported treatment (RST). In contrast, nonspecific therapies, such as "social work counseling," "case management," "family therapy," and "supportive psychotherapy," were much more commonly taught than RSTs. Fewer than half of the social work programs provided both didactic instruction and clinical supervision in *any* empirically supported therapy. This does not bode well for the effectiveness of the services these graduates will subsequently go on to provide their clients, and further suggests that compliance with the CSWE's own accreditation standards is problematic.

Another interesting point notable in the psychiatric residency standards is the clear requirement that, over the past 5-year period, of those psychiatrists who completed their residency training, at least 50% must have passed the specialty examinations required for credentialing as a psychiatrist. The analogous situation in academic social work is the proportion of the graduates of a given program who pass the LCSW examination. Rather than this information being open and transparent, available to applicants, current students, and faculty, LCSW pass rate information is not advertised at all by the individual programs and is virtually impossible to obtain. For example, Florida has more than half a dozen MSW programs located within the state. In 2008, the pass rate for first-time LCSW test takers ranged from 50% to 69% across the varying programs; in 2007, it was 42% to 78%, and in 2006, 43% to 69% (Thyer, 2011). It seems obvious that a clinical social work program that has less than 50% of its graduates passing the state's licensure examination is doing a worse job at preparing social workers to legally practice than the one which has more than 70% passing. It would be helpful for social work programs to be held to an expectation that a certain percentage (say 50%?) of their clinical graduates who take their state's LCSW test (almost all states require the same nationally used examination) actually pass the test required to legally practice! Law programs employ the pass rate to the state bar as one standard for continuing accreditation, and apparently psychiatry has a similar standard. Social work would be wise to emulate this reasonable benchmark.

# LAX ETHICAL STANDARDS PROMOTE PSEUDOSCIENCE

In terms of ethical standards applicable to the practice of professional social work, the *COE* developed by the NASW is the major player (NASW, 2006). There are other social work ethical standards, such as those promulgated by the Clinical Social Work Association (see www.clinicalsocialworkassociation.org/content/ethics-code), a much smaller group, and of course many social workers chose to have a primary membership in a non-NASW organization, such as, for example, the American Association for Marriage and Family Therapy, which offers its own ethical standards (see www.aamft.org/imis15/content/legal_ethics/code_of_ethics.aspx). The NASW *COE* only applies to persons who actually belong to the NASW, and most social workers do not belong. Nevertheless, the NASW *COE* remains the disciplinary benchmark for ethical behavior among social workers in the United States.

Given this influence, imagine if you will that the NASW *COE* contained the following provisos:

- *Social workers* who engage in assessment, therapy, teaching, research, organizational consulting, or other professional activities maintain a reasonable level of awareness of the current scientific and professional information in their fields of activity.
- *Social workers* rely on scientifically and professionally derived knowledge when making scientific judgments in human service provision, or when engaging in scholarly or professional endeavors.
- *The social worker* always has the responsibility to recommend scientifically supported most effective treatment procedures. Effective treatment procedures have been validated as having both long-term and short-term benefits to clients and society.
- Clients have a right to effective treatment (i.e., based on the research literature and adapted to the individual client).
- *Social workers* are responsible for review and appraisal of likely effects of all alternative treatments, including those provided by other disciplines and no intervention.
- In those instances where more than one scientifically supported treatment has been established, additional factors may be

considered in selecting interventions, including, but not limited to, efficiency and cost-effectiveness, risks and side effects of the interventions, client preference, and practitioner experience and training.

- *Social workers* who use . . . assessment techniques do so for purposes that are appropriate in light of research.
- *The social worker* collects data, or asks the client, client–surrogate, or designated others to collect the data needed to assess progress within the program.
- *Social workers* do not use public statements that are false, deceptive, misleading, or fraudulent, either because of what they state, convey, or suggest, or because of what they omit, concerning their research, practice, or other work activities.
- *Social workers* do not solicit testimonials from current clients or patients or other persons who because of their particular circumstances are vulnerable to undue influence.
- *Social workers* do not exaggerate claims for effectiveness of particular procedures.

If ethical standards such as these were in place and stringently enforced, pseudoscience within social work would be dramatically curtailed. Unfortunately, the laudable guidelines mentioned earlier are not to be found within the NASW *COE*. They are contained within the *Guidelines for Responsible Conduct for Behavior Analysts* (see www.bacb .com/index.php?page=57) developed by a related discipline, behavior analysis, as formulated by the Behavior Analyst Certification Board. Just substitute the phrase *behavior analyst* for *social worker* to get the original wording for the quotes mentioned earlier. By way of disclosure, one the authors of this book, Bruce Thyer, is a board-certified behavior analyst. He is also an LCSW, and a past member of the NASW's Academy of Certified Social Workers (ACSW). It would be impossible for any social worker to ethically provide or advocate for the delivery of pseudoscientific or bogus assessment or treatment services were standards analogous to those developed for behavior analysts modified and adopted by the profession of social work.

Sentiments such as those mentioned earlier have been suggested in the past. In an article titled "Should Social Work Clients Have the Right to Effective Treatment?" Myers and Thyer (1997) argued that the answer to this question is an unambiguous yes. These authors cited the guidelines promoted by social worker Robert Ackerman (1996), such as:

- Social workers should be aware of the state of the art treatment for specific disorders as represented in the scientific literature and endorsed by government health agencies. If the worker cannot treat with specificity, then the client should be referred for proper treatment. The impression should not be given that all treatments are equal or that treatments of demonstrated efficacy are simply alternatives. (p. 11)
- Social workers should learn and utilize effective treatments which are clearly supported in the literature. They should not substitute unproved, doctrinaire or general approaches when proven techniques are available. (p. 12)
- Social work schools...should provide instruction based on current information and accepted state of the art treatments.... Utilization of proven, accepted, specific, effective techniques in mental health treatment are highly consistent with the primary mission of social work. (p. 13)

Ackerman's views are also similar to those of social worker Leslie Tutty who suggested that "it is important to provide the most effective treatment available. This entails professionals keeping current on the research on treatment effectiveness for their particular client populations" (Tutty, 1990, p. 13).

Thyer (1996) also provided some specific guidelines for practitioners relating to the topic of the clients right to effective treatment, including, among others:

- Social workers should make use of practice methods that are supported by empirical research. (p. 121)
- Social workers should engage in the systematic evaluation of their own practice through the use of single system research designs (SSRDs) and other appropriate research methodologies. (p. 122)
- [Social workers should] Become competent in the use of relatively reliable and valid methods of assessment...Make appropriate *use* of these empirically supported methods of assessment in your practice...Avoid the use of structured assessment methods which lack credible research support as reliable and valid measurement techniques. (p. 122)

- [Social workers should] Become competent in the use of social work treatments that possess credible empirical support...Actually *use* these methods in your work with clients as your first choice treatment option, taking into account other factors such as unique aspects of the client, the client's wishes, agency resources, etc....Only make use of less well-supported methods of intervention after those which possess greater levels of empirical support have been given a reasonable clinical trial and shown (with data) not to produce improvements. (p. 123)

Analogous guidelines were suggested for social work educators, supervisors, and students.

What does the NASW *COE* actually have to say on this matter of providing effective treatment? The *COE* is a complex document and addresses many diverse issues, but in examining it for content related to any expectation that social workers provide empirically supported services, relatively few points emerge. Among these are the following (NASW, 2006):

- Social workers' primary responsibility is to promote the well-being of clients. (Standard 1.01)
- (a) Social workers should provide services to clients only in the context of a professional relationship based, when appropriate, on valid informed consent. Social workers should use clear and understandable language to inform clients of the purpose of the services, risks related to the services...relevant costs, reasonable alternatives...Social workers should provide clients with an opportunity to ask questions. (Standard 1.03)
- (b) Social workers should provide services in substantive areas or use intervention techniques or approaches that are new to them only after engaging in appropriate study, training consultation, and supervision from people who are competent in those interventions or techniques. (Standard 1.04)
- (c) When generally recognized standards do not exist within an emerging area of practice, social workers should exercise careful judgment and take responsible steps...to ensure the competence of their work and to protect clients from harm. (Standard 1.04)
- Social workers should not engage in physical contact with clients when there is the possibility of psychological harm to the client

as a result of the contact (such as cradling or caressing clients). (Standard 1.10)

- (a) Social workers should refer clients to other professionals when the other professionals' specialized knowledge or expertise is needed to serve clients fully or when social workers believe that they are not being effective or making reasonable progress with clients and that additional service is required. (Standard 2.06)
- Continuing education and staff development should address current knowledge and emerging developments related to social work practice and ethics. (Standard 3.08)
- (b) Social workers should critically examine and keep current with emerging knowledge relevant to social work. Social workers should routinely review the professional literature and participate in continuing education relevant to social work and social work ethics. (Standard 4.01)
- (c) Social workers should base practice on recognized knowledge, including empirically-based knowledge, relevant to social work and social work ethics. (Standard 4.01)
- Social workers should not participate in, condone, or be associated with dishonesty, fraud, or deception. (Standard 4.04)
- (c) Social workers should critically examine and keep current with emerging knowledge relevant to social work and fully use evaluation and research evidence in their professional practice. (Standard 5.02)

In many ways, the aforementioned standards are laudable, but the devil is in the details. In 1992, the NASW's National Committee on Lesbian and Gay Issues (NCOLGI) prepared a position statement condemning as unethical so-called reparative therapies aimed at changing the sexual "preferences" of homosexuals to heterosexual. Among the reasons marshaled for the position were the following:

> Proponents of reparative therapies claim—without documentation—many successes. They assert that their processes are supported by conclusive scientific data which are in fact little more than anecdotal. NGOLGI protests these efforts to "convert" people through irresponsible therapies...empirical research does not demonstrate that...sexual orientation

(heterosexual or homosexual) can be changed through these so-called reparative therapies. (NCOLGI, 1992, p. 1)

Now at the time, one of the authors (BAT) who was a member of the NASW thought that this was a fine position indeed for his major professional organization to take. NCOLGI was absolutely correct. There was indeed very little scientifically credible evidence that reparative therapies worked, and that it is indeed unethical to attempt such a treatment, in part on that basis, but also of course because of the message such treatment conveys relating to the supposedly pathological nature of homosexual orientation as something that requires repairing, as if it was a defect of some sort. The NASW's more recent statement on this issue (National Committee on Lesbian, Gay, and Bisexual Issues, 2000) says:

Lesbians and gay men often are pressured to seek reparative or conversion therapies which cannot and will not change sexual orientation…NCLGB believes that such treatment potentially can lead to severe emotional damage…No data demonstrate that reparative or conversation therapies are effective, and in fact they may be harmful. (www.socialworkers.org/diversity/lgb/reparative.asp)

This is a great precedent, our major professional association issuing a statement saying that a given intervention does not work, and may even be harmful, and social workers should not provide it. Those that do so are in violation of our *COE*. Similar position statements have been issued by related groups such as the American Psychological Association (www.apa.org/news/press/releases/2009/08/therapeutic.aspx; www.apa.org/about/governance/council/policy/sexual-orientation.aspx), the American Psychiatric Association, and the American Counseling Association.

With these NASW statements in mind, several years ago, one of the authors, who had been a member of the NASW for 25 years (BAT), sought further advice from the NASW ethics office, and sent them a letter requesting written answers to the following three general questions:

1. Is a social worker who provides an intervention that lacks any scientifically credible evidence that it helps clients acting unethically?

2. Is a social worker who provides an intervention that scientifically credible studies have shown to be ineffective acting unethically?

3. Is a social worker who provides an intervention that scientifically credible studies have shown to be harmful to clients acting unethically?

Bruce eagerly awaited a written response from the NASW, hoping to obtain in writing some statement that would be used to promote the tenets of evidence-based practice, some answers such as (a) not necessarily, (b) yes, they are acting unethically, and (c) yes, they are acting unethically. Such straightforward answers would seem consistent with the NASW's own *COE*, principles enumerated earlier, such as basing practice decisions on research evidence and avoiding doing harm to clients. In due course, he did get a letter but it simply stated that the NASW Ethical Consultation office did not provide answers in writing to queries like his, but they would be happy to have him call them on the telephone and raise his questions with a staff consultant, who would point him to the relevant sections of the *COE* that seemed to apply to his queries. In other words, the NASW declined to state in writing that it is unethical for a social worker to provide a therapy that research evidence has shown to be harmful!

This reluctance to condemn the provision of demonstrably ineffective or even harmful treatments has led to the practice situation described as follows:

> The present state of service delivery in the human services is most charitably characterized as being in disarray. Observers less benevolent than the author would use terms such as 'irresponsible,' 'unethical,' 'inhumane,' and 'incredible.' Once one has graduated with a professional degree (PhD, MD, MSW, etc.) and obtained a state license to practice as a mental health services provider, there are few if any strictures as to what constitutes suitable treatment…Quite literally it does not matter whether a psychotherapist competently provides intervention well supported by sound clinical research, and actually achieves favorable outcomes with clients, or if she or he lacks clinical skills in effective interventions and provides nonspecific conversation and attention which do not help clients with meaningful problems. If one maintains a license,

doesn't engage in libidinous activities with clients, or fraudulently bill them, one can have a long and financially rewarding career. (Thyer, 1995, pp. 93–94)

Given the inability or reluctance of the discipline's major professional association to ethically condemn the provision of harmful or ineffective clinical social work services, it is not surprising that pseudoscientific and other bogus practices are being provided by LCSW. It gets worse. We recently used the Internet to search for LCSWs who provide *magical* practices, and we found many examples of professional social workers who use their legal credentials in the context for advertising that they use tarot cards, astrology, shamanism–witchcraft, extrasensory perception, and clairvoyance to read clients' auras and to help clients communicate with spirits and ghosts. These practitioners openly advertise these services, with no apparent professional sanctions being imposed by the NASW or state licensing board. Why are pseudoscientific practices so widespread in professional social work? Because they are not deemed to be unethical by the major professional organizations charged with the oversight of services provided to the public, and no proactive steps are made to curtail such practices.

We would like to emphasize that we are not arguing against innovation in professional practice or for the ability of clients to request preferred treatments. We are arguing against *social workers* providing untested therapies, those which have been tested and found to be not useful, above and beyond nonspecific placebo and relationship factors, and those which have been previously tested and shown to be actively harmful. We are also condemning making unwarranted claims about the presumptive effectiveness of one's services, which is characteristic of many of the pseudoscientific practices we have addressed. We believe that those social workers offering an alternative or complementary therapy are ethically obligated to inform the client of the treatment's evidentiary foundations, or lack thereof. We concur with the position of social worker Frank Bruno, who said:

> There is no immorality or injustice in trying the best possible method, even though one is not sure that it is correct or not, if at the same time its experimental method is acknowledged and the social worker watches its results with an open

mind, ready to change his point of view or his method as the results suggests. He cannot be expected to use a method of precision, exactly appropriate to the dynamics of a situation, when neither the causes nor even the visible phenomena are exactly known. But he can be held to the duty of using the very best methods available, and of attempting to improve them in the light of his experience. (Bruno, 1934, pp. 589–590)

With respect to reparative therapy, Jenkins and Johnston (2004, pp. 558–559) maintained this perspective: "Social workers cannot offer a service (conversion therapy–reorientation) they cannot deliver. It is unethical in many situations to even offer this service." We believe this standard should be much more broadly applied within professional social work, than being apparently restricted to the provision of reparative therapies. Most ethics complaints processed by the NASW deal with sexual activity with clients, dual relationships, and other boundary violations (Strom-Gottfried, 2003).

There are many other examples of workable ethical standards found in other fields, which actively discourage providing pseudoscientific therapies by practitioners. The World Medical Association promotes the *Declaration of Helsinki*, wherein it is asserted:

*Use of Placebo*

33. The benefits, risks, burdens and effectiveness of a new intervention must be tested against those of the best proven intervention(s), except in the following circumstances:

Where no proven intervention exists, the use of placebo, or no intervention, is acceptable; or where for compelling and scientifically sound methodological reasons the use of any intervention less effective than the best proven one, the use of placebo, or no intervention is necessary to determine the efficacy or safety of an intervention and the patients who receive any intervention less effective than the best proven one, placebo, or no intervention will not be subject to additional risks of serious or irreversible harm as a result of not receiving the best proven intervention.

Extreme care must be taken to avoid abuse of this option.

*Unproven Interventions in Clinical Practice*

37. In the treatment of an individual patient, where proven interventions do not exist or other known interventions have been ineffective, the physician, after seeking expert advice, with informed consent from the patient or a legally authorised representative, may use an unproven intervention if in the physician's judgement it offers hope of saving life, reestablishing health or alleviating suffering. This intervention should subsequently be made the object of research, designed to evaluate its safety and efficacy. In all cases, new information must be recorded and, where appropriate, made publicly available. (Retrieved November 6, 2014, from www.wma .net/en/30publications/10policies/b3)

Again, the preceding quotation provides something for social work to consider adapting to its own professional services.

The American Medical Association offers equally, if not more so, strict ethical guidelines:

*Opinion 8.083—Placebo Use in Clinical Practice*

A placebo is a substance provided to a patient that the physician believes has no specific pharmacological effect upon the condition being treated. In the clinical setting, the use of a placebo without the patient's knowledge may undermine trust, compromise the patient-physician relationship, and result in medical harm to the patient.

Physicians may use placebos for diagnosis or treatment only if the patient is informed of and agrees to its use. A placebo may still be effective if the patient knows it will be used but cannot identify it and does not know the precise timing of its use. A physician should enlist the patient's cooperation by explaining that a better understanding of the medical condition could be achieved by evaluating the effects of different medications, including the placebo. The physician need neither identify the placebo nor seek specific consent before its administration. In this way, the physician respects the patient's autonomy and fosters a trusting relationship, while the patient still may benefit from the placebo effect.

A placebo must not be given merely to mollify a difficult patient, because doing so serves the convenience of the physician more than it promotes the patient's welfare. (Retrieved November 6, 2014, from www.ama-assn.org/ama/pub/ physician-resources/medical-ethics/code-medical-ethics/ opinion8083.pageon)

We have often heard social work practitioners justify the use of placebo-type pseudoscientific practices on the grounds that they can produce beneficial outcomes, even if they only amount to nonspecific treatment and relationship effects. Other disciplines require that their practitioners inform clients of the evidentiary status of the services they provide and to not deliver placebo treatments in lieu of research-supported therapy, except under fairly restricted circumstances and with client informed consent.

## LAX CONTINUING EDUCATION STANDARDS PROMOTE PSEUDOSCIENCE

All social workers are expected to engage in a lifelong and continuous process of continuing professional education. This is drilled into them in their BSW and MSW programs, is required by the NASW *COE*, and is mandated by the states and other jurisdictions that provide for the licensing and other legal regulation of social work practice. The *NASW Standards for Continuing Professional Education* (NASW, 2003, p. 12) state that "social workers shall complete 48 hours of continuing professional education every two years," with each hour being required to last for a full 60 minutes. This standard is similar to that of other professional disciplines, but again, the devil is in the details. One may accrue continuing education hours (CE) by attending formal organized learning events, such as courses provided by accredited social work programs, seminars, and staff development training workshops sponsored by the NASW or other approved groups. However, CE can also be fulfilled by attending conferences, symposia, panel discussions, and other activities sponsored by social work or allied disciplines. Finally, one may fulfill this CE requirement by, according to the NASW standards, "writing papers and books for presentation or publication; making presentations on major professional issues or programs; reading professional journals and books; preparing for initial consultation, teaching, or training assignments; and engaging in *independent study, research or tutorial projects*" (NASW, 2003, p. 13, italics added). Hence, one may fulfill the NASW standards by studying at home alone or reading a book or a journal. Obviously, there is a quality control issue here.

Although continuing education is expected of all professional social workers according to the NASW, the reality is that obtaining formal CE is *mandated* by one's state board, if one is a licensed social worker in most (but not all) states (Seelig, 1990). Most social work boards require between 30 and 35 CE hours every 2 years, although this varies across the states. The licensure of social workers is the function of the individual states, not the NASW or any other national body. The individual state and provincial boards have formed the Association of Social Work Boards (ASWB; www.aswb.org), which develops the written examinations used by almost all jurisdictions to license social workers. Licensure itself may be available for individuals with the BSW, MSW, or doctorate, but the most common licensing credential is known as the LCSW, and permits the independent practice of clinical social work, and the practice of psychotherapy. Indeed, social workers comprise the largest professional discipline delivering psychotherapy services in the United States, and it is a very big business. Many private and state organizations that hire social workers themselves require that one possess the LCSW. Recall that in most states, each LCSW needs CE, and a number of entities are approved providers of CE for LCSWs, and there are several large umbrella groups that approve CE providers. The major players in this regard are the national office of the NASW, the NASW state chapters, the ASWB, graduate academic social work programs, and an array of multimillion-dollar companies. There are also numerous smaller stand-alone organizations and individuals who provide CE training. If a person or entity offers a CE program that is approved by one of these organizations, then the large market of LCSWs needing CE is opened up to them.

The traditional and still common CE platform is a conference put on by a social work organization. In return for attending the conference, one could earn CE. Sometimes one simply signs a form at the end of the conference indicating which sessions one participated in, with the total number of hours, and pays a CE fee, and in due course one receives a CE certificate indicating the number of hours earned. With a sufficient number of CE hours completed at the end of the 2-year cycle, one has fulfilled one's mandated CE required for licensure. This conference model of CE is expensive, including travel, conference registration fees, meals, and time off from work, a particular concern for social workers in private practice. So there has been, in effect, a race to the bottom in terms of providers offering CE courses "approved" by the NASW, state NASW chapters, or numerous other groups, provided in a more convenient format.

Many continuing education (CE) providers now allow one to sign up for a CE topic online through a website, read designated materials, take the quiz online, and if one passes, then print out the certificate of completion stating the numbers of CE completed. Again, earn enough of these over time, and you will have fulfilled the state's licensure requirement for CE. Some online CE programs allow the social worker to immediately retake the quiz if he or she initially fails to earn a passing grade. It is not usually difficult to pass after one or two tries. Some of the less rigorous CE providers take some publicly available document, say a fact sheet on some mental disorder prepared by the National Institute of Mental Health, post it online, and offer the quiz on its content for an hour or so of CE credit. Sometimes if you get stuck on a question you can leave the quiz, rereview the brochure or article, and return to the quiz where you left off. You complete the quiz and if you fail, you can immediately retake it, with or without a rereview of the course content. In the experience of one of the authors (BAT), some programs like this seem to devote very little attention to the composition of a legitimate quiz, with the result that the test can be very easy to pass. On some occasions, it was not even necessary to have read the materials in order to pass the quiz and earn an hour or two of CE hours, because the correct answers to the quiz were so transparently obvious. This laxity, although convenient for the LCSW, provides *no* assurance to the public that the social worker is indeed coming into contact with useful information, that "new knowledge is acquired, skills are refined, professional attitudes are reinforced, and individual's lives are changed" (NASW, 2003, p. 1), which is the avowed purpose of requiring CE. However, such lax programs do ensure the CE provider of a steady stream of revenue from LCSWs seeking an easy way to complete their CE requirements. There are obvious financial incentives to make earning CE as simple as possible so that the provider can earn greater income from its students.

Nowadays, one can acquire a designated book, or read a given journal article on some topic, complete a written multiple-choice quiz, and send it in for scoring. One of the authors (BAT) recently received a thick CE booklet in the mail offering an array of programs. The written information was in the brochure, as was the quiz required of each module. One course was a state-required 3-hour program on "Ethics and Boundaries." After the 13 pages of text content, there is a 5-item multiple-choice quiz. You can complete this quiz and mail it in, or complete it online. Here are two of the five questions found on this quiz:

3. Informed consent services should only be provided when valid informed consent can be obtained.
   a. True
   b. False
4. Buying property from a disaster client at far below market value is an inappropriate ethical violation.
   a. True
   b. False

The reader may judge for herself or himself the degree of professional training and knowledge of disciplinary ethics required to complete such a test of one's ability to practice safely. If you score above a certain level (e.g., 75% is a very common threshold), you can earn a certain number of CE hours (1, 2, or more hours), depending on the length and complexity of the material. This approach avoids the expense and inconvenience of attending a conference. Listening to approved CDs or watching DVDs is another medium through which one can earn CE. Is describing the CE business as a "race to the bottom" hyperbole?

To be sure, some CE programs are of a relatively higher quality. For example, the Society for Social Work and Research (www.sswr.org) offers CE for attending selected sessions during its annual conference. One must be present the entire time, and have his or her CE attendance form signed off by a moderator at each session. At the end of the conference, you turn in your attendance sheet, sign a statement of assurance that you did indeed attend the indicated sessions, and you eventually receive your CE certificates. However, not all approved CE providers have such quality-control standards in place, and even under the best circumstances, there is no evidence that a person who attended a particular session actually acquired an accurate understanding and good grasp of the material presented.

The comments mentioned earlier mostly pertain to the *process* of earning CEs. We will now turn to a review of the *content* of selected CE programs. In the fall of 2014, one of the authors (BAT) received a lengthy colorful course catalog from the Kripalu Center for Yoga and Health, a self-described nonprofit educational organization, the mission of which is to teach the art and science of yoga. The Kripalu Center is located on a beautiful 350-acre campus near Lenox, Massachusetts, and was founded in 1983 by Yogi Amrit Desai, an advocate, among other things, of strict celibacy among his followers. It is one of the largest and most sophisticated yogic schools in North America and has more than 15,000 visiting students a year. Amrit Desai was forced to leave in 1994, after it was discovered that the married yogi was having sex with three of his students (Carlson, 2002), but the organization continues to thrive in his absence. While paging through the catalog, Bruce was intrigued to discover that a large number of the Kripalu classes could be taken by LCSWs to earn CE needed for their licensure renewal (see www .kripalu.org/cecredits). This website says that the social work programs have been approved for CE by the NASW. Well, with the imprimatur of the profession's largest organization behind it, the Kripalu Center's social work CE programs must be credible and legitimate, right? Look over some of the programs offered in their Fall 2014 catalog—the following are only a few of the social work–approved CE courses listed—and arrive at your own judgment:

*Evidence-Based Qigong Certification* (Earn 8.5 CE Credits)
> "The Chinese word 'qi' is identical in meaning to the Sanskrit word 'prana.' Come deepen your understanding of the spiritual root common to all Eastern energy practices. The nurturing, relaxing, and core-strengthening benefits of qigong offer a perfect complement to your existing yoga practice."

*SomaSoul: Moving Your Body's Story* (Earn 25 CE credits)
> "In this workshop, you
>
> Access your body's energy through expressive movement explorations focusing on heart, legs, pelvis, gut, and spine.
>
> Experience the deepest reservoirs of emotion and energy through somatic/visceral movement exercises.

Rewrite elements of your body's story, from tension and pain to freedom and healing.

Transform limiting beliefs through a dynamic expressive-arts process."

*Lightworkers Healing Method Intensive: Angelically Guided Energy Healing* (Earn 29.5 CE)

"Experience the joy of channeling divine guides, angels, and light beings. When you learn to be a vessel for higher-dimension healers, miracles happen in your healing practice and in your life."

*The Art of Reiki: Reiki I* (Earn 8.5 CE)

"In Reiki 1, you

Explore the applications of Reiki through slide show and discussion.

Receive attunements to empower yourself as a conduit for channeling life-force energy.

Practice Reiki on yourself and others."

*Let Your Yoga Dance Teacher Training: Chakra Fusion, Module 2* (Earn 22 CE)

*Activating Your Chakras: Awaken Your Energy Body* (Earn 15.5 CE)

"You've heard about chakras and the energy body. You might even know where your blocks are and the gifts you want to bring forth. But do you know how to activate your chakras to harvest the energy within?

Through a unique combination of yoga and bioenergetic techniques, Anodea Judith, best-selling author and world-renowned teacher of the chakra system, has developed a method for awakening and enhancing your energy body and channeling that energy into specific chakras.

Flow through the liberating current of the chakras using asana, chanting, meditation, partner work, and illuminating discussions on the psychology of the chakras. Suitable for beginners and advanced practitioners alike, this workshop offers you a deeper sense of yourself and a potent set of tools for growth."

We find it odd that so many of these social work CE offerings at the Kripalu Center seem more oriented toward improving the health and well-being of the clinical social worker, as opposed to conveying skills to enhance one's ability to provide safe and effective services to the public. Keep in mind that the Kripalu Center is more akin to a spa, as it offers onsite massage, facials, seaweed masks, exfoliation, whirlpools, cranial-sacral therapy, Reiki, delicious meals, hikes, yoga exercise classes, and suites with queen-size beds, private baths, and your choice of mountain or lake views. It would be a good thing if the Kripalu Center was an anomaly in providing CE for training in pseudoscientific therapies, but it is not.

In 2010, the Association for Spirituality and Psychotherapy (an approved provider of social work CE) advertised a National Congress on Spiritual Sexuality and Sexual Healing. Clinical social work faculty at this conference were to offer workshops on "Energy Psychology and Healing from Sexual Trauma" and "Music and Movement." Other speakers taught "The Path of Sexual Priestess" "The Tao of Sexual Secrets" and "Sex, Spirit and Shamanism" (see www.spiritualawak-eningprocess.com/2010/09/national-congress-on-spiritual.html). There is an annual Canadian Energy Psychology Conference (epcca-nada.ca/?page_id=19) that offers social work CE for practitioners to learn about these elaborate placebo-based therapies. Many accredited social work graduate programs offer CE in pseudoscientific therapies, an offense to common sense made more egregious by using the prestige of distinguished universities to lend credibility to these bogus treatments. Simmons College School of Social Work offered a 2-day workshop in which one could learn when and how to utilize imagery, hypnosis, breathing techniques, and the Tapas Acupressure Technique to reduce stress, build resources, and prepare for using EMDR.

> The Tapas Acupressure Technique is an exquisite relaxation process that is a self-administered mind/body approach to restructuring the neuro-pathways that have been damaged by repeated stress. Developed by Tapas Fleming, an acupuncturist, it utilizes meridians around the eyes and the back of the head to quickly dissolve traumatic stress, emotional pain, and transform negative beliefs. (see www.thelifeworkscenter.com/techniques.htm)

The LCSW providing this workshop also provides training in thought field therapy, emotional freedom technique, and hypnosis and imagery, all interventions of no scientifically credible value. The School of Social Work at the State University of New York in Buffalo offered CE programs in the Spring of 2010, including a workshop on the theory and practice of sensorimotor psychotherapy, an intervention the CE brochure itself described as lacking evidence from experimental or quasiexperimental studies, and as being solely based on clinical observations and long-standing clinical practice that have not been subjected to empirical tests. We would submit that any profession worthy of the name would not approve of CE training in treatments with such flimsy evidence. A more recent CE course offering from this program titled "Self-Care in Trauma Work" stated, "Our activities will include mindfulness exercises, meditation, art, movement, writing, and breathwork." And a 2009 workshop offered by the Buffalo program was titled "The Body Remembers Stress and Trauma: Enhancing Healing by Moving the Breath and Body in Harmony." It was directed for social workers who "wish to incorporate breathing and rhythmic body movements (yoga-based) as well as mindfulness techniques into treatment with adults and adolescents."

In keeping with what we found through Internet searches, in a 2007 to 2008 survey conducted by one of us (MGP) of LCSWs throughout the United States (Pignotti & Thyer, 2012), respondents were asked an open-ended question about what CE seminars, workshops, or certification trainings they attended in the past 2 years. Responses included seminars on a number of questionable approaches. Here is an informal list of just a few that were named: bioenergetics, brainspotting, critical incident stress debriefing, critical incident stress management, dreams, electrical magnetic frequency balancing, energy psychology, thought field therapy or emotional freedom technique (aka meridian tapping therapies), Ericksonian therapy, Imago relationship therapy, internal family systems (this is not the more conventional family systems approach and often involves dealing with "alters"), neurofeedback, somatic experiencing, and Sufi psychology.

The authors' alma mater, the University of Michigan School of Social Work, arguably one of the profession's most distinguished programs, has succumbed to providing training in pseudoscientific practices. It has offered its graduate students a clinical course that taught the techniques of thought field therapy (Pignotti, 2007), a method discussed elsewhere in this book, and shown to essentially be an elaborate placebo treatment (Pignotti, 2005). Generally, graduate classes may be taken by LCSWs to fulfill CE requirements. Also, the Michigan Program offered six CE for a workshop on adventure-based therapy, an intervention for youth closely aligned with wilderness therapy programs that we reviewed in Chapter 3. Michigan faculty have justified the inclusion of pseudoscientific practices into the social work curriculum in part on the grounds that these techniques are so widely popular among the general public. It was claimed that:

> It is therefore critical that social workers become apprised of the evidence base for CAM (complementary and alternative medicines) and learn clinical assessment and communication skills that facilitate CAM disclosure and allow for the development of integrative treatment planning and case management–specific nonpharmacological treatment skills in CAM; such mind-body practice therapies are also appropriate educational techniques to teach future social work professionals. (Gant, Gioia, Been, & Seabury, 2009, p. 410)

We agree that social workers need to be informed about complementary and alternative medicines (CAM), especially the legitimate evidentiary foundations (or lack thereof) related to each individual approach, and social workers should be able to provide informed guidance to clients related to CAM. However, we think it professionally irresponsible to actually teach MSW students the *use* of pseudoscientific CAM such as thought field therapy as legitimate interventions when they are demonstrably ineffective, according to the scientific evidence to date. Additionally, where CAM is taught, students need to be taught to critically evaluate the claims, including the methodology of any research conducted on a particular intervention.

If a client wishes to use homeopathic "medications," products that are essentially water with no active ingredients, to treat a child who is sick with an earache, and asks the social worker's advice, the social worker should be able to provide informed guidance. If the client wishes to treat her family member's cancer with thought field therapy (TFT), which is claimed to help this disease, as well as dengue fever, malaria, irritable bowel syndrome, and postnatal depression (truly a panacea therapy!; see www.rogercallahan.com/news/tft-and-cancer-teleclass-recording-now-available/thought-field-therapy), we believe that the responsible professional role of the social worker is to acquaint the client with the facts about TFT's bogus claims and advise against such treatment, and most certainly not provide it, even if the social worker was trained in the method at the University of Michigan! Yet Michigan offered an MSW class titled "Complementary, Alternative, and Indigenous Healing Systems" in 2003 and 2005, a course that surveys treatments such as polarity therapy, Reiki, acupuncture, acupressure, reflexology (treating people by pressing on the bottoms of their feet!), and iridology (diagnosing people by examining their irises, a practice of no credibility). They included content on voodoo, spiritualism, chiropractic, and homeopathy. The class visited various practitioners of these arcane arts. In 2005 and 2006, further MSW classes actually taught skills in some of these CAM. Not simply *about* them, but how to *do* them! They conclude by asserting that social workers "must have a strong background in theories related to health behavior and promotion, risk reduction, pathophysiology of disease, nutritional sciences, and *practice of complementary therapy approaches*" (Gant et al., 2009, p. 412, emphasis added).

We find it a professional embarrassment for a social worker to get involved in, endorse, and advertise himself or herself as providing certain forms of CAM. For example, we can read on the website of *Bottoms Up Colonics* (see bottomsupcolonics.com):

> Sue Wilson has come from a 20 year Social Work background working with children and families from abuse backgrounds with learning and behaviour disorders. She has now complemented this work with alternative therapies and nutrition working with the complete system of Mind, Body and Spirit to heal and balance people's health. The experience she gained in working in this counselling field benefits the colonic clients as often when we are releasing physically, emotional releases will coincide with this. The old saying of you have s##t on the liver and that all of your emotions are in your tummy is true. We do hold on to our emotions and these are often released with a colonic treatment. This is where Sue can guide you through this experience so when you complete your treatment you have released emotionally as well as physically...The bottom line [Authors' note: Was this a pun?] is that having a colonic is like having a week's

detox in one hour. It will hasten your recovery. I have worked and continue to work with people who will say I have been sick for twenty years and after one colonic I felt 100% better.

It is amusing that as far back as 1919, physician Richard C. Cabot (1919) recommended that social workers be taught to give clients enemas during home visits and to find that now, almost 100 years later, Dr. Cabot's vision for the future of social work is finally "coming to pass!"

CAM is creeping its way into social work education via textbooks, chapters, and articles, a sort of retrograde evolutionary process that threatens to undo much of the progress made in the past two decades on placing the field on a sounder evidence-based footing. For example, the School of Social Work at Arizona State University offers a graduate certificate in integrative health modalities (ssw.asu.edu/admissions-degrees/scholarships/aihm_certificate). Classes included in this certificate include "Ancient Healing Traditions," "Introduction to Holistic Therapies: Mind, Body and Energy," and "Treating the Whole Person." Topics covered include traditional Chinese, ayurvedic, homeopathic, naturopathic, and indigenous medicines. Also see readings, largely uncritical, by Block (2006); Cook, Becvar, and Pontious (2000); Dziegielewski and Sherman (2004); and Lee, Ng, Leung, and Chan (2009). One laudable aspect of this latter textbook is that it contains a lengthy chapter on the ethics of social workers providing CAM to their clients. However, their conclusion is essentially that, with proper guidelines, it is ethical do to so, as it respects clients, and is in other ways consistent with the NASW *COE*. We disagree if the particular CAM has no known credible evidence that it helps clients. Take, for example, the following menu of interventions recommended in *Integrative Body-Mind-Spirit Social Work* (Lee et al., 2009, p. 299):

Treatment techniques related to body process as utilized in Integrative Body-Mind-Spirit Social Work involve many senses and primarily include the following activities:

- Treatment techniques related to breathing exercises
- Kinesthetic: physical movement and exercises, dance, massage, and stretching
- Taste: bitter tea, the mindful eating of rice, and herbal drinks

- Visual: mental imagery, color imagery, eye massage, and mental camera
- Touch: drumming, percussion, hand massage, and acupressure
- Sound: singing, mantra, humming, bells, and music
- Diet: health eating habits, mindful appreciation of food, and balanced and simple meals

It is tempting to give in to despair to think that this is being conveyed as the latest advanced form of contemporary clinical social work practice. And it is both maddening and ironic that the subtitle of this text is *An Empirically Based Approach to Assessment and Treatment*.

With respect to CAM, we support the position put forward by Fontanarosa and Lundberg (1998):

> There is no alternative medicine. There is only scientifically proven, evidence-based medicine supported by solid data or unproven medicine, for which scientific evidence is lacking. Whether a therapeutic practice is "Eastern" or "Western," is unconventional or mainstream, involves mind-body techniques or molecular genetics is largely irrelevant except for historical purposes of cultural interest...as believers in science, we must focus on fundamental issues—namely the patient, the target disease or condition, the proposed or practiced treatment, and the need for convincing data on safety and therapeutic efficacy...until solid evidence is available that demonstrates the safety, efficacy, and effectiveness of specific alternative medicine interventions, uncritical acceptance of untested and unproved alternative medicine therapies must stop. Alternative therapies that have been shown to be of no benefit (aside from possible placebo effect) or that cause harm must be abandoned immediately. (pp. 1618–1619)

This is a very strong position and flies in the face of the conventional epistemological egalitarianism, relativism, and postmodernist subjectivism currently fashionable in social work, which asserts that all interventions are basically equivalent in terms of effectiveness. We address the consequences and fallacies of this misguided view in the next and concluding chapter.

CAM and other pseudoscientific therapies are just as amenable to scientific evaluation as more conventional treatments. A November 1998 issue of *JAMA* was devoted to this topic, and included sound outcome studies on chiropractic, moxibustion, Chinese herbal medicine, acupuncture, yoga, and the use of saw palmetto as a dietary supplement. A federally funded National Center on CAM (nccam.nih.gov) finances such studies. Sometimes they are shown to be useful, but many times, they are not. The proponents of pseudoscientific treatments and CAM have just as great a responsibility to keep up to date with this literature, according to common sense and the NASW *COE*, as do more conventional practitioners. There is no bias or disposition against unproven treatments. There is a bias against social work practitioners providing these in the context of earning fees from privately paying clients and from third-party vendors, while making unsupported claims as to the effectiveness of certain pseudoscientific interventions. A recent systematic review sponsored by the Cochrane Collaboration found that a CAM involving a zinc preparation was actually effective in preventing the frequency and severity of the common cold (Singh & Das, 2011). This is great news. We urge that other CAM be subjected to similar comprehensive evaluations. Pseudoscientific treatments carry their own risks. For example, acupuncture can cause serious complications (Yamashita, Tsukayama, Tanno, & Nishijo, 1998), and many over-the-counter dietary supplements are of uneven quality and purity (Parasrampuria, Schwartz, & Petesch, 1998). One of the authors (BAT) once had an MSW student become seriously ill during one semester, experiencing dizziness, muscle weakness, confusion, and incapacity. She was extensively tested and no diagnosis could be made, until it was found that she was drinking a tea made of over-the-counter St. John's wort as a self-medication for depression, while she was concurrently taking a prescribed antidepressant. The two different classes of drugs produced serious side effects due to their interactions. When she stopped the herbal tea, she was "cured" of what had been thought to be the onset of multiple sclerosis.

The fifth edition of a very widely used textbook on social work treatments (Turner, 2011) contains chapters on chaos theory, constructivism, existential social work, narrative therapy, neurolinguistic programming, postmodern social work, transactional analysis, and transpersonal social work, all sharing the common element of not yet having been shown to be of genuine help to clients, beyond the level of individual testimonials and clinical judgment (e.g., Greene, 1988). Just as Abraham Flexner's (1910) report on medical education helped enhance the standards of medical training in that discipline, we need a similar purging of the social work educational equivalents of magnetic healing, chiropractic, naturopathy, bleeding, and purging, practices commonly encountered in medical training today more than 100 years ago. More on this is provided in the final chapter.

Social work needs to advance far beyond the professionalized delivery of placebo-based treatments. Deblanco made this point in regard to traditional (so-called allopathic, although this is a misrepresentation) medicine and CAM:

> Focusing on quality of life, comfort, and hope, alternative practitioners have much to teach the allopath who short-changes such human needs. For such fundamental aspects of care, do we really need to put each intervention in a scientific test? If a clinician spends ample time laying on hands and addressing issues warmly and hopefully with a patient, we don't need a controlled trial demonstrating the value of such interchange. But daggers flash when alternative clinicians claim their wares are not only entirely safe but also effective beyond the placebo effect. (Delbanco, 1998, p. 1561)

If what some social workers are seen to legitimately provide is in actuality really nothing more than elaborate mechanisms to engender, hope, optimism, and generalized placebo effects, what, pray tell (pun intended), is the need for 2 years of graduate training for MSWs? Does good practice need to include relationship factors, time, attention, warmth, and so on? Obviously, but it also requires empirically supported interventions (where these have been developed) to augment those outcomes engendered by general clinical support, acumen, and bells and whistles like laying on of hands, eye movements, tapping, gizmos, or the patter of invisible forms of "energy" being manipulated (Thyer, 2007).

## BOGUS SOCIAL WORK PROGRAMS

A bogus social work program is one that offers its students the BSW, MSW, or doctorate in social work, but one in which the awarding institution/university/college is not itself accredited by one of the major higher education accrediting bodies in the United States. See www.chea .org/degreemills/frmPaper.htm for a brief description of the problem of diploma mills in the United States and abroad. Programs offering the BSW or MSW degree are also likely bogus if these degrees are not fully or provisionally accredited by the CSWE, and are not making a good faith effort to earn such accreditation. Bogus programs are often easy to recognize, once one learns what to look for. Table 7.1 lists some of the characteristics that tend to be associated with diploma mills or other academic institutions of less than legitimate standing. The CSWE is not responsible for the existence of bogus degree programs in social work, and when unaccredited MSW programs have been offered in the United States, the CSWE has taken action to close them down (e.g., LaSalle University, in the 1980s), and indeed it is rare to find a bogus BSW or MSW program. However, illegitimate "doctorates" are common and sometimes MSWs are tempted to acquire one for the purposes of self-promotion, prestige, or career advancement. One of the authors (BAT) had a faculty colleague with a legitimate MSW and a doctorate from Oxford Graduate School listed on her curriculum vitae. Now, the real University of Oxford is an institution of immense status, and anyone receiving a doctorate from such a program would legitimately be seen as having obtained a very distinguished credential indeed. However, when Bruce Googled "Oxford Graduate School," he found that *this* Oxford program was a small religiously affiliated school located in the state of Tennessee, and at the time was unaccredited! One can obtain doctorates from any number of religiously affiliated institutes that require minimal attendance or scholarly activities on the part of its students. And there are PhD programs in various odd or fringe disciplines that are not evident to the public when the holder simply lists PhD after his or her name.

For example, here in Florida, where the authors are living, one may enroll in the American Academy of Clinical Sexologists (AACS), and earn a PhD in that field (see www.esextherapy.com/catalog.htm). This costs about $9,000 in tuition, and the program acknowledges that it is unaccredited, noting:

> The American Academy of Clinical Sexologists is not an accredited institution. Therefore, the acceptance of the transfer of credit to another institution is up to the transferring institution. As well, lack of accreditation by an agency recognized by the United States Department of Education will affect the ability of a student to apply for federal financial aid and/or credits may not be accepted by employers.

**TABLE 7.1**
**What Questions Should I Ask to Determine Whether a**
**Degree Provider Is a "Mill?"**

If the answers to many of the following questions are "yes," the degree provider under consideration may be a "mill":

- Can degrees be purchased?
- Is there a claim of accreditation when there is no evidence of this status?
- Is there a claim of accreditation from a questionable accrediting organization?
- Does the operation lack state or federal licensure or authority to operate?
- Is any attendance required of students, either online or in class?
- Are few assignments required for students to earn credits?
- Is a very short period of time required to earn a degree?
- Are degrees available based solely on experience or resume review?
- Are there few requirements for graduation?
- Does the operation fail to provide any information about a campus or business location or address and rely, for example, only on a post-office box?
- Does the operation fail to provide a list of its faculty and their qualifications?
- Does the operation have a name similar to other well-known colleges and universities?
- Does the operation make claims in its publications for which there is no evidence?

Also

- Is the college or university located in a less-developed country, with lax oversight of its educational programs?
- It is solely a "cyber-university" or does it have a "bricks and mortar" campus you can physically visit?
- Does it advertise master's thesis or doctoral dissertation requirements than seem unrealistically easy (e.g., a 20-page thesis, double-spaced, or submitting previously published articles that appeared in trade journals)?
- Discounts on tuition are offered if you "pay now"
- Packages of diplomas, transcripts, and letters of recommendation are offered for purchase
- The graduation date listed on the diploma can be altered to suit the request of the graduate
- There are no proctored or objective examinations
- Program faculty are themselves found to have bogus degrees
- The program offers a flat-rate tuition
- A list of so-called accrediting agencies that themselves are not recognized by the U.S. Department of Education, agencies that are basically cover or fronts for legitimate accreditation. Sometimes diploma mills do obtain state registration, which actually says little about the program's quality. It is more akin to having a business license from the state

*(continued)*

TABLE 7.1 (*continued*)
**What Questions Should I Ask to Determine Whether a
Degree Provider Is a "Mill?"**

---

- Little opportunity to interact with professors via telephone or face to face
- The name of the questionable institution (e.g., Washington International University, located in the British Virgin Islands) is very similar to a widely recognized and reputable university (Washington University, located in St. Louis, MO)

---

*Source:* Retrieved from www.chea.org/degreemills/frmPaper.htm

The entire institution has 10 faculty, most of whom obtained their own PhDs from Maimonides University, an unaccredited program, now defunct, formerly located in Miami. The AACS itself appears to be the successor to Maimonides University, in that almost all the latter faculty now appear on the roster of the former. Included on the faculty are three Florida LCSWs with MSWs from legitimate social work programs and "PhDs" from Maimonides University. In other words, social workers with degrees from a diploma mill are on the faculty of a new diploma mill granting bogus degrees to social workers! The AACS is oriented to granting the "PhD" to legitimately licensed mental health professionals, including LCSWs. Dissertations granted by this institution include titles such as "The Use of Nudity in Therapy with Gay Men," "The Secret and Not so Secret Life of Swingers," and "Erotological Examination of Cunnilingus and Relevant Techniques for Stimulating Female Sexual Response." We must grudgingly admit that these topics possess a bit more frisson than the usual dissertation research project emerging from more traditional social work PhD programs. And with a degree from this program, one is transmogrified from Mary Richmond, LCSW, to Dr. Mary Richmond, PhD, LCSW.

Alternatively (pun intended), an LCSW could earn his or her PhD from the Indian Board of Alternative Medicine. The entire program costs $850, and courses are completed by mail. You are sent the textbook for your course, and some questions to answer. When these are completed, you are mailed a take-home written test. In this manner, all courses are completed. There is an optional (not mandatory) clinical practicum involving healing methods such as using healing magnets, Bach Flower Remedies, and the like (see www.altmedworld.net/alternative-medi-cine-phd-program.htm).

The University of Holistic Theology is another option for the aspiring social worker. It states that:

> We only offer educational programs that prepare students for religious, spiritual, metaphysical, and holistic vocations as ministers, professionals, or lay-persons in the following categories: ministry, pastoral and spiritual counseling, theology, education, administration, teaching, media communications, parapsychology, **social work**, spiritual, complementary, holistic healing, intuitive and spiritual development. (see www.universityofholistictheology.com/tuition.htm, boldface added)

Complete tuition is a modest $3,300 for the PhD, and the package to earn the bachelor's, master's, and PhD in holistic theology can be had for only $7,000. Classes require no tests or examinations, only written papers, and the PhD requires a dissertation of no less than 10,000 words, roughly 30 to 40 double-spaced pages! The entire program is to be completed within 18 months. Sadly, one can Google "LCSW" and "holistic theology" and find examples of social workers who have earned or are earning a degree from this diploma mill (e.g., www.cylex-usa.com/pre%20marital%20counseling.html).

Wilson State University offered the PhD in social work, and the following are some of the attractive features of their program.

> If you want to get your Doctorate degrees online on the basis of prior life experience, the eligibility requirements... for the degree may be satisfied in any of the following ways:
> - Prior job experience in any field
> - Previous educational achievements
> - Employer-sponsored training and attendance of workshops
> - Participation in organizations, both professional and nonprofessional
> - Personal goals, lifestyle, hobbies, and travel
> - Participation in volunteer activities and community service
> - Independent reading, viewing, listening, or writing

If you have the required work or **life experience**, click below to apply for a **life experience college degree** in your desired major and get it in just 7 days!

**Fee Structure**

The complete Doctorate degree online package costs only $449 with free shipping.

The package includes the following documents:

- One Original Accredited Degree
- Two Original Transcripts
- One Award of Excellence
- One Certificate of Distinction
- One Certificate of Membership
- Four Education Verification Letters

## PLUS YOU CHOOSE THE GRADUATION YEAR!

Obviously, earning a PhD in social work in 7 days, for a tuition payment of less than $500, seems like a good deal. Diploma in hand, or on the wall, the social worker could now claim to be "Dr." That the degree is completely bogus will matter not to the type of applicant attracted to such a program to begin with. It spears that Wilson State University is now closed (it was operating at least until 2010), but similarly bogus institutions continue to proliferate and seduce unwary and ill-informed students into applying. Others attract social workers simply looking for a "shortcut" way to put themselves before the public as "Dr."

There are legitimately accredited distance education programs, such as those offered by Walden University, Capella University, the University of Phoenix, and Argosy University, and some of these offer doctorates in social work, for example, www.capella.edu/schools_pro-grams/social_behavioral_sciences/dsw/social_work.aspx and www.waldenu.edu/Degree-Programs/Doctorate/18085.htm. However, most social workers, faculty, and practitioners alike, who earned their doctorates via 5 years or more of full-time residential study at a traditional bricks-and-mortar institution hold ambivalent feelings about the overall quality of online or other distance-learning format doctoral studies. It is common for doubts to be raised about the quality of the research or clinical training afforded by online education. But they are legitimate degrees, in terms of being housed in properly accredited (by CHEA and its affiliates) universities, and its graduates can honestly add PhD after their name, and rightly call themselves Doctor. Potential clients will have no way of knowing if their doctorally trained LCSW social worker with the PhD earned it traditionally, or via distance learning. Of course it is always good to ask.

The Commission on Higher Education Accreditation posts a list of unaccredited colleges and universities (see www.michigan .gov/documents/Non-accreditedSchools_78090_7.pdf) and any social worker with degree from such institutions could have obtained a bogus degree (see also www.maine.gov/education/highered/Non-Accredited/a-am.htm). Periodically the U.S. Government Accounting Office investigates federal employees who are studying at, or who have earned degrees from, unaccredited colleges and university and diploma mills (see www.gao.gov/new.items/d04771t.pdf). It is a serious problem that degrades the value of legitimate degrees and places individuals at risk who are receiving services from someone who may have the training and educational background they claim to have.

## SUMMARY

There are many troubling aspects of the world of academic and professional social work, as well as within the array of services provided by state and federal agencies, that promote the tolerance, proliferation, and encouragement of members of the discipline providing pseudoscientific practices to the public.

The NASW *COE* standard in this regard is remarkably lax, and when asked if it was unethical for a social worker to provide a therapy that research showed was harmful to clients, the NASW's ethics consultation office refused to provide an opinion to one of the authors. The accreditation standards used by the CSWE are similarly flaccid with respect to promoting the teaching of empirically supported treatments and of evidence-based practice. Major professional associations and academic programs accredit CE programs that teach pseudoscientific treatments and complementary and alternative therapies with no credible evidentiary foundations. Clinical social workers can fulfill their state-required mandate for CE by enrolling in personal self-help classes focused on weight loss, yoga, and spurious energy therapies. Social workers include their degrees and state licenses when they advertise providing massage services, colonic (e.g., high-volume enemas) therapies, and the healing of auras, and the professional bodies charged with the oversight of clinical practice do little to discourage this. Some social workers obtain bogus degrees from diploma mills and present themselves as possessing legitimate doctorates.

The features mentioned earlier are not mainstream, or characteristic of the profession. The vast majority of social workers are conscientious, well intended, and competent. But just as the presence of a couple of bad apples can spoil a barrel of them, the existence and toleration of social workers who provide pseudoscientific services, deliver bogus CE, and advertise illegitimate degrees erodes the entire profession. Our national organizations, accrediting body, and state licensing boards need to be more proactive in purging such members from the profession.

# REFERENCES

Accreditation Council on Graduate Medical Education (ACGME). (2007). *ACGME program requirements for graduate medical education in psychiatry.* Chicago, IL: Author. Retrieved March 10, 2011, from http://www.acgme.org/acWebsite/downloads/RRC_progReq/400_psychiatry_07012007_u04122008.pdf

Ackerman, R. (1996, March). *Beyond current values of informed consent in mental health.* Paper presented at the meeting of the Ethics and Professional Standards Committee, NASW New York Chapter, New York, NY.

American Psychological Association. (2007). *Guidelines and principles for accreditation of programs in professional psychology.* Washington, DC: Author.

Baker, L. R., Stephens, F., & Hitchcock, L. (2010). Social work practitioners and practice evaluation: How are we doing? *Journal of Human Behavior in the Social Environment, 20,* 963–973.

Bledsoe, S. E., Weissman, M. M., Mullen, E. J., Ponniah, K., Gameroff, M. J., Verdeli, H.,…Wickramaratne, P. (2007). Empirically supported psychotherapy in social work training programs: Does the definition of evidence matter? *Research on Social Work Practice, 17,* 449–455.

Block, P. (2006). Alternative, complementary, and integrative medicine in a conventional setting. In S. Gehlert & T. A. Browne (Eds.), *Handbook of health social work* (pp. 773–707). Hoboken, NJ: John Wiley & Sons.

Bloom, M., Fischer, J., & Orme, J. G. (2009). *Evaluating practice: Guidelines for the accountable professional* (6th ed.). Boston, MA: Allyn & Bacon.

Bruno, F. (1934). *The theory of social work.* New York, NY: D. C. Heath.

Cabot, R. C. (1919). *Social work: Essays on the meeting ground of doctor and social worker.* Boston, MA: Houghton and Mifflin

Carlson, P. (2002, September 2). Gurus get in scandalous positions. *The Sun Sentinel*, p. 1D.

Cook, C. A., Becvar, D. S., & Pontious, S. L. (2000). Complementary alternative medicine in health and mental health: Implications for social work practice. *Social Work in Health Care, 31*(3), 39–57.

Council on Social Work Education. (2008). *Educational and policy accreditation standards.* Alexandria, VA: Author. Retrieved February 23, 2011, from http://www.cswe.org/Accreditation/41865.aspx

Delbanco, T. (1998). Leeches, spiders, and astrology: Predilections and predictions. *JAMA, 280*, 1560–1562.

Dziegielewski, S., & Sherman, P. (2004). Complementary therapies: Tips and techniques. In S. Dziegielewski (Ed.), *The changing face of health care social work: Professional practice in managed behavioral health care* (2nd ed., pp. 422–438). New York, NY: Springer Publishing Company.

Flexner, A. (1910). *Medical education in the United States and Canada: A report to the Carnegie Foundation for the Advancement of Teaching.* New York, NY: Carnegie Foundation.

Fontanarosa, P. B., & Lundberg, G. D. (1998). Alternative medicine meets science (editorial). *JAMA, 280*, 1618–1619.

Gant, L., Gioia, D., Been, R., & Seabury, B. (2009). Incorporating integrative health services in social work education. *Journal of Social Work Education, 45*, 407–425.

Greene, G. (1988). Analysis of research on the effectiveness of transactional analysis for improving marital relationships: Towards close encounters of the single kind. *Transactional Analysis Journal, 18*, 238–248.

Jenkins, D., & Johnston, L. B. (2004). Unethical treatment of gay and lesbian people with conversion therapy. *Families in Society, 85*, 557–561.

Kazi, M. A. F. (1998). *Single-case evaluation by social workers.* Brookfield, VT: Ashgate.

Lee, M. Y., Ng, S.-M., Leung, P., & Chan, C. (2009). *Integrative body-mind-spirit social work: An empirically based approach to assessment and treatment.* New York, NY: Oxford University Press.

Myers, L. L., & Thyer, B. A. (1997). Should social work clients have the right to effective treatment? *Social Work, 42*, 288–298.

National Association of Social Workers. (2003). *NASW standards for continuing professional education.* Retrieved from https://www.socialworkers.org/practice/standards/NASWContinuingEdStandards.pdf

National Association of Social Workers. (2006). *Code of ethics.* Washington, DC: NASW Press. Retrieved February 23, 2011, from http://www.socialworkers.org/pubs/code/code.asp

National Committee on Lesbian and Gay Issues. (1992). *Position statement on reparative therapies.* Washington, DC: National Association of Social Workers.

National Committee on Lesbian, Gay, and Bisexual Issues. (2000). *"Reparative" and "Conversion" therapies for lesbians and gay men. Position Statement.* Washington, DC: National Association of Social Workers.

Parasrampuria, J., Schwartz, K., & Petesch, R. (1998). Quality control of dehydroepiandrosterone dietary supplement products (letter). *JAMA, 280,* 1565.

Pignotti, M. (2005). Thought field therapy voice technology vs. random meridian point sequences: A single-blind controlled experiment. *The Scientific Review of Mental Health Practice, 4*(1), 72–81.

Pignotti, M. (2007). Questionable interventions taught at top-ranked school of social work. *The Scientific Review of Mental Health Practice, 5,* 78–82.

Pignotti, M., & Thyer, B. A. (2012). Novel unsupported and empirically supported therapies: Patterns of usage among licensed clinical social workers. *Behavioural and Cognitive Psychotherapy, 40,* 331–349.

Seelig, J. M. (1990). Mandatory continuing education. *Journal of Independent Social Work, 4*(3), 75–80.

Singh, M., & Das R. R. (2011). Zinc for the common cold. *Cochrane Database of Systematic Reviews,* Issue 2. Art. No.: CD001364. doi:10.1002/14651858. CD001364.pub3

Strom-Gottfried, K. (2003). Understanding adjudication: Origins, targets, and outcomes of ethics complaints. *Social Work, 48*(1), 85–94.

Thyer, B. A. (1995). Promoting an empiricist agenda within the human services: An ethical and humanistic imperative. *Journal of Behavior Therapy & Experimental Psychiatry, 26,* 93–98.

Thyer, B. A. (1996). Guidelines for applying the empirical clinical practice model to social work. *Journal of Applied Social Sciences, 20,* 121–127.

Thyer, B. A. (2007). Social work education and clinical learning: Towards evidence-based practice? *Clinical Social Work Journal, 35,* 25–32.

Thyer, B. A. (2011). LCSW examination pass rates: Implications for social work. *Clinical Social Work Journal, 39,* 296–300. doi:10.1007/s10615–009–0253–x

Thyer, B. A., & Myers, L. L. (2007). *A social workers' guide to evaluating practice outcomes.* Alexandria, VA: Council on Social Work Education.

Turner, F. J. (Ed.). (2011). *Social work treatment: Interlocking theoretical approaches* (5th ed.). New York, NY: Oxford University Press.

Tutty, L. (1990). The response of community mental health professionals to client's rights: A review and suggestions. *Canadian Journal of Community Mental Health, 9,* 1–24.

Weissman, M. M., Verdeli, H., Gameroff, M. J., Bledsoe, S. E., Betts, K., Mufson, L.,...Wickramaratne, P. (2006). National survey of psychotherapy training in psychiatry, psychology and social work. *Archives of General Psychiatry, 63,* 925–934.

Yamashita, H., Tsukayama, H., Tanno, K., & Nishijo, K. (1998). Adverse events related to acupuncture (letter). *JAMA, 280,* 1563–1564.

# CHAPTER 8

# Promoting Science and Discouraging Pseudoscience: The Way Forward

*The great enemy of the truth is very often not the lie—deliberate, contrived and dishonest—but the myth—persistent, persuasive and unrealistic. Belief in myths allows the comfort of opinion, without the discomfort of thought.*—PRESIDENT JOHN F. KENNEDY

Thus far in this book, we have reviewed the features of pseudoscience, shown how it negatively impacts the profession of social work, and described the types of bogus assessment methods and treatments some social workers are providing. We have examined how pseudoscientific therapies are used in assessment and in practice with adults, with young persons, with children with disabilities and their families, and how incorrect, inaccurate, or fraudulent practices are conveyed in social work educational programs, abetted in this by lax practice, and ethical and accreditation standards of the profession's major organizations. It might be useful at this point to balance this litany of woes by reiterating the message that the authors have been proud to be practicing social workers, to have worked in the field for several decades, to be licensed, and to have taught in social work educational programs. We believe that in many ways the profession is in a very solid position within the eyes of the general public, the academy, and mainstream social science. However, every field has an undetermined number of fringe practitioners (Field, 2009; Lilienfeld, Lynn, & Lohr, 2015; Ross & Pam, 1995), most of whom are probably well intentioned, but nevertheless are individuals who use their professional credentials to provide ineffective and sometimes harmful methods of assessment and treatment. Psychiatry has its share, with Bruno Bettelheim and his Orthogenic schools for autistic children, Wilhelm Reich and his orgone therapy, and Arthur Freeman and his traveling lobotomy clinic (Johnstone, 1989; Valenstein, 1986). Many German psychiatrists adopted pseudoscientific eugenic theories, which Hitler used to justify the Holocaust (Roder, Kubillus, & Burwell, 1995) against Jewish people, the Romy, gays and lesbians, the intellectually disabled, and various eastern European peoples. Even today, distinguished psychiatrists who receive undisclosed income from pharmaceutical companies issue public statements and write articles extolling the virtues of the latest drug (claims that later turn out to be exaggerated). Psychology had its flirtations with phrenology and graphology, and continues to endorse the invalid ink blot test as a legitimate means of assessing clients. Early on, it promoted IQ testing as a means of classifying individuals, to the detriment of intelligent persons from non-Western European backgrounds trying to immigrate to the United States (Lilienfeld, Lynn, & Lohr, 2003, 2015). Moreover, many practicing clinical psychologists are holders of the PsyD degree, which is often offered in proprietary freestanding (although accredited) schools that often have less rigorous standards than university-based PhD programs. A substantial proportion of contemporary professional psychological practice seems to be built on pseudoscientific myths (Dawes, 1994). Contemporary nursing has its share of practitioners of so-called therapeutic touch (see www.therapeutic-touch.org/newsarticle.php?newsID=1), yet another of the unending variants of laying on of hands, ala Mesmerism, magnetic healing, Reiki, acupressure, and polarity therapy. Note that each of these approaches has its own different and conceptually distinct theory as to how touching a client with one's hands, or simply holding one's hands close to the client, can promote healing, above and beyond placebo influences. All these theories cannot be correct because they often contradict each other. Good evidence exists that Mesmer's hypothesized "magnetic fluid" does not exist, and controlled trials show that the practitioners of therapeutic touch cannot actually detect the supposed energy field around someone's body. The philosophical principle of parsimony, common sense, as well as scientific evidence, indicates that these "therapies" exert little more (but it can be significant) than placebo influence (Jopling, 2008).

Thus, when we compare social work to other human service fields, we have no more to be ashamed of than do members of other human service and health care disciplines. But perhaps it might be contended that our oft-claimed unique focus on caring for marginalized and other historically oppressed groups lays upon social work a particular burden to ensure that the services provided to these individuals are not yet another way of exploiting their hopes and needs. And, to reiterate an earlier point, the public expects professional social workers to provide services that deliver benefits above and beyond those obtainable via placebo treatments. Here is how Professor Alan Barsky recently addressed this issue:

> When we choose to offer clients particular models of intervention, we need to have sound rationale for using them. We should identify the best research evidence available, so we can help clients select the interventions that are most likely to be effective. We should be cautious about using untested interventions. (Barsky, 2014, p. 5)

The principles of evidence-based practice (EBP) can be applied in one of at least two ways. What we call negative EBP consists of describing and exposing pseudoscientific and ineffective interventions and assessment methods, in the hope that these will be discarded by the profession. This is a huge undertaking, akin to playing a never-ending game of Whack-a-Mole, that carnival game wherein you bash at the heads of mole-like creatures with a mallet as the moles pop up randomly on a table. One's professional life could be consumed with such a focus, which can be a very useful contribution to the field. Examples include the developmental psychologist Jean Mercer and one of the authors' (MGP) criticism of and activism exposing injurious holding, coercive restraint, and attachment therapies (Mercer, Sarner, & Rosa, 2003; Pignotti & Mercer, 2007), and the psychologist, renowned for her research in eyewitness reports and memory, Elizabeth Loftus's (Loftus, 2003; Loftus & Ketcham, 1994) work on the often questionable content of repressed memories relating to childhood sexual abuse, said to be uncovered in psychotherapy. Another side of the coin can be said to be positive EBP, highlighting assessments and interventions that are valid, in the sense they "work," as determined by credible scientific investigation, and are pragmatic, ethical, and acceptable to clients and family members. Having largely emphasized negative EBP thus far, the balance of this chapter reviews some suggested ways in which social work can move forward, by reducing the practice of pseudoscience by members of our profession, and promoting the teaching and practice of EBP within our field. Although it may be unrealistic to hope to reduce the larger public's demand for ineffective therapies (just stroll through the complementary and alternative medicine (CAM) and homeopathic medicines section of your local drug store), steps can be taken to help ensure that professional social workers are not the purveyors of the psychosocial equivalents of such nostrums.

## IMPROVING SOCIAL WORK EDUCATION

The Council on Social Work Education is the nationally designated body responsible for the content and quality of social work academic training. As described in the previous chapter, the accreditation standards are rather lax and weakly enforced, so that bachelor's degrees in social work (BSW) and master's degree in social work (MSW) programs can freely include pseudoscientific content and still be in compliance with educational mandates. We identified some additional accrediting standards that could be adopted in future versions of the *Educational Policy and Accreditation Standards (EPAS)* and its successor documents to tighten up on the expectation that classroom and field instruction content is scientifically current, accurate, and reflective of the latest developments in intervention research. At present, a small number of social work MSW programs have adopted EBP as the conceptual framework around which their curriculum is based. Among these are Washington University in St. Louis, the University of Tennessee in Knoxville, Abilene Christian University in Texas, and the former Department of Social Policy and Social Work at the University of Oxford (now known as the Department of Social Policy and Intervention). The *EPAS* certainly permit such a focus, and it is very compatible with current educational thinking in other disciplines. There is a growing literature on the topic of adopting EBP within academic social work, which additional programs could draw upon in restructuring their curriculum (e.g., Bellamy, Bledsoe, Mullen, Lin, & Manuel, 2008; Howard, McMillen, & Pollio, 2003), with attention being given to field instruction and international applications (Thomlison & Corcoran, 2008; Thyer & Kazi, 2004).

Social work has seen the establishment of various institutes devoted to promoting EBP, in the United States, in Canada, and abroad (Hannes,

Claes, & the Belgian Campbell Group, 2007; Sundell, Soydan, Tengvald, & Antilla, 2010), and a number of initiatives have been undertaken to examine the feasibility of teaching existing practitioners the model of EBP (Manuel, Mullen, Fang, Bellamy, & Bledsoe, 2009; Parrish & Rubin, 2011). A national survey of almost 1,000 social work faculty found that a large majority of them had favorable views of EBP (Rubin & Parrish, 2007). This approach is also generally endorsed by federal agencies that fund research and social care programs, including the office of the Surgeon General, the Centers for Disease Control and Prevention, the various National Institutes of Health, and the Substance Abuse and Mental Health Services Administration. Across the Atlantic, the United Kingdom's National Health Service and other leading national agencies have similarly adopted EBP as a guiding framework for the research they sponsor and the services that are provided.

Existing faculty can undertake steps within their existing programs to more closely align the training they provide to be consistent with EBP by offering content in practice and other classes primarily based on scientific justification, *where such content is available.* We cannot stress this latter point enough. EBP does not depend on the existence of well-conducted randomized controlled trials in order to guide practice. It requires that one consult the best available evidence, and if this means quasiexperiments, or preexperiments, then that is completely compatible with EBP. And where these forms of evidence are lacking, perhaps single-subject investigation, theories, or clinical opinions are the best available evidence. Particularly ambitious faculty could try and develop an explicit track or specialization within their curriculum, focusing on EBP. This may take both time and persistent effort, but the possible benefits could be immense. When individual faculty become aware of other instructors within their program who teach pseudoscientific practices, some face-to-face counseling as to why this is unacceptable may be one approach to try and remove such content from the curriculum. One hard-hitting tactic is to write up the equivalent of an exposé on pseudoscientific content being taught and seek to publish this in a professional periodical or local newspaper (i.e., Pignotti, 2007). When our social work journals publish scientific claptrap, this practically calls out for a vigorous response. Journal editors often welcome well-documented critical responses to works that have been recently published, which, in the opinion of the responding authors, reflect pseudoscientific practices (i.e., Albright & Thyer, 2010; Pignotti & Mercer, 2007; Pignotti & Thyer, 2009).

Many social work programs offer continuing education (CE) classes to licensed clinical social workers (LCSWs). EBP-inclined faculty can proactively offer to teach classes on the latest research-based methods of assessment and intervention for any of a wide array of disorders or conditions commonly encountered by social workers in their practice. By being first at the table in terms of offering content, there is less opportunity for pseudoscientific, bogus, and magical CE programs being sponsored by your own institution, or the state chapter of the National Association of Social Workers (NASW). There is a great hunger in the practice community for information on psychosocial interventions that really seem to work, and EBP-inclined faculty can take advantage of this need to provide such content.

Apart from improving the content of social work education, another initiative the Council on Social Work Education (CSWE) could undertake to reduce the likelihood that a professional social worker seeks and obtains a bogus degree would be for the CSWE to proactively request that diploma mills and other fringy degree-granting institutions halt offering degrees labeled as social work or social welfare. It is not reasonable to expect the diploma mills to shut down. Like dandelions they close up, relocate, and spring up anew, often in countries where U.S. authorities hold no sway, in response to the lucrative profits they reap. But when programs are identified as offering bogus doctoral and other degrees variously named as "social work" or "social welfare," a firm but polite letter to the offending institution asking it to desist would be a good first step. Those who refuse, if in the United States, could be followed up via a letter to the state educational office, asking them to look into the matter, and questioning the legitimacy of the degree-granting institution. Perhaps a list could be posted on the CSWE website listing diploma mills (use the list provided by the National Council on Higher Education Accreditation [CHEA]) that offer social work degrees, with language warning social workers and others to avoid obtaining such degrees.

The NASW could more vigorously enforce its own ethical standards relating to social workers being prohibited from claiming credentials, including degrees, to which they are not legitimately entitled. A few well-publicized stories of social workers possessing bogus credentials being sanctioned by the NASW may deter other members of the profession from obtaining or advertising them. Similarly, state licensing boards could demand that clinical social workers cease using bogus degrees in their professional advertising. Setting a positive example for other boards to hopefully follow, the Oklahoma Social Work Licensing Board, whose members are to be commended, ordered an LCSW practicing in that state with a diploma-mill PhD who was using the title "Dr." or "PhD" in his advertisements to stop misrepresenting his credentials (see www.casewatch.org/board/sw/post.shtml). The individual has since moved on to another state, although he is no longer practicing as a licensed social worker. He was also reported to have received hundreds of thousands of dollars of government money for treating children with controversial forms of "attachment therapy," which at least two former clients as well as some former staff have complained about in the media (see hamptonroads.com/2008/07/practitioner-controversial-therapy-moves-his-base-hampton-roads). Nevertheless, boards taking such steps will at least withdraw the support of and distance the social work profession from such individuals, and this would be helpful in reducing the demand for these academic shortcuts.

## WHAT CAN SOCIAL WORK STUDENTS DO?

There is sometimes a very fine line for a faculty member between the joy of having students who are reflective, scientifically skeptical, and critical thinkers and students who are a constantly challenging pain in the backside. The classroom is not a place to play the game of "gotcha," but it is above all a place where it should be safe to ask meaningful questions. Recall the principles contained within the NASW *Code of Ethics*, principles such as:

> Social workers who function as educators, field instructors for students or trainers should provide instruction only within their areas of knowledge and competence and *should provide instruction based on the most current information and knowledge available in the profession.* (NASW, 2006, Section 3.02(a), emphasis added) (and)
>
> Social workers should critically examine and keep current with emerging knowledge relevant to social work (NASW, 2006, Section 401(b)) (and)
>
> Social workers should base practice on recognized knowledge, including empirically based knowledge, relevant to social work and social work ethics (NASW, 2006, Section 4.01(c))

It is clear that social work faculty should be imparting accurate and current information in their classes. With these principles in mind, Thyer (1996) offered some suggestions to faculty and students aimed at moving social work education into closer adherence to the NASW *Code of Ethics*. For example, it was suggested that faculty teaching about theories of human behavior should focus their instructions on those theories of human behavior and development that are relatively well supported by empirical research, and avoid promulgating theoretical perspectives that contemporary research suggests are largely invalid. For example, the theory of cognitive development taught by Piaget is no longer considered to be accurate within the larger field of developmental psychology, but current social work texts often continue to review it, with little attention given to the fact that it is considered outmoded. Faculty should distinguish in their instruction between content that is currently considered to be empirically supported, that which lacks research support, and that which we are pretty sure is not true, but is being covered for historical review purposes. Similarly, practice instructors should focus their teaching on psychosocial methods of assessment and intervention, which are reasonably well supported by appropriately designed and published research studies. And correspondingly, avoid teaching, as legitimate methods of helping, approaches that lack such a foundation. If this strikes you as too stringent a standard, ask yourself if you would find it an appropriate standard for medical education? If you do not believe that a given area of social work practice enjoys a substantial level of research support that can so inform practice, make sure you have consulted the scientific literature to be sure you are correct. Do not assume, because *you are not aware of* potentially effective treatments in a given area, that these do not exist. There is a great distinction between saying "I do not know" versus "There is no such body of literature." Until one has actively looked at current research, it can be a mistake to assume no empirical findings exist to guide one's teaching and practice.

Obviously, there are many areas in the social work curriculum in which strong evidence is either lacking or irrelevant. Instruction in social work ethics, the history of social welfare, and some areas of social policy are ones in which scientific research support is an inappropriate benchmark. But when it comes to trying to theorize about human behavior, and to intervene at the interpersonal, group, organizational, community, or policy level, scientific considerations are of vital importance and can only be neglected at one's professional peril.

Students have some things they can do to help avoid being indoctrinated in pseudoscientific course content. At the beginning of each relevant course, privately approach the instructor and enthusiastically tell him or her how much you are looking forward to learn about empirically supported content related to the class's subject matter (e.g., human behavior in the social environment, practice methods, substance abuse, mental health, school social work, child welfare, domestic violence). In class, when being presented with an approach to assessment or intervention, ask, with a bright smile and chirpy tone, if this method is reliable and valid, or has been shown through controlled studies, to really help social work clients, and with what types of problems or issues. Maybe you and your friends can rotate this assignment each class, so none of you gets tagged as a nag. An honest instructor will reply along one of the following lines:

- "Great question! Thanks for asking" and then proceed to describe relevant studies, AND provide references. You can check these out, and verify the instructor's summary of the research. If the references do not support what was taught, you bring it back with a puzzled look (perhaps privately, not during class), pointing out what you see as a different interpretation, and ask the instructor to clarify things.
- "Great question! You know, I am not sure. I will follow this up and get back to you next class." And then actually does so in the next class.

A dishonest or pseudoscientific teacher will reply differently, perhaps saying:

- "I am not sure, but it is irrelevant. This technique has been very widely used for decades and the consensus of clinical opinion is that it works!"
- "I am not sure, but it is irrelevant. I have seen it used successfully many times, and you should trust my expertise-authority-credibility-credentials in this matter."
- "I am not sure, but it is irrelevant. The influence of social work intervention is too subtle to be detected by the crude and constrictive methods of positivistic science. We rely on other sources to inform our practice, such as intuition and client testimonials."

- "It doesn't matter which intervention you use because it is the therapeutic relationship that counts."

Or worse of all:

- "How dare you question my authority! I am the instructor here and you are the learner!"

Obviously, faculty who listen to such questions respectfully are positively reinforced by the students, with public words of thanks in class, saying how helpful it was, the way they responded, or privately during individual meetings during office hours with the teacher. And end-of-term course evaluations are similarly positive. Dismissive faculty, or those who inappropriately deny the value of scientific research when it comes to informing social work theory and practice, should receive poor course evaluations. If instructors cross the line, presenting clearly bogus content in class as legitimate approaches to social work, perhaps when the class is over and grades are turned in, brave students can meet privately with the offending faculty member and relate how distressed they were that pseudoscientific techniques were taught in class, and ask the faculty member to amend his or her ways, gently and respectfully. If this is ineffective, complain formally to the program director, dean, or if need be, the dean of undergraduate or graduate studies. Follow all rules for filing complaints. Be respectful and polite, and focus on the transmission of pseudoscientific content, not personalities, when making your complaints. You are not looking to receive an apology. You are looking to enhance the scientific rigor of program content.

Now, if you, the reader, think this is unrealistic advice, imagine a social work faculty member who presented reparative therapy as a legitimate and effective method for changing homosexuals into heterosexuals. Would not this rightfully engender student protest? Would not most other faculty smile benignly on the students' activism, proclaiming it laudable advocacy, or even join with the students in halting the promulgation of such content? How about teaching the so-called holding therapy, discussed in Chapter 3, wherein parents are taught to lay on top of their child's supine body, or the even more dangerous prone facedown restraint procedures (which puts the child at risk for asphyxia) until the child becomes unquestioningly compliant. We are not advocating disrespectfully and publicly challenging everything that the faculty teach. But when specific claims are made regarding the legitimacy of a taught theory, or of a method of social work practice, it is incumbent on the teacher to include balanced coverage on the current scientific foundations of this subject. And if this is not provided proactively, it is both right and proper for the students to request it.

Practice faculty can make students aware of websites and other credible resources that focus on research relating to the evaluation of psychosocial methods of assessment and intervention useful in clinical work, and analogous sources pertaining to macro-level practice. We particularly recommend the following resources as useful in this regard:

- The Cochrane Library of Systematic Reviews (www.cochrane.org)
- The Campbell Library of Systematic Reviews (www.campbellcollaboration .org)
- The website listing research-supported (formerly empirically supported) treatments for major mental health disorders, sponsored by the Society for Clinical Psychology (www.div12.org/Psychologi calTreatments/index.html)
- The U.S. Federal Substance Abuse and Mental Health Services Administration National Registry of Evidence-based Programs and Practices (www.nrepp.samhsa.gov)
- The Center for Evidence-Based Policy (www.ohsu.edu/xd/research/ centers-institutes/evidence-based-policy-center/index.cfm)
- The Clinical Practice Guidelines prepared by the National Institute on Health and Clinical Excellence, in the United Kingdom (www.nice .org.uk)
- therapyadvisor.com/default.aspx, which provides information on research-supported treatments in the fields of child and adult mental health, and in the area of substance abuse
- www.quackwatch.com, which provides various quack-type therapies being offered in health and mental health care

When one is looking for clinical interventions, programs, community-based practices, and policies that have credible evidence that they are helpful, the aforementioned resources can be very useful. They can also provide information about interventions that do not seem to work, or that have not yet been rigorously tested. Such content could and, in our opinion, should form the centerpiece of the social work curriculum, as well as for useful CE programs.

## BE A WHISTLE-BLOWER

If you encounter a social worker who advertises having a degree that turns out to be from a diploma mill or is otherwise bogus, who offers a therapeutic service that is known to be harmful, or makes unrealistically optimistic claims (e.g., promising to "cure" otherwise intractable conditions), follow the NASW *Code of Ethics*, which says:

> Social workers should not participate in, condone, or be associated with dishonesty, fraud, or deception (NASW, 2006, section 4.04)... and...
>
> Social workers should ensure that their representations to clients, agencies and the public of professional qualifications, credentials, education, competence. affiliations, services provided or results to be achieved, are accurate. Social workers should claim only those relevant professional credentials they actually possess and take steps to correct any inaccuracies or misrepresentations of their credentials by others. (NASW, 2006, Section 4.06(c))

The most straightforward way to deal with such a situation is to contact the possible offender yourself, by phone, e-mail, or in person. Explain your concern and ask the social worker to provide you with any additional information that might help clarify the claims. If this is done to your satisfaction, you can let the matter go. If it is not, then you can respectfully and politely ask the social worker to desist, citing professional ethics. For example:

- "Well, the program you obtained your PhD from is listed by the Council on Higher Education Accreditation as a diploma mill, and it is unethical for you to advertise having such a degree. Please rearrange your advertising to omit this degree, otherwise I will have to file a complaint with the state NASW Chapter (if the offender is a member of the NASW) or the state social work licensing board."
- "I see that you are offering facilitated communication as a therapy for persons with autistic disorder. This treatment has been said to be determined to be ineffective by the American Psychological Association, the National Speech and Hearing Association, and the American Pediatric Association. I believe, on this basis, that it is

unethical for you to provide this service to the public. I must ask you to stop providing this therapy, otherwise…etc."

## EDUCATING OUR CLIENTS TO BE DISCERNING MENTAL HEALTH CONSUMERS

Given the multitude of bad experiences people have had with various harmful and/or ineffective interventions, the question arises of how we might prevent this from ever occurring in the first place. It has been our experience that all too often, state boards are reluctant to take any action against a licensed mental health professional unless the case involves egregious sexual misconduct. This means that, whether we like it or not, the burden of prevention often falls on the shoulders of the prospective client and/or on a social worker providing referrals, to be a discerning consumer when hiring a mental health professional.

Unfortunately, all too often, people ask better questions of a car dealership when purchasing an automobile than they would of a mental health professional. This may be because mental health consumers make unwarranted assumptions that someone who is licensed is necessarily qualified to provide services to them and will not provide ineffective or even harmful services. Unfortunately, this is not always the case. Although important to determine, the mere fact of being licensed is necessary but not sufficient evidence that the consumer will be provided with the most effective interventions available. Therefore, we have put together a series of questions that we recommend people ask when interviewing a prospective psychotherapist.

This list of questions can also apply to social workers who work in agencies and need to investigate various referral sources so that clients of those agencies can be provided with the best services. Here, this is a matter of social justice. Clients of such agencies often have no choice and must go to the treatment providers the agency sends them to. Given that often these are some of the most economically disadvantaged clients and/or legally mandated clients, they are in a highly vulnerable position. In the interest of social justice, these clients ought to be equally entitled to the highest quality interventions available, but in order for this to happen, social workers employed by such agencies need to learn to be good consumers on their clients' behalf. Therefore, we offer these questions as guidelines of what to ask when hiring a mental health professional, whether it be via a referral from an agency or an individual consumer.

1. *What is your educational background? Specifically what degrees do you hold and in what fields and from which institution?*

    This will establish whether or not the person has had the degree of education required to qualify for licensure. In most states, in social work, this means holding a MSW from a CSWE-accredited institution. In some states, people who hold BSWs can be licensed, but they are not allowed to practice independently. A list of CSWE-accredited institutions is available at www.cswe.org/Accreditation/organizations.aspx. If the person uses the title "Dr.," it is important to find out what their doctorate is in. Is their degree an MD? A PhD? An EdD? A PsyD? If the degree is a PhD what field is it in? This is important to ask because some people who put the initials PhD after their name may not necessarily have that PhD in a mental health–related area or may have a PhD from a diploma mill. For instance, if someone has a PhD in English Literature, that would not qualify them to be practicing as a mental health professional. If your therapist displays his or her impressive-looking diploma on his or her office wall, reflecting that he or she earned a PhD in Christian Counseling from the Tripp Bible Institute, a real place (see www.trippbibleinstitute.com), it would be good to know that admission to this school of higher education does not require a high school diploma, and all coursework is completed entirely by postal mail! If the person is in independent (private) practice and does not hold at least an MSW or an MA/MS in a mental health–related field, our advice would be to politely discontinue the interview with that person immediately and find someone else. Such an individual would not meet even the minimum qualifications to practice, and thus has no business doing so.

2. *Are you licensed? If so, what is your licensure and in what state/states?*

    If the person is not licensed in the state where you are being treated, unless he or she is working directly under the supervision of a licensed individual responsible for the person's work, we recommend going no further. If a person is not licensed, in the event that you need to file a complaint, you would have no recourse unless the person broke the law and could be criminally prosecuted. A person's licensure gives you recourse to complain, should the need arise. In most states, the licensure for a social worker that entitles them to practice independently is an LCSW. You can check with your state licensing board to see what that is for your particular state. You can also check on most state licensing board websites to determine if any actions have been taken against that person due to complaints that were filed. Other valid forms of licensure include licensed marriage and family therapists (LMFT) and licensed clinical psychologists who may hold a PhD or a PsyD. Again, we wish to emphasize that while it is important that the person is licensed, licensure alone is not sufficient to guarantee that this person is fully competent to help an individual with a particular type of problem. What being licensed means is that the person has the requisite level of education, has passed a written (and in some states an oral) state licensing examination, and has successfully undergone a period of supervision, in most states, 2 years. Beyond that, there are no guarantees, other than the fact that you will have a mechanism for complaint, should the need arise. Thus, further questions are necessary.

3. *What are your areas of expertise? In what way do you qualify to claim such expertise?*

   This is an important question, especially in the age of the Internet, because the term "expert" has been bandied about a great deal, accompanied by hyperbole such as "internationally acclaimed expert" or "leading expert," but may have very little actual substance. For example, someone could claim to be an "expert" in thought field therapy, past-life regression, or attachment disorders, and the training and certifications they received may not be based on any kind of scientific evidence. This would be a very different situation from someone who has received specialized training in a field that does have empirical support, such as applied behavior analysis, and delivers empirically supported interventions. It is important to keep in mind that there are no restrictions on using the term "expert" and so make sure the "expert" you hire is not an emperor with no clothes. Unfortunately, there are many associations with names that sound credible, but on close inspection, turn out to be, at best, marginal. One can join the American Psychotherapy Association (www.americanpsychotherapy. com/about) and become credentialed as a *professional counselor, PTSD clinician, PTSD counselor, relationship therapist, master therapy, fellow,* or *diplomate* in psychotherapy. The reality is that these credentials, which come with nice certificates suitable for display on an office wall, require minimal advanced training, and are largely invisible within the larger field of legitimate psychotherapists. The American College of Forensic Examiners' Institute (members.acfei.com/_catalog.php) offers the *certified master forensic social worker* credential, another professionally undistinguished credential requiring minimal advanced qualifications beyond an MSW. One of the authors (BAT) contacted this organization and confirmed with them that they do not even require licensure as a clinical social worker in order to obtain their "advanced" credential. This same group offers a weak credential called the *board certified posttraumatic stress disorder clinician*, only requiring a 15-hour online continuing education course.

4. *Are you under any kind of supervision? If so, with whom and what information about my case will be shared with that individual/individuals?*

This is important to ask for two reasons. First, the person needs to inform you with whom he or she intends to share your information and, second, you can find out the qualifications of the supervisor. Being in supervision can be very positive, but not necessarily so, if the supervisor is not adequately qualified and/or is himself or herself practicing methods that lack adequate empirical support. Some consumer guides emphasize the importance of peer supervision. Again, although this can be positive, it really depends on who the "peers" are. If the peers are into a pseudoscientific practice, they may merely be reinforcing one another's harmful practice and make matters even worse. It is also important to find out if the person participates in any Internet forums such as listservs and to what extent they rely on information provided there. Are adequate precautions taken to protect the confidentiality of cases discussed in those types of forums? A therapist should never, under any circumstances, be discussing a client by name or using any sort of identifying information.

5. *What specific interventions do you plan to use with me? What specific training do you have in the interventions you will be using? What is the evidence that supports their effectiveness? Are there any research-supported alternatives to the interventions you are offering? If so, where are those available?*

If the person immediately begins to give you testimonials and anecdotes as evidence for the effectiveness of their treatment approach, claims high success rates, and offers you no specific research evidence to support those claims, that is the time to say your good-byes and walk out the door. If the person offers you an intervention lacking in published research evidence and claims it is superior to those interventions that do have such evidence, again, it is time to say good-bye to that therapist. Also be wary of the therapist claiming that the treatment is "evidence-based" or "research-based" but failing to provide you with citations from peer-reviewed journals. Some Internet websites present "research" that has not been published in peer-reviewed journals or that has been published in journals or newsletters that are owned by companies that promote a particular brand name therapy. For example, thought field therapy has a newsletter called *The Thought Field* that has reported on a number of research studies that have not been published in reputable peer-reviewed journals and, on further examination, are highly flawed. A decade or more ago, asking about research was a fairly simple matter. It either existed in reputable publications or it did not. Nowadays, however, with the increasing emphasis on research-supported interventions (although this is a good thing), the downside is that the term has been misused and abused and has been used to describe therapies that have not even met minimal criteria to qualify as empirically supported (see Mercer & Pignotti, 2007; Pignotti & Mercer, 2007, for some examples). If no treatments exist that fully qualify as empirically supported for the problem for which you are seeking assistance, then the person needs to provide you with what the available treatment options are and what the degree of research evidence is for each. How will the therapist ensure that the treatments will be delivered safely? Have there been any reports of harm? If so, find out the details. You may also need to do your own investigation of this. Doing an Internet search on the intervention through a search engine such as Google or Yahoo can be helpful, although recognize that not everything on the Internet is necessarily true, so check carefully how conclusions being presented were arrived at.

*6. How do you perform your initial assessment and diagnosis?*

By asking this question, you can determine whether or not the therapist is using assessment tools that have adequate reliability and validity (see Chapter 2 on assessment). If a therapist is making quick, snap decisions about you without doing a careful assessment, it is a serious red flag! For example, some therapists make the assumption that all overweight clients who walk through their door, regardless of what problem they present with, have been sexually abused and if they do not remember such abuse, they are repressing memories of abuse when there is no evidence to support this notion. Another current fad diagnosis is telling a client that he or she had a narcissistic parent and doing an Internet search will reveal a number of websites on this topic. This is a one-size-fits-all (or nearly all) type of diagnosis that some therapists are so impressed with that they may attribute having had a narcissistic parent to a wide range of current difficulties being experience by clients. There is no possible way a therapist can diagnose a parent or other family member who is not present in the session and while some clients have felt that the traits of narcissism describe their parent, there is no way such a secondhand diagnosis can be reliably performed, nor is there evidence that having a narcissistic parent is the cause of various problems.

7. *How will you be evaluating our progress? If the intervention you are using is not working or making me worse, what will be our next steps?*

Even if the therapist is using an empirically supported intervention, no intervention is 100% effective and, thus, for some individuals, it may not work. That is why it is very important for therapists to be monitoring the progress of each client with assessment tools that have adequate reliability and validity (see Chapter 2 on assessment for details).

8. *What are your fees? Do you charge for the initial consultation? What is your policy on missed appointments?*

The therapist has an obligation to provide you fully with all this information, prior to beginning therapy. Do they work on a sliding scale (a client pays according to the client's income)? If so, they should provide you with a schedule of income-based fees. It is also important to find out if fees may change, depending on results. Some of the pseudoscientific approaches have people at various levels of training and a bait-and-switch tactic is employed to refer a client to a higher level, more "advanced" and (of course) more expensive practitioner. The person might be under the impression that the therapy is quick and relatively inexpensive, but if it does not work for him or her, he or she may be switched to a more advanced, highly expensive form of the treatment.

*9. Are there additional products you sell to your clients or additional activities in which you involve your clients?*

If the person is offering additional products to clients, such as nutritional supplements, or is attempting to involve you in his or her favorite cause, this is a serious ethical violation as it constitutes a dual relationship. A psychotherapist should be only your therapist, not a product vendor or a friend. There have even been some cases we are aware of where therapists have attempted to involve their clients in business ventures, book clubs, or spiritual study groups, which, again, is strictly forbidden as a dual relationship under the various professional codes of ethics. If you live in a small town, contact with the therapist may be unavoidable (e.g., a client working in or even owning a local store). However, in that case, although permissible and unavoidable, the therapist, not the client, is responsible for assuring that no abuses of power occur. In the age of the Internet, there may also be issues with social networking sites such as Facebook. Under no circumstances should a therapist be "friending" clients on such personal websites because this opens the door to highly inappropriate boundary violations, although it would be permissible for the therapist to have a strictly professional Facebook page.

*10. About how long do you expect the therapy to last? Approximately how many sessions will I need and when should I expect to be seeing results? Will I need to get worse before I get better?*

Although the exact time needed may vary from person to person, the therapist should be able to give you a ballpark figure, suggested by research. Be very wary of therapists who tell you that you will likely get worse before you get better. This line and rationalization for clients becoming worse while in treatment has been employed by some of the trauma and recovered memory therapists we discussed in Chapter 4 who used it as a rationalization for convincing clients to stay in therapy who were actually not getting better and deteriorating from the treatment. Their solution has been to continue doing the more of the same treatment, sometimes with devastating results. Clients who find themselves worse and less able to function in life after beginning therapy, need to see this as a serious warning sign that they may have gotten involved with a therapy that does more harm than good.

11. *Can significant others (e.g., family members, partners, close friends) in my life be involved in my therapy if I wish? If so, in what way?*

Although there are varying philosophies about involving the client's significant others, it is helpful to know in advance, if and how they can be involved and again, whether there is any research on the helpfulness of involving family members or other important people in the client's life. For example, with treatments for obsessive-compulsive disorder (OCD), involvement of significant others has been shown to be helpful.

12. *Will I be asked to sever ties with people family members or others in my life with whom I am close?*

If the answer is yes and you find that most of that person's clients have cut ties with family members and/or close friends, this is a major warning sign. Although there are undoubtedly some cases where abusive situations (e.g., sexual abuse, spousal domestic abuse) have been proven to exist that are putting the client in physical danger and severing ties may be the best choice to make, therapists who are routinely recommending this for clients who are not in such extreme situations of danger, may be luring the client into a controlling, abusive, and cult-like relationship with the therapist (Singer & Lalich, 1996).

13. *How do you decide if a client is appropriate for the form of intervention or therapy you are offering?*

This will provide you with further insight into how the therapist thinks about the treatments being offered. Does the therapist see them as one-size-fits-all treatments or is he or she discerning?

14. *Have you ever been sued for malpractice or have there been any complaints to your licensing board about you? If so, what can you tell me about the circumstances, and how it was resolved?*

Although a topic that most practitioners may be uncomfortable with, it is certainly justifiable for a potential client to ask such questions. Most state licensing boards also provide information on disciplinary actions taken against a given practitioner.

The question often arises whether it is important for a therapist to have personally been in therapy. Although there are arguments, both pro and con, for this position, there is no actual research evidence that having been in personal therapy will make the person a better, more effective therapist. Some clients feel more comfortable with therapists who have personally experienced what they themselves are going through. Again, however, there is no evidence that this is necessarily helpful. The pro is that the therapist may have inside knowledge of experiences the client had and have an awareness of aspects someone who has not had the experience may lack. However, the downside also exists, that the therapist may impose his or her own experiences onto those of the client, thinking that they are more alike than they actually are, thus failing to recognize and listen for important differences.

For some therapies, support group work with other clients who are experiencing the same problem may be helpful. A good demonstration of an empirically supported group treatment for OCD was provided in the recent television reality series called *The OCD Project* where clients with OCD lived together in a house for a period of time and participated in an empirically supported exposure-based treatment for OCD called exposure and response prevention. This, however, is not necessarily the case for all types of problems. For example, peer support groups for adolescents with conduct disorders have been found to do more harm than good (Lilienfeld, 2007).

In addition to asking these factual questions, it is important to make sure that the therapist hired is someone the client feels comfortable speaking and sharing his or her innermost feelings with. This, of course, is subjective and a therapist who may be compatible with one client, may not be compatible with another. Your initial interview with that therapist should be the time when you can explore and determine this. Always remember that you, the client, is the one who ultimately will be hiring the therapist.

## OTHER OPTIONS FOR CLIENTS

Apart from the previously mentioned list of questions, social work clients have other options available to them. For example, if a client has a problem for which one or more psychosocial interventions exist that have strong levels of research support, and their social worker provides them instead with something pseudoscientific, bogus, or magical, particularly when he or she is not informed of potential alternative empirically supported therapies, then in our view the client has legitimate grounds for complaint. This can be expressed verbally to the social worker in person, over the phone, or in writing. Depending on the egregiousness of the social worker's services in this regard, complaints may be taken up by the lines of authority, to the agency or other supervisor, the NASW state chapter to file an ethics complaint, or to the state licensing board. Where harm has been caused, recourse to a lawsuit may be socially just. If, for example, a social work client did not receive an empirically supported intervention to help him or her, and was provided something pseudoscientific instead, he or she is "harmed" in terms of delayed access to legitimate therapy, the costs of paying for the bogus treatment, and perhaps other more serious consequences (e.g., a troubled adolescent who cut her wrists following months of ineffective care; a client who commits suicide; or a socially phobic person who loses his or her job because he or she was not effectively helped). These *may be* grounds for a successful lawsuit, *if* more effective alternative therapies were available, these alternatives were not discussed or offered, or the social worker made unjustifiable claims regarding the presumptive effectiveness of the pseudoscientific treatments he or she wished to provide. To the best of our knowledge, no social worker has been successfully sued on such grounds by a disgruntled client, but if and when such a legal ruling in favor of a client's right to effective treatment, where these are known to exist, is passed, this has the potential to revolutionize social work practice. Very quickly, LCSWs and other social workers would cease offering bogus treatments and would perforce be required to learn about more scientifically justifiable methods of service.

We want to make a rather obvious point here, in that we are not asserting that social workers should be held culpable or guilty of malpractice if their clients do not improve. By the right to effective treatment, we are not asserting that clients have a right to be "cured" somehow and that any outcome less than this represents misconduct. By right to effective treatment, we are referring to expecting professional social workers to use scientifically supported interventions, not any kind of guarantee that clients' problems are resolved.

We also think it would be a good thing if insurance companies began requiring licensed social workers who receive third-party payments to accurately describe the nature of the therapies they provide their clients. Reimbursements should be provided to legitimate therapies that are specifically known to have been helpful for the types of clients being treated, and declined for conspicuously pseudoscientific or otherwise bogus interventions. It would be insurance fraud, for example, for a social worker providing something else to label it, for the purposes of insurance reimbursement, *cognitive behavioral therapy* (CBT), for example, if CBT was not really what was being delivered.

## SOCIAL WORK SHOULD EMULATE ENGINEERING

The idea that social work is more akin to the applied discipline of engineering than to the social sciences is not a new one. For example, a small textbook appearing in 1936 was titled *Handbook on Social Work Engineering* (Guild & Guild, 1936), and this theme was picked up decades later by the distinguished social work academic Walter Hudson (Hudson & Hill, 1973). A recent essay by Horgan (2011) describes what he called "the malaise of social 'science.'" He says that social scientists are roughly divided into two camps, the softies, more closely aligned with the humanities, and the hardies, who wish to emulate the harder sciences like physics. This is simply a reworking of Snow's (1959) concept of the "Two Cultures" found more broadly within academia and certainly also applies to social work. Here is what Horgan observes with respect to social science, views that we believe have particular relevance to our field:

> Social scientists are especially dangerous when they insist— and convince others—that they have discovered absolute truths about humanity, truths that tell us what we are and even what we should be. Hence social scientists—more than any other scientists—should be humble or at least modest, in making claims. Here's a more specific suggestion: Social scientists should be identifying not with the hard sciences or the humanities but with engineering.... [engineers]...They don't seek "the truth", a unique and universal explanation of a phenomenon or solution to a problem. In fact, engineers would scoff at such a formulation of their work. They merely seek answers to specific, localized, temporary problems,

whether building a bridge with less steel or a more efficient solar panel or a smartphone with a bigger memory. Whatever work, works. In the same way, social scientists should eschew the quest for truths about human behavior. They should instead focus more intensely on finding answers to specific problems...In spite of its weaknesses, social science—when applied wisely—can do even more than the hard sciences to make the world a better place. (Horgan, 2011, p. 1)

During the annual convention of the American Psychological Association, Jerome Wiesner, the Provost of the Massachusett's Institute of Technology told psychologists that " 'social and behavioral scientists should get out of their ivory tower.' He called for the establishment of a new profession of social engineering to apply the findings of the social sciences to pressing social problems,... 'I can't understand why the great weight of social sciences can't be put behind worthy causes' " (cited from Nelson, 1969, p. 1103). Wiesner was asking for psychologists to develop this focus of social engineering, but it was a social worker who subsequently noted that "Wiesner, like many others, needs to be informed that such a profession does exist, that being social work. The profession of social work has historically both interpreted and applied social science knowledge and has focused its attention on the 'pressing social problems' confronting modern society...I doubt that we need another profession. Why not use the one that exists and make it more effective and increasingly socially relevant" (Dailey, 1969, p. 1353). Fox (1982) made a similar suggestion that clinical psychology was the discipline best suited to apply social science to solve social problems, going too far as to suggest that doctoral-level psychologists should conduct hospital discharge planning! He too seemed unaware of the ideal position that the existing profession of social work was in to undertake the task of social engineering, a point made by Thyer (1984) in response to Fox's assertions.

Social work education requires training in the social and behavioral sciences, but there should be dramatically less emphasis on testing theories in favor of using the tools of social science to evaluate the plethora of existing social service programs that are already in place. Far too few of them, even immense programs such as everyday state-provided mental health and substance abuse services, have credible evidence that they actually help their clients. Use the opportunities of the dissertation research requirement, universally found in our doctoral programs, to encourage students to undertake high-quality evaluations of existing services, or to develop and test newer more effective interventions. Too much social work research focuses on the descriptive features, correlates, precursors, and phenomenology of social problems (e.g., homelessness, mental illness, domestic violence, child abuse), work which at best has potential implications to practice. Far too little involves seeing if the services the clientele of social work agencies are materially (and in other ways) benefiting from the care social workers and other health care providers are providing. Research on the outcomes of social work practice has the potential to yield more direct applications to practice, not merely implications. Harrison and Thyer (1988) argued this point, which has been made before and since by many other writers—namely evaluation research is the most valuable form of scientific inquiry social workers can undertake (also see a review of this topic in Chapter 1 in Royse, Thyer, & Padgett, 2010). Such an applied focus, akin to engineering's emphasis on solving problems rather than on testing theories or discovering universal truths, would make our discipline's science much more relevant to practitioners than is presently the case.

Again, this is not a new idea. For example, Fraiberg presented the following statement relating to social work research:

> As an applied science, a user of other sciences, social work is obliged to put its borrowings to a pragmatic test. Is this theory useful to our field? we ask. Does it explain things better? Does it suggest new and better remedies for our problems? (Fraiberg, 1961, p. 87)

We need less of what has been variously termed zombie science, junk science, or cargo cult science, studies that follow the procedures, often with weak rigor, of conventional scientific inquiry, or which investigate issues of trivial importance. The more removed a social work inquiry is from the direct concerns of social work clients and their well-being, or of the effectiveness of social welfare policies and programs, the more it resembles mainstream social science and less an applied field. As noted by Thyer (1759, pp. 487–488), "The end of all knowledge is to understand what is fit to be done, for to know what has been, and what is, and what may be, does but tend to that."

# SUMMARY

As American social work moves into its third century, social work is a thriving profession. There are hundreds of thousands of BSWs and MSWs providing mental health and other clinical services across the United States. A large proportion of these services are helpful, ethical, and in many cases grounded in credible empirical research. The practitioners are well trained, conscientious, and properly place the client's well-being of paramount importance. There are a number of professional practice organizations that provide a supportive community for social workers, and ethical complaints and malpractice lawsuits are relatively and gratifyingly rare in our field. Relatively speaking, professional education and practice standards are considerably enhanced compared to just a few short decades ago. The number of accredited academic programs are expanding and clinical social workers provide a important segment of mental health care and other clinical services across a wide array of problem areas. As humanists, we look with pride on distinguished social workers such as Jane Addams, who received a Nobel Peace Prize (en.wikipedia.org/wiki) and Irena Sendler, who rescued hundreds of Jewish children from the Warsaw ghetto during World War II (en.wikipedia.org/wiki/Irena_Sendler).

We can also look with disciplinary pride at world-class clinical researchers who have advanced cutting-edge developments in the care and effective treatment of persons with serious psychosocial problems, individuals such as the late Gerard Hogarty, MSW, who did so much to advance the psychoeducational approach to helping persons with chronic mental illness; Myrna Weissman, MSW, PhD, codeveloper of interpersonal psychotherapy, an effective treatment for persons with serious depression; Gail Steketee, MSW, PhD, whose research advanced the care of persons experiencing OCD, posttraumatic stress disorder, and who initiated the earliest sound clinical descriptions and treatment investigations of persons who engage in compulsive hoarding; Steven Schinke, MSW, PhD, who has engaged in 30 years of rigorous work in treating adolescent substance abuse, as well as in other important areas; and Carl Leukefeld, DSW, who has also made significant contributions in the field of substance abuse, including a long-term follow-up study demonstrating the lack of effectiveness of the widely used Drug Abuse Resistance Education (DARE) program.

Our field will be advanced by cultivating the rigorous scientific thinking and research skills exemplified by these individuals.

We hope that our description of the nature and variety of various pseudoscientific practices to be found among a small segment of social worker professionals, in our journals and textbooks, taught in some of our social work programs, and conveyed through officially sponsored continuing education events, will serve as a wake-up call that all is not healthy in the profession. In 1984, Prince Charles of the United Kingdom once described a proposed architectural plan for a building in London as "a monstrous carbuncle on the face of a much-loved and elegant friend." We view pseudoscientific theory and practice within contemporary social work in much the same light and with equal distaste. The treatment for carbuncles may be painful. It can involve lancing, draining, disinfectants, and sunlight, and in some cases, surgical removal. We believe that the words of Oliver Cromwell addressing the British Rump Parliament in 1653 have currency with respect to pseudoscientific practices in social work: "You have sat for too long for any good you have been doing. Depart I say, and let us have done with you. In the name of God, go!" We close with a pertinent passage from Hebrew scripture.

> All counselors praise the counsel they give
> But some give counsel in their own interest
> Be wary of a counselor
> And learn first what is his interest
> For he will take thought for himself. (Sirach 37:7–9)

## REFERENCES

Albright, D. L., & Thyer, B. A. (2010). Does eye movement desensitization and reprocessing (EMDR) reduce posttraumatic stress disorder in combat veterans? *Behavioral Interventions, 25,* 1–19.

Barsky, A. (2014, Fall). Ebola and the ethics of using unproven drugs. *The New Social Worker,* pp. 4–5.

Bellamy, J. L., Bledsoe, S. E., Mullen, E. J., Lin, F., & Manuel, J. I. (2008). Agency-university partnerships for evidence-based practice in social work. *Journal of Social Work Education, 44,* 55–75.

Dailey, D. M. (1969). Social work—Dr. Wiesner! (letter). *Science, 165,* 1353.

Dawes, R. M. (1994). *House of cards: Psychology and psychotherapy built on myth.* New York, NY: Free Press.

Field, T. (2009). *Complementary and alternative therapies research.* Washington, DC: American Psychological Association Press.

Fox, R. (1982). The need for a reorientation of clinical psychology. *American Psychologist, 37,* 1051–1057.

Fraiberg, S. (1961). Psychoanalysis and the education of social workers. *Smith College Studies in Social Work, 48,* 87–106.

Guild, J. P., & Guild, A. A. (1936). *Handbook on social work engineering.* Richmond, VA: Whittet & Shepperson.

Hannes, K., Claes, L., & the Belgian Campbell Group. (2007). Learn to read and write systematic reviews: The Belgian Campbell Group. *Research on Social Work Practice, 17,* 748–743.

Harrison, D. F., & Thyer, B. A. (1988). Doctoral research on social work practice. *Journal of Social Work Education, 24,* 107–114.

Horgan, J. (2011, February 13). A prescription for the malaise of social "science." *The Chronicle Review.* Retrieved March 20, 2011, from http://chronicle.com/article/A-Prescription-for-the-Malaise/126311/

Howard, M. O., McMillen, C. J., & Pollio, D. E. (2003). Teaching evidence-based practice: Toward a new paradigm for social work education. *Research on Social Work Practice, 13,* 234–259.

Hudson, W. W., & Hill, C. T. (1973). Social work. *Engineering Education, 63,* 352–355.

Johnstone, L. (1989). *Users and abusers of psychiatry.* New York, NY: Routledge.

Jopling, D. A. (2008). *Talking cures and placebo effects.* New York, NY: Oxford.

Lilienfeld, S. O. (2007). Psychological treatments that cause harm. *Perspectives on Psychological Science, 2,* 53–70.

Lilienfeld, S. O., Lynn, S. J., & Lohr, J. M. (2003). *Science and pseudo science in clinical psychology.* New York, NY: Guilford Press.

Lilienfeld, S. O., Lynn, S. J., & Lohr, J. M. (2015). *Science and pseudoscience in clinical psychology* (2nd ed.). New York, NY: Guilford Press.

Loftus, E. F. (2003). Make-believe memories. *American Psychologist, 58,* 867–873.

Loftus, E. F., & Ketcham, K. (1994). *The myth of repressed memories.* New York, NY: St. Martin's Press.

Manuel, J. I., Mullen, E. J., Fang, L., Bellamy, J. L., & Bledsoe, S. E. (2009). Preparing social work practitioners to use evidence-based practice: A comparison of experiences from an implementation project. *Research on Social Work Practice, 19*, 613–627.

Mercer, J., & Pignotti, M. (2007). Shortcuts cause errors in systematic research synthesis: Rethinking evaluation of mental health interventions. *The Scientific Review of Mental Health Practice, 5*, 59–77.

Mercer, J., Sarner, L., & Rosa, L. (2003). *Attachment therapy on trial: The torture and death of Candace Newmaker.* Westport, CT: Praeger.

National Association of Social Workers. (2006). *Code of ethics.* Washington, DC: NASW Press.

Nelson, B. (1969). Psychologists: Searching for social relevance at APA meeting. *Science, 165*, 1101–1104.

Parrish, D. E., & Rubin, A. (2011). An effective model for continuing education in evidence-based practice. *Research on Social Work Practice, 21*, 77–87.

Pignotti, M. (2007). Questionable interventions taught at top-ranked school of social work. *The Scientific Review of Mental Health Practice, 5*, 78–82.

Pignotti, M., & Mercer, J. (2007). Holding therapy and dyadic developmental psychotherapy are not supported and acceptable practices: A systematic research synthesis revisited. *Research on Social Work Practice, 17*, 513–519.

Pignotti, M., & Thyer, B. A. (2009). Some comments on *Energy psychology: A review of the evidence:* Premature conclusions based on incomplete evidence? *Psychotherapy, Theory, Research, Practice, Training, 46*, 257–261.

Roder, T., Kubillus, V., & Burwell, A. (1995). *Psychiatrists: The men behind Hitler.* Los Angeles, CA: Freedom Publishing.

Ross, C. A., & Pam, A. (1995). *Pseudoscience in biological psychiatry: Blaming the body.* New York, NY: John Wiley.

Royse, D., Thyer, B. A., & Padgett, D. (2010). *Program evaluation: An introduction* (5th ed.). Belmont, CA: Cengage.

Rubin, A., & Parrish, D. (2007). Views of evidence-based practice among faculty in Master of Social Work Programs: A national survey. *Research on Social Work Practice, 17*, 110–122.

Singer, M. T., & Lalich, J. (1996). *Crazy therapies: What are they? How do they work?* San Francisco, CA: Jossey-Bass.

Snow, C. P. (1959). *The two cultures and the scientific revolution.* Cambridge, England: Cambridge University Press.

Sundell, K., Soydan, H., Tengvald, K., & Antilla, S. (2010). From opinion-based to evidence-based social work: The Swedish case. *Research on Social Work Practice, 20,* 714–722.

Thomlison, B., & Corcoran, K. (Eds.). (2008). *The evidence-based internship: A field manual.* New York, NY: Oxford University Press.

Thyer, B. A. (1984). A reorientation of clinical psychology? Look before you leap. *Journal of Clinical Psychology, 40,* 865–867.

Thyer, B. A. (1996). Guidelines for applying the empirical clinical practice model to social work. *Journal of Applied Social Sciences, 20,* 121–127.

Thyer, B. A., & Kazi, M. A. F. (Eds.). (2004). *International perspectives on evidence-based practice in social work.* Birmingham, England: Venture Press.

Thyer, R. (Ed.). (1759). *Samuel Butler.* London, England: J. & R. Tonson.

Valenstein, E. S. (1986). *Great and desperate cures.* New York, NY: Basic Books.

# Index